Ned Sherrin
In His Anecdotage

BOOKS BY CARYL BRAHMS AND NED SHERRIN

Cindy Ella, or I Gotta Shoe
Rappel 1910
Benbow was his Name
Ooh! La-la!
After you, Mr Feydeau
Paying the Piper (play translation)
Song by Song
Too Dirty for the Windmill (memoir)

BOOKS BY NED SHERRIN

A Small Thing like an Earthquake
Cutting Edge, or Back in the Knife Box, Miss Sharp
TW3 (ed., with David Frost)
1956 and All That (with Neil Shand)
The Metropolitan Mikado (libretto, with Alistair Beaton)
Loose Neds
Ned Sherrin's Theatrical Anecdotes

NED SHERRIN

IN HIS ANECDOTAGE

*A Classic Collection from
the Master Raconteur*

This edition published in Great Britain in 1993 by
Virgin Books
an imprint of Virgin Publishing Ltd
332 Ladbroke Grove
London W10 5AH

ISBN 1 85227 426 3

Typeset by Phoenix Photosetting, Chatham, Kent
Printed in Great Britain by
Mackays of Chatham PLC, Chatham, Kent

For Alistair Beaton
who devised the original *Loose Ends* monologue
for me, and continued to write it
throughout the programme's first two years,

and for
Neil Shand, Andrew Nickolds,
Ian Brown, James Hendrie, Pete Sinclair, Steve Punt,
Mike Coleman, Richard Stoneman and Ged Parsons
who took up the challenge

Introduction

I enjoyed enormously writing *Theatrical Anecdotes* for Virgin Books, though so many of the theatre stories triggered memories for me – other anecdotes, incidents, gossip, shafts of wit – which disappointingly fell outside the scope of that book.

The present volume gives me wider brief to roam over further hints, chestnuts, rumours, fragments and apocrypha which have intrigued me in the fields of literature, the law, politics, history, music, movies, sport and the Royal Family. It has also given me a second chance with theatre stories which I forgot for the earlier book, which have come to light in biographies published since, or which readers were encouraged to send me.

Perhaps not all the entries in this book qualify strictly as anecdotes but they have all stuck in my mind.

I don't know where a passion for handing on anecdotes, gossip, *bonmots* comes from. I do vividly remember an early piece of theatrical information which excited me greatly. During the war I lived on a farm in Kingweston, Somerset. The 'big house' had been taken over as headquarters of the Searchlight Brigade for the area. The officers of the Mess worked hard to keep on good terms with the villagers. Among other delights we were asked to ENSA concerts. On one occasion a half a dozen village children were the entire audience for a hard-working but not very proficient company from the nearby town of Wells. The military had wisely decided to give them a miss and they had to suffer the indignity of performing for us. They did so with ill-grace. On another evening my parents, my brother and I were asked to an Officers' Mess cocktail party. My mother and father hated cocktail parties and sent my brother and me to represent the family. I must have been twelve or thirteen. I was a devoted reader of *Picture Post*, drawing all my theatrical knowledge from its glossy photo-features. I remember clutching a glass of lemonade and hearing a conversation between two officers' wives who towered above me. They were discussing the theatre. 'I hear Ivor Novello has inherited the mantle of Owen Nares,' said one to the other. This was priceless news to me and I cherished it until I realised that there was no one to whom I could pass it on. No one I knew would derive the same pleasure that it had given me. It is the essence of anecdotage to pass on. I hope that it will be easier for these stories to find an audience.

At about the same period I adopted a possessive attitude to English history – particularly the Wessex kings who had burnt cakes and manufactured candle-clocks and fought Danes and Vikings across the fields and moorland where I grew up. English history, particularly in its early days – say up to Henry VII – has been a romantic and personal passion, a storehouse of murder, betrayal, greed and bravery, which I have converted to anecdotage here. Many of the incidents have royal echoes today.

It is impossible to recall a lifetime of collecting trivia without *aides-mémoire* and in the course of checking a number of anthologies I have also found some new favourites.

I am particularly indebted to my friend Michael Hill for access to his unpublished book of Royal Quotations, and to the following works:

> Elizabeth Longford's *Oxford Book of Royal Anecdotes*.
> *The Oxford Book of Literary Anecdotes* edited by James Sutherland.
> *The Oxford Book of Political Anecdotes* edited by Paul Johnson.
> *The Oxford Book of Legal Anecdotes* edited by Michael Gilbert.
> *Jazz Anecdotes* (Oxford University Press) edited by Bill Crow.
> *The Faber Book of Art Anecdotes* edited by Edward Lucie-Smith.
> *Hollywood Anecdotes* (Ballantine) edited by Paul F. Boller, Jr. and
>   Ronald L. Davis.

I read that Lady Thatcher has had a little local difference with the publishers of her memoirs, who demanded 'more anecdotes'. She has had to summon a think-tank of devoted acolytes to recall the rib-tickling moments of her years in office. I wonder if she has been reminded of her tribute to the sterling qualities of Lord Whitelaw, 'Every Prime Minister should have a Willie'? In his book *A View from the Wings*, her speech-writer, Sir Ronald Millar, records that 'When the explosive burst of laughter that greeted this observation subsided she frowned and said sternly, "Everything that's said in this room is confidential. You realise that?" '

Confidentiality is against the spirit of anecdote – and somehow her failure to spot Sir Ronald's joke, 'Keep taking the tablets' – 'Why can't I say "pills", Ronald?' has also leaked out.

It has been interesting to watch the Baroness develop her public sense of humour since she came to fame. I remember her on the pilot for *Quiz of the Week* (a successful BBC TV precursor of today's *Have I Got News For You*) in 1970, when she got all her answers right and did not venture a joke. By 1992, when I was following her at the Hilton at a Persons of the Year Luncheon, she had developed a highly effective and amusing way of ending her speech at my expense: 'Well, I must finish now,' she said to an audience which had come to hear her, 'I'm only warming up for the principal speaker.'

It remains for me to thank Sally Holloway, who has been a patient and constructive editor; Christine Motley, who, having ploughed her way through my *Theatrical Anecdotes*, has now typed every page of this book without complaining; and finally Marie Reynolds, who did a wonderful job publicising the previous volume and who I am delighted to know will be responsible for this one as well.

Ned Sherrin
Chelsea, 1993

Acknowledgements

I am grateful for permission to reproduce the following material: on page 50, extracts from Alan Clark's *Diaries*, reprinted courtesy of Weidenfeld & Nicolson, London, 1993; on page 55, selected passages from the works of Cyril Connolly, reproduced by kind permission of the Estate of Cyril Connolly, c/o Rogers, Coleridge and White Ltd; on page 57, letter from John Moffat, courtesy of the author; on page 60, extract from an article by John E. Cunningham, first published in the *Spectator*; on pages 133 and 134, extracts from poems by Donald Hall, reproduced by kind permission of David R. Godine Publishers, Boston, USA; on page 165, extract from an article by John Naughton, first published in *The Observer*; on page 171, selection of 'Overheards' by Miles Kington, first published in *The Independent* and reproduced by kind permission of Rogers, Coleridge and White Ltd on behalf of the author; and on page 273, extracts from *Truman* by Roy Jenkins, reproduced by kind permission of William Collins, an imprint of HarperCollins Publishers Ltd.

Every effort has been made to contact the copyright holders of quoted material. If however there are items which I have unintentionally overlooked, I can only apologise for the omission. Any such material will of course be properly credited in any future edition.

N. S.

Ned Sherrin
In His Anecdotage

— A —

AARONSON, Boris. The great Russian-American designer worked on a wide variety of shows but is perhaps most closely associated with the spectacular appearance of the Sondheim/Prince shows *Company*, *A Little Night Music*, *Pacific Overtures*, and Jerome Robbins's production of *Fiddler on the Roof*. He had two simple rules of show business:

1 Every show has a victim.
2 Don't be that victim.

ADDISON, Joseph. I have a special interest in the late seventeenth- and early eighteenth-century poet and essayist Joseph Addison since I played him in Sally Potter's film of Virginia Woolf's *Orlando*. I was asked to play the poet Pope, but I didn't think that would carry conviction and besides Pope had over twenty lines and I did not reckon that I could learn more than Addison's six.

Addison served as MP for Malmesbury for a long period but he never spoke in the House. He tried once and so loud were the cries of 'Hear him! Hear him!' that he fell back in his seat without a word. However, he did become secretary of state and took, as his senior under-secretary, one Temple Stanyon. Unfortunately he lent him money and from then on Stanyon slavishly agreed to everything he proposed. Finally the exasperated Addison yelled, 'Sir, either contradict me or pay me my money!'

Unfortunately this fine scene is not relevant to the plot of *Orlando*.

ALFRED the Great (reigned AD 871-99). Alfred is the richest source of anecdotes of the early English kings. His grandfather was Egbert, a contemporary of Charlemagne, who spent time at the French Court and returned to unite the kingdoms of Kent and Wessex. Egbert was succeeded by his son Aethelwulf whose four sons, Ethelbald, Ethelbert, Ethelred I and Alfred, were all to reign between 858 and 900.

Alfred came to the throne in AD 871, by which time the Danish army was all over the south and west. Alfred retreated to the most inaccessible hideouts in Wessex, holing up on the Isle of Athelney by Easter 878.

Here is where anecdotage sets in. Schoolboy history credits him with the invention of the candle-clock, a simple device by which a taper burning down through various layers of coloured wax measured the passage of time; and then improving on that with a more sophisticated water-clock.

Then there is shadowy authority for the story that during his unhappy, on-the-run, anonymity at Athelney – still there on the railway line from Castle Cary to Taunton – a peasant woman who was hiding him left him, at a time when food was hard to come by, to watch cakes baking on her hearth. Obsessed by his problems Alfred's mind wandered to the re-conquest of his kingdom and when the woman came back the cakes were burnt and ruined. Alfred was savaged by her tongue.

In this rumour-threaded age Alfred also had a vision of St Cuthbert, Bishop of Lindisfarne, who promised that the King would regain his kingdom. He added that his companions would soon return laden with fish. Both prophesies were happily fulfilled – though the first took longer than the second.

Another anecdote has Alfred disguising himself as a minstrel and gaining access to the banqueting hall of the leader of his Viking enemies. He took his time to sum up the strength of the enemy and after a few heavy ballads returned to his colleagues convinced that he could whack the indolent Danes.

This he did – enforcing Christianity on those enemies who chose to stay in his realm.

Alfred also has a reputation as a great advocate of education. When he was twelve his mother showed him an illuminated book of poems. She promised to give it to the first son who could read it. Alfred found himself a teacher and won the contest and the book.

He married Aelswith, daughter of a Midland nobleman, in AD 868 when he was nineteen, three years before he became King.

He later cleverly cemented his authority over more of England by marrying his intellectually formidable daughter, Ethelflaed, to Ethelred, a Prince of Mercia, the Midland territory. She famously became known as the Lady of the Mercians. He made another alliance further north with Eadwulf, a Northumbrian heavy.

In all these campaigns, barterings and negotiations Alfred emerges as both brave and statesmanlike; but more merciful than was fashionable among his contemporaries. However, in cases of persistent backsliding, oathbreaking and marauding he could deal harshly, on one occasion ordering the execution of the entire crew of a Danish ship.

Alfred's own verdict on his reign was modest. 'He did not dare set down much of his own writ, for he did not know how it would like them that came after.' However, he did inspire a Boswell, the monk Asser, who records his later years in glowing terms.

His exercise of wise government; his invitations to scholars; his creation of schools and universities to the advancement of learning; especially his writing and translating for his subjects in their own language, and his encouragement of invention are counterpointed farcically with his lacerating piles, which apparently crippled him, even on his wedding day. Legend suggests he welcomed this distraction from earthly delights – though legend doesn't tell us how Aelswith felt about it.

When he died, Edward, his oldest son, buried him at Winchester in the monastery he had founded. However, the monks made the heir pay dearly to lay his father's bones to rest and then spread ugly rumours that Alfred's spirit did not lie easy but haunted the grounds. Edward rescued the remains and placed them in a new abbey at Hythe.

Alfred's great jewel, engraved 'Alfred Made Me' sits in the Ashmolean Museum at Oxford.

ALLEN, Maude. Maude Allen was notorious in the early years of this century for her *Salome* Seven Veils Dance. An MP accused her of lesbianism in an article daringly entitled 'The Cult of the Clitoris', and Ms Allen sued him for libel. A backwoods peer, Lord Albemarle, visiting his club during the much-publicised lawsuit, remarked vaguely, 'I've never heard of this Greek chap Clitoris they're all talking about.'

AMECHE, Don. Don Ameche starred with Claudette Colbert in *Midnight* in 1939 and played one of the best in the tiresome history of practical jokes on his co-star. He paid the most decrepit ancient extra on the set to knock on her dressing room door and, when she opened it, ask for her autograph saying, 'Miss Colbert, I've adored you ever since I was a little boy.'

When I was producing the first Marty Feldman movie, *Every Home Should Have One*, shooting was nearly brought to a standstill when an extra (Terry Pritchard – now it can be told) persuaded a girl to go up to Marty's clever but insecure co-star Shelly Berman (famous for his LP of funny telephone calls) and ask for his autograph, claiming that she had always loved his 'Driving Instructor' LP, the huge hit by his rival Bob Newhart. He duly exploded.

ANGLO-SAXON SUCCESSORS to King Alfred. Eight English Kings (crafty or craven) descended from Alfred and sat on the throne in the hundred years after Edward's death. Three were assassinated, two were notorious womanisers, one was a rude rebellious teenager, another combined cowardliness with brutality and licence in equal parts. A jealous murdering stepmother and a rich traitor fill out the colourful cast.

Edward the Elder, who died in AD 925 having succeeded his father Alfred in 900, yields little in anecdote – on the other hand, the birth of Edward's son Athelstan springs from an anecdote recorded by the church historian William of Malmesbury. His mother, Egwina, according to an ancient ballad was 'the daugher of a neat-herd'. She was said (or sung) to be so beautiful that even as a child she attracted everyone's attention. An unidentified professional dreamer dreamt that she would become the mother of a powerful king. The rumour fascinated an old woman who had nursed King Alfred's five children. Determined to meddle in the course of history she took Egwina into her household and in a rapid Saxon finishing course transformed her from a simple neat-herd's daughter into a girl with prospects. When Edward the Elder, still an aetheling, found time to drop in on his old nurse, Egwina was not only beautiful - she was also presentable. A son, Athelstan, and a daughter, Editha, were the fruits of this out-pouring of mutual affection. William hints that no marriage ceremony blessed their union but Pingard, a poetess of the same period, disagrees, calling Egwina 'partner to Edward's throne', a very different matter from partner to his bed.

Athelstan is the first king to be accorded a precise physical description. He was of average height, his flaxen hair shot through with golden threads. The two-tone effect topped off a ruddy face and a strong and energetic physical presence – essential for royal survival in those days. He inherited some of his grandfather's versatility, collected relics with enthusiasm and was reluctant to punish wrong-doers who showed signs of genuine repentance. His Aunt Mercia brought him up as a formidable soldier and in her victory at the Battle of Brumanburgh five kings and seven earls from Ireland and the son of a king of Scotland were killed.

Athelstan ran a busy marriage market for his many sisters, although two became nuns and one an abbess. He placed others with husbands whose titles included France, Meaux, Paris, Saxon Germany, Aquitaine and in one case that of 'a Prince whose name is not recorded but whose dominions lay among the Alps'. The favourite for this mystery husband is Conrad the Peaceable of Burgundy, but sadly 'in two generations the English Royal Family had lost all trace of her'. The export of Royal sisters went hand in hand with burgeoning trade on the Continent.

Athelstan's death was a cue to the Danes to invade, but his eighteen-year-old brother, Edmund I, had not fought alongside his brother for nothing. Having successfully defended the kingdom he lost his life intervening in a scuffle between one of his stewards and an outlaw. His brother, Eadred, succeeded him, but his successful reign was ended by a long sickness in AD 955.

This let in Eadwig, Edmund's fifteen-year-old son. He was an impetuous, argumentative adolescent with striking blond good looks. Eadwig's riotous coronation has gone into legend. Between the ceremony in Westminster Abbey and the official feast which was to follow, Eadwig disappeared. Dunstan, the Abbot of Glastonbury, and the Bishop of Lichfield found him crownless and in bed with two ladies, a mother and daughter working together. The prelates dragged the anointed King from the pair's protecting clutches back to the banquet. In a speedy sequel Eadwig married the daughter and Dunstan was banished.

Eadwig was succeeded four years later by his younger brother Edgar, a more sober sixteen-year-old. Dunstan was brought back from exile to advise him as Archbishop of Canterbury and eventually crowned him at Bath. Edgar took his job seriously and soon after the ceremony he was rowed – on the River Dee – by eight Northern and Scottish kings as an act of homage.

When he died on 8 July 975, his two marriages and two surviving sons were a recipe for trouble. Edward, his son by his first wife, matched his uncle Eadwig in confused and violent adolescence. If Eadwig had offended Dunstan, Edward was happy to make enemies across the board. His murder after three years qualifies as the crime of the century in an age when challenges for the title are not hard to find. The scene was Corfe Castle where his stepmother, Queen Elfrida, a 'pampered beauty', set a trap. Tired and thirsty from hunting, Edward called on her as she lived nearby. 'On his arrival, alluring him to her with female blandishment, she made him lean forward, and, after saluting him while he was eagerly drinking from the cup which had been presented, the dagger of an attendant pierced him through.' Edward dropped the cup of mead and staggered to his horse which dragged him, half-mounted, to Wareham, where the wicked stepmother's retainers, led on by an all too obvious trail of blood, finished the job, covering his body with turf and little ceremony.' A year later Edward's bones were translated to the care of nuns at Shaftesbury. William of Malmesbury, relishing more sensational accounts, reports strange happenings around his first grave. 'Lights were shown above . . . there the lame walked, there the dumb resumed the faculty of speech; there every malady gave way to health.' Word travelled quickly and 'The murderess, excited by it, attempted a progress thither.' However, her horse declined to carry her forward, 'in spite of whips and clamours'. She ordered a Mercian lord to remove the bones from Shaftesbury, but for his pains, 'Within a year he was eaten by vermin we call lice'!

Elfrida's son Ethelred therefore entered into his inheritance under a cloud – just as he had entered the world. At his baptism he 'fouled the font', which prompted Dunstan, who was officiating, to announce, 'By God and his mother, this will be a very sorry fellow.' His reign was said to be 'cruel in the beginning, wretched in the middle and disgraceful in the end'.

His popularly received nickname Ethelred the Unready is a corruption of 'unraed', which is nearer to uncounselled' or even 'ill-advised'. Ethelred deserves a Freudian biographer. He is reported as weeping uncontrollably at his stepbrother's death and then being 'beaten with candles' by his mother, who thought he should show more gratitude for his succession which she had engineered. He feared candles for the rest of his life.

His coronation – Dunstan's fourth ceremony – was a cue for the Danes to return to rape and pillage. One of their victims was Dunstan's successor, Elphege, whom they took prisoner. When he refused to ask for ransom from his tenants they stoned and hacked him to death. It was a cue for another legend. Elphege's blood, scattered over the ground turned dead sticks of wood overnight into thriving green saplings – transforming the Danes instantly from murderers into worshippers. They gave the battered corpse safe passage to London. There it lay for ten years. When it was removed to Canterbury it proved to be 'free from every taint of corruption' and continued, according to William of Malmesbury, 'fresh . . . its soundness unimpaired . . . a miracle that a carcass should be divested of life and not decay.'

Ethelred's second wife was Emma, daughter of Richard, Duke of Normandy, known – rather like an Edwardian musical comedy heroine – as 'The Pearl of Normandy'. His son, Edmund, succeeded him briefly in 1016 but died, murdered by a traitor's ruse. The villain, one Edric Streona, arranged for his killers to find Edmund 'as he was sitting down for a necessary purpose' and drive an iron hook into his bowels. Canute or Cnut, the Danish leader, took the crown, adding a patina of legitimacy by marrying Emma, Ethelred's widow, and preparing the ground for one of the great folk anecdotes in English history – and the most misinterpreted. Openly ambitious to gain the support of the English Church he had himself baptised before leaving Denmark, and finding himself in barely disputed possession of England he embraced its religious practices with a convert's zeal. However, the incident which converted him in English memory from cruel usurper (he had in early raids severed his enemies' ears and noses and in some cases 'unmanned' them) to lovable folk hero is described in the simplest terms by Maria, Lady Calcott in her *Little Arthur's History of England*.

One day when Canute was walking with the lords of the court by the sea-side, some of them, thinking to please him by flattery began to praise him very much indeed, and to call him great, and wise and good, and then foolishly talked of his power, and said they were sure he could do everything he chose and that even the waves of the sea would do what he bade them.

Canute did not answer these foolish men for some time. At last he said, 'I am tired, bring me a chair.' And they brought him one: and he made them set it close to the water; and he said to the sea, 'I command you not to let the waves soil my feet.' The flattering lords looked at one another, and thought King Canute must be mad to think the sea would really obey him, although they had been so wicked as to tell him it would the moment before. Of course the sea rose as it does, every day, and Canute sat still till it wetted him and all the lords who had flattered him so foolishly. Then he rose up and said to them, 'Learn from what you see now, that there is no Being really great and powerful but GOD! He only, who made the sea, can tell it when to stop.' The flatterers were ashamed, and saw that Canute was too good and wise to believe their false praise.

Canute was not so perfect that he could do without a mistress – Aelgifu – a Northampton girl whom he sent to govern Norway, where she became a byword for harsh government.

Edward the Confessor, Emma's son by her first husband, Ethelred, was the last anointed king before the Norman invasion, and his received image – benign, ascetic, pious – is not the stuff of anecdote. He married Edith Godwin, sister of Harold – who was to fight at Hastings. Rumour said that the marriage was never consummated and Edward had a reputation for being a Virgin King five hundred years before Elizabeth annexed the female version of the title.

He rebuilt Westminster Abbey to provide himself with a suitable tomb and died on 4 or 5 January 1066 – just as his resting place was completed – the last ruler of his line.

ANNE, Queen. Queen Anne was the second child of King James II by his first wife, Anne Hyde, daughter of Lord Clarendon. Neither she nor her sister Mary could produce surviving heirs to the throne - Bishop Burnet hints that this may have been due to a syphilitic infection inherited from their father. 'The violent pain that his eldest daughter had in her eyes and the gout which has so early seized our present Queen, are through the dregs of a tainted original, upon which Willis, the great physician, being called to consult for one of his sons, gave his opinion in these words *Mala stamina vitae*, which gave such offence that he was never called afterwards.'

Queen Anne was 'the Quintessence of orderliness', shy, unimaginative, serious, and short-sighted as well as a martyr to her gout. She was also tiny and married to a dim Danish Prince by whom she had seventeen children, all of whom died. William, Duke of Gloucester, lasted longest, dying in 1701 aged eleven. She was able to enjoy the great Duke of Marlborough's victories – Blenheim,

Ramillies, Oudenarde and Malplaquet – but was continually beset by quar-
relling politicians. She was the last of the wayward Stuarts.

At fifteen she was emphatic on the subject of Roman Catholicism: 'The more
I see of these fooleries and the more I hear of that religion the more I dislike it.'

Uncharacteristic scandal attached itself to her at seventeen. Letters were discovered from Lord Mulgrave, a bachelor favourite of Charles II, eighteen years
her senior, from which people drew the inference of too great an intimacy. He
was banned from court in November 1682 and given the nickname 'King John'.
He was sent off to Tangiers for a spell, and although the gossip was probably
exaggerated, Anne's older sister Mary could bemoan the fate of 'my pore sister'
[sic] and with a dash of hypocrisy add, 'not but that I believe my sister very innocent'.

The incident had two positive results: it speeded her marriage to the dim
Dane Prince George, and facilitated her friendship with Sarah Jennings, who
was to become Duchess of Marlborough. Poor George was the butt of many
court jokes – from King Charles's 'I've tried him drunk and I've tried him sober,
but there's nothing in him' to the rehabilitated Mulgrave's suggestion that his
fits of asthma were 'put on so that he should not be taken for dead and taken
away and buried'.

Soon after her succession he forgot all his ambitions and lived for 'his news,
his bottle and the queen'.

Sarah Jennings entered the Princess Anne's service in 1683 on her marriage to
Prince George. Their friendship was intense and had provoked endless speculation. After Sarah's marriage to Churchill the Queen said, 'We four must never
part till death mows us down with his impartial hand.' The Duchess (who
according to Lady Clarendon 'looked like a mad-woman and talked like a
scholar') saw that this was not to be the case. While the friendship held the
Princess demanded that the two women should behave as equals. Sarah was Mrs
Freeman in this charade and the Princess Mrs Morley.

The Queen's coronation in 1702 was marred by a particularly vicious attack
of gout – she is unique among English monarchs in being carried to the ceremony in an open sedan chair. Within two weeks England declared war on
France. King Louis joked, 'It means I'm growing old when ladies declare war on
me.'

The lady had the last laugh with Marlborough on her side. A Colonel Parke
took eight days to ride across Europe with news of the victory at Blenheim –
then he had to wait for a wind before his ship could sail the next stage. The
Queen was playing dominoes at Windsor when the Colonel turned up with the
message, addressed to Marlborough's wife on the back of a tavern bill: 'I have
not time to say more, but to beg you will give my duty to the Queen, and let

her know her army has had a glorious victory.' Parke got a thousand guineas for his sore seat (as well as a miniature of the Queen) and the country went mad.

Parliament continued to be a thorn in her side, 'I have changed my ministers,' she told the new Tory cabinet in 1711, 'but I have not changed my measures: I am still for moderation and will govern by it.'

Anne had more to suffer from gout and the erysipelas inflammation of which she died. Worse were the remedies applied: bleeding, blistering, emetics and a shaven head added pain and indignity to the pretence of treatment. Five days before she died she was asked how she was. Not surprisingly, she murmured, 'Never worse. I am going.' Dr Arbuthnot, her physician, told Dean Swift, 'I believe sleep was never more welcome to a weary traveller than death was to her.'

ARRAN, 8th Earl of. 'Boofy' Gore was an amiable, eccentric columnist and member of the House of Lords who in the sixties introduced a valuable bill for homosexual reform. On another occasion he demonstrated his wide range of concerns by leading a campaign to protect the badger.

These acts were summed up by a fellow peer as 'teaching people not to bugger badgers and not to badger buggers'.

Badgers are still endangered.

ATKINS, Eileen. Eileen Atkins, one of the most gifted and sensitive of actresses, has a knack of attracting put-upon roles which belie her keen off-stage wit. Apart from inventing *Upstairs Downstairs* and *The House of Elliot* with her friend Jean Marsh, her career has stretched from tap-dancing as a juvenile in working men's clubs to touring her one-woman show as Virginia Woolf. While playing Virginia Woolf in Los Angeles she got a call from Paramount Studios asking her to play a CIA agent in a movie. There were two conditions. She must have a perfect American accent and she must be able to get out of her show. She thought for a moment and said 'no' on both counts. On the latter she added, 'Besides it's a one-woman show.' The brash reply came without hesitation: 'Close it.'

Ms Atkins's mother always regretted that she 'never did a play with a few laughs in it – a nice play I can talk to the neighbours about.'

After Eileen Atkins's great success in T. S. Eliot's *The Cocktail Party* and her character's macabre fate, she went home one Sunday reckoning that the notices of her triumph might have penetrated the family circle. 'Once I'd admired the new lino, been up to the allotment and through everybody's illnesses, I finally asked, "Did you read any of my reviews?"' 'Oh yes,' her mother said. 'You weren't the *Daily Mirror*'s idea of a martyr.'

My favourite Atkins story concerns the size of her breasts. She says herself, 'I've never worried about having small tits.' However, on one occasion, on her way to Harrods three construction workers leered at her from the scaffolding. 'Cor!' yelled one. 'It wasn't worth that one burning her bra.' She went inside in a rage and as she did her shopping her indignation festered. When she came out she strode up to the three men and said, 'I dare say you've all got small cocks, but I don't shout about it.'

As she stalked away feeling vindicated she noticed that their faces were completely blank and puzzled. A few yards further up the road she realised she had come out of a different door and they weren't the same workmen.

Ms Atkins has firm views on accents. Recently she said, 'It's a damn shame we have this immediate thing of ticking off in the mind about how people sound. On the other hand, how many people really want to be operated upon by a surgeon who talks broad cockney?'

ATKINSON, Rowan. I like this Rowan Atkinson story so much that I have not dared to check its authenticity. Atkinson had been filming one of his credit card commercials, I think in Florida, and when shooting was over he flew back in the same aeroplane as the crew – Atkinson in first class, the crew in business class. Also in first class was a particularly objectionable drunk who kept calling for drinks during the in-flight entertainment – which happened to be episodes of Atkinson's 'Mr Bean' series. The drunk laughed uproariously until the lights went up and he looked around the cabin for the first time.

Catching sight of Rowan he was so bemused and shocked that he had a heart attack and died.

ATTENBOROUGH, Sir David and Richard, Baron. This story has all the qualities of an urban myth so once again I have not dared to check its authenticity with the principal actors.

When David Attenborough lived in Chelsea his older brother visited him one evening, unwisely leaving his Rolls-Royce unlocked outside the door. When he left he found that his brief case (surely containing the only copy of the script of some epic film) had been stolen.

Dickie returned to his brother's house and they telephoned the Chelsea police station. Eventually a copper rode up on his bike and came into the house to take down the facts. Having done so he delivered a long and pompous lecture, pointing out the unwisdom of leaving a car unattended, its doors unlocked, with valuable property inside. Chastened and already annoyed at their mistakes the Attenboroughs listened patiently to the monologue.

Eventually the policeman left and they were settling down to a consoling drink when the door bell rang.

It was PC Plod, who asked if he might use the telephone in the hall. From the drawing room they heard his conversation. 'Chelsea Police Station? Bert, it's me. Can you send a squad car round. Some bugger's stolen my bike!'

ATTLEE, Clement, 1st Earl. Attlee had the unenviable task of following Churchill as Prime Minister in 1945 and achieved the feat of being one of the most successful peacetime premiers. Famous for his dormouse appearance and clipped, abrupt, Haileybury-military manner he was aware of the contempt in which Churchill in particular held him. This is instanced in many jibes, some probably apocryphal. 'Major Attlee is a modest man; but then he has much to be modest about'; 'A sheep in sheep's clothing'; 'An empty taxi drew up in Downing Street and Attlee got out'. And, when Attlee settled in as a confident PM 'Feed a bee on royal jelly, and it becomes a queen.'

When he was to be installed a Knight of the Order of the Garter at Windsor he penned five uncharacteristic lines:

> Few thought he was even a starter
> There were many who thought themselves smarter.
> But he ended PM,
> CH and OM,
> An Earl and a Knight of the Garter.

Occasionally he gave as good as he got, replying succinctly to a Churchill broadside, 'I must remind the Right Honourable gentleman that a monologue is not a decision.' On Conservatives in general he commented, 'If we have to have Tories, at least they should be gentlemen' – a remark which has even more resonance and relevance in the eighties and nineties than in the decade in which it was uttered.

John Vincent's review of Kenneth Harris's worthy biography of Attlee in 1982 is a better verdict on the book than the life: 'The result is a well-proportioned portrait of an annoyingly uninteresting paragon. Blamelessness runs riot through six hundred pages.'

Attlee's well-known terse manner applied both in general and in specific cases. On democracy he said, 'It means government by discussion, but that is only effective if you can stop people talking.' This he famously did in several classic encounters. After the war, in 1945 when the coalition ended, Attlee received a letter from Harold Laski, the new chairman of the Labour Party. 'The continuance of your leadership is a grave handicap to our hopes of victory in the coming election . . . your resignation of the leadership would now be a great service to the party. Just as Mr Churchill changed Auchinleck for Montgomery before Alamein, so I suggest you owe it to the party to give it the chance to make a comparable change on the eve of this greatest of our battles.'

The stark reply read, 'Dear Laski, Thank you for your letter, contents of which have been noted. C. R. Attlee.' Attlee's final verdict on Laski was equally terse: 'Rum thing about Harold: he never got the hang of it.'

When a cabinet minister, John Strachey, wanted to publish a volume of poetry he was reminded that protocol demanded that he seek the Prime Minister's permission. He duly submitted the manuscript to Attlee and after some delay phoned Downing Street to ask for the verdict. Attlee was direct: 'Can't possibly publish. The lines don't scan.'

In sacking he was just as direct. One unsuspecting junior minister responded to a summons and asked hopefully, 'What can I do for you, Prime Minister?' 'I want your job,' said Attlee. Collapse of junior party. 'But . . . why, Prime Minister?' 'Afraid you're not up to it.' His verdict after the Chancellor, Hugh Dalton's indiscreet downfall was as merciless: 'He always was a loud-mouthed fellow.' This contrasts vividly and ironically with the self-deception in Dalton's own account of his resignation. 'I was moved to see that he was much more deeply moved than I was at this moment. He said he hated – hated – he repeated the word several times – hated to lose me.'

Mrs Attlee's driving was a continuing tale of accidents even after she defiantly passed an advanced driving test. She was the terror of the roads of Hertfordshire and, according to Douglas Jay, who inherited Attlee's official driver when he became President of the Board of Trade, 'George' testified that Attlee never spoke to him except to say 'Good morning, George' at the beginning and 'Good night, George' at the end of the day. 'The only time he ever spoke to me was once when we were driving to Chequers for the weekend and a car overtook us and nearly sent us into the ditch. Mr Attlee said furiously, "Who's that bloody fool?" I said, "That was Mrs Attlee, sir." "Best say no more about it."'

The story is borne out by a BBC crew who interviewed Attlee much later at his retirement home. The interviewer, Derek Hart, and the producer, Michael Hill, hearing that the old man was going in to Westminster offered him a lift. He accepted gratefully. Then Lady Attlee appeared and reminded him that she was driving him to town. Plainly alarmed he insisted on 'sparing her the trouble' and riding in the BBC car.

In his preface to his collection of political anecdotes, Paul Johnson recalls a late meeting with Attlee when, after a television interview, he asked him to sign his book of lectures, *From Empire to Commonwealth*. Attlee spent a long time in a corner writing in it and finally handed it back closed. Johnson's curiosity was excited: but when he finally found a tactful moment to look at the inscription he found the single word, etched in a quavering hand – 'Attlee'. Once again Attlee accepted a lift in Johnson's BBC car; typically he had not bothered to ask for one. He asked to be dropped off: 'Army & Navy Stores . . . off to India tomorrow. Must get kitted up.' He disappeared through the doors in Victoria Street, the last Johnson saw of him.

AYER, Sir A. J. (Freddie). Freddie Ayer, the Oxford philosopher, soccer fan and notable womaniser, overstepped the mark in the latter respect when he was having an affair with the stage and film designer Jocelyn Rickard, by acquiring seven more mistresses.

In her autobiography, *The Painted Banquet*, she claims that she broke off the affair not out of jealousy but because there were not enough nights in the week.

AYLETT, Sydney. Sydney Aylett, a barrister's clerk, was involved in a divorce action in the days when 'inchastity' between the granting of a decree nisi and a decree absolute would invalidate a divorce if it got to the ears of the King's Proctor. The barrister in this case warned the client that he must cease to cohabit with the lady he intended to marry until his decree came through. The man was dismayed. 'Good heavens, what am I going to do?'

'I suggest,' Aylett's barrister said dryly, 'that you buy a goat.'

The day that the decree nisi was made absolute Aylett sent the client a telegram: YOU CAN NOW KILL THE GOAT.

— B —

BALDWIN, Stanley, 1st Earl Baldwin of Bewdley. Stanley Baldwin's most quoted remark was provoked by the *Daily Mail*. The Editor, signing himself 'Editor, *Daily Mail*', attacked Baldwin over the disappearance of 'an immense fortune' left to him by his father. His piece concluded, 'It is difficult to see how the leader of a party who has lost his own fortune can hope to restore those of anyone else, or his country.' Baldwin took legal counsel and was advised that he could sue. Nowadays he probably would have done so if the example of contemporary Prime Ministers is followed. However, Baldwin took advantage of a public meeting in the Queen's Hall during the course of a Westminster by-election when the press lords, Rothermere and Beaverbrook, put up their own candidate in opposition to Duff Cooper to highlight the issue of Empire trade. Baldwin finished, 'I shall not move in the matter, and for this reason – I should get an apology and heavy damages. The first is of no value and the second I would not touch with a barge pole. What the proprietorship of these papers is aiming at is power, and power without responsibility – the prerogative of the harlot through the ages.'

Lady Diana Cooper observed the effect on the press: 'I saw the blasé reporters, scribbling semi-consciously, jump out of their skins to a man.'

Lord Longford, or Frank Pakenham as he was in the thirties when he was a fledgling Tory politician, once asked Baldwin who was his greatest political influence. Baldwin said it was Sir Henry Maine. Longford pressed – 'What was Maine's supreme contribution?' Baldwin thought hard and then said, 'Rousseau argued that all human progress was from contract to status. But Maine made it clear once and for all that the real movement was from status to contract.' Then there was another pause, followed by a look of horror on Baldwin's face. 'Or was it,' he said, 'or was it the other way round?'

Baldwin's involvement in the abdication crisis is the stuff of drama rather than anecdote, but I like the explanation he gave for excluding Churchill from his 1935 Cabinet. 'I feel we should not give him the post at this stage,' he wrote with uncanny foresight. 'If there is going to be a war – and no one can say that there is not – we must keep him fresh to be our war Prime Minister.'

B A L L , Lucille. In her early days in Hollywood Lucille Ball was under contract to Harry Cohn at Columbia Pictures. It had not been a happy association and near the end of her term Cohn still owed her $85,000. To avoid paying her he sent her a script he knew she must refuse. Seeing through his ploy, she accepted enthusiastically, aware that if she turned the film down she would be in breach of contract and would lose the money he owed her. Cohn was forced to make the picture and pay her the money. Meanwhile, Cecil B. De Mille wanted her for a major picture which she was keen to accept. Halfway through the Columbia film she realised that she was pregnant. In these circumstances Cohn could dismiss her for natural causes. She couldn't tell Cohn and she couldn't tell De Mille in case it got back to Cohn.

However, having completed the Columbia movie and collected her cash she and her husband, Desi Arnaz, called on De Mille to make a clean breast of it and apologise. When De Mille realised that there was no chance that she could make his film he was determined to be magnanimous, 'You're the only woman I know who's ever screwed Desi Arnaz, Harry Cohn, Paramount Pictures and Cecil B. De Mille all at the same time!'

B A R B E R , Rector. Rector Barber was head of my college, Exeter, at Oxford. He was a dry stick, a meticulous scholar and an expert on Propertius, a particularly difficult and grammatically idiosyncratic Latin poet. Asked what he thought of Propertius 'as a poet', he looked contemptuous. 'Oh!' he said. 'You mean the *slush* side of poetry.' He claimed that 'Exeter was the second oldest college in Oxford – unless you count lodging houses, in which case it is the fourth.'

I remember him once looking quizzically at an undergraduate who was claiming direct descent from a medieval head of college at whose portrait on the wall in Hall he was pointing. 'How interesting,' said Barber. 'Of course you realise that all Rectors were celibate in those days.'

B A R K E R , Robert. Robert Barker and Martin Lucas, King's Printers under King Charles I, printed an edition of 1,000 copies of the Bible. A dramatic misprint caused them to be summoned before the Star Chamber, the edition to be called in and the printers fined £300.

In it, the Seventh Commandment read 'Thou shalt commit adultery.'

BARRIE, Sir James. According to Mrs Comyns Carr's memoirs Barrie was present at a picnic with his favourite Llewelyn-Davies children when one of the children was rebuked by Sylvia Llewelyn-Davies for eating too many chocolates. 'You'll be sick tomorrow if you eat any more,' she insisted. 'No,' replied little Jack, 'I shall be sick tonight.' Barrie was so delighted with the reply that he asked if he could use the line in a play. He offered Jack Llewelyn-Davies a royalty of 'a halfpenny a performance' for the copyright. The child agreed and it turned out to be a profitable deal. The play was *Peter Pan*.

BEECHAM, Sir Thomas. At the beginning of the eighties Caryl Brahms and I wrote a play about Sir Thomas Beecham – the Disraeli, Wilde, Shaw or Mencken of music, so often and so widely is he quoted. In his mouth innumerable quips have been placed by re-tellers anxious to clothe a suspect story with more authority and the promise of laughter. We began at Arthur Lowe's prompting – his accountant had done the same job for Beecham and told Arthur how alike in appearance they were. Unfortunately Arthur wanted us to write in Mrs Lowe as all the seductive women in Sir Thomas's hectic love life so we kept to our original concept and in the end we were lucky enough to get Timothy West, who harboured a keenness to conduct, to play the part.

As we talked to Sir Thomas's old colleagues and adversaries the familiar jokes were dusted down and as the show went into rehearsal more were offered by post and telephone. Neville Cardus has even confessed to making up and circulating one Beecham story, and Beecham accused him of fabricating one about a singer in his opera company which turned out to be true in character but not in fact. The singer confided in the great man about his son. 'He'll be leaving Oxford next year. I've spent a lot of money on him and he doesn't know what sort of job to take up.'

Beecham stroked his chin. 'Aren't you going to make a singer of him?'

'Oh no, Sir Thomas.'

'Why?'

'Well, he hasn't got a voice, not really.'

'Ah,' said Sir Thomas in dulcet tones, 'Ah, I see – a family failing.'

That joins the brood of 'offspring' foisted on Beecham, like 'Try anything once except incest and folk dancing,' which we used shamelessly in our play, but which can be traced to Sir Arnold Bax's *Farewell My Youth*, published in 1943. We also used another story with a doubtful provenance. It has Beecham in Fortnum & Masons accosted by a stately woman fan and struggling to identify her and not admitting that he cannot. He tried all the routine questions: 'How's your husband?' 'He's very well.' 'How are your children?' 'Oh, they're very well,' and so on until, getting nowhere, he enquired, 'And how is your brother?'

To which she replied, 'Still king.' It is probably only a matter of time before Beecham is awarded W. S. Gilbert's reply to a musically illiterate woman who asked if Bach was still composing – 'No, madam, decomposing,' came the answer.

Cardus in his *Memoir* (1961) was elegant and perceptive on Beecham's humour. 'He was a comedian. Or, as this is a term which the English associate with red-nosed buffoonery, I had better describe him as an artist in comedy. But he was not a wit in the epigrammatic way of Oscar Wilde . . . Sir Thomas indulged not so much in wit as in waggery.'

Beecham's was a Lancastrian family, 'enriched by the manufacture of pills'. One of his earliest excursions into studied humour was a commission from his father to produce a version of a Christmas carol which would promote the family product. Young Thomas came up with:

> Hark! the herald angels sing!
> Beecham's pills are just the thing.
> Two for a woman, one for a child . . .
> Peace on earth and mercy mild.

'These sentiments,' he explained later, 'especially the ellipsis, seemed to me admirably to express the rapture which is occasioned by a good effortless release.'

To a musical ignoramus like me, Beecham was a spirited introduction to its literature. Music itself is so elusive a target that it plays hell with easy formula definitions. 'Music,' said Dr Johnson to Boswell on their way round the Hebrides, 'is a method of employing the mind without the labour of thinking at all,' which reduces it to much the same as washing up. But Johnson also said, 'Of all noises I think music the least disagreeable.'

'A musicologist,' Beecham enjoyed saying, 'is a person who can read music but can't hear it.' Oscar Wilde argued on one hand that 'Music is the condition to which all other arts are constantly aspiring'; but in his novels and plays he was not so admiring. 'If one hears bad music it is one's duty to drown it by one's conversation' (*The Picture of Dorian Gray*); 'You see, one plays good music, people don't listen, and if one plays bad music people don't talk' (*The Importance of Being Earnest*); 'Musical people are so absurdly unreasonable. They always want one to be perfectly dumb at the very moment when one is longing to be absolutely deaf' (*An Ideal Husband*).

Frank Zappa has a zappier verdict on musical appreciation: 'Most people wouldn't know music if it came up and bit them on the ass.' Or as Ulysses S. Grant put it, 'I only know two tunes. One of them is "Yankee Doodle"; and the other isn't.'

George Herbert said the only sound thing *against* music: 'Music heals not the toothache.' Baudelaire confined his antagonism to that of Wagner: 'I love Wagner, but the music I prefer is that of a cat hung up by its tail outside a window and trying to stick to the panes of glass with its paws.' Jimmy Durante said, 'I hate music, especially when it's played.'

Charles Lamb was often on the attack, in verse:

> Some cry up Haydn, some Mozart –
> Just as the whim bites, for my part
> I care not a farthing candle
> For either of them or for Handel . . .

And in prose: 'A carpenter's hammer, in a warm summer noon, will fret me into more than midsummer madness. But those unconnected, unset sounds are nothing to the measured malice of music.'

Beecham's contempt was directed towards the inferior, the unadventurous, the pretentious and the foreign: 'Why do we in England engage at our concerts so many third-rate continental conductors when we have so many second-rate ones of our own?' He knew his own worth, of course: 'I am not the greatest conductor in this country. On the other hand, I'm better than any damned foreigner.' As far as English music was concerned, Beecham was determined to make it better: 'British music is in a state of perpetual promise. It might almost be said to be one long promissory note.' He knew his public, too: 'The English may not like music but they absolutely love the noise it makes.' He had two golden rules for an orchestra: 'Start together and finish together. The public doesn't give a damn what goes on in between.'

Cardus once caught Beecham being cavalier with the last act of *Siegfried* at Covent Garden in the thirties. The first two acts were a dream, 'In the third act Beecham went berserk.' The conductor answered Cardus's criticism forthrightly: 'You critics are inhumane. I chanced to look at my watch, laid on my desk before me, and we were still not half-way through Act III. It was getting on for eleven o'clock. In the audience were many poor souls who had to go home to such remote habitations as Putney, Streatham and Swiss Cottage. And the public houses would close at eleven, and my orchestra, slaving away since six o'clock, were thirsty. So I just let Wagner rip!'

Beecham believed that 'Nearly all the questionable works of the great musical geniuses have been prompted by religion. Wagner's *Parsifal*, the *Requiem* of Brahms, and Elgar's *Gerontius*, described by my friend George Moore as holy water in a German beer barrel. Each is, I think, my most potent aversion. Too much counterpoint. Protestant counterpoint. What dreadful crimes have been committed in the name of religion.'

Beecham was the ace when it came to explosions between singers, players and conductors. However, lashing an orchestra tends to be one-sided, though soloists can answer back. 'You are here and I am here; but where is Beethoven?' Artur Schnabel once enquired of a conductor. But a player in one of Barbirolli's orchestras paid a parking fine confessing, 'I prefer to face the wrath of the police than the wrath of Sir John Barbirolli.' Stokowski boasted, 'I am more than a martinet – I am martinetissimo!'

To one player Beecham said silkily, 'We cannot expect you to be with us all the time, but perhaps you could be good enough to keep in touch now and again.' To another, 'Cor anglais, kindly give me some indication of your presence at four bars after the letter G.' When an oboist called on to give an A came up with a wide vibrato, he looked around the orchestra and said simply, 'Take your pick.' With Jean Pouquet, the violinist, he appeared with an orchestra so overawed that their opening rehearsal bars were disastrous. Beecham persevered and they got better. 'Don't look now,' he said, leaning towards Pouquet, 'But I believe we're being followed.' Again: 'Gentlemen in the clarinet department, how can you resist such an impassioned appeal from the second violins? Give them an answer, I beg you.'

Perhaps the cruellest Beecham anecdote features the player who arrived late for rehearsal. Beecham asked his name. 'Ball, sir.' 'I beg your pardon?' 'Ball, Sir Thomas.' 'Ah, Ball! How very singular!' Or is it beaten by the comment to an inadequate cellist? 'Madam, you have between your legs an instrument capable of giving pleasure to thousands and all you can do is scratch it.'

His attitude to women in an orchestra was unequivocal. 'If they are attractive it will upset my players and if they are not they will upset me.'

Beecham's grapeshot splattered singers and orchestras impartially. He stopped a rehearsal of *La Bohème* because the tenor was inaudible. The man was lying on the bed upon which Mimi was also dying. Beecham yelled, 'Mr Nash, I can't hear you. Sing up!' 'How do you expect me to sing my best in this position, Sir Thomas?' said Nash. 'In that position, my dear fellow,' replied Beecham, 'I have given some of my best performances.'

Diaghilev's Russian dancers had no language in which to protest when Beecham upped the tempo on their first London appearance. 'I made the little buggers hop,' he smiled.

'How would you like it, tonight, madam?' he enquired tetchily of a soprano. 'Too fast or too slow?' An Australian soprano had trouble with the score of the *Messiah*, but pleaded that she would be all right for the performance. She said that she had been working hard on the score for months, taking it to bed with her every night. 'In that case,' he reassured her, 'I'm sure we shall have an immaculate conception.'

However, from the hero of Dame Ethel Smyth's maritime opera *The Wreckers*, which he rehearsed for its first performance in 1909, Beecham had to cope with some of his own medicine. The tenor stopped. 'What's the matter, Mr Coates?' asked Sir Thomas. 'I was just wondering . . .' said Coates. 'Is this the place where I'm supposed to be drowned by the waves or the orchestra?'

Conductors have composers, singers and players as targets: but most especially they have each other. Take Beecham on Von Karajan: 'a sort of musical Malcolm Sargent'; on Toscanini, 'a glorified Italian bandmaster', and 'Much is made of the fact that he conducts without a score – Toscanini is so short-sighted that he would not be able to use a score . . . but though it is generally known that Toscanini invariably conducts from memory and though it is generally known that Toscanini is blind, nobody apparently is aware that he is also tone-deaf!' On Sir John Barbirolli: 'He has done splendid work with the Hallé since they brought him back from New York . . . a good, strong, north of England orchestra, masculine and vigorous . . . Barbirolli . . . has transformed it into the finest chamber orchestra in the country'; on Sir Adrian Boult: 'He came to see me this morning – positively reeking of Horlicks': on Malcolm Sargent: 'Malcolm is an extremely accomplished musician and an incredibly accomplished conductor. I appointed him my deputy . . . take my advice, if ever you appoint a deputy, appoint one whom you can trust technically, but his calibre must be such that the public will always be glad to see *you* back again.'

On hearing that Mr Sargent had become Sir Malcolm, Beecham retorted, 'I didn't know he'd been knighted. I knew he'd been doctored.' Beecham heard that Sargent, whose nickname was Flash Harry, had been in Tokyo. 'Malcolm in Tokyo? What was he doing?' 'Conducting,' came the reply. 'Ah, I see. A flash in Japan.' On that same Japanese tour, a news report claimed that a gun had gone off in the audience one night when Sir Malcolm was conducting. 'I had no idea the Japanese were so musical,' Sir Thomas mused.

Edgard Varèse, the composer, made a distinction between European and American conductors: 'In Europe when a rich woman has an affair with a conductor she has a baby. In America she endows an orchestra for him.' Beecham was more sweeping: 'All the arts in America are a gigantic racket run by unscrupulous men for unhealthy women.'

Beecham also enjoyed to kick around the reputations of composers. On Vaughan Williams: 'I very much like some of Vaughan Williams, for example his *Fantasia on a Theme of Thomas Tallis*. Unfortunately, in his compositions published subsequently he omitted to take the precaution of including a theme of Thomas Tallis.' After conducting Vaughan Williams's Pastoral Symphony for the BBC he leaned over to the celeste player and said briskly, 'A city life for me!' On a symphony by Bruckner in which the composer fails to organise and develop an idea: 'In the first movement I took note of a dozen pregnancies and half a dozen miscarriages.' On a symphony which Elgar declined to allow him to cut, 'Elgar's A-flat symphony is a large work . . . the musical equivalent of St Pancras Station, Neo-Gothic, don't you know!'

He was sharp with Beethoven. 'The best of Beethoven's music, excepting the first four of his piano concertos, and the third, fourth and sixth of his symphonies is second-rate measured by the values set up by Mozart.' Of the third movement of Beethoven's Seventh Symphony: 'What can you do with it? It's like a lot of yaks jumping about.'

Mozart alone escaped Beecham's sallies. (Poor Stockhausen! 'Have you conducted Stockhausen, Sir Thomas?' 'No, but I've stepped in a lot.') Mozart was the only composer he would never 'misconduct'. 'The only thing that is really important, in playing, in conducting – yes, even in misconducting – is this. Whatever you do, do it with conviction.'

Beecham's second wife was the pianist Betty Humby. After she had rehearsed a piece in the Fairfield Halls in Croydon, Beecham saw two stage hands arrive to move the piano off stage. 'Don't bother,' he told them. 'After that performance it will probably slink off.'

Lady Beecham died while they were touring in South America. On his return he met an old friend who had not heard the news. He enquired, 'How's Betty?' 'On tour,' said Sir Thomas, 'with Vaughan Williams.'

Beecham also had it in for harpsichords: 'The harpsichord sounds like two skeletons copulating on an iron roof – in a thunderstorm.'

In the course of diligent research for our Beecham play I asked Leonard Bernstein if he had any suitable stories. 'Not really,' he told me. 'We had a dressing room together once at the Met. We were sharing a ballet programme. He was extremely kind to me – but that's not really what you want, is it?'

At a lunch to celebrate his seventieth birthday telegrams were read out. Each was received with loud applause, especially those from the great surviving composers who included Strauss, Sibelius and Stravinsky. Maintaining his reputation for waggery Beecham waited until the final round had died down and then asked hopefully, 'Nothing from Mozart?'

BEERBOHM, Sir Henry Maximilian. Such was Max Beerbohm's aesthetic, dandyish pose at Oxford that when someone asked him if he was going down to the river to watch the boats during Eights Week he murmured, 'What river?'

BENNY, Jack. Judy Garland was born in a trunk according to the song in *A Star is Born*. For touring theatricals, 'the trunk' is home of all their make-up, wigs, costumes and effects, and was a key possession.

Legend has it that when Jack Benny was touring the Midwest of America in a vaudeville show a colleague – who was particularly fond of his mother – heard just before curtain-up that the old lady had died three days earlier, giving him no chance to get home for the funeral. Distraught, he wept. He was a perfect son. However, he was also a professional so as the time came for curtain-up he pulled himself together. 'Ah well,' he said, 'I suppose it could have been worse.'

Benny expressed shock. 'Could have been worse? What could be worse?'

His old friend sighed, 'Well, imagine losing your trunk!'

BERLIN, Irving. Great success, of course, breeds great jealousy. Towards the end of his active career (the early sixties) Irving Berlin came up with a spectacular flop, a patriotic musical, *Mr President*. Two song writers met on the sidewalk outside the Broadway theatre where the show was playing. 'Are you in there?' asked one. 'At the Irving show?'

'Yes,'said the other.

'How is it?' said the first.

'It's even worse than I'd hoped!'

BERNHARDT, Sarah (Rosine Bernard). Recent biographies have highlighted more of the eccentricities of Sarah Bernhardt. Her Jewish mother, a prostitute, would have preferred her daughter to have followed her into that profession, as Sarah's younger sister indeed did. The disappointed mother's advice, on which her actress daughter was inclined to act, was always to have two lovers, a younger one for pleasure and an older one for financial support.

When she was twenty years old the actress was made pregnant by a Belgian prince. When she broke the news to him he showed her the door saying, 'If you sit on a pile of thorns you can never know which one has pricked you.'

She was later the mistress of Charles Haas, the model for Proust's Swann and a Jewish member of the Jockey Club and a friend of the Prince of Wales. In this role she was not his only mistress and when he tired of her he pensioned her off.

During the 1871 Commune she followed her mother's advice. Arthur O'Connor, an aristocratic young Irishman attached to the French National Army whom she snatched from the professional bed of her younger sister, provided the pleasure, and Jacques Stern, a rich banker, the cash.

In later life her financial security enabled her to abandon the old and concentrate on the young – including the handsome young actor Jean Mounet-Sully, the artist Gustave Doré, Lou Tellegen, a good-looking 27-year-old actor, whom she took on one of her farewell tours of America when she was 66, and a bisexual Greek called Aristides.

BEST, George. The exquisite creative football of George Best is perhaps best summed up in Sir Matt Busby's team talks to Manchester United. Best was often told not to turn up. The reason? As Sir Matt explained it, 'It wasn't worth his coming. It was a very simple team talk. All I used to say was: "Whenever possible, give the ball to George." '

BETHELL, Sir Richard. When Bethell (later Lord Westbury) was Attorney-General in the mid-nineteenth century he enjoyed a long feud with Lord Chancellor Campbell. On the day of Campbell's elevation to the Chancellorship they met in a freezing Westminster Hall. Campbell had taken the precaution of enveloping himself in a huge fur coat. Bethell affected not to recognise him. Campbell remonstrated. 'I beg your pardon, my lord,' Bethell replied, 'I mistook you for the Great Seal.'

BETJEMAN, Sir John. When John Betjeman became engaged to Penelope Chetwode, the daughter of Field-Marshal Lord Chetwode, a former Commander-in-Chief in India, the veteran soldier considered how his rather unsuitable future son-in-law should address him. Rejecting 'father' and 'sir' he thought for a while and then pronounced, 'Call me "Field-Marshal".'

BEVIN, Ernest. When Ernest Bevin, the burly, Bristolian ex-docker, was Foreign Secretary in Attlee's Labour Cabinet in 1947, he went into hospital for what an official described as 'an internal operation'.
   'Call it piles, lad,' Bevin told him. 'Call it piles.'
   On a visit to the United Nations in 1948 Bevin was installed in the Waldorf Astoria. Eager to please on the first evening, the chef enquired what Bevin would like for dinner. Back came the somewhat cryptic message, 'Just steak and chips with some newts.' Bewilderment reigned in the kitchens and the cellars. Finally the manager phoned the British Embassy. An amused official solved the riddle. All old Ernie wanted with his steak and chips was a bottle of his favourite wine, Nuits St-Georges.

BIGGINS, Christopher. At a recent Royal charity polo occasion at the Guards Polo Club at Windsor the commentator was at pains to explain the finer points of the sport to newcomers. Helpfully he announced, 'In polo we change ends after a score.' From the stands the theatrically trained voice of Christopher Biggins boomed out: 'Just like in life, my dear.'

BIOGRAPHY. Biography and autobiography have been getting a bad press recently. Indeed it was always so. 'Autobiography,' wrote Lord Altrincham (John Grigg – he disclaimed his title) in 1962, 'is now as common as adultery and hardly less reprehensible.' Franklin P. Adams said, 'An autobiography usually reveals nothing bad about a writer except his memory.' Quentin Crisp sees it as 'an obituary in serial form with the last instalment missing'. An American publisher, Roger Jellinek, was sceptical, but accurate: 'The purpose of Presidential Office is not power or leadership of the Western world, but reminiscence, best-selling reminiscence!' Marshal Pétain believed that 'To write one's memoirs is to speak ill of everybody except oneself.' Evelyn Waugh viewed the task without enthusiasm – perhaps too much of his life had already surfaced in his fiction: 'Only when one has lost all curiosity about the future has one reached the age to write an autobiography.' Philip Guedella saw it as 'an unrivalled vehicle for telling the truth about other people'.

'Biography,' Guedella felt, 'like big game hunting, is one of the recognised forms of sport, and it is as unfair as only sport can be.' Wilde said, 'Every great man nowadays has his disciples and it is always Judas who writes the biography.' 'A well-written life,' in Carlyle's view, 'is almost as rare as a well-spent one.' J.B. Priestley had 'never read the life of any important person without discovering that he knew more and could do more than I could hope to do in half a dozen lifetimes.'

BLAKE, Eubie. Eubie Blake, the composer authologised in the musical *Bubbling Brown Sugar*, celebrated his hundredth birthday with the widely quoted remark, 'If I'd known I was going to live this long I'd have taken better care of myself.' (Though Adolph Zukor may have said it before him.)

Three years earlier – after two marriages and several strings of romances – when Blake was ninety-seven, he was asked 'How old do you have to be before the sex drive goes?'

He answered, 'You'll have to ask somebody older than me.'

Zukor did not say that.

BLOM, Eric. Eric Blom, the distinguished musicologist, was the *Observer* music critic in the early fifties and the editor of the fifth edition of *Grove's Dictionary of Music*. At his cremation it was planned that a Bach Chorale should be played. The organist misheard the instructions and the congregation were treated to Offenbach's 'Nuit d'amour'. He thought he had been asked for a 'barcarolle'.

BOGDANOVICH, Peter. The ex-movie critic and momentary directorial wunderkind of Hollywood – *The Last Picture Show, Paper Moon, What's Up, Doc?* – Peter Bogdanovich, inspired one of Billy Wilder's most acid comments before he hit the doldrums. 'It isn't true that Hollywood is a bitter place, divided by hatred, greed and jealousy,' Wilder said. 'All it takes to bring the community together is a flop by Peter Bogdanovich.'

BOOTHBY, Robert John Graham, Baron. In 1932 Lord Boothby – then Robert Boothby MP – visited Germany and was invited to meet Adolf Hitler. At the Chancellery in Berlin Boothby walked the length of the very long room towards Hitler who was seated at the end. Not until he reached the desk did the Führer look up, spring to his feet, raise his right arm in his personal salute and shout, 'Hitler!' Boothby responded by clicking his heels together, raising *his* right arm and shouting back, 'Boothby!'

BORGE, Victor. Victor Borge escaped from occupied Denmark on the arrival of the Nazis – his real name, Borg Rosenbaum, would not have promised a secure future. His well-known line in his one-man show, 'The shortest distance between two people is a smile', was practised on two Russian diplomats who smuggled him by plane to an American boat in Finland.

On his application for an American visa he was told, 'You can have it if you can make the people of America laugh as much as you have made people laugh in Scandinavia.'

He arrived with little English and had his Danish scripts translated so that he could appear on the Bing Crosby radio show. Even without understanding the words he was reading he was elected Radio Find of 1940.

Much later in his career he recalled 'a charming theatregoer who spoke to me after the show and said, "I feel I know such a lot about you, Mr Borge, because my mother has all your records." For once I was too delighted to make the old wisecrack about wondering where I lost them.'

The theatregoer was the Queen.

BOTTOMLEY, Horatio William. Horatio Bottomley was very much the Robert Maxwell of his day. After the Great War, he swindled the public out of thousands of pounds with his bogus Victory Bonds and phoney competitions and lotteries in his magazine, *John Bull*. One day an office boy was brought before him for pinching a postal order from the magazine. The great swindler frowned for a moment, then relaxed, smiled and said, 'Damn it all, it's only sixpence and I suppose he has to begin *somewhere*.'

Bottomley eventually (unlike Maxwell) found himself in Wormwood Scrubs. At the same time he was required to appear in the Bankruptcy Court. On these occasions he had to change from prison uniform into civilian clothes. One acquaintance who met him in court pointed out the creases in his rumpled coat. Bottomley was casual about it. 'Never mind, when I get back, I change for dinner.'

After his release he was lunching in Romano's in the Strand. At a neighbouring table sat Sir Henry Curtis-Bennet, a notably fat barrister. At the end of his meal he crossed over to Bottomley and said how well he looked. Bottomley cast his eye over Bennet's paunch and said, 'Yes – it changed my life. And it looks as if three years wouldn't do you much harm.'

BOWEN, Charles, Lord. Lord Bowen, a nineteenth-century judge, has two claims to inclusion in any gallery of witty lawyers. On one occasion judges were composing an address to Royalty. Many took exception to the phrase 'Conscious as we are of our shortcomings . . .' Considering it too humble and craven, Bowen slyly suggested a change to 'Conscious as we are of one another's shortcomings'.

In his book of *Legal Anecdotes* Michael Gilbert, on the evidence of Sir Henry Cunningham, credits Bowen with originating one of the most hardy chestnuts used by after-dinner speakers. He refers to the story of Daniel, perhaps about to be eaten, in the lion's den and then points out that Daniel had one great advantage, one consolation; 'He knew that when the dreadful banquet was over, at any rate it was not he who would be called upon to return thanks!'

BOXING. David Belasco, the flamboyant theatrical writer, director and impresario, was at one time a boxing promoter. 'Boxing is show business with blood,' he insisted.

Boxing has produced moments of eloquence – or, more often, bravura. In 1902 Bob Fitzsimmons memorably said, 'The bigger they are, the harder they fall,' before facing the enormous Jim Jeffries. Some eighteen years later Jack Dempsey had a similar thought: 'Tall men come down to my height when I hit 'em in the body.' Asked by a woman reporter whether he watched his opponent's eyes or his gloves, Terry Downes flashed back in reply, 'His gloves, dear: never bin 'it by an eye in me life.'

When Theodore Roosevelt asked one Frank Govan why he had given up dentistry to box, the ex-dentist knew exactly why: 'It pays me better to knock teeth out than put them in.'

Muhammad Ali, the champion of the off-the-cuff boxing chat from his days as Cassius Clay, said, 'I figure I'll be champ for about ten years and then I'll let my brother take over – like the Kennedys down in Washington.' His manifesto as Muhammad Ali ran 'Float like a butterfly, sting like a bee. His hands can't hit what the eye can't see.' (Was Ali's couplet, incidentally, an echo of the 'Ballad of Joe Louis', lyrics by Richard Wright, music by Count Basie, sung by Paul Robeson in 1942? 'Rabbit say to the bee, "What makes you sting so deep?" The bee say, "I sting like Joe and rock 'em all to sleep." ')

Ali was particularly hard on Joe Frazier: 'He's so ugly they ought to donate his face to the Wild Life fund'; and 'That man can't sing. He's the only nigger in the world ain't got rhythm.' Ali was also the source of wit in others. 'I'd like to borrow his body for just forty-eight hours,' said Jim Murray in 1964. 'There are three guys I'd like to beat up and four women I'd like to make love to.' Even Ali's doctor was quotable: 'They're selling video cassettes of the Ali–Spinks fight for $89.95. Hell, for that money Spinks will come to your house.'

Among boxing managers, Jack Hurley, whose character is summarised by the title of his autobiography, *Don't Call Me Honest, You'll Ruin Me*, typifies the mean sub-Runyon literature of boxing disenchantment. 'Looking at a fighter who can't punch is like kissing your mother-in-law'; 'Putting a fighter in the business world is like putting silk stockings on a pig'; 'I think every young man should have a hobby. Learning to handle money is the best hobby'; and: 'I've had more operations than any human being alive. I've had twenty-seven sinus operations and now they say you shouldn't have any. That's how they found out.'

BOYCOTT, Geoffrey. When the great Yorkshire and England batsman was a very young man playing for Barnsley, he got a trial for Yorkshire and his success was confirmed by a telegram asking him to report for duty at Headingley the next day. Legend has it that the message arrived during a match and was delivered to Boycott in the middle of his innings. Allegedly, he declared the innings closed and walked from the field. When the opposition captain asked him what was happening he said simply, 'I've finished with this sort of cricket.' And he had.

Denis Compton tells a story of a man in a curry house in Sheffield. He asks for a Vindaloo. The owner urges him to try a Boycott. At first he resists; but pressed he asks the difference between a Boycott and a Vindaloo. 'They taste the same,' says the owner, 'but with a Boycott you get the runs more slowly.'

BOYLE, Sir Edward. The progressive Tory MP Edward Boyle, a Cabinet Minister under Harold Macmillan, recalled that after his father, a landed

Conservative, had listened to one of J. B. Priestley's famous, albeit somewhat radical, wartime broadcasts, he remarked, 'The feller sounds as though he's after my dining room clock.'

My father had much the same opinion of Priestley.

BRAHMS, Johannes. André Previn tells a story of a young composer who came to Brahms and asked if he might play for the master a funeral march which he had composed in memory of Beethoven. Permission was granted and the young man played away. When he had done he asked Brahms for his verdict.

'I'll tell you,' said Brahms, candidly, 'I'd be much happier if you were dead and Beethoven had written the march.'

(An original, later, source is perhaps a Oscar Levant comment. He said much the same to a young composer in similar circumstances after George Gershwin died in 1937.)

BRANDSTRUP, Ludwig. Poor Mr Brandstrup has been sold short in my book of *Theatrical Anecdotes* and this is the first opportunity I have had to right the wrong. A Danish correspondent, Hansgeill Rasmussen, gave me the following anecdote for the previous book:

> Christian Gottschalk was a Danish actor working in Copenhagen at the beginning of the German occupation in World War Two. He came on stage to face an audience of German officers, entering with his right arm raised straight up in the air. The young Germans jumped up and lifted their arms in a 'Heil Hitler' salute. Gottschalk faced them for a few seconds and then said, 'The snow was THAT high outside my front door this morning.'

Mr Rasmussen has now written to me enclosing a copy of the Copenhagen newspaper *Berlinske Tidende*, dated 10 April 1940. Mr Rasmussen had got the name wrong – the witty and courageous Dane was in fact not Christian Gottschalk but Ludwig Brandstrup.

Apologies all round!

BRITISH BROADCASTING CORPORATION. In the early days of broadcasting in the 1920s, when everything was new and the technology was erratic, the then Bishop of London was invited to deliver an epilogue, finishing with a blessing. After praying that the Lord should bless and keep the listeners, Amen, he appeared to add the ironical aside: 'I don't think.'

In fact the wretched Bishop had been cut off while saying to his producer, 'I don't think that was too bad, was it?'

It is difficult to know which of the lunacies committed by the BBC is most worthy of inclusion; but at least this one was unfamiliar to me. In the 1930s the

Corporation broadcast the popular song 'Ain't it grand to be blooming well dead'. Many people accused the BBC of encouraging suicide. Performances of the song were discontinued with a statement by a BBC official that 'Although people like ourselves may find it amusing, I very much question whether, in the present state of the country, it can have other than a lowering effect upon public morale.' (Pre-echoes of the newscaster Martin Lewis's plea for more Good News bulletins?)

Although James Joyce's *Ulysses* had been published in 1922 Lord Reith would not allow it to be mentioned on the BBC in 1931. At a literary luncheon in his honour that year, Joyce, by then blind and gloomy, was told of the ban by Harold Nicolson. He cheered up immediately.

BRITTEN, Sir Benjamin. The edited letters and diaries of Benjamin Britten and the biography by Humphrey Carpenter have revealed most of what there is to be told about the composer and his relationship with Peter Pears and with young boys (blameless).

Reviewing the letters, John Amis remembered once asking Britten why, after the opera *Paul Bunyan*, produced during his self-imposed exile in North America from May 1939 to March 1942, he had never asked Auden for another full-length libretto. Britten answered, 'Well, you see, Johnny, when writing an opera the composer *must* wear his trousers. But with Auden one never could.' Amis guffawed at this and was rewarded by one of Britten's characteristic dismissals: he 'was out in the cold for a year'.

David Hemmings was Britten's famous first boy soprano as Miles in *The Turn of the Screw*, and much admired by Britten and Pears. As they walked on the shingle at Aldeburgh one day the two men asked young Hemmings what he wanted to be when he grew up. 'A doctor,' he said.

'Why?' they asked with visions of an angelic child who wanted to devote his life to the selfless service of others.

Hemmings soon disillusioned them. 'So I can see all those women naked,' he said.

Britten and Pears attracted light versifiers. Michael Flanders sent them sky-high in a revue song in *Airs on a Shoestring*. Their fans were dismissed as 'The Doggy, Doggy Few'; *Gloriana* became Orgy and Bess, and the Sweep's cry in *Let's Make and Opera*, 'Don't send him up again!', was neatly transposed to the composer and his favourite singer. All the culprits were out in the cold for ever.

So, probably, was the clerihew contributor to *Punch* who observed:

> There's no need for Peter Pears
> To give himself airs.
> He has them written
> By Benjamin Britten.

BROADHURST, Henry. The Victorian MP for Stoke was aware of the value of catching the eye of popular cartoonists in trying to make his mark. He adopted a famous pair of enormous boots. He knew that he had succeeded when he was announced on a public platform and heard the crowd roar: 'We know 'im! We know 'im! We've seen 'is boots in *Punch*!'

BROOKFIELD, Charles. Charles Brookfield was a Victorian actor, a companionable club man and raconteur who charmingly invented an appropriate conclusion for his own obituary: 'Never a great actor, he was invaluable in small parts. But, after all, it is at his club that he will be most missed.'

BROWN, George (Lord George-Brown). Labour Foreign Ministers have often been the subject of anecdote, from Ernest Bevin's attempt to kiss Lady Diana Cooper in the lift of the British Embassy in Paris to some of George Brown's indiscretions.

George Brown is sadly only remembered, if at all, by a new generation as the master of the gaffe who inspired in *Private Eye* the euphemism for drunkenness: 'tired and emotional'. At a reception at Buckingham Palace Harold Wilson could sometimes be heard to mutter, 'Tighten your seat-belts, here comes George.' However, Woodrow Wyatt has claimed that he first said, 'I'd rather have George Brown drunk than Wilson sober.'

Brown was bold in his answer to these charges. 'What do you think went wrong?' he asked Wyatt after Wilson defeated him for the leadership of the Labour Party. 'You must face it, George,' said Wyatt. 'It's because you're so dreadfully rude to people when you're drunk.' George did not back down. 'What makes them think I'm rude to them just because I'm drunk.'

Wyatt reported – in his review of Peter Patterson's excellent biography of Brown called, of course, *Tired and Emotional* – a dinner party at his house where George, by now Foreign Secretary, sat next to Edwina Erlanger, a famous beauty not in her first flush but still a handsome woman. He talked to her briefly and drunkenly and then shouted, 'Shut up, you old bag. I've talked to you long enough. Now I'm going to talk to this pretty girl on my other side.'

It was as Foreign Secretary that his gaffes became the stuff of legend. When he wanted a fire on a cold night in Brussels and the Ambassador said that the staff had gone home he got the Ambassador's wife out of bed to make and light one.

Perhaps his finest hour in Brussels was at a dinner given by the Belgian Prime Minister: 'I'll tell you who's been defending Europe,' he bellowed. 'The British Army. And where, you may ask, are the soldiers of the Belgian Army tonight? I'll tell you where the soldiers of the Belgian Army are. They are in the brothels of Brussels!'

He could call Giscard d'Estaing 'that frog' to his face, and could arrange a state dinner for the Turkish President Sunay and his very homely wife at Hampton Court and amidst his rambling speech congratulate the man on being married 'to the most beautiful woman in the world'. Topping that, having booked the Royal Ballet at the special request of the President he could tug him away in the middle of their performance, saying, 'You don't want to listen to this rubbish – let's go and have a drink.'

The general public was not aware of his low tolerance for alcohol until he made a maudlin appearance on television on the evening of President Kennedy's assassination. Earlier he had nearly come to blows with the American actor Eli Wallach because Wallach had never appeared in a play by the excellent Ted Willis, a long-time friend of George Brown – or even heard of him.

However, the public was not privy to the most endearing George Brown 'tired and emotional' anecdotes. This one could be apocryphal. Both Auberon Waugh and Peter Patterson quote the authority as Lord Chalfont. Patterson says that Chalfont described it to him with such vivid detail that he thought he must have witnessed it – then he found out by diligent research that George Brown had never visited Brazilia where the scene is set. Waugh sets the story – equally sure that he has Chalfont's authority – in the Balkans. He heard it from Chalfont in 1976 and printed a version which did not name George on 2 May 1976.

I shall stay with the South American version because it's a more exotic location and that's the way I've been telling it since the 1970s. I have preferred not to check with Alun Chalfont in case he now wishes to forget it.

George was at a state reception in Brazilia and when, late in the evening, the band struck up he asked a gorgeously scarlet-robed figure to dance. 'No,' said the invitee. 'There are three reasons why I will not waltz with you, Mr Brown. In the first place you are drunk. In the second this is not a waltz. It is the National Anthem of Peru. In the third and most important place, I am the Cardinal Archbishop of Lima.'

His end was sad. He abandoned his lifelong membership of the Labour Party for the SDP. He left his high Anglican faith for the Catholic Church. He left his wife of many years, the long-suffering Sophie, for his secretary, many years younger; and when he made his speech of resignation from the party it lost its impact when he was photographed by countless paparazzi collapsed helplessly in the gutter the same evening saying, 'I wish I could do this sort of thing standing up.'

BROWNE, Coral. One of Coral Browne's classic remarks which was unaccountably omitted from my *Theatrical Anecdotes* stems from the time when she was filming Frank Marcus's *The Killing of Sister George* with Beryl Reid and

Susannah York. There is a scene in the film where Sister George's lover, played by Ms York, is stolen from her by the BBC executive played by Coral Browne. In a steamy meeting she goes down on Ms York's character. Before filming started, the director, Robert Aldrich, called the two actresses to his office and said that if they had any objections would they please voice them now. He did not want embarrassing trouble in the studio on the day of filming. He put the question to Coral first. Her reply was unequivocal: 'I'll eat through the mattress if you don't say cut!'

BUCCLEUCH, Mary, Duchess of. Mary, Duchess of Buccleuch, died in 1993 at the age of 92. She was a descendant of Charles II and Nell Gwyn and brought taste and organisation to her three palatial homes – Drumlanrig, Bowhill and Boughton. She was by all accounts a friendly but formidable hostess, giving guided tours which her guests were not allowed to avoid, and insisting on punctuality at meal times. To one young man who was late for dinner she was stern in her disbelief of his excuses. 'You got lost on your way from your bedroom?' she said. 'Well, remember in future to turn right at the Rembrandt and left at the Leonardo.'

BURGON, John William. Burgon was to become Dean of Chichester; but while he was an undergraduate at Oxford in 1845 he won the Newdigate Prize for an English poem. The subject was Petra. Most of it was fairly routine stuff but the judges pounced on one couplet which they judged exceptional:

> Match me such a marvel, save in Eastern clime –
> A rose-red city, half as old as time.

So praised and quoted was the couplet that it was inevitably parodied – notably with reference to an elderly don at Trinity called Short. The parody was:

> Match me such a marvel, save in college port,
> That nose-red liquor, half as old as Short.

BUSH, George. While 'Reaganism' referred to a government ideology, no one uses 'Bushism' in this way. A 'Bushism' means the ex-president's funny way of talking: rambling, often incoherent; staccato sentences with no pronouns; weird mixed metaphors and non-sequiturs.

This semi-coherent style may appear to some as sincerity and lack of artifice – he tries to come on as 'a regular guy'. 'When I need a little free advice about Saddam Hussein, I turn to country music.'

Jacob Weisberg of the *New Republic* compared Bush to 'a big, clumsy, golden retriever, drooling and knocking over the furniture in eagerness'. Faced with an extreme right-wing challenge from David Duke, 'We have – I have – want – to be positioned in that I could not possibly support David Duke because of his racism and his bigotry and all of that.'

What does one make of 'I had a good long talk bilaterally with François Mitterand this morning'? It recalls a pompous film mogul in Wardour Street who once told me, 'I shall have to make a hemisphere-to-hemisphere call before I can make a decision on this.' He meant he had to call New York.

Asked what it was like to sit opposite Gorbachev at the Malta summit, Bush's answer was 'I'm not the most articulate emotionalist.'

He got mightily confused about his relationship with Barbara Bush and their dog. 'It has been said by some cynic, maybe it was a former president, "If you want a friend in Washington, get a dog" . . . I don't need that, because I have Barbara Bush.' A month later Barbara and the dog were on his mind again. 'I'm delighted that Barbara Bush is with me today, and I – she got a good, clean bill of health yesterday. But I'm taking another look at our doctor. He told her it's OK to kiss the dog – I mean – no – it's okay to kiss your husband, but don't kiss the dog. So I don't know exactly what that means.'

Sometimes he had an odd set of political priorities: 'Get this [economic plan] passed. Later on, we can all debate it.' Under the heading 'For whom the bell knells', *New Republic* highlighted his reluctance to make an election prediction in 1988. 'I don't want to get, you know, here we are close to the election – sounding the knell of over-confidence that I don't feel.'

One of Bush's more insensitive alleged asides concerns a tour of Auschwitz: 'Boy, they were big on crematoriums, weren't they?' The obvious was easier: 'It's no exaggeration to say the undecideds could go one way or another.' Toasting the Prime Minister of Pakistan, Benazir Bhutto, at a White House dinner he admitted, 'Fluency in English is something that I'm often not accused of' – however he insisted on controlling the content of his speeches, 'Inarticulate as though I may be.'

Sometimes he just sounded 'hypoactive'. During a Bush-Dukakis debate he complained, 'These are two hypo-rhetorical questions'; and a year later from the Oval office, 'I'm not going to hypothecate that it may – anything goes too fast.'

One of the most touching George Bush anecdotes stems from his second campaign for the Presidency. In the line of duty he visited an Old Folks' – a Sunset Home. Confronted by a bed-ridden, aged incumbent he bent forward in concern. Kindly, he said, 'Do you know who I am?' The nonagenarian was used to this approach. 'If you don't know who you are,' she shot back, 'you'd better ask at reception.'

However, none of Bush's curious constructions did him as much damage as the impeccably literate 'Read my lips. No more taxes.' Maybe he knew what he was doing messing up the language.

BUTLER, Samuel. Having rejected holy orders because of religious doubts and his preferred alternative, sheep farming in New Zealand, which he took up in 1859, Butler returned to England in 1894 to study painting, and in 1872 published *Erewhon* anonymously. From works of scientific controversy and on art and travel he wrote *The Authoress of the 'Odyssey'* based on his theory of the feminine authorship of the *Odyssey*. In April 1902, when he was 67, he was staying in an hotel in Rome. With another guest he discovered their mutual interest in Homer. 'Oh! In that case,' said his new acquaintance, 'you ought to meet old Butler.'

'I am old Butler,' was his reply.

— C —

CAMPBELL, Kim. Canada's first woman Prime Minister, Kim Campbell, who succeeded Brian Mulroney as leader of the ruling Conservative Party, seems to have taken a leaf out of the book of the Australian Prime Minister, Paul Keating, when it comes to invective.

An official portrait photograph early in her campaign earned her the title of 'The Madonna of Canadian politics', and her more acid dismissals of opponents have inspired a Montreal publisher to issue a slim volume of quotations: she has called opponents of her party 'enemies of Canada' and apathetic voters 'apathetic SOBs', and has talked of the 'evils of the papacy', in spite of the fact that Roman Catholicism is the principal religion of her country. Of one opponent she said, 'I wish I'd known him before his lobotomy.' On becoming Defence Minister, her best line was 'Don't mess with me. I got tanks.' And of the opposition in general: 'I suspect some of them haven't read this bill. I suspect after three pages their lips get tired.'

CAMPBELL, Mrs Patrick. Since the publication of my *Theatrical Anecdotes*, William Hartley has reminded me of two more Mrs Patrick Campbell anecdotes. Dismissing one rival she said, 'Such a clever actress. Pity she does her hair with Bovril.'

Another of her Hollywood indiscretions was provoked by the well-known actor Joseph Shildkraut, who, when he first saw her, had not heard of her or her formidable reputation. He asked around about her. Apprised of his researches Mrs Pat was irritated and bided her time until they were introduced. She pretended not to know him and asked his name. It was his turn to be annoyed. 'Joseph Shildkraut,' he snapped. 'Oh well,' she said, 'you could always change it.'

CAMROSE, Viscount (William Berry). Lord Camrose, proprietor of *The Daily Telegraph*, was one of three Berry brothers: the others were Seymour, who became Lord Buckland, and Gomer, who was to be Lord Kemsley. William Berry, the son of a stern Victorian mayor who was Mayor of Methyn, bought *The Sunday Times* during World War One and the *Telegraph* in 1927. He was not an automatic Tory eulogist. He fired off daily memoranda of the order of ' I dislike intensely the fulsome adulation of Mr Baldwin . . . no wonder people describe the paper as a "hack party" journal'; and 'We have fallen too easily for the trouble in Spain. It is notorious that the Spanish Government is a bad one. It by no means follows that the people rebelling against it are extremists or Bolsheviks.'

William Deedes, reviewing a biography of *William Camrose: Giant of Fleet Street* in the *Sunday Telegraph* by Camrose's son, Lord Hartwell, recalled a cluster of anecdotes which might otherwise have got away. A reporter once telephoned the canteen with a peremptory order for a ham sandwich 'with mustard', unaware that he had inadvertently dialled Camrose's extension. The sandwich was delivered promptly with a follow-up call from the proprietor enquiring, 'I trust your sandwich has arrived?' A colleague covered his premature baldness by wearing a hat at all times in the office – at all times, that is, except when Camrose telephoned him, when he respectfully took it off. Yet another, on a meagre £12 a week at the *Telegraph*, was offered £15 by the *Daily Herald*. He reported this to his boss, who asked what they were offering. The reply was £17. 'I will raise your salary to £15,' said Camrose.

Also on his staff was Hugo Wortham, the editor of the 'Peterborough' column, a cantankerous wine buff. He made a practice of criticising the claret which Camrose served at office lunches. On one occasion he exclaimed loudly, 'Oh God, they've boiled the claret again!' Camrose heard the complaint in silence but a few months later when Wortham was again invited the claret was chilled. Camrose waited his moment and then as a silence fell on the room enquired loudly, 'Claret to your taste, Mr Wortham?'

CANNING, George. Canning, a brilliant orator, and, for me, a schoolboy hero, was both Foreign Secretary (in 1807) and, for only four months, Prime Minister in 1827.

He had a legendary quick mind and thought too fast for (pre-shorthand) dictation and for his own lightning pen. Once when gout in his hand stopped him writing he did manage to dictate two despatches simultaneously – one on Greek affairs to George Bentinck, and the other on South American policy to Howard de Walden. He will, however, probably be best remembered for his couplet summing up two Prime Ministers:

Pitt is to Addington
As London is to Paddington

(Major is to Thatcher
As Rat is to Catcher?)

Shelley dismissed Canning's rival, Castlereagh (who was to commit suicide, his mind having gone, in 1822), in another couplet after the Peterloo Massacre in 1819:

I met murder on the way!
He had a mask like Castlereagh.

CANNON, Jimmy. Jimmy Cannon, who died in 1973, was one of the wittiest of that tough-guy school of American sportswriters. He went to the heart of his profession with 'A sportswriter is entombed in a prolonged boyhood.' He had a vivid turn of romantic phrase: 'Philadelphia is an old wino sleeping it off in a doorway littered with busted dreams. Its teams are doomed to lose and its fans are cruel and crabbed.' 'However, he protested that he was against the romantic school. 'Sportswriting survives because of the guys who *don't* cheer'; and 'Hemingway was a sportswriter . . . he was the only guy who could make fishing sound interesting to me. Fishing with me has always been an excuse to drink in the daytime.'

Cannon had a healthy contempt for sportsmen too: 'Let's face it, sportswriters, we're not hanging around with brain surgeons!'

CARMAN, George, QC. George Carman has become one of the most celebrated libel lawyers, defending Norman Tebbit against an action brought by a Labour council, and winning £35,000 damages for Jason Connery over a claim that he had shown cowardice. Other successes on criminal charges were his defences of Jeremy Thorpe, Peter Adamson, Maria Aitken and Ken Dodd. Barred from a Fleet Street wine bar, he is alleged to have said to the barman as he left: 'If you tell me why, I will sue you.'

Defending South Yorkshire police against Arthur Scargill, he said in court, 'Entrusting Arthur Scargill with upholding civil liberties was as dangerous as trusting Satan to abolish sin.'

CAUSLEY, Charles. The poet Charles Causley tells an affectionate story of his aged countrywoman mother watching an early television transmission. 'Some Greek Tragedy, and all these ladies from RADA sitting around in smocks on rocks and saying, "Woe". My mother said, "What's the matter? Why don't they go out and get a job like I did?" '

It reminds me of my mother, who, after lunch one Boxing Day when she was very old, was watching the energetic Debbie Reynolds and a troupe of dynamic dancers. My mother was half asleep but as they romped and tumbled over and through a haystack in the opening sequence of *The Unsinkable Molly Brown*, she opened one beady eye and said disapprovingly, 'I do hope those aren't local children.'

CÉZANNE, Paul. Cézanne seems to have been remarkably careless about the disposition of his canvases – in spite of the fact that he was often hard up. Renoir tells of meeting him in the street dragging a picture. Cézanne explained that there was no money left in the house and that the canvas was for sale – it was in fact the superb *Bathers*. Meeting Renoir again a few days later, Cézanne told him joyfully that he had had a great success with his picture. 'It has been taken by someone who really likes it!' Renoir assumed he had found a buyer. However, it turned out that a poor musician had gone into such ecstasies over the canvas that Cézanne gave it to him for nothing.

On another occasion Cézanne complained to Renoir that Estaque, a favourite resort of artists in the Midi, had been ruined by building. Renoir went to check and found it virtually unspoilt. He also – by accident – found a Cézanne. When his companion Lauth was caught short with violent diarrhoea they had looked around for some large leaves. Renoir spotted a sheet of paper lying amidst some rubble. However, he could not let it relieve his companion's distress. A look revealed that it was one of Cézanne's finest watercolours. He had slaved over it for some twenty sittings and then, displeased, cast it away among the rocks. Renoir retrieved it for his own pleasure.

CHANEL, Coco. Coco Chanel, the great French dress designer, was mistress to a great many men, including famously the Duke of Westminster. However, during the war she had an affair with a German officer and when hostilities were over she was accused of collaborating. She answered the charge fiercely. 'My heart is French but my cunt is international.'

CHAPPELL, Greg. The competitive Australian cricket captain Greg Chappell used extraordinary tactics to win a final Benson & Hedges limited-over Test Match between Australia and New Zealand in Melbourne in 1981. The teams were one-all in the three-match series and New Zealand needed six runs off the last ball to win. To ensure that the New Zealand No. 10, Brian McKechnie, did not hit the ball out of the ground Chappell told his brother Trevor to bowl *underarm*. McKechnie could not hoist the ball into the air and Australia won the series. The letter of the law, if not the spirit had been observed. It provoked the pungent New Zealand suggestion of a new underarm deodorant: 'It's called Chappell and it stinks.'

CHARLES I. King Charles I was the son of James I and a better art patron than a politician. At loggerheads with Members of Parliament, from the start of his reign he attempted to rule without them. Fortunately he did not inherit his father's personal idiosyncrasies – sadly he *did* inherit his absolutism and belief in the Divine Right of Kings. He made a politically imprudent but personally happy marriage to the Catholic French Princess Henrietta Maria. She arrived in England with instructions from the French Clergy to be a missionary for Catholicism. According to Trevor Roper, her 'ideas of missionary activity were somewhat elementary, and consisted of breaking into an Anglican service in the royal household with a pack of beagles and interrupting the preacher with hunting noises.'

They first met when Charles was Prince of Wales and the sixteen-year-old Henrietta Maria, wanting to show that although she was small she was not wearing high-heeled shoes insisted, 'Sire, I stand on mine own two feet; I have no helps by art: this high am I, neither higher nor lower!'

According to John Aubrey, Charles made an early enemy when he 'had complaint against one Henry Martin for his wenching. It happened that Henry was in Hyde Parke one time when his majestie was there going to see a race. The King espied him, and sayd aloud, "Let that ugly rascal be gonne out of the parke, that whore-master, or else I will not see the sport." So Henry went patiently *sed manehat alta mente repostum* ("but the sarcasm remained deep within him"). That sarcasm raised the whole county of Berks against the King . . . shortly after he was chosen Knight of the shire of the county . . . and proved a deadly enemy to the King.' Not the way to make friends and influence subjects.

The struggle between King and Parliament came to a head in 1642 when Charles had been on the throne seventeen years. The King invaded the House of Commons to arrest five MPs, including Pym and Hampden. To Speaker Lenthall he said, 'Well, since I see all the birds are flown I do expect that you shall send them unto me as they return hither. If not, I will seek them myself, for their treason is foul and such a one as you will thank me to discover . . . ' This evoked from the Speaker the famous reply 'May it please your Majesty, I have neither eyes to see nor tongue to speak in this place but as this House is pleased to direct me, whose servant I am.'

Thomas Wentworth, 1st Earl of Strafford, was impeached by the Long Parliament for corrupting the King and setting him against them. When Strafford heard that the King had agreed, although under duress, to the bill of attainder, he delivered the bitter quotation, 'Put not your trust in princes nor in the sons of men for in them there is no salvation.' The truth of this was brought home to the King when Strafford was executed on Tower Hill.

Charles suffered his final defeat at the hands of the Parliamentary party at the Battle of Naseby in 1646. His older sons, Charles and James, escaped to the Continent and Charles I's execution was imminent. He said farewell to his two younger children, Elizabeth and Henry, Duke of Gloucester, who was only eight. 'They will cut off my head,' he told him, taking him on his knee, 'and perhaps make thee King: but mark what I say, you must not be King so long as your brothers, Charles and James, do live – for they will cut off your brothers' heads when they catch them, and cut off thy head too, at last: and therefore I charge you do not be made a King by them.' Bravely the child replied, 'I will be torn in pieces first.'

The execution, on 30 January 1649, took place at the Banqueting Hall in Whitehall. The King had risen early, telling his attendant, 'I have a great work to do this day . . . this is my second marriage day: I will be trim today as may be, for before tonight I hope to be espoused to my blessed Jesus.' The organisation of the execution was botched. In bitter cold the King had to wait several hours instead of the few minutes he had expected. The execution team had the unbelievably appropriate names of Hunks, Hacker and Colonel Axtell.

On the scaffold Charles remembered Strafford, saying, 'An unjust sentence that I suffered to take effect, is punished now by an unjust sentence on me.' Seeing one of the team of officials fingering the axe the King remarked, 'Hurt not the axe that may hurt me.' Charles described himself as 'the Martyr of the People' and added 'Death is not terrible to me: I bless God I am prepared. I am going from a corruptible to an incorruptible crown where no disturbance can be.'

A young witness in the crowd saw the axe fall. He said he would remember as long as he lived the sound that broke from the crowd: 'Such a groan as I never heard before, and desire I may never hear again.'

The shirt which Charles was wearing is preserved at Windsor. His tomb was opened in 1813 and one of his vertebra was removed and fashioned into a salt cellar. His coffin shared a vault with Henry VIII's. He lost a finger bone at the same time, which was used to make a knife handle!

CHARLES II. The eldest son of Charles I and one of most colourful English kings, Charles II fled the country after losing to Cromwell at the Battle of Worcester in 1652, subsequently living an impoverished and dissolute life on the Continent. He returned as King in 1660. Tall and handsome, his saturnine features framed by a black periwig, he had a keen intellect and a special interest in science which belied his nickname, the 'Merry Monarch'. He achieved the prodigious feat of fathering thirteen illegitimate children – eight sons and five daughters – without producing a legitimate heir by his Spanish wife Catherine of Braganza. Sex apart, he was a competent monarch, reviving the Exchequer and the Royal Navy to leave a prosperous England. Despite the usual Stuart rows with Parliament he saw the introduction of habeas corpus, which if taken literally as 'you must have the body' might well serve as his private epitaph.

He was a witty conversationalist. After listening to a catalogue of his sins before being crowned in Scotland in 1651, he commented ironically, 'I think I must repent, too, that ever I was born.' After his defeat at the hands of Cromwell his escape was famously exciting. Sheltered in the Penderels' house in a nearby forest he and a Colonel Carlis then hid in the leafy branches of a great oak which has lent its name to a hundred Royal Oak public houses. By this ruse they avoided the Roundhead soldiers who were offering a £1,000 reward. When they left, the Penderels stayed loyal, cut Charles's hair to disguise him and he further darkened his white skin first with fireside soot and later with walnut juice. He escaped to the Netherlands where a string of minor German princesses were suggested as brides, 'Odds fish, but they are dull and foggy,' he moaned.

His Restoration took place in 1660 when the country showed itself in favour of a restored parliament and a restored monarchy. Samuel Pepys, a 26-year-old clerk in the Exchequer, was on board the *Royal Charles* which brought him back from Holland. At the disembarkation he recorded that, 'One of the King's footmen, with a dog that the King loved (which shit in the boat, which made us laugh and me think that a King and all that belong to him are but just as others are) went in a boat by ourselves.'

It is Charles II's amours which fascinated his subjects – and their descendants. One of his rare failures was Frances Stuart ('La Belle Stuart'). In 1662 he wrote a poem to win her: 'Oh, then 'tis, oh, then I think there's no Hell/Like loving too well.' At 32 he really might have done better or viewed it more critically. The same year Frances Stuart married the Duke of Richmond, though Barbara Villiers, Lady Castlemaine, another mistress, insisted that La Belle Stuart had led him on, 'Increasing his ardour without diminishing her virtue by making the final sacrifice.' The King was more philosophical. He wrote to his sister Minette, 'If you are well acquainted with a little fantastical gentleman called Cupid as I am, you would neither wonder nor take ill any sudden changes which do happen in the affairs of his conducting.' He often wrote to Minette (Mary of Orange), and when she was about to give birth in 1665, yet another mistress, the Duchess of Portsmouth, had just produced a girl. 'I am very glad,' he wrote, 'that your indisposition of health has turned into a great belly . . . I am afraid your shape is not so advantageously made for that convenience as *hers* is; however a boy will recompense two grunts or more.'

In the year that he was rejected by Frances Stuart, he met and married Catherine of Braganza. She landed at Portsmouth. 'It was happy for the honour of the nation. I was not put to the consummation of the marriage last night, for I was so sleepy, by having slept two hours on my journey, that I was afraid that matters would have gone sleepily.' He was more optimistic to Lord Clarendon after the ceremony. 'I cannot tell you how happy I think myself and must be the worst man living (which I think I am not) if I am not a good husband.'

Barbara Villiers, Lady Castlemaine, was the most termagant of his mistresses – and the most unfaithful. He caught her with John Churchill (to be rewarded by a later monarch with the title Duke of Marlborough) in her apartments. He reacted coolly – 'Go, you are a rascal, but I forgive you because you do it to get a living.' Lady Castlemaine, frequently hysterical, was more likely to threaten 'to massacre her children and burn the palace over his head'.

He met his two favourite actresses, 'Moll' Davis, whose hit song was 'My lodging is on the cold ground', and Nell Gwyn, at Tunbridge Wells in the summer of 1668. Contemporary gossip said that the ballad 'raised the fair songstress from her bed on the cold ground to the royal bed'. Pepys's verdict was dismissive. He found her 'a most impertinent slut'. On the other hand Nell Gwyn had graduated from orange seller at Covent Garden to comedienne at the Theatre Royal, Drury Lane. She vowed that she was 'but one man's whore, though I was brought up in a bawdy house to fill strong waters for the guests'. On one occasion the mob mistook her for the King's Catholic French mistress, the Duchess of Portsmouth. 'Be civil, good people,' Nell shouted from her coach. 'I am the Protestant whore!' which delighted and disarmed the ugly crowd.

Another mistress was Winifred Wells, a Maid of Honour to the Queen. He treated them all generously. Arranging for the upkeep of their children and enobling them. Nell Gwyn was in the habit of calling their child, affectionately, 'You little bastard', and when Charles protested she replied, 'I have nothing else to call him.' At her persuasion he founded the Chelsea Hospital for veterans and on his deathbed he requested, 'Let not poor Nelly starve.'

His judgements were often peremptory. Presbyterianism was 'Not a religion for a gentleman'. The Divorce Debate in the House of Lord was 'Better than a play!' When Lord Rochester quipped that the King 'Never did a foolish thing and never said a wise one', he replied, 'My words are my own and my actions are my ministers.' When he drew the bed curtains around Prince William of Orange and his niece Mary – the future William and Mary – he yelled, 'Now, nephew, to your work! Hey! St George for England!' Did he know that the task might not be much to William's taste?

On his page and later his Lord Treasurer, Sydney Godolphin, he was equally brusque: 'Never in the way and never out of it.'

When he dissolved Parliament in 1678 over a bill to exclude his brother James from the throne: 'I will submit to anything rather than endure the gentlemen of the Commons any longer.' Dissolving Parliament again in 1682 he announced, 'You had better have one King than five hundred.'

When an astrologer offered his services to the King he was taken to Newmarket and asked, 'to foretell winners'.

Having survived the plague and the Great Fire of London he died in 1685. 'I am sorry, gentlemen,' he apologised on his deathbed, 'for being such an unconscionable time a-dying'; and his last words were, 'Open the curtains that I may once more see day.' He was fifty-five.

CHARLES V. Charles V was a Holy Roman Emperor in the sixteenth century. On one occasion at least his judgement approached the wisdom of Solomon. Two ladies contended for precedence at his court. They appealed to the Monarch for a decision. Deftly he replied, 'Let the elder go first.'

No more was heard of the dispute.

CHILD STARS. I have dealt with Jackie Cooper and Jackie Coogan elsewhere, but there are a few more who warrant consideration. When W. C. Fields was asked how he liked children he famously growled 'par-boiled', and when he was cast opposite the scene-stealer Baby Le Roy he spiked the kid's orange juice with gin and told the director to walk the groggy boy around: 'Walk him around, he's no trouper. Send him home.'

Shirley Temple, whose career took off in 1931, set off an anthology of stories. Her father, a bank teller in Santa Monica, complained that women were writing to ask him to father their child. He reported the fact to Darryl Zanuck, asking him to promise not to tell Mrs Temple – 'She'd be ashamed of her sex,' he told the studio chief.

Little Shirley soon had an inflated idea of the importance of Hollywood. When she met Pershing, a World War One general, she showed him her autograph book full of Hollywood stars. Pershing was unimpressed, having heard of few of them. 'How did he ever get to be a general?' was the brat's comment.

Nor was she pleased when Santa Claus asked for her autograph in a Los Angeles department store. She knew he could not be Santa – 'He said he'd seen all my movies.'

She was equally clear-eyed after meeting H. G. Wells. She was told he was the most important person in the world. 'God is the most important person in the world,' was her verdict, 'and the Governor of California is second.' Darryl Zanuck, her studio boss, was dismayed that she was not encouraged to name him as the third.

Hard on Temple's heels came Mickey Rooney, who was once greeted by a fan in the Midwest and asked if he remembered his accoster. Rooney confessed that he didn't. Furious, the man stomped off saying, 'But I saw you in *Love Finds Andy Hardy*.'

Rooney idolised Clark Gable, and as a teenager became notorious for copying Gable's mannerisms, dress trends, and taste in cars. 'Some day I'll play a dirty trick on that kid,' Gable stormed. 'I'll wear a sarong and drive around in a hearse.' Pity he didn't.

CHURCHILL, Lord Randolph Henry Spencer. Everyone resigning from government to advance their careers should remember Lord Randolph Churchill – Sir Winston's father, the husband of Jenny Jerome. Lord Salisbury made him Chancellor of the Exchequer in 1886; six months later Churchill, in a bid for power, staged a theatrical resignation which backfired. Two days later he was lunching with a group who deplored his action. He said that he did not expect his resignation to be accepted. No one could think of a replacement except his hostess, who suggested Goschen, a former Liberal minister and financial expert who was now a Liberal Unionist. As Lady Bracknell said, 'We ask them in after dinner'. Lord Randolph poo-poohed the idea, casually, with 'I had forgotten Goschen.' Months later he and his hostess met again. By now Goschen had got the job and Lord Randolph said to her, sadly, 'You were quite right. I forgot Goschen.'

Earlier he had tried to define Tory Democracy. 'To tell you the truth I don't know myself what Tory Democracy is. But I believe it is principally opportunism.'

His sad end – the result of catching syphilis, perhaps even at his stag night before his marriage to Winston Churchill's mother – provoked a sympathetic epitaph from Lord Rosebery, who had watched with admiration his refusal to submit and his determination to carry on with the political life. 'There was no retirement, no concealment. He died in public, sole mourner at his protracted funeral.'

CHURCHILL, Randolph Frederick Edward Spencer. Randolph Churchill – though a political failure and perhaps a failure in life – had many of his father Sir Winston's domineering traits. According to Alan Brien, who often researched for him, he was undismayed by the prospect of death. In hospital for a lung operation he dominated his doctors and ridiculed the concept of Doctor's Orders. 'I'm paying,' he would say. 'It's my lung. I give the orders. I take advice, but I give the orders.' He demonstrated to a dragon matron how to make a proper cup of tea, and when a piece of him was cut out he demanded to see it before it was thrown away. 'It was rather nasty-looking really,' he told Brien, 'like a fat mutton chop you wouldn't give to a dog. Well rid of that, I'd say.'

He was a friend of Lord Beaverbrook and also his sparring partner. Calling one day at Arlington House, the press baron's London home in St James's, he was told by the butler, 'The lord is out walking in the park.'

'On the lake, I presume,' replied Randolph.

It is apocryphal that he once said, during an audience with the Pope, 'Ah, Roman Catholic! You must know my friend Evelyn Waugh?'

Not apocryphal, since he records it in his diaries, is Waugh's comment in 1964. Churchill had gone into Sister Agnes's hospital for the removal of that lung. It was announced that the piece removed was not malignant. Waugh commented that it was a 'typical triumph of modern science to find the only part of Randolph that was not malignant and remove it'.

CHURCHILL, Sir Winston. Churchill stories tend to revolve around his addiction to brandy: 'Always remember I have taken more out of alcohol than alcohol has taken out of me'; sweeping statements on service subjects: 'The traditions of the navy – rum, buggery and the lash' and 'In my experience officers with high athletic qualifications are not equally successful in the high ranks'; and anticipation of Roland Rat's rescue act at TV-am ('Rat saves sinking ship') with a comment on a failed Tory who tried to stand as a Liberal, 'The only instance in history of a rat swimming towards a sinking ship.'

Any trawling of Churchill anecdotes is going to yield a rich catch of chestnuts – this is a less well-known one which Hugh Foot (Lord Caradon) told my friend Michael Hill.

When Churchill was returning from a visit to the USA as Prime Minister in the 1950s he stopped off in Jamaica. Resting in Government House after the flight he was told by Sir Hugh Foot, who was Governor, that the people of Kingston, hearing of the presence of the great man, had expressed an overwhelming desire to see him. Although tired, Churchill made a tour of the city in an open car to much acclaim. Back again in Government House, sipping his brandy, he beamed at Foot and said, 'Haven't seen so many blackamoors since Omdurman.'

On to the chestnuts. Lady Astor provoked the first. 'If you were my husband, Winston,' she said, 'I should flavour your coffee with poison.' 'Nancy,' he replied, 'if you were my wife I should drink it.'

Bessie Braddock, the redoubtable Liverpool Labour MP, inspired another. 'Madam, you are ugly,' he fired. She retorted, 'Sir, you are drunk.' Which he capped with 'Yes, but in the morning I shall be sober.'

On Sir Stafford Cripps; 'There but for the grace of God goes God.' (A similar sentiment occurred to Herman Mankiewicz on sighting Orson Welles.)

On Field Marshal Montgomery: 'In defeat unbeatable: in victory unbearable.'

On Anthony Eden's speeches: 'They consist entirely of clichés – clichés old and new – everything from "God is Love" to "Please adjust your dress before leaving." '

On Stanley Baldwin: 'He occasionally stumbled on the truth, but hastily picked himself up and hurried on as if nothing had happened.' On Baldwin's retirement he commented, 'Not dead. But the candle in the great turnip has gone out.'

He discussed a forthcoming visit to America and how he should greet President Roosevelt with his secretary Edward Marsh, who suggested, 'I am in favour of kissing him on both cheeks.' 'Yes,' Churchill grunted, 'but not on all four.'

His definition of political ability was pointed: 'It is the ability to foretell what is going to happen tomorrow, next week, next month and next year. And to have the ability afterwards to explain why it did not happen.' To Churchill politics were 'as exciting as war . . . and quite as dangerous. In war you can only be killed once. In politics – many times.' He defined democracy as 'the worst form of government, except for all those other forms that have been tried from time to time.'

He despaired of getting through the Yalta conference with Stalin and Roosevelt quickly. 'I do not see any way of realising our hopes about a world organisation in five or six days,' he cautioned the optimistic Roosevelt. 'Even the Almighty took seven.'

His verdict on Joseph Chamberlain has been prolifically plagiarised: 'Mr Chamberlain loves the working man. He loves to see him work.'

Churchill's comment has had far more revamps than F. E. Smith's on another Chamberlain, Austen, 'Austen always played the game and always lost.'

Neville Chamberlain was the most vulnerable member of the family. According to Churchill, 'In the depths of that dusty soul is nothing but abject surrender'; he was 'a good Lord Mayor of Birmingham in a bad year'. To Lloyd George, Chamberlain 'saw foreign policy through the wrong end of a municipal drainpipe'.

In 1937 Aneurin Bevan found him a handy target: 'Listening to a speech by Chamberlain is like paying a visit to Woolworth's: everything in its place and nothing above sixpence.' A few years later he added, 'The worst thing I can say about democracy is that it has tolerated the Right Honourable gentleman for four and a half years.'

Back to Churchill. His cruel verdict on Ramsay Macdonald requires more explanation nowadays – he called him The Boneless Wonder after a circus act popular in his youth. It was a remark provoked by Macdonald's hold on power in spite of a string of defeats. 'He is the greatest living master of falling without hurting himself.'

During the Second World War General Sikorski, leader of the Polish government in exile, in France and then in Britain, attempted unsuccessfully to raise a loan in the City to pay his troops.

Finally, in desperation he appealed to Churchill in French, their only common language. Churchill, whose command of this language was notoriously poor, replied sorrowfully, 'Non, mon general, quand je suis avec les vieux Dames de Threadneedle Street je suis impotent.'

When Churchill was writing the last volume of *The World Crisis* in the 1920s, he needed some vital information from Lloyd George, in whose government he had served. He asked his PPS, Bob Boothby, if he thought Lloyd George would agree to meet him. Boothby, an intimate of Lloyd George, assured him he would and arranged the encounter. After Lloyd George had gone, Boothby found Churchill in a mood of deep introspective gloom. Collecting himself, Churchill agreed that the meeting had yielded all he needed to know: but, in Boothby's account, 'a hard look came into his face and he went on; "Within five minutes the old relationship between us was completely re-established. The relationship between master and servant. And I was the servant."'

Lloyd George had earlier recalled Churchill's interview with a throat specialist. He ended it sharply by saying, 'I entirely disagree with your diagnosis.'

In 1924 when Baldwin offered Churchill the Chancellorship of the Exchequer with the words, 'Will you go to the Treasury?' Churchill recorded that he would have liked to reply, 'Will the bloody duck swim?' In fact, he answered more grandiloquently, 'This fulfils my ambition. I still have my father's robes as Chancellor. I shall be proud to serve you in this splendid office.'

In his last years in the House of Commons he overheard two newish MPs whispering behind their hands. One said, 'Poor old Winston, he's gaga.' He turned to them and snapped, 'Yes, and he's deaf too.' In his twilight years he spent much time on the Riviera, which Lady Churchill disliked. When he was staying with friends in a villa in Monte Carlo, his host invited Mrs Daisy Fellowes, the Singer sewing-machine heiress, to join them. Soon after lunch began, Winston closed his eyes and seemed to drop into a deep sleep. Mrs Fellowes turned to her host and said, 'What a pity that so great a man should end his life in the company of Onassis and Wendy Reves' – an American whose interest in Churchill had occasioned some malicious gossip. To the dismay of the whisperers, one of Churchill's eyes opened and he said, 'Daisy, Wendy Reves is something you will never be. She is young, she is beautiful and she is kind.' With that, he closed his eye again.

CLAIBORNE, Craig. Craig Claiborne is the star cookery writer long associated with *The New York Times*. He recently published an autobiography and also a volume of recipes based on his salt-free diet. The autobiography contains some rather sordid revelations. I was delighted to get a letter from my friend Gerald Asher, who had just read it. 'He describes,' he wrote, 'his seduction by his father with whom he had an affair. The trouble with dishing up a story like that in Chapter One, when the final chapter deals with your new salt-free diet, is that if the end and the beginning are tasteless, who can be sure about the middle?'

CLAIRE, Ina. Ina Claire, who died recently in her nineties, had been a Ziegfeld Girl, a distinguished stage high comedienne and a stylish supporting actress in movies. When she married John Gilbert at the height of his fame, an unwary film reporter asked her how it felt to be married to a great star. 'I don't know,' she told him. 'You'd better ask Mr Gilbert.'

CLARK, Alan. The retirement from office of Alan Clark promised a series of sharp, indiscreet memoirs packed with seditious anecdotes. He has already provided a vignette of returning with Mrs Thatcher and Sir Geoffrey Howe in a VC10 from the Italian summit on Lake Garda. Howe went to change into a dinner jacket because on arrival he was due to address a meeting in Douglas Hurd's constituency. On his reappearance Clark's response was to say 'Bring us two large gin and tonics and keep the change . . . Prime Minister, the maître d'hôtel wants to know what you'd like to drink.' According to Clark, 'Geoffrey was wearing the half-unhappy smile which always marked his demeanour when she was around.'

He awards Nigel Lawson the palm for the best rejoinder he ever heard to Mrs Thatcher. 'Early in 1987 we had this ludicrous Nationalised Industries Bill before us, which had come in under the auspices of the Treasury and which everybody hated. So she started off by saying that, personally, she thought it was complete rubbish and then asked various people what they felt – which was much the same. She then turned to Lawson and said, "Chancellor, this comes from the Treasury, am I quite alone in thinking that it doesn't carry the support of the whole Cabinet? Tell me, Chancellor, an I *quite* alone?"

'To which Lawson replied, "Well, Prime Minister, only you can judge whether you are alone, but even if you were, I've no doubt your views would carry great weight." '

One comment which will stick is Clark's dismissive verdict on Michael Heseltine (which he attributes to their colleague Michael Joplin): 'A man who bought his own furniture.'

COE, Sebastian, MP. Poor Sebastian Coe, the star middle-distance ruuner, fell into the embarrassing celebrity trap of saying 'Don't you know who I am?' on a visit to the Lords. The staff there are famously rude, but the club servant on this occasion managed to be witty as well.

Coe had presented himself at the wrong entrance gate. He was brusquely told to find his way round to a different point of entry. He remonstrated and uttered the fateful words, 'Don't you know who I am?'

'No' said the gateman.

'I am Sebastian Coe.'

'Right then, you'll be able to run round all the quicker, won't you?'

COHN, Al. Al Cohn, saxophone player and arranger, had a sharper line in repartee than many jazz men. He defined a gentleman as someone who knows how to play an accordion and doesn't. When a bum tapped him for money at a bus station he hesitated: 'Hey, how do I know you won't spend this on food?' When a colleague complained that his drummer's tempos varied – slowing down with sticks, hurrying with brushes – he offered, 'Tell him to play with one of each.' Asked on a tour of Europe if he'd tried 'Elephant Beer', he said, 'No. I drink to forget.' And to another barman's 'What'll you have?' the answer was, 'One too many.'

Finishing an album featuring 24 mandolin players he was asked where it was possible to find so many. 'Well,' he said, 'all day today you couldn't get a haircut in Jersey City.'

COHN, Harry. The Columbia Pictures tycoon, Harry Cohn, was one of the most ruthless and certainly the most vulgar of Hollywood moguls. He started life as a song plugger and always had a good instinct for what the public wanted. His dictum on critics is often paraphrased. 'Screw the critics. They're like eunuchs. They can tell you how to do it: but they can't do it themselves.'

His 'infallible' test for the popular appeal of a film was 'If my fanny squirms, it's bad. If my fanny doesn't squirm, it's good.' Herman Mankiewicz's comment was succinct: 'Imagine – the whole world wired to Harry Cohn's backside!'

His dictatorial attitude to Columbia employees was expressed simply: 'I am the King here. Whoever eats my bread sings my song.' He explained his ruthless drive by a reference to his boyhood suffering. He behaved the way he did 'So *my* sons won't have to sleep with their grandmother.'

Cohn interfered at every stage of production. Of one writer he demanded 'a speech that every person in the audience will recognise immediately'. 'You mean like Hamlet's soliloquy?' the writer suggested.'No! No! I mean something like "To be or not to be".'

When Cohn got wind of a story called the *Iliad* by an author called Homer he scented commercial possibilities and urgently demanded a treatment. Having read it he was not so sure. 'There are an awful lot of Greeks in it.'

Another of Cohn's Goldwynesque slips was to demand changes in a biblical script where the words 'no, Sire', and 'yes, Sire' appeared. 'I may not be a college man,' he bellowed, 'but I know goddam well that in biblical times people did not go around saying, "Yes, siree" and "no, siree".' Clifford Odets, one of the writers harangued, said quietly, 'We'll fix it, Harry.'

Cohn was a vivid phrase-maker and inspired a few. Hedda Hopper said of him, 'You had to stand on line to hate him'; and Elia Kazan remarked, 'He liked to be the biggest bug in the manure pile.' Budd Schulberg called him 'The meanest man I know. An unreconstructed dinosaur.' Of Cohn's brother Jack, Harry Kurnitz said, 'He's sometimes known as Harry Cohn without charm.' Cohn had a fair idea of his own popularity, 'If I wasn't head of a studio who would talk to me? . . .' 'I don't have ulcers, I give them.' He took unlimited advantage of his position as studio head for sexual favours, saying, 'It's better than being a pimp.'

Cohn's end inspired one of the great catty Hollywood remarks – generously attributed to a number of other sources on different but similar occasions. At his funeral someone asked Red Skelton why there were such enormous crowds of people attending. Skelton said, 'Give the public what they want, they'll all show up.' (Some credit the comment to Samuel Goldwyn speaking of Louis B. Mayer.)

COLE, John. The BBC's long-time political reporter John Cole told an endearing story on *Desert Island Discs* of a lunch with Roy Hattersley which dealt simultaneously with both their Achilles' heels – as far as caricaturists are concerned – Cole's outlandish Ulster accent and Hattersley's appetite.

When it was time to order the wine, Cole, the host, handed the wine list to Hattersley saying, 'You order the wine, Roy. You know about these things.' Hattersley became serious. 'John,' he said with intensity, 'we must scotch these rumours that I know everything about lunch and you have a funny voice.'

'But Roy,' said Cole, 'I do have a funny voice.'

COLE, Nat King. Nat King Cole was an admired jazz pianist before he became a world star as a singer. In the thirties, however, he found that it was convenient to break up the monotony of an instrumental session by the King Cole trio with a few vocals, and noticed that the customers wanted more. Quite early on a customer requested a song he didn't know; he offered 'Sweet Lorraine' instead and it netted the trio fifteen cents – a nickel apiece. The big spender requested another tune. Again Cole didn't know it. He asked if there was anything else the man would like. 'Yeah,' he said, 'I'd like my fifteen cents back.'

When Nat King Cole moved into a white suburb of Los Angeles, neighbours petitioned against undesirables. Cole found out where it was being passed around and asked if he could sign it. He wasn't keen on undesirables either.

COLEFAX, Sybil. Sybil Colefax was one of the prominent London hostesses of the 1920s and 30s. Her husband, Sir Arthur, was often described as talented and with high ideals. He also bored for England. He was boring beyond belief. Indeed, Lord Berners wickedly started a rumour that Sir Arthur Colefax had been offered £30,000 a year to bore the Channel Tunnel. (Cheap at the price judging by current estimates.)

Berners merits an entry of his own but this story must creep in under Sybil Colefax's skirts – anyway she was probably present at the first night in question. Dilettante, exquisite, a composer, Berners wrote the music for Diaghilev's Russian Ballet production *Triumph of Neptune*. The first night was a success and the impressario tried to persuade his composer to take a curtain call. Lord Berners refused, saying that his aunt had threatened to disinherit him if ever he went on the stage.

COLEMAN, David. It is perhaps unfair that the excellent and versatile sports commentator has given his name to 'Colemanballs" – those inadvertent howlers, grammatical errors and self-contradictory slips made under pressure which have been immortally anthologised by *Private Eye*.

My favourite Coleman contribution which helped to set the form is 'The pace of this match is really accelerating, by which I mean it is getting faster all the time.' Then there was Garth Crooks on LBC, a local radio station in London: 'Football is football; if that weren't the case, it wouldn't be the game it is.'

Ian St John and Jimmy Greaves have borne their share of this burden: 'The only thing that Norwich didn't get was the goal they finally got,' was Greaves's solo. And with St John as straight man: Ian St John: 'Is he speaking to you yet?' Greaves: 'Not yet, but I hope to be incommunicado with him in a very short space of time.'

Perhaps the best comes from the lugubrious John Motson on the BBC. 'There's been a colour clash: both teams are wearing white.'

COLETTE, Sidonie Gabrielle Claudine. When Colette was the mistress of H. G. Wells, they were both invited to dine with Lord Beaverbrook. Wells warned Colette that the Beaver was in the habit of asking unexpectedly direct questions of his guests, particularly new ones. At the start of dinner the Beaver eyed Colette speculatively. Taking the initiative she looked across at him and said, 'Tell me, Lord Beaverbrook, have you fucked any interesting women lately?'

CONDON, Eddie. In Bill Crow's fascinating anthology of *Jazz Anecdotes* (OUP) many of the tales treat of spectacular instrumental feats, hirings and firings and a distressing number of pranks, put-ons and practical jokes. An exception is the chapter on Eddie Condon, who, in addition to playing banjo and guitar, organised record dates, produced jazz concerts, and kept a saloon. More important, he had a caustic tongue and ready opinions.

When asked what he thought of jazz as an art form he said dismissively, 'Canning peaches is an art form.' To a woman with extravagant headwear: 'Is that a hat or a threat you're wearing?' When the French jazz critic Hugues Panassie gave him a generally favourable notice he commented, 'I don't see why we need a Frenchman to come over here and tell us how to play American music. I wouldn't think of going to France and telling him how to jump on a grape.'

At a party where an Eddy Duchin record was spinning on the gramophone a fellow guest said, 'Don't you adore Eddy Duchin, Mr Condon? He really makes the piano talk, doesn't he?' Condon replied, 'He certainly does. And what the piano says is, "Please take your clumsy hands off me."'

After working for Red Nichols he commented, 'Red thought he played like Bix [Beiderbecke], but the similarity stopped the minute he opened his horn case.'

His first 'Eddie Condon's' Club was on West 3rd Street. He had special names for employees – the men's room attendant, for instance, was 'Flush Gordon'; and his club policy was 'We don't throw anybody in, and we don't throw anybody out.'

He was not a fan of way-out music. When a waiter dropped a tray of plates and cutlery at West 3rd Street he looked up from his drink and muttered, 'None of that progressive jazz in here.' Asked the capacity of his club at its launch, Condon replied, 'Oh, about 200 cases.' His recommended hangover cure was 'Take the juice of two quarts of whisky.' Invited by a friend to dine at a Middle Eastern restaurant he declined politely, saying, 'The aftertaste of foreign food spoils the clean, pure flavour of gin for hours.'

He drank a great deal but held it well, adding this note to one of his record albums: 'A Mr Dewar from somewhere in the British Isles was also in the studio at the time, very welcome indeed, although exhausted at the end of the ceremony.' When his wife compiled a warning list of musicians they knew who had died of liver complaints, he glanced at it and handed it back with the words, 'There's a drummer missing.' Hearing that English hotel guests could order alcohol at any hour of the day or night he announced, 'I'm taking out papers.'

When seriously ill and given a blood transfusion he said, 'This must be Fats Waller's blood. I'm getting high.' The disease was acute pancreatitis. He could take food neither orally nor intravenously. The doctor suggested the only alternative which he felt was undignified. The doctor tried to persuade him that it would be like having a drink. At this he capitulated, turning over and saying, 'See what the boys in the back room will have.'

Faced by a fake electric fire in a friend's suite at the Warwick Hotel in New York he suggested, 'It's cold in here. Could you please throw another bulb on the fire.'

In spite of his own relish for liquor, he did attempt to keep another legendary consumer, Pee Wee Russel, straight when he worked for him. Russel was so soaked in alcohol that on one occasion, when playing in a Boston Jazz Club, he was puzzled by a couple who greeted him warmly. He looked blank. The woman said, 'Pee Wee, don't you remember us? You stayed at our house for six months while you were working in St Louis.' All Russel could manage was an uncomfortable shrug and 'If you say so.'

CONNOLLY, Cyril. 'Literature,' said Cyril Connolly, 'is the art of writing something that will be read twice; journalism what will be grasped at once.' Connolly was to write a great deal of both and edit more. He could turn a neat near-clerihew too:

> M is for Marx
> And clashing of classes
> And movement of masses
> and massing of asses.

Married three times and savagely remembered by his first wives, he wrote: 'In the sex war, thoughtlessness is the weapon of the male, vindictiveness of the female.'

He could be a cutting critic, of himself as well as of others: 'Those whom the gods wish to destroy they first call promising.'

He also summed up his disappointment at the limits of his own fame in a verse:

> At Eton with Orwell,
> At Oxford with Waugh,
> He was nothing afterwards
> And nothing before.

CONTI, Prince of. The Prince of Conti, a noted eighteenth-century rake, eventually realised that his sexual prowess was waning. 'It is time for me to retire,' he said philosophically. 'Formerly my civilities were taken for declarations of love but now my declarations of love are taken for civilities.'

COOGAN, Jackie. Jackie Coogan was the biggest child star of his day, especially after Chaplin's first feature film, *The Kid*, in 1920. On reaching his majority he found that his parents and squandered most of his hard-earned money. A 'Coogan Act' to protect child stars was the one good result.

Coogan's hardest money came from crying, which he found hard to do on cue. In *Oliver Twist* he could not summon up a tear for the line 'My mother is dead, sir.' Frank Lloyd, the director told him to imagine his own mother was dead. That didn't help. Finally Coogan himself had an idea: 'Sir,' he asked, 'would it be all right if I imagined that my dog is dead?'

And that was before he knew what his mother was doing with his money.

COOLIDGE, Calvin. The President of the United States and his First Lady were visiting a government farm in the 1920s. Passing the chicken coops, Mrs Coolidge enquired how often the rooster made love each day. 'Dozens of times,' was the answer. 'Please tell that to the President,' she said. When Coolidge passed the pen and was told about the rooster, he asked, 'Same hen every time?' 'Oh no, Mr President, a different one each time.' He nodded slowly; 'Please tell that to Mrs Coolidge.'

COOPER, Jackie. Like his predecessor, Jackie Coogan, Jackie Cooper, child star of the thirties, had trouble crying on cue. Filming *Skippy* for his uncle Norman Taurog in 1931 he had three crying scenes. For the first Taurog raged and ranted at the dry-eyed kid to no effect − only when he brought another child in an identical costume to the side of the set did Cooper, thinking he was going to be sacked, burst into tears.

In the next crying scene he was with a dog he adored and he was so happy that once again he could not cry. Eventually, Taurog took the dog away out of sight and ordered a shot to be fired. He told Cooper that he had killed the dog and again got the desired effect. Then the dog was restored to the child.

That left a third crying scene and the same subterfuge would not work again.

However, Cooper's mother was on the set. She did something that no one had thought to do before. She took her son to one side, quietly explained the scene to him and pointed out how devastated Skippy would be at the death of his beloved dog. He started to weep and continued to do so copiously through the scene. No doubt these torrential tears contributed to his Oscar nomination.

A couple in New York, who sound more like Coogan's parents than Cooper's, took their son to see Cooper in *Sooky*, the quick follow-up sequel to *Skippy*. The boy adored it. He voted it even better than *Skippy* – especially the happier ending. 'But it doesn't end happier,' his mother argued. 'Doesn't Sooky's mother die?' 'Oh, sure,' said her son, 'but in *Skippy* the dog died.'

CORRIGAN, Laura. In the 1930s Laura Corrigan, an immensely rich and snobbish American society hostess, arrived in London. She was notorious also for her malapropisms, such as calling her house in Grosvenor Square 'my little *ventre-à-terre*'.

At one dinner party she placed a man on her right in the belief that he was the Duke of Lancaster. When told that he was merely Mr Lancaster she exclaimed, 'Oh dear, what a terrible mistake!' and shouted down the table, 'Who's the next-ranking dook?'

COWARD, Sir Noel Pierce. In my book of *Theatrical Anecdotes* I attempted to exonerate Sir Noel Coward of his popular but perhaps tasteless comment on the huge Queen Salote of Tonga and the tiny Emperor Haile Selassie of Abyssinia (Ethiopia) who shared a coach in the coronation procession of Queen Elizabeth II. Coward was reputed to have said, when asked who was the little man opposite the enormous queen, 'Her lunch.'

I understood that Coward had denied the remark; however, the actor John Moffat has written to correct my correction.

Noel Coward may have regretted that he ever made the famous Queen Salote comment but I can assure you that he did . . . for he made it to me! I was appearing with Noel at the Haymarket Theatre at the time of the coronation. A small group of the company (including Hugh Manning and me) had watched the procession from the front of the Haymarket Theatre. Later, an hour or so before the performance, Hugh and I were chatting to Noel just inside the stage-door. Noel had watched the procession on television and was impressed and pleased that we had waited all night on the cold pavement. Queen Salote had been the star of the parade . . . in her open carriage waving and beaming with joy in the light sunlit drizzle she was a magnificent sight . . . and we were speaking of Star Quality. One of us . . . I can't now be sure whether it was Hugh or me . . . asked Noel 'Who was that little man sitting beside her?' Noel (and I can point out the exact spot where he was standing . . . indeed have several times done so during my subsequent appearances at the Haymarket) raised his forefinger and said 'I think . . . ' (and here came that little pause for better effect) '. . . it was her lunch.' Those were the exact words.

John Humphry may also have been present – my memory doesn't serve me well enough – but it was Hugh and I who were initially responsible for the spreading worldwide of that remark and it has constantly come back to me in vastly inaccurate variations.

Some years later I told Isobel Dean that Coward had said it to me.'Oh yes, yes, yes,' replied that delightfully acerbic lady. 'Hugh Manning always claims he said it to *him*.' 'He did,' I replied triumphantly. 'He said it to both of us.'

Now a further correction. A contemporary photograph shows Salote in her coach waving happily; but opposite her sits HH Ibrahim, Sultan of Kelantan, in all the full splendour of Malay court dress with silk baju and ceremonial head-dress.

When it began to rain he asked to have the hood raised. This was vetoed by Salote – so he got colder and colder despite having invested in a pair of long johns at Austin Reed, having been told it would be chilly in the Abbey. He complained that it was 'all very well for the Queen, she was dressed in tree bark!'

Another piece of Coward legend came my way the other day – again, it could be apocryphal but it has the ring of a genuine Coward retort. A compulsive American approached him in a lift in the Hassler Hotel in Rome and said, 'I bet you can't guess my raunchiest sexual fantasy.' Coward said, 'No, but I'm sure you're going to tell me.'

'My raunchiest sexual fantasy is to imagine Gina Lollobrigida is going down on me slowly murmuring her name "Gi-na Loll-llo-bri-gee-da!" ' and he made a meal of the word.

'Thank God,' said Coward crisply, 'it wasn't Anna Magnani!'

CRICKET. As the finest game, it is not surprising that cricket has come in for the neatest and meetest of judgements. Back to the great claim of the Duke of Dorset, who said in 1777, 'What is life but a game of cricket?' to an opponent, Archbishop Temple, who dismissed it as 'organised loafing'. More thoughtful was Lord Mancroft, who said, 'Cricket is a game which the English, not being a spiritual people, have invented to give themselves some concept of eternity.'

The concept of eternity has little to do with fast bowling today. Mike Brearley, the England captain of the early 1980s, was vivid on the subject of Jeff

Thomson's 90-mile-an-hour onslaughts in Australia: 'Broken marriages, conflicts of loyalty, the problems of everyday life fall away as one faces up to Thomson!'

Jonathan Rice's *Curiosities of Cricket* reveals some odd royal involvements with the game. In 1300 Edward I paid John Leek, a monk, £6 to coach his son Prince Edward at 'creag', an early form of the game – in which the Prince seems to have made little headway; presumably Piers Gaveston did not share his enthusiasm.

As related elsewhere, Frederick, Prince of Wales was killed by a cricket ball in 1751. It was recorded that year only that 'Prince Frederick took an interest in cricket'. However, the royal star was George VI, to whom *Wisden* accorded an obituary: 'When Prince Albert, he performed the hat-trick on the private ground on the slopes below Windsor Castle where the sons and grandsons of King Edward VII used to play regularly. A left-handed batsman and bowler, the King bowled King Edward VII, King George V and the present Duke of Windsor in three consecutive balls.'

CROMER, George Rowland Stanley Baring, 2nd Earl of. In 1961 the Earl of Cromer was offered the Governorship of the Bank of England by Harold Macmillan. He duly asked the advice of a senior member of the Baring banking family. The distinguished, elderly Baring suggested he should decline, remarking, 'After all, the Bank of England is only the East End Branch of the Treasury.' Cromer did not take his advice.

CUKOR, George. George Cukor, literate, witty, sophisticated, was an exception in the early days of Hollywood and a rare example of a director with a Broadway background making the change to movies – albeit more adept with actors than with cameras.

He was surrounded by a court of friends and favourite actresses and actors. When he was directing *Camille* with Garbo she was surprised to see the same actor appear for no logical reason in several different scenes. 'Who is he?' Garbo asked. 'What part is he playing?' 'That man is Rex Evans,' Cukor replied. 'And he's playing the part of a friend who needs a job.'

Similarly a friend once asked Cukor why the camera lingered curiously long on a handsome young man in a swordfight in *Romeo and Juliet*. There didn't seem to be any very good reason, said the friend. 'Oh yes,' Cukor teased him. 'There was a *very* good reason.'

If Cukor was unlucky to be run off *Gone With The Wind* because of Clark Gable's protests (Cukor's biographer Patrick McGilligan suggests that Gable had had one drunken sexual encounter with Bill Haines, a gay friend of Cukor's, and was not keen to hear Hollywood whispering, 'George is directing one of Billy's old tricks') he was perhaps lucky to get on board Jack Warner's production of *My Fair Lady*. His preferred rivals were Jerome Robbins and Vincente Minnelli, but Cukor's powerful agent, 'Swifty' Lazar, kept badgering Warner, who one day found himself - just by coincidence, of course - sitting next to Cukor on a plane. Warner asked, 'How'd you like to do *My Fair Lady*?' Cukor said, 'Yes,' without hesitation and added, 'I'd love to – and you're making a very intelligent choice.'

Garbo became a confidante of Cukor's who agreed to arrange a meeting between her and Ivor Novello, who was visiting Hollywood in the thirties. The introduction was to be especially secret and Garbo was not to be called Garbo. The fiction employed was that her name was Harriet Brown. The meeting went well, Novello observed the fiction and called her 'Miss Brown', and they saw each other a second and third time at Cukor's house. Finally Novello said, 'Miss Brown, now that we know each other so well, do you think I might call you Harriet?'

Cukor directed Jack Lemmon early in his career and the actor was disconcerted by the number of times the director said 'Less.' After a day of 'Less' he protested politely, 'Mr Cukor, if you keep it up I won't be acting at all.' Cukor replied, 'You're beginning to get it, my boy!'

CUNNINGHAM, John E. Mr Cunningham has no real place in this book, but I so enjoy his fictional anecdote that I am resolved to include it. In a *Spectator* competition in 1987, inviting participants to give a description, tinged with disapproval, by an historical or fictional character of a scene which is obviously unfamiliar, he submitted the following.

> It being much talked of upon the Town, to Piccadilly to see an old play, *The Caretaker* by Mr Pinter that was a Player and is now trade-fallen. But Lord! What a dull insipid thing it was – but three poor actors and not one did know his lines but did repeat them o'er and o'er that it was mere foolery and no sense in the world and methought a whole Act was lost wherein the company should go to *Sidcup* that is in Kent.
>
> So to the Piazza to see the strumpets & a saucy piece, her hair all draggled, did climb into the coach and offer me safe sex: but minding my promise to Mercer I did but toy with her, so she mighty bold did ask Did my Mistress know I was out? Resolved to give up such plays & company hereafter.

CURTIZ, Michael. Many people – notably David Niven – have recorded the odd adventures with the English of Michael Curtiz, the émigré Hollywood movie director, immortal for his instruction, while directing *The Charge of the*

Light Brigade, to 'Bring on the empty horses!' However, a recent book about one of the movies he directed, *Casablanca*, provides one I had not heard before. He was yelling on set for 'a poodle, a black poodle' which he needed urgently for a street scene. Anything for local colour, the prop man thought – hitherto unaware that black poodles were characteristic of wartime North Africa. Anyway Curtiz was temperamental and the prop man did not fancy an argument. It was his lucky day. He phoned around, tracked one down and had it on the set inside an hour. 'Is very nice,' said Curtiz, 'but I want a poodle.' The prop man insisted that this was a poodle. He reached for its pedigree. Curtiz went mad. 'I wanted a poodle in the street! A poodle of water! Not a goddam dog!'

Curtiz won an Oscar in 1943 for *Casablanca* and delivered the most incomprehensible speech ever. 'So many times I have a speech ready but no dice. Always a bridesmaid, never a mother.'

On another notable occasion he said, 'The next time I send a dumb sonofabitch to do something, I go myself!'

CURZON, George Nathaniel, 1st Marquess. 'My name is George Nathaniel Curzon. I am a most superior person' is the popular verdict on Lord Curzon of Kedleston – one of his many enormous country houses. There were others at Hackwood and Montacute.

A grandee who never quite recovered from his promotion to the office of Viceroy of India in 1898 when he was only 39, Curzon saw the rest of his existence as an anti-climax, especially when he failed to become Prime Minister. The office of Viceroy was filled with pomp and ceremony and for seven years he was followed by long strings of elephants and retinues of native servants. According to Lord Beaverbrook, for Curzon it was 'a journey to heaven'.

Curzon was famous for his extravagant opinions – 'Gentlemen never wear brown in London'; 'Gentlemen never take soup at luncheon.' He even instructed his second wife, Grace, in the art of making love: 'The lady never moves.' He once took a bus. 'This omnibus business is not what it is reported to be. I hailed one at the bottom of Whitehall and told the man to take me to Carlton House Terrace. But the fellow flatly refused.' When he saw soldiers on leave in a swimming pool: 'Good heavens! I never knew the working classes had such white skins.'

In 1918 as a very grand and super-sophisticated Foreign Secretary, Curzon was reading out a minute at a Cabinet Meeting in connection with the Peace Celebrations. He came across the apparently unfamiliar word 'beano'. Not having heard of it before he pronounced it 'be-ano', as if it were Italian.

While Foreign Secretary he was telephoned at Kedleston by his private secretary at the Foreign Office, Robert Vansittart, who conveyed the news of the death of a foreign diplomat. Curzon was not impressed: 'Do you realise that to convey to me this trivial piece of information you have forced me to walk the length of a mansion not far removed from the dimensions of Windsor Castle?'

Lord Derby said of Curzon, 'He makes one feel so terribly plebeian'; and reported an incident when he kept the cabinet waiting with no explanation or apology. At last an office messenger turned up carrying the green baize footstool which Curzon used to rest his leg when phlebitis attacked him. Derby rose and bowed to the footstool saying, 'The Marquess himself has not arrived but we see premonitory symptoms.'

His great disappointment was not to be asked to form a ministry in 1923 as Bonar Law's successor. Summoned to London from Montacute to meet George V's Private Secretary, he was sure he was to get the call. However, on his arrival he found that Lord Stamfordham's job was to break the news that the King had sent for Stanley Baldwin on the advice of a former Prime Minister, Arthur Balfour, who nursed a grudge against Curzon. He collapsed and wept and moaned that he had forgotten Baldwin (shades of Lord Randolph Churchill's 'I forgot Goschen'). To Curzon, Baldwin was 'not even a public figure. A man of no experience. And of the utmost insignificance. Of the utmost insignificance.'

His second wife's support was more than moral. Grace was an heiress on whom he depended financially. When Balfour returned to his seat in Norfolk after advising the King to send for Baldwin, his house party was anxious to hear the latest news. 'And will dear George be chosen?' enquired one woman. 'No, dear George will not,' said Balfour, well pleased. 'Oh – I am so sorry. He will be terribly disappointed.' 'Oh, I don't know,' said Balfour scathingly, 'he may have lost the hope of glory but he retains the means of Grace.'

Curzon built an elaborate tomb for his first wife in Kedleston church and prepared another to match it for himself. After his death Grace, Lady Curzon, when down into the vault to look at his coffin. On a nearby ledge lay a postcard. She recognised her late husband's handwriting. It read: 'Reserved for the second Lady Curzon.'

CUTFORTH, René. René Cutforth was a distinguished Australian reporter for BBC radio and television. He once engaged in a classic battle with the BBC accounts department, which ranks with the brilliant Muir and Norden gambit. (Frank Muir and Dennis Norden were commissioned to write a radio programme about Paris. They were paid some expenses to cover a research visit. Then the Powers That Be changed their minds and cancelled the programme before they could make their trip. BBC accounts sent a peremptory memorandum asking for their money back. Muir and Norden laboured for a morning to produce the perfect bureaucratic reply to frustrate any further attempt by the

BBC to recover the money. At last they found it. They replied: 'We are afraid we have no machinery for returning this money.' They never heard another word.)

Cutforth's situation was more dangerous. Reporting from Poland, he entered lunch expenses for entertaining a high-ranking Polish general once a week. A new broom in BBC accounts grew suspicious and asked for details of the general. Chancing his luck, Cutforth invented a name, a regiment and even a number for his general. As ill-luck would have it, a Polish Army list had just surfaced in London. The new broom obtained it and found no mention of Cutforth's general. He pointed out in no uncertain terms in a telex to Cutforth that his meal ticket did not exist.

Cutforth was equal to the charge. He telexed back: 'The man is clearly an imposter. I shall have nothing further to do with him.'

— D —

DANISCHEWSKI, Monja. According to Frank Muir, Monja Danischewski, a compulsive punster, was lunching in a fish restaurant in Duke Street with his wife and some American film people when his wife said that she suddenly felt ill. She began to feel worse and worse and pleaded, 'Take me home.' With that she fainted and her head dropped into the fish on her plate. 'Ah well,' said her husband, rising to extricate her, 'there's no home like plaice.'

DARLING, Charles John (Lord Darling). When a magistrate committed a burglar to appear before Lord Darling in the early years of this century, it was because he reckoned him to be an habitual criminal who deserved a more severe sentence than he could give. After a lengthy debate the prisoner made a last effort to save his skin.

'I don't see why they call me a professional crook,' he argued. 'I've only done two jobs and each time I've been nabbed.'

Mr Justice Darling was equal to the challenge. 'It has never been suggested that you are *successful* in your profession.'

DARROW, Clarence Seward. The American lawyer Clarence Darrow is best remembered for his demolition of William Jennings Bryan in the Scopes case (concerning man's descent, or not, from monkeys); and for his defence in 1924 of Leopold and Loeb, the student murderers. Both have been celebrated on stage and in films.

He had two memorable exchanges with judges, one good-natured the other not. When he was defending a Mrs Simpson, who actually shot her husband while he was on the witness stand petitioning for a divorce, the prosecution subpoenaed the judge who had presided as a witness. The attorney insisted on calling him 'Your Honour'. Darrow protested that this form of words should only be used when His Honour was on the bench. The judge in the murder trial intervened. 'Clarence,' he said, 'I took you to lunch once and you called me "Your Honour".'

'Sure,' said Darrow, 'but that was because you paid the bill.'

In the second case Darrow was annoyed with a judge who interrupted the case to ask him how long he had practised law in Chicago.

'Twenty-one years, Your Honour. How long have you practised?'

'Twenty-eight years, Mr Darrow,' said the judge smugly.

Darrow considered the statement for a moment and then said dismissively, 'Now that we have both acquired additional knowledge, may we proceed with the case?'

DAVIES, Marion. The bright, funny girl whom William Randolph Hearst made his mistress, and on whose relationship with Hearst Orson Welles based his film *Citizen Kane,* held the key to the great secret of the film. What infuriated Hearst about the movie was that Welles had found out that 'Rosebud' was the lovers' private name for Ms Davies's genitalia. And particularly because in the film Kane dies with the word 'Rosebud' on his lips.

DE GAULLE, Madame Charles. General de Gaulle's cry of exasperation ('How can you govern a country which has five hundred-odd cheeses?') is better known than his dexterity in extracting Madame de Gaulle from an embarrassing situation.

Lady Dorothy Macmillan once asked her what she wanted for the future. When she replied 'a penis' there was general consternation until the General leaned over and explained, 'In English, it is pronounced "happiness".'

DEGHY, Guy. When Guy Deghy, the mittel-European writer and actor, died in 1992 Keith Waterhouse supplied an idiosyncratic postscript to his obituaries in his *Spectator* diary. Keith used it to illustrate the indignities character actors have to put up with. As an actor Deghy specialised in baddies of foreign extraction. The American director Stanley Donen was interviewing him for a Hungarian role and asked him if he could do a Hungarian accent. To one whose last assignment had been to play an Austrian of Dutch extraction who has spent many years in Paris, this was child's play. 'I am Hungarian by birth, Mr Donen,' he told the director. 'I lived in Budapest until I was in my late twenties.'

'Yes, but can you do the accent?'

'I am speaking to you now in a Hungarian accent, Mr Donen. It is my natural accent.'

'But can you sustain it?'

Deghy had come from improbably noble stock; his grandmother, brought up in a castle in Transylvania, spoke only French, keeping her Hungarian for conversations with the cook. As family fortunes fluctuated Deghy tried acting and being a lavender water salesman. After Munich he settled in London and after a spell with the Hungarian section in Bush House he moved to BBC Radio in Leeds. Caught drinking fifteen minutes after hours and fined £1 by the magistrates, he had to bid farewell to that austere profession and fall back on acting. Frequently this meant working in the flood of half-hour quickies turned out for TV by the Danziger brothers in three days flat at the Equity minimum of £7 a day. He also worked for Harry Alan Towers. The difference was that Towers paid a little better and made his movies even faster. In a chase sequence in one Towers production, he and John Le Mesurier were required to hide behind a packing case. Told by the director to crouch even lower, Deghy protested, 'This is just about as low as we can get.'

The cameraman's voice cut through the darkness: 'You could be working for the Danzigers!'

DE MILLE, Cecil B. Cecil B. De Mille had a massive ego which was frequently fed by those who worked for him. Jesse Lasky Jr was employed by De Mille in 1958 on *The Buccaneer*. 'Do you believe in God, Jesse?' De Mille asked him. 'Yes, sir. I think so,' Lasky hesitated. 'Think so?' De Mille picked up. 'But don't you know?' 'I believe in you, sir,' said Lasky handing over his script. 'Not a bad beginning,' conceded De Mille.

He got rougher treatment from a pair of extras. He was indulging his passion for lecturing his crowd actors before breaking for lunch when he noticed two women talking. He called them to him and invited them to share whatever they were discussing over the microphone if it was so important. One of them plucked up the courage to say, 'I was just asking my friend when that old, bald-headed son-of-a-bitch was gonna let us have lunch.' De Mille grabbed the microphone from her and yelled, 'Lunch!'

The director was much mocked for his vast epics. His name proved a temptation for critics who could write about 'run-of-De-Mille' pictures, the 'De Millennium' and 'a movie for De Millions'. W. C. Fields, who lived near him, said, 'Some day the bastard is going to be crushed under one of his own epics!' His mixture of bare flesh and high principles was also mocked. *Time* magazine called *Samson and Delilah* 'Biblical ersatz with an Edgar Rice Burroughs flavour'. 'Scripterama' was another popular phrase. Often De Mille opened himself up to mockery. 'My father studied for the ministry and read the Bible in our home,' he once said. 'And this picture is dear to my heart. Furthermore, we have to take in seven million dollars to break even.' It gave the *New Yorker* the headline 'FURTHERMORE DEPARTMENT'.

During the shooting of *The Ten Commandments* De Mille had trouble getting the extras to look suitably awestruck when Moses came down with the tablets. His trick was to announce that a member of the crew had died and left a widow and eight children. Then he called for two minutes' silence, having warned the cameras to roll. Having got the correct reverent reaction at last he admitted that no one had died.

On *Samson and Delilah* an assistant tried to improve on the Bible, which called for Samson to slay Philistines with 'the jawbone of an ass'. 'This is a De Mille picture,' he told the screenwriters. 'We gotta use the whole ass.'

De Mille's mixture of sex, religion and spectacle never stopped him taking liberties with history – a habit which produced this quatrain:

> Cecil B. De Mille
> Much against his will
> Was persuaded to keep Moses
> Out of the War of the Roses.

In a sweeping defence of his methods De Mille spoke his own epitaph, 'I didn't write the Bible and I didn't invent sin.'

DENNING, Alfred, (Baron). Lord Denning once heard an appeal in a bestiality case. The defendant's victim was a duck. The defence called a psychiatrist, who had the mannerisms of a Viennese stage psychiatrist, who gave evidence that he had treated the man for a long time and that he was 'showing a marked improvement'.

Denning asked if that meant that he was 'about to graduate up through the animal and bird kingdom until he gets to little boys and girls?'

'Oh no, my Lord,' replied the psychiatrist, 'he always sticks to ducks.'

DERBY, Edward George Villiers Stanley, 17th Earl of. Tory Grandees were still very powerful in the 1920s in Baldwin's incoming government. Lord Derby and the Duke of Devonshire were influential if not informed. They met at Devonshire House some months before it was demolished to make way for a car showroom. Confident in their own inadequacy in the Lords, Duke and Earl were not sure of the competence of their colleagues in the Commons. Devonshire suggested, 'Let's get some clever lawyer.' Derby offered, 'I know the very man; someone was telling me about him the other day, a fellow called Pig.' 'The only Pig I know,' said the Duke, 'is James Pigge in Surtees.'

Thus did Sir Douglas Hogg, 1st Viscount Hailsham, transfer from being an expensive QC to an MP and later Lord Chancellor.

DEVONSHIRE, Dukes of. The 10th Duke of Devonshire, Edward William Spencer Cavendish, was presiding over a committee meeting at Pratt's (a club he owned) to elect new members during the Blitz in 1940 when a bomb fell, extinguishing the lights and bringing down the ceiling. When the lights came on again a slightly dishevelled but imperturbable Duke enquired, 'I can't remember, did we elect the feller or not?'

His son, Andrew Cavendish, the present Duke (married to Deborah Mitford, he re-named the musical *The Mitford Girls* 'La Triviata') was no admirer of Anthony Eden, Prime Minister at the time of the Suez crisis. He referred to President Nasser as 'the camel that broke the straw's back'.

DEXTER, John. Stories of John Dexter at work in the theatre are legion. Many of them hinge on his tendency to victimise the weakest member of a cast, but they are balanced by others that bear testimony to his brilliance in staging intractable material – such as with *The Royal Hunt of the Sun*, where his imagination was immediately excited by reading the apparently impossible stage direction 'They climb the Andes.' Perhaps his most inspired rebuke was to a playwright he often directed successfully, Arnold Wesker: 'Shut up, Arnold, or I'll direct this play the way you wrote it!'

He was fiercely opposed to privilege and I had to outmanoeuvre him on one occasion when we were filming Leslie Thomas's novel *The Virgin Soldiers*. We interviewed hundreds of young actors for the principal leading roles who were required to look like what the average sergeant-major would call 'a complete shower'. One of the candidates was a conventionally handsome Columbia Pictures contract actor, Christian Roberts, who had already had a good part in *To Sir With Love* with Sidney Poitier. He was also the son of the owner of Job's Dairies – the large South London milk distributors – and the two things most likely to annoy Dexter were the thought that he was being pressured by Columbia, who were financing the film, to cast a contract player and the fact that Christian was comfortably off. His good looks made it improbable that we would engage him but he deserved an unbiased hearing, so just before he came in to be interviewed I said to John, 'Interesting chap – his father's a milkman.' All Dexter's proletarian sympathies were engaged and he gave Christian a very thorough hearing. As I expected, he was not suitable and indeed left the profession for a time to work in the family business: but he has now returned with great success in leading roles in the rock musicals *Return to the Forbidden Planet* and *From a Jack to a King*.

DICKENS, Charles. This concerns Dickens the editor, not Dickens the novelist. A young poet, Laman Blanchard, sent Dickens some verses which he hoped he would publish in *Household Words*. He called them 'Orient Pearls at Random Strung'. Dickens's rejection note was succinct: 'Dear Blanchard, too much string – Yours, C.D.'

DILKE, Sir Charles. Sir Charles Dilke was a rising star of the Liberal Party with a place in Gladstone's second Cabinet in the 1880s and a safe seat in Chelsea, where he also lived, in Sloane Street. He comprehensively blotted his copy book by having an affair with a young married woman, Mrs Crawford, who accused him of luring her into bed, teaching her 'every French vice' and sharing her favours simultaneously with Fanny, one of his servant girls. It was *the* political–sexual scandal of the second half of the century and inspired a music hall song. It went:

> Charlie Dilke spilt the milk
> On the way to Chelsea.
> The papers say that Charlie's gay,
> Oh what a wilful wag.
> This noble representative
> Of ev'rything good in Chelsea,
> Has let the cat, the naughty cat,
> Out of the Gladstone bag.

What was extraordinary was Dilke's behaviour, at a time when he was hoping for political rehabilitation. He was staying at the Glen, the Scottish home of the rich Tennant family – Margot Tennant was Herbert Henry Asquith's second wife – and made a pass at Margot's younger sister Laura. She may not have been quite as sharp as Margot, who, when called 'Margott' by Jean Harlow, was to say, 'No – the "t" is silent as in Harlow'; but when the old goat met her in a passage on her way to bed and said, 'If you will kiss me, I will give you a signed photograph,' she had the good sense to reply, 'It is awfully good of you, Sir Charles, but I would rather not, for what on earth should I do with the photograph?'

DIMAGGIO, Joe. When the great baseball star Joe DiMaggio was married to Marilyn Monroe he accompanied her to Korea where she was to entertain the troops. Her reception was stupendous and she turned to DiMaggio to say, 'Joe, you've never heard such cheering.' Her husband assured her quietly, 'Yes, I have.'

DISRAELI, Benjamin (Lord Beaconsfield). The extraordinary devotion of Mary Anne Disraeli to her husband, Gladstone's great Tory rival, is worth celebrating. She swore that she would never go to the House of Commons until he was Prime Minister; but once she did travel with him as far as the gates because he had a particularly important speech to deliver. As he got out her fingers were painfully trapped in the carriage door but she did not let him know, fearing it might ruin his speech. On another important occasion, travelling to stay at Hatfield she fell and cut her face. Again she dissembled, first staying in her room with a 'headache', later asking to be seated far away from him, saying, 'He has lost his eye-glass and . . . he will never see what a condition I am in.' It was two days before he became aware of the accident.

She was committed to his comfort, always staying up, with lights blazing, fires burning, a hot meal waiting, until he returned from the House. Once, having turned down an invitation to celebrate at the Carlton Club, he arrived home to find a tempting pie and a bottle of champagne waiting for him. 'My dear,' he said, 'you are more like a mistress than a wife.'

Mistresses he had had earlier in his career included a complicated period when he and his first patron, the Lord Chancellor, Lord Lyndhurst, shared the favours of Henrietta, the wife of Sir Francis Sykes, and heroine of Disraeli's novel *Henrietta Temple*. He was at the same time also involved with Sykes's mistress, Mrs Bolton, the wife of a Park Lane doctor.

For such a flamboyant character as Disraeli, some of his statements seem out of character: 'Men destined to the highest places should beware of badinage . . . an insular country, subject to fogs, and with a powerful middle class, requires grave statesmen.' Contrariwise, he had started his career as a sort of out-of-town try-out for Oscar Wilde. He was both dandy and novelist. 'Let me die eating ortolans to the sound of soft music' will do for dandy; the fledgling author supplied 'a want of tact is worse than a want of virtue', and 'I rather like bad wine, one gets so bored with good wine'. He decided early that 'affectation tells . . . here better than wit'; and he would soon find, like Wilde, that affectation was a way of making people pay attention. In Taper, a politician in his novel *Coningsby*, he created a mouthpiece for himself: 'I am all for a religious cry . . . it means nothing, and, if successful, does not interfere with business when we are in.'

Disraeli's parliamentary debut was a disaster. During his maiden speech he was howled down and retired shouting, 'Gentlemen . . . the time will come when you will hear me!' He developed a talent for sustained invective, with Peel as his first whipping boy. This was an act of revenge: he and his wife had both solicited Peel for office, which Peel denied him. He cut his teeth on the Free Trade debates with an elaborate metaphor in which the inconsistency of Peel's policy in power was contrasted with his protestations in opposition. He was represented as a suitor whose behaviour 'in the hours of possession' contrasted unfavourably with his previous conduct, 'during the hours of courtship'. As the debates continued Disraeli found new similes. Peel was Lord High Admiral of the Turkish navy, betraying his Sultan; 'organised hypocrisy'; a nurse dashing out the brains of her charge in 'a patriotic frenzy'. Nor did he confine himself to policy. He was happy to be personal: 'The Right Honourable Gentleman's smile is like the fittings on a coffin' . . . 'The Right Honourable Gentleman is like a poker. The only difference is that a poker gives off occasional signs of warmth.'

When Peel did a U-turn in his policy on the Corn Laws Disraeli accused him of a career of political dishonesty. In his memorable attack he said, 'The Right Honourable gentleman caught the Whigs bathing and walked away with their clothes. He has left them in full enjoyment of their liberal position and he is himself a stout conservative of their garments.' Peel asked why, if Disraeli so despised his character and conduct, he had once asked to serve under him. Had he not been 'ready, as I think he was, to unite his fortunes with mine in office'? In a brazen lie or in panic Disraeli denied the charge, 'With respect to my being a solicitor for office, it is entirely unfounded.'

For some reason Peel decided not to confront Disraeli with his letter of supplication. Robert Blake suggests that this may be because 'Peel, who had the hyper-sensitivity on points of honour of a man only half belonging to the patrician world, refrained because it would be unfair to read out a personal communication.' It is one of the great 'ifs' of history to conjecture what would have happened if Peel had behaved as would most fully paid-up patricians.

It was his opposition to Peel that brought Disraeli to the unfavourable notice of Queen Victoria. When he came to power his first task was to win her confidence with flattery. 'Everyone likes flattery,' he said to Matthew Arnold, 'and when it comes to Royalty you should lay it on with a trowel.' After the publication of her *Highland Journal* he could refer to 'We authors, Ma'am', and he told her she was 'the head of the literary profession'. He defined his formula for handling her: 'I never deny, I never contradict; I sometimes forget.' Gladstone, she complained, addressed her as a public meeting; Disraeli treated her 'with the knowledge that she was a woman'.

Disraeli was unique in combining an orchidaceous style with the responsibilities of high office. 'Life is too short to be little,' he said, and 'Revolutions are not made with rosewater.' 'I believe that nothing in the newspapers is ever true . . . and that is why they are so popular, the taste of the age being decidedly for fiction.' (*Endymion*). 'The fun of talk is to find what a man really thinks, and then contrast it with the enormous lies he has been telling all dinner, and, perhaps, all his life.' 'No man is regular in his attendance at the House of Commons until he is married.' When he was asked to speak up in the House, he retorted calmly,

'What I say is to enlighten you. If I bawled at you, you would leave this place as great a fool as you entered it.'

Disraeli, 'the great panjandrum', gave, and so it was necessary that he should also take. 'He is a self-made man and worships his creator,' said John Bright. Carlyle called him a 'Hebrew conjuror' and asked, 'How long will John Bull allow this absurd monkey to dance on his chest?' As proud of his Jewish ancestry as he was protective of the Church of England he replied to Daniel O'Connell's attack by saying, 'Yes, I am a Jew, and when the ancestors of the Right Honourable Gentleman were brutal savages in an unknown island, mine were priests in the Temple of Solomon.' To a heckler who shouted that Disraeli's wife had picked him out of the gutter he was more predictable: 'My good fellow, if you were in a gutter, no one would pick you out.'

The climax to Disraeli's career was his confrontation with Gladstone. His invective was still spirited but his years, his honours and his increased responsibility, confronted by his monumental, solemn and righteous opponent, contrived to turn his sallies from glancing wit to a head-on assault. When he came in for the kill he characterised Gladstone as 'intoxicated by the exuberance of his own verbosity.' He conjured up a triumphant simile to describe Gladstone's dying ministry. It reminded him of 'those marine landscapes, not very unusual on the coast of South America, with their range of exhausted volcanoes. Not a flame flickers on a single, pallid crest.' Privately he could turn lightly to Gladstone's daughter and refer to a diplomat as 'the most dangerous man in Europe, myself excepted as your father would say: your father excepted – I should prefer to say.'

A Disraeli chestnut has been liberally adapted by subsequent politicians and is indeed a sort of precursor of the good news–bad news joke. 'If Mr Gladstone fell into the Thames *that* would be a misfortune, and if anyone pulled him out, *that*, I suppose, would be a calamity.'

His words as, while dying, he corrected the proofs of his final speech – 'I will not go down to posterity talking bad grammar' – retain to the end the light, dilettante, detached wit which he did not allow to sabotage his other achievements.

DOCHÉ. The nineteenth-century French actress and *grande horizontale* was the original *Dame aux Camélias* of Dumas *fils* – 'better than Bernhardt', according to some who saw both. She rejected Napoleon III as a lover before he became Emperor, as well as the Earl of Pembroke – or rather she failed to arrive for an assignation with him at the Star and Garter. He never spoke to her again and settled an enormous sum on a ballet dancer. Doché's secret? 'She was beautiful? No. Was she clever? No. I think it must be because she had such beautiful shoulders,' said one admirer.

She took a new lover while she was appearing as Camille and living near the theatre on the sixth floor in the rue de Rivoli. Her admirer, a young marquis, was required to crawl up the stairs like a dog holding between his teeth a diamond necklace selected by her at Dumorets in the rue de la Paix.

When an older lover collapsed and died in her bed she sent a message to his wife, 'Madame, I regret to inform you that your husband has just died in my rooms. I wish you would take all necessary steps at once to remove him, *car son cadavre chez moi est très embarrassant.*'

DORSEY, Tommy. The sharp tongue, tough manner and high standards of musicianship of the legendary bandleader Tommy Dorsey are best exemplified by his comment when looking for a trumpet player. One of his musicians made a suggestion adding, 'He's a nice guy.' Dorsey was not impressed. 'Nice guys are a dime a dozen,' he said. 'Get me a prick who can play!'

Dorsey followed a practice of making his band members pay forfeits – buying drinks for the band if they were late. Buddy Rich, frequently late, had somehow got away with it, so on an occasion when the pianist Joe Bushkin was the culprit he agreed to buy wine for everyone except Rich. When a bottle of wine arrived for Rich Bushkin sent it back. A fight between the two men immediately ensued outside. 'Well, it was a fighting band,' said Bushkin later. What amused him was that when Dorsey tried to stop the fight it transpired that he wasn't worried about the welfare of his players but the fate of their band uniforms. 'Take the jackets off!' he yelled; 'The jackets. We've got another set to play.'

One young player, Terry Gibbs, who joined Dorsey's band in California, soon realised he had made a mistake. He wasn't interested in playing dance music and stood little chance of playing jazz solos. He gave in his notice to the manager, to Dorsey's fury. When they next met Gibbs feared a physical assault. 'Did you just quit my band?' threatened Dorsey. Before Gibbs could explain he added, 'Nobody quits. You're fired.' Gibbs saw his chance: 'Well, if you fire me you gotta pay my way home.'

'No, you quit! You pay your own way home.'

DRIBERG, Tom (Lord Bradwell). Tom Driberg, one of the Labour movement's last great eccentrics and outsiders, stays in the public memory largely for his sexual adventures. He 'cottaged' public lavatories devotedly all his life and made a habit of introducing his current rent boy as 'one of my young constituents'. His behaviour was tactfully overlooked for years by parliamentary colleagues, and other scandals – like the suggested improper advances made to two striking marchers whom he had asked to his house – were hushed up at

Lord Beaverbrook's insistence. In 1951 he unaccountably married a Yorkshire widow of whom he complained: 'She broke her marriage vows; she tried to sleep with me.'

In Edinburgh when he was approaching 70 he picked up a burly Scottish sergeant and took him to bed. Pinned down with his head buried in the pillows in the middle of the act he turned to ask if his partner would not prefer to be doing it with a girl. 'Och no,' said the soldier. 'This is for men. Girls are for cissies.'

DRINKWATER, John. Drinkwater (1882-1937) was a popular poet and playwright in the early 1920s who comes off badly in this little tale.

Sybil Thorndike and Lewis Casson had commissioned Laurence Binyon to write a play about St Joan. When Bernard Shaw, who had long contemplated this subject, saw Sybil Thorndike's Beatrice Cenci he knew he had found his Joan. The news that he was at work reached the Cassons. When they wrote to Shaw he replied simply, 'Nonsense! Of course Sybil plays my *Saint Joan*; someone else can do the other one. I warned off Masefield and Drinkwater, but I forgot Binyon.' Binyon behaved like a wise gentleman and did not protest or compete. Shaw was less gentlemanly. When asked later why he wrote the play he replied, 'To save Joan of Arc from John Drinkwater.'

DRYDEN, John. The seventeenth-century Poet Laureate is an unlikely subject for an amusing story, but the immensely unreliable nineteenth-century book by Sir James Prior, a *Life of Edward Malone with Selections from his Anecdotes*, suggests that Dryden, something of a shot-gun husband at the hands of his wife's brother, then neglected his wife. When she remonstrated with him over the time he spent so long poring over his books, she added, 'I wish I were a book, and then I should have more of your company.' 'Pray, my dear,' her husband is supposed to have replied, 'if you do become a book, let it be a calendar, for then I shall change you every year.'

DURHAM, John George Lambton, 1st Earl of. Lord Durham was one of the early nineteenth-century stars of Ranelagh, the London pleasure garden. He was a laid-back peer known affectionately as 'King Jog' because he once remarked he thought '£40,000 a year a moderate income – such a one as a man might jog on with'.

There was perhaps an unconscious echo of 'King Jog' in Grey Gowrie's reason for resigning as Arts Minister – that he could not get by in London on less than £40,000 a year . . .

— E —

EDDISON, Robert. The late Robert Eddison features in my *Theatrical Anecdotes*, but this story had not yet appeared in the programme for Simon Russell Beale's *Edward II* when the book went to press. Eddison played Lightborn, the poker-packing murderer, in an earlier production, which starred Ian McKellen. 'Lightborn must surely be one of the very best small parts in the whole of theatrical literature,' Eddison testified. 'Indeed I doubt the need of any qualification. I was finally (and delightedly) convinced of this when, quite two years after playing him, as I disembarked from a taxi the driver turned and contemplated me . . . "Aren't you," he said, "that low bugger who did in Edward II?" '

EDWARD I. As a young man Edward had often been rash, hasty, ill-advised and extravagant. He sketched a pattern for princes of irresponsible youth and dramatic reform which Shakespeare was to have Henry V perfect and which Edward VII was to attempt to retrace. His obsession with tournaments, the polo of the age (it unseated princes even more frequently), made him neglect his estates and his other responsibilities.

In 1270 Edward set out for the Holy Land bound for a crusade – the last in the old medieval tradition. His princess, Eleanor of Castile, accompanied him; a more welcome companion than Berengaria on her unhappy honeymoon with Great Uncle Richard. Eleanor was in her tent when the Emir's envoy arrived and delivered his letters. As Edward studied them the Saracen reached into his robes again. This time he drew out a dagger and aimed it at the Prince, who, seeing it just in time, managed to raise his hand to ward off the blow but received a savage wound in his arm. He kicked the man before he could strike again, wrenched the dagger from him and killed him with it. Edward's attendants came running, and the Court minstrel, squaring up bravely to a corpse, knocked the dead man's brains out with a footstool, earning a rebuke from Edward. As the days passed, the flesh around his wound grew black. A romantic notion grew up that Eleanor lovingly sucked the wound clean, but in fact the blackened flesh was hacked away by surgeons, and fifteen days later, as he had been promised, Edward was well enough to ride again. The Sultan sent ambassadors denying complicity in the Emir's plot, and provoked from Edward one of his first recorded statements in English, 'You pay me worship but you have no love for me.'

News of the deaths of his uncle, Richard, of his two sons, John and Henry, and then of his father, Henry III, reached Edward on his way home. Confident in his succession, the new King took his time over the last part of the journey, allowing himself a last, nearly fatal, exercise in irresponsibility before he sailed for England. The Count of Châlons, near Lyon, challenged him to a monster tournament, a 'mêlée'. Against everyone's advice – invariably a spur to him – Edward agreed and sent to England for a crack party of knights. He mustered a thousand, but as they entered the arena they were plainly outnumbered and the Count made straight for the King. The exercise in chivalry developed into a fight, 'the little Battle of Châlons' – the Count's unsporting intention all along. A giant, he lunged to drag Edward from his horse, but his target was too nimble for him and leant forward. The Count hit the ground heavily, and, shocked by the fall, lay on the turf and begged for quarter. The King exploded in one of his famous rages and whacked the stunned Count soundly, refusing contemptuously to accept the sword of surrender with his own hands.

On his return, the new King, who had a glimmering of an idea of Britain, spent most of one year in Wales seeking to impose the best of English criminal law – not a strong point with the Welsh – while respecting Welsh civil customs. Where Edward went the Queen accompanied him, and her third son was born at Caernarvon Castle in 1284. A convenient tradition attributes the choice of birthplace to statesmanship, which is unlikely. Another apocryphal story tells how the Welsh nobles asked for a Welsh prince, and Edward promised to present them with one who spoke neither English nor French. Then he revealed his infant son. Tradition alone locates the Tower and the room in which the boy was born. A year later, with the death of Prince Alphonso at the age of twelve, Prince Edward became the heir apparent to the English throne.

In 1290 when Edward was setting off to subdue the Scots he heard of his Queen's sickness. Eleanor was near him in Nottinghamshire, and he reached her before she died on 28 November. He followed her bier through thirteen bitter, cold days of progress from Grantham to London, ordering a service at every resting place. At each halt he erected a cross in memory of his 'chère reine'; the last was just before the entry to Westminster Abbey. (By a simple process of colloquialisation, it became 'Charing Cross'.) Eleanor was buried at the feet of her father-in-law in his Abbey.

After remarriage (to a French princess) and drawn-out conflict with the dissident Scots William Wallace and Robert Bruce, Edward made arrangements in the spring of 1305 to knight his son at Westminster. To contemplate the character of Edward of Caernarvon cannot have given his father great confidence. The Prince lost large sums of money at pitch and toss, he travelled with a lion and a troupe of Italian fiddlers, two trumpeters, a horn player, a harpist and a drummer. His favourite companions were young grooms and servants with whom he could swim and horse around. His physical prowess exploded into energetic ditch-digging, hunting and racing as well as swimming. He was a medieval prototype for a rich, not particularly bright, handsome, bodybuilding twentieth-century bisexual, dividing his ample leisure between the gym and doubtful bars. Unfortunately, he was born to be King.

His more serious misdemeanours included insulting a judge who gave sentence against a favourite servant. (His father made him apologise.) On another occasion he broke into the Bishop of Lichfield's park and killed his deer. This time the King banished Piers Gaveston, the prince's companion.

Gaveston, a Gascon contemporary and Edward's greatest friend and influence, was loyal and genuinely fond of the prince, but acquisitive and on the make. Darkly handsome against Edward's fair complexion and bright curly hair, Gaveston's great charm and his downfall lay in his wounding wit, sprayed irrelevantly on all who crossed his path. He was a great maker of enemies and Edward needed friends.

When the Prince of Wales asked his by now sick and ageing father to grant Royal estates to Gaveston, the King, in a rage, tore handfuls of hair out of Prince Edward's head and once again dismissed the Gascon under oath to leave England and not come back. 'You base-born whoreson,' he shouted at his son, 'do you want to give away lands now, you who never gained any!'

On his death bed, the King exacted reluctant promises from the Prince of Wales. He wished his heart to be taken to the Holy Land with a hundred knights. He did not want his body buried until the Scots were defeated. The bones were to be carried from battlefield to battlefield so that he could still lead his army to victory. It was not enough for him to work his exhausted carcass until he died – he wanted his boiled-down bones to labour on after death. He ordered that Gaveston should never be recalled without the consent of the nation. He died, aged sixty-eight, on Friday, 7 July 1307. It was a matter of moments before Edward II broke all the promises that he had made.

EDWARD II. Edward II's reign began with the recall of his favourite,

Gaveston, and a journey to France with his stepmother to claim her niece as his bride. Her Coronation and the feast which followed it were organised by Gaveston, but she was upstaged by the splendour of the young man's retinue, and his catering arrangements went badly awry. No food reached the Queen's or any other table before darkness fell. When it did arrive it was badly cooked and badly served. There were few things more dangerous than an angry medieval Baron with a rumbling belly and if Gaveston had a hope of salvation he lost it over dinner.

Gaveston's Mitford-like zeal for giving the barons nicknames did not endear him to them either. The Duke of Lancaster (an eccentric dresser) was 'the actor'; the sallow and skinny Earl of Pembroke was 'Joseph the Jew'; and the choleric Earl of Warwick was 'the wild boar of Arden'. The Queen too was aware of the way her husband and his lover mocked her behind her back. Eventually the net closed on Gaveston, and he surrendered to Pembroke and Warwick. His personal safety was guaranteed. Near Deddington Pembroke called a halt. His prisoner asked to rest and, as the Countess of Pembroke was at a neighbouring manor, Pembroke left to spend the night with her, unaware that his progress south through the Midlands was monitored by the Earl of Warwick. With 'Joseph the Jew' away with his lady, 'the wild boar of Arden' came out from Warwick, his truffle hunt rewarded in the early hours of the morning by the discovery of Gaveston and his guards in the house of the local rector.

Gaveston's elegant clothes were thrown aside and he was dragged downstairs in the first rough covering that came to hand. Barefoot and bareheaded, he was hustled to a dungeon in Warwick Castle. With the summary justice of a lynch mob, two Welshmen in Lancaster's service then beheaded Gaveston on the green of Blacklow Hall in front of a crowd shouting with joy and blowing horns. In a macabre division of spoils, Lancaster's men saved him Gaveston's head while four cobblers carried his trunk back to Warwick on a ladder. The Earl declined to receive it and eventually it found a temporary resting place with the Dominicans at Oxford. Even they did not dare bury it in consecrated ground as Gaveston had died excommunicate.

When the King was told the news he was too shocked to say more than, 'By God, what a fool he was. I could have told him not to get into Warwick's hands.' Edward was alone again. He lost himself in physical activity. Seven days a week he dug ditches around Clarendon Park, burying his grief in fatigue until his first son was born and provided a distraction.

Gaveston was replaced as the King's favourite by Hugh Despenser, but the Queen – who now had a champion in Roger de Mortimer, Earl of March – captured Despenser at Bristol and had him brought to the Mortimer stronghold of Hereford. In the presence of the 'she-wolf', he met a horrible death, his genitals cut off and burned in front of him for being a heretic and a sodomite. When the torture could wrack him no more he was beheaded and the head displayed on London Bridge, 'with much tumult and the sound of horns in the presence of the Mayor and commonalty'.

Edward's downfall was unavoidable. Articles of Deposition were drawn up, tabulating his dangerous corruptness and incompetence. Monks and earls, knights and citizens, abbots and barons set off on the road to Kenilworth to take part in one of the nastiest spectacles of public humiliation witnessed in England. Bishop Adam Orleton was their enthusiastic spokesman. Clothed in a simple, black shift and not lacking physical courage, Edward preserved his composure until Orleton's invective shifted from accusations to threats that if he did not agree to resign, not only he but his sons and the whole Plantagenet line would be deposed. Warming to his task, the Bishop of Hereford had the satisfaction of seeing the King faint at his feet and then, as he continued his relentless diatribe, interrupt the threats with groans mingling distress and assent. Eventually he sobbed out his sorrow that he had betrayed his people, his trust in his accusers and his joy that his son was accepted as his successor. Homage was renounced, and his household was dissolved as the Steward, Sir Thomas Blount, broke his staff of office and the crown, sceptre and orb were surrendered in fresh paroxysms of weeping.

The disgraced ex-King still posed a problem for the security, if not the conscience, of his supplanters. To conceal his whereabouts the prisoner was moved from place to place, to Corfe, to Bristol and to Berkeley. With every move, even more discomfort was heaped upon him. One attempt at rescue in July 1327 was foiled, but it gave Queen Isabella and Mortimer an unpleasant shock and stiffened their determination to be rid of him, especially as their popularity was not increasing. It was not until his 'dark and dreadful' death that Edward's life was raised from weak inadequacy to stark tragedy; but public opinion was beginning to change, as tales spread of the Queen's adultery and Mortimer's greed (which outstripped Despenser's). As he was denied food and water and clothing: as he was teased from sleep, crowned with hay and shaved with muddy water culled in an old helmet from a stagnant ditch, the 'she-wolf' complained to his guards of their overkind treatment.

At Berkeley Castle two new gaolers, Thomas Gurney and William Ogle, took charge. On 21 September, by accident or by design, Thomas, Lord Berkeley, spent time away from the castle at his manor of Bradley. During the night hideous shrieks rang against the echoing stones of the castle. 'Many a one woke and prayed to God for the harmless soul which was passing that night in torture.' In the morning, with suspicious speed, Edward's unblemished body was exhibited to the citizens of Gloucester to prove that he had died of natural causes. Tradition has it that his jailers killed him by stuffing a red-hot poker up his anus through his bowels and into his stomach, and that this barbarous torture, nastily combining criticism of his lifestyle with discreet murder, left only his contorted features as testimony to sow doubt among the citizens of Gloucester, who were given no more than a quick frontal view of the corpse next day. Modern opinion is divided on the story; but the body was interred, hugger-mugger, in Gloucester Cathedral, and Isabella had yet another chance to indulge her gift for theatrical tears.

EDWARD III. Edward III's reign did not begin in earnest until he had rid himself of the influence of his mother and her lover. Although he held his father in some affection, he could not prevent his downfall. All he could do was harden a determination not to be politically inept and criminally incompetent, especially since Isabella and Mortimer had become the unconscious architects of a precedent for the removal of a useless King, deposed not only by his own resignation but by the common consent and unanimous counsel of the Lords, the whole clergy and the people. Young Edward stood by as Mortimer enriched himself and his family with the Despenser estates and engineered a truce with Scotland on humiliating terms. He threw in the King's five-year-old sister, Joan, as bride for Robert Bruce's eldest son, David, to seal the bargain. (At four, David Bruce was the younger man.)

Chafing at his political impotence, and at his mother's rapacity and her lover's vulgar ostentation, both exercised at the expense of his dignity, Edward determined to remove them. He was strengthened in 1328 by his own marriage to Philippa of Hainault. The couple soon saw that the 'she-wolf' had feathered her love-nest with Mortimer at their expense. An empty purse did not inhibit the passion of the teenage lovers, though, and by 1330 the Queen, an early royal advocate of breast-feeding her child herself, was suckling another Edward, born at Woodstock in June and known later as the Black Prince. A tournament held at Cheapside to celebrate the event gave Philippa an opportunity to endear herself to the people of London, an affection she never lost. Some scaffolding collapsed, endangering the lives of the Queen and her ladies: no one was injured, but the King, exploding in a good Plantaganet rage, threatened the offending carpenters' lives. Philippa, coming out of shock, pleaded publicly for the men in an unconscious rehearsal for her later appeal on behalf of the Burghers of Calais. She pacified her husband and secured her place in the affections of the citizens.

The royal couple's plot to unseat Mortimer was carefully laid, but some suspicion of danger got through to him in 1330. He and Isabella shut themselves up in Nottingham Castle behind bolted gates and guarded battlements, and the keys were laid nightly on Isabella's pillow, but these precautions proved inadequate. The conspirators were planning an inside job. Edward joined the party, entering through a secret passage, and reached the chamber where Isabella and Mortimer were preparing for bed. The Queen's screams to her son to 'have pity on gentle Mortimer' did not impress him. 'Gentle' Mortimer (a magnificent misnomer) was roughly rushed to London, there to be drawn and hanged as a traitor, the first victim of the brand-new gallows at Tyburn. The King treated his appalling mother better than she deserved, and installed her in some comfort in her favourite Castle Rising in Norfolk with a handsome allowance, freedom to roam the countryside hawking, and an ample supply of romances to occupy her infinite spare time. Punctiliously he paid her an annual visit. A life of mean and grasping crime had been crammed into only thirty-six years, and she survived in cushioned imprisonment for another twenty-eight. Then she was buried at Newgate in a double funeral with her daughter Joan, whom she had married so young to David Bruce. The two solemn processions converged on the church from the roads entering London from the East and the North. The coffins of murderous mother and unlucky daughter met at the high altar.

By 1330 Edward III was impatient to rule and to be seen to rule, determined to prove that he was neither his unfortunate father nor his awful mother. A quarter of a century later he would be able to look back with no doubts that he had proved his point, happily unaware that only decline and dotage lay ahead. St George's Day 1358 marked the public celebration of his greatest achievements. His interests did not lie in literature and the arts, though Philippa could commission the chronicler Froissart and enjoy Chaucer. Edward wanted a shrine to chivalry, and Windsor was the place. In the early years of his reign, forty young English knights had adopted a silk eyepatch and sworn that no man would see out of two eyes until he had performed some notable deed of honour on foreign soil. The King was their inspiration. Edward enjoyed war above everything, and if there was no territory for which to fight then tournaments were his joy. His statesmanship was instinctive and practical, owing little to any carefully conceived master plan.

Enormous sums were spent in flamboyant display at Windsor, where Edward built the great Round Hall in 1344 to house his Order of the Round Table. No sooner was one Order re-established than another was new minted, and whether the Order of the Garter sprang from the Countess of Salisbury's dropped ribbon as some suggested, or from an earlier source, it needed a home. More vast sums of money were spent on building the St George's Chapel. Windsor became an All-England Championship course for tournaments, jousting parties and hunting expeditions. Rings of smaller houses surrounded the castle providing lavish accommodation for visiting princes and nobles. Hunting lodges, scattered through the Great Park, gave the King and his guests easy access to any part of the forest within convenient range of food and stabling. Days at Windsor were crammed with exercise and martial arts; nights were filled with balls and feasting. It was the Hickstead of its day.

Edward III would reign for nineteen more years after the Windsor tournament in 1358. His Queen died eight years before him in 1369. Philippa's final illness lasted some two years. All her sons except the youngest, Thomas, were fighting on the Continent when she died. However, Edward was with Philippa at her death, and he pensioned the ladies of her bedchamber in accordance with her last wishes. One such lady, Alice Perrers, was not included. The King had taken up with her even before the Queen's death, and she was assured of a bigger benefit. The King's orders have the enfeebled ring of infatuation: '. . . know all, that we give and concede to our beloved Alice Perrers, late damsel of the chamber of our dearest consort, Philippa, deceased, and to her heirs and executors all the jewels, goods and chattels that the said wife left . . .'

The 'said wife' had provided a particularly congenial background for her exciting, explosive, soldier husband. She was engaged to a child, married an adolescent, bore the sons and daughters of a lusty, six-foot sportsman, caught the danger signs of his flashing eye, anticipated his less politic eruptions and introduced an atmosphere of some scholarship, family security and order into a court which on her death fell apart in sickness, family intrigue and senile foolishness.

The King's dotage was saddened by deaths and disfigured by disloyalty. He was happier taking sweets from the fingers of Alice Perrers than believing dispatches setting out the schemes of the King of France, and news of the King's senility and his dependence on corrupt officials and on his meddling mistress became common currency. Alice manipulated him, kept him from state affairs, exploited her position into a public scandal and even sat beside judges in the courts.

The Commons, who had had the support of the Prince of Wales, now moved to rid the King of his mistress. They triggered a pitiful collapse. Edward begged them to deal gently with Alice 'for the sake of his love and honour'. His honour was in tatters and Dame Alice was banished. With the death of the Black Prince, the Duke of Lancaster, John of Gaunt, gained control and restored his father's mistress, sabotaging the King's remaining faculties the more swiftly. Edward had reigned for fifty years and now retired to his palace at Sheen where 'Dame Alice' cheerfully took bribes to plead unworthy causes or gave unsuitable petitioners access to the old man.

As Edward grew weaker, Alice talked of the hunting and hawking expeditions on which he would embark the next day. In June 1377 his voice failed and he lay between distraction and death. Choosing her moment, Alice removed his jewels, picked the rings from his fingers and tiptoed from the room. Her departure was a signal to the other courtiers to leave the sinking ship, with a speed not seen around a royal deathbed since William the Conqueror. One priest alone remained to hear the King's voice come back and croak the two words, 'Jesu miserere,' and to give him the cross to kiss. Soon afterwards he died, sixty years old, and King for fifty-one of them. His death did not approach the horrors of his father's; but it provided its own inglorious pathos.

EDWARD IV. Edward IV was born at Rouen in 1442. He was the eldest son of Richard, Duke of York and Cicely Neville, the twenty-third child of the prolific Earl of Westmorland. Her nickname was the 'Rose of Raby', and her two attributes which survive in history are her piety and her blonde good looks. Edward was to inherit the latter (he was sometimes called 'The Rose of Rouen') but not the former. Shakespeare welcomes him with two of his most famous lines, spoken by his deformed younger brother, Richard, Duke of Gloucester:

> Now is the winter of our discontent
> Made glorious summer by this sun of York . . .

Edward, in contrast to Gloucester, was handsome, tall (his coffin was opened in 1789 to reveal a skeleton of 6ft 3½ins) and proudly conscious of his appearance, showing it off at the least provocation although he grew fatter as he grew older as a result of his excesses. He acknowledged three bastard children and probably fathered more. 'I had three concubines which in three diverse properties diversely excelled: one the merriest, another the wiliest, the third the holiest harlot of the realm, as one whom no man could get out of church lightly to any place but it were to his bed . . .'

His long-time mistress was the wife of a London merchant. She was famously known as Jane Shore but recent research suggests that her name was Elizabeth. She was 'the merriest . . . this Shore's wife, in whom the King therefore took special pleasure,' recorded Sir Thomas More, who knew her in old age; 'For many he had, but her he loved.'

When Edward came to the throne (he was proclaimed King on 4 March 1461), the London court took on a new character. The handsome, affable, confident nineteen-year-old King, popular with the citizens, and especially with their wives, recalled his young brothers from their refuge in Utrecht, creating the older, George, Duke of Clarence and the younger, Richard, Duke of Gloucester. As the King indulged himself in a pleasant round of 'wine, women and pageantry', the reins of government slipped easily into the hands of the Neville clan of Warwick, the King Maker, who had done much to assure his accession. So it would always be with Edward IV. To make money was a congenial hobby, but his easygoing nature encouraged him to give the day-to-day administration of the realm into other hands and then, when he found his confidence misplaced and his trust betrayed, he was always able to summon up the speed, skill and courage to pull his chestnuts out of the fire

While Warwick was consolidating the new King's position and seeking to strengthen it by a political marriage, Edward had other ideas, focused on Elizabeth Woodville. Elizabeth was the daughter of Henry V's eldest brother's widow, Jacquetta of Luxembourg, and her second husband, Richard Woodville, Lord Rivers, reputed to be the most handsome man in England. Elizabeth herself had been married, but was now widowed with two sons.

Tradition places the first romantic meeting between Edward and Elizabeth in the forest of Whittlebury, where he was hunting near her mother's castle at Grafton. She waylaid him under a Northampton oak holding her two orphaned sons by her and pleading for the restoration of her inheritance. She brought off the scene at the 'Queen's Oak' triumphantly and the King, finding an age difference of seven years no obstacle to his passion, granted her request and followed his generosity with an improper suggestion. 'My liege,' she countered, 'I know I am not good enough to be your queen, but I am far too good to be your mistress.' Her managing mother came to her aid with a welter of intrigue of which the climax was a secret early morning wedding near Stony Stratford with no witnesses apart from the Dowager Duchess, a priest, 'two gentlewomen and a young man who helped the priest to sing'. The King rode off to hunt as soon as the ceremony was over and returned at night when the Duchess was sure that the rest of the house slept. After a few days, Edward invited himself formally to stay with Lord Rivers. Again Jacquetta made sure that the royal feet pattered discreetly to her daughter's bedroom after lights out.

The King, who relished a comfortable home life, achieved it by falling in with his wife's whims inside their palaces, and gratifying his own outside the walls. His brother Clarence, stung by Elizabeth's opposition to his second marriage (she had earmarked the young Burgundy girl as a possible prize for *her* brother, Lord Rivers), arrived in the Council Chamber the worse for drink and muttering slanders against the Queen. At her prompting, Edward, who was inclined to view his brother as a nuisance rather than a threat, had him arrested, arraigned and sentenced to death, though he hesitated over his execution. However, he was eventually put to death – according to tradition, in a butt of Malmsey wine, an end which does something for poetic justice, if not for historical accuracy.

In 1482, Edward's pleasure-plied body fell an easy victim to malaria or typhoid, and propped up on pillows, pleading with his ministers, Hastings and Stanley, to protect his two sons, he died at the age of 42 on 9 April.

EDWARD V. Edward V, son of Edward IV, reigned for only 75 days after he suddenly became King, aged thirteen, on his father's death in April 1483. His immediate problems were the ambition of his uncle, Richard of Gloucester, the Protector, and the unpopularity of his mother's family, the Woodvilles.

His father had carefully arranged his education, 'his special knowledge of literature which enabled him to discourse elegantly, to understand fully and to declaim most excellently from any work whether in verse or prose that came into his hands, unless it were from among the more abstruse authors . . .'

On his father's death, however, England looked with little confidence on the prospect of a king who was a minor, surrounded by the grasping, upstart Woodvilles. The potential opposition was led by the Duke of Gloucester and experienced statesmen like Edward IV's loyal chamberlain, William, Lord Hastings, and the Duke of Buckingham.

Edward's reign was little more than a sharp, unequal struggle for power between the two groups. It was inevitable that, once again, the crown, won by a strong man, would be lost by the weakness of his son.

His brief reign ended when he and his brother were almost certainly murdered in the Tower on the orders of the Lord Protector.

EDWARD VI. Edward VI was Henry VIII's only legitimate son and his reign was only six years long. He succeeded his father at the age of nine. Short, slight, and consumptive, he was precocious and a devoted Protestant. When his tutor, John Cheke, was taken very ill he said confidently, 'He will not die at this time, for this morning I begged his life from God in my prayer and obtained it.'

His Lord Protector was the Duke of Somerset, his uncle. The Duke's brother, Lord Seymour, insisted to the King that Somerset was too old for the job, saying 'It were better that he should die.' However, Seymour was to go first. Wishing to gain private access to the King, which had been denied him, Seymour foolishly tried to enter from the Private Garden, attended by two servants and armed with pistols. The young King, however, had bolted an inner door from his side and left his small dog on guard in the corridor. When Seymour approached, the dog sprang at him barking and Seymour unwisely shot him. He was arrested, having failed to realise that a child is unlikely easily to forgive the shooting of his pet dog.

Protector Somerset did not last long. 'Methinks I am in prison,' said the King when Somerset installed him against his will at Windsor Castle. 'Here be no galleries nor no gardens to walk in.' When Somerset was executed the boy entered bleakly in his journal: 'The Duke of Somerset had his head cut off upon Tower Hill between eight and nine o'clock in the morning.'

He turned down a request from Charles V that he should tolerate his older sister Mary's attendance of Mass, saying, 'I would not set light God's will, thereby to please an Emperor.'

As he was dying, the Duke of Northumberland, who had succeeded Somerset as the Protector, persuaded him to sponsor the claims to the succession of his daughter-in-law, Lady Jane Grey – a plan which Edward, mindful of her Protestantism, went along with in his will, causing sister Mary no end of trouble.

EDWARD VII. The second child and eldest son of Queen Victoria and Prince Albert, Edward VII spent the first 60 years of his life as the King-in-Waiting, a rakish, formidably human Prince of Wales, acquiring the nicknames 'Roger the First' and 'Tum-Tum' as his appetite for mistresses and food matched those of Henry VIII – his other obsession, shooting, coming a bad third. His popularity was the reverse coin of his mother's. Where she had been remote he was accessible. 'We live in radical times,' he wrote to his mother about her withdrawal from public life after the death of Albert, 'and the more the People see the Sovereign the better it is for the People and the Country.'

His mother early judged him stupid, and the traditional Hanoverian antipathy between sovereign and heir apparent was established. He was eleven when he realised that he would become King – hitherto he had assumed his older sister Vicky would succeed. By his fifteenth year he had discovered Paris – a life-long obsession, and asked the Empress Eugénie if he might stay on after his parents had completed their State visit. She suggested that they would miss him. 'Not do without us!' he exclaimed. 'Don't fancy that! They don't want us, and there are six more of us at home!'

On a visit to Canada in 1860, Blondin, the famous tightrope walker, offered to carry the nineteen-year-old Prince of Wales across Niagara Falls. He took up the challenge but, not surprisingly, was prevented from doing so. A few years later even Blondin might have doubted his ability to carry 'Tum-Tum' across.

He was twenty when scandal first hit him. While he was with fellow officers in Ireland in the Curragh under canvas they spirited a young actress, Nellie Clifton, into his tent, a gesture of which he took enthusiastic advantage. His parents were horrified. Albert wrote to him in the strongest terms and when the Prince Consort died of a chill a few weeks later Victoria blamed his death on anxiety over 'Bertie', as he was called in the family: 'Oh that boy – much as I pity him I never can or shall look at him without a shudder, as you can imagine.'

His engagement to Princess Alexandra of Denmark may have begun as a damage-limitation exercise but the night before he proposed to her he wrote to her mother: '. . . though rather shy we conversed a good deal together, and I fell in increasing love toward her every moment.' Alexandra wrote to his sister, Princess Victoria of Prussia, 'You may think I am marrying Bertie for his position but if he were a cowboy I would love him just the same.'

The wedding in St George's Chapel, Windsor, was distinguished by the antics of the bridegroom's nephew – the future Kaiser – who, having thrown the cairngorm from his dirk across the floor bit two of his other uncles, the Princes Arthur and Leopold. Then further confusion reigned as the train took the guests back to London with Disraeli having to sit on his wife's knee, and the Duchess of Westminster, in half a million pounds' worth of jewels, consigned to a third-class carriage.

Wit was not in Bertie's repertoire but he enjoyed playing practical jokes, like putting his drunken friend Christopher Sykes to bed in a stupor and placing a dead seagull beside him. The next night he placed a live trussed rabbit in the same place. He would pour brandy over Sykes or burn his hand with a cigar. Sykes, terminally snobbish, invariably responded with 'As your Royal Highness pleases!' Another favourite trick was to place the hand of the blind Duke of Mecklenburg on the arm of the grossly fat Helen Henneker and enquire of the Duke, 'Don't you think Helen has a lovely waist?' Like many practical jokers he did not take kindly to the roles being reversed, and having established a beguilingly louche atmosphere he would turn on the over-familiar guest and cut him, or arrange for his bags to be packed before breakfast, a carriage called and the offender sent on his way.

The 'Marlborough House Set' which the Prince of Wales gathered about him was so fast that it is not surprising that he was involved in scandals. In the Mordaunt case in 1870 he was subpoenaed when Sir Charles Mordaunt brought a divorce suit against his wife. She had confessed to 'doing wrong' with the Prince and others and although the royal letters read out in court were innocuous, the damage was done and Sir Henry Ponsonby wrote that 'London was black with the smoke of burnt confidential letters'. By this time poor Lady Mordaunt was in a mental home.

In 1891 there was the Baccarat Scandal. The Prince's dancing days were now done and cards became his after-dinner diversion. Staying at Tranby Croft conveniently to attend the St Leger, the Prince heard that there were five witnesses to Sir William Gordon-Cumming's cheating at baccarat. Sir William denied it but promised never to play again if the matter was hushed up. When the rumour spread he brought a civil action against his accusers which in the end discredited both sides. Unthinkably the Prince was again subpoenaed. 'It seemed to the mass of the nation as though the Prince of Wales were on trial.' (Philip Magnus.) Gordon-Cumming lost, was dismissed from the army, expelled from his clubs and ostracised – 'Thank God!' wrote Edward to his son Prince George, 'the Army and Society are now well rid of such a damned blackguard!' However, Gordon-Cumming quickly married a rich American girl, Miss Garner, while Edward had to face his mother's wrath. 'The monarchy almost is in danger if he is lowered and despised,' she wrote, '. . . It is not this special case but the light which has been thrown on his habits which alarms and shocks people so much, for the example is so bad.' A German comic paper published a cartoon of the Prince of Wales feathers changing the motto from 'Ich Dien' to 'Ich Deal'. *The Times* regretted in a leader that the Prince had not signed the same assurance that he would not play cards again as Sir William.

In the same year the Prince, who was carrying on a famous affair with 'My Darling Daisy' Brooke, later Lady Warwick (the after-effects of which his son would have to settle), attempted to retrieve a compromising letter she had written to Lord Charles Beresford with whom she had previously had an affair. When Lady Beresford got hold of it she lodged it with the leading society solicitor of the day, Arthur Lewis, as a weapon to be used against any recurrence of the romance.

Lewis refused to give the letter to the Prince of Wales though he did allow him to read it. Beresford called the Prince 'a coward and a blackguard' and all but struck him. The Prince retaliated by ostracising both Beresfords. Sir Charles then decided that he must publish the entire incident – the number of pamphlets produced was limited but the Duchess of Manchester used to entertain her guests by reading one aloud at her dinner parties.

Back in 1871 another crisis – not of the Prince's making – distressed the nation. He went down with typhoid at Sandringham. The Archbishop of Canterbury telegraphed a prayer for his recovery to be read in churches – another first! The concerned Princess of Wales was instructed not to enter his bedroom in his delirium lest it over-excite him – so she used to crawl in on her hands and knees. She showed similar concern when dining next to the elderly Disraeli, who cut his finger on a knife at dinner when it slipped off a rock-like roll. She wrapped it in her handkerchief and the old boy said, with a mock groan, 'When I asked for bread they gave me a stone; but I had a Princess to bind my wounds.'

Princess Alexandra appears to have been tolerant of her husband's mistresses – actresses like Lillie Langtry, and Hortense Schneider, and La Goulue, the Moulin Rouge dancer, and the society women to whose bedrooms he padded during country-house weekends, though not so happy about his involvement with pseudo-socialist Lady Warwick. She was amused that Mrs Keppel, his last mistress, though twenty years younger than she was, had grown a great deal stouter.

Husband and wife shared a suspicion of Germany. The Princess's was a traditional Danish distrust of a powerful neighbour. When her son, later George V, was given honorary command of a Prussian regiment during a State visit to

Berlin in 1890 she said, 'And so, my Georgie boy has become a real live, filthy, blue-coated Pickelhaube German soldier!!! Well, I never thought to have lived to see *that*!' As Queen she was able to dismiss a long harangue by the Kaiser with 'Willy, dear . . . I am afraid I have not heard a single word you were saying.' Edward, who did much to switch public sympathy towards France and the Entente Cordiale, vowed, 'You can tell when you have crossed the frontier into Germany because of the badness of the coffee.' As King he insisted that King Kalakua of the Sandwich Islands should take precedence over the Crown Prince of Germany – 'Either the brute is a king or else he is an ordinary black nigger, and if he is not a king, why is he here?' Of the Kaiser, he was dismissive: 'Willum is a bully and most bullies when tackled are cowards.' In 1908 he complained to Lord Knollys about having to meet the Kaiser, 'The Foreign Office, to gain their object, will not care a pin what humiliation I have to put up with.'

Domestic politics, art and literature did not greatly occupy him. 'We are all Socialist nowadays,' he said in a Mansion House speech in 1895. He re-arranged the pictures and furniture at Windsor enthusiastically, saying, 'I do not know much about Art but I think I know something about Arrangement.' He 'preferred men to books and women to either'. Hosting, against his wishes, a dinner to celebrate the new *Dictionary of National Biography* he was puzzled to see Canon Ainger, who had contributed entries on Charles and Mary Lamb. 'Why is he here?' he barked. 'The little parson? He is not a writer.' Told that he was 'a very great authority on Lamb', he was thoroughly confused and set down his knife and fork muttering, 'Oh, *lamb*!' A reference to Lord Rayleigh, a great authority on electro-magnetism, prompted the remark 'Well, Lord Rayleigh, discoverin' somethin', I suppose!' Then he turned to a woman nearby and said, 'He's always at it!'

Appearances concerned him. When he saw Lord Harris at Ascot in a brown bowler he enquired, 'Goin' rattin', 'Arris?' Very unfairly he told Haldane, 'Mr Haldane, you are too fat.' When Lord Rosebery's evening clothes did not please him it was, 'I presume you have come in the suite of the American Ambassador!' Though when he *finally* got into his Coronation robes ('I don't mind praying to the eternal Father, but I must be the only man in this country afflicted with an eternal Mother') he said to his grandchildren: 'Am I not a funny-looking old man?'

Sir Frederick Ponsonby was reprimanded for wearing a tail-coat during a pre-luncheon visit to an art exhibition, 'I thought everyone must know that a *short* jacket is always worn with a silk hat at a private view in the mornin'.'

When the Russian Ambassador asked if it was correct for him to go to race-meetings while in mourning: 'To Newmarket, yes, because it means a bowler hat, but not to the Derby because of the top hat.' In fashion he was both a con-servative and an innovator. On the traditional side he clung to the frock-coat and tried to bring back knee-breeches with evening dress; and he despised the Panama hat. On the other hand he was the pioneer of a forebear of the dinner jacket, conveniently worn on a voyage out to India. His use of the Norfolk jacket, a felt hat brought back from Homburg, and a green Tyrolean hat from Marienbad were three more fashions he popularised and his 'tum-tum', which required him to leave the bottom button of his waistcoat undone, meant that every other gentleman followed suit. He loved foreign uniforms – often out-landish, like the short coats of the Portuguese cavalry which 'showed an inmense expanse of breeches'. An odd act of *hommage* as he referred to the Portuguese nobility as 'waiters in a second-class restaurant'.

His coronation in 1902 was delayed because of an emergency operation for appendicitis. Queen Alexandra wanted to be present but was persuaded by Sir Frederick Treves to wait in the next room. She was later to conquer her fear of visiting those badly wounded and mutilated in the war. 'I thought I could not do it; but then, of course, there is simply nothing one cannot do.' She had a lame leg which she owed to a severe illness and rheumatism after her first pregnancy. Visiting another wounded soldier who had just been told his leg would always be stiff she rallied him with 'My dear, dear, man, I hear you have a stiff leg; so have I. Now just watch what I can do with it.' And she lifted her skirt and swished her bad leg safely over his bedside table.

If Queen Alexandra was tolerant of his ladies – their stall at the Coronation was called 'The Loose-Box', he had to put up with her notorious unpunctual-ity. Once, when she had kept him waiting a half an hour, she finally entered say-ing to a courtier, 'Keep him waiting, it will do him good!' On another occasion she appeared for a formal audience billed for noon at 1.50. She seemed radiant and unconcerned, murmuring, 'Am I late?'

There is some dispute over one of her remarks – barbed or innocent? She was told that the King had a new car. 'A new cow?' she enquired. 'No, Ma'am, a new *car*.' 'Yes, yes, I hear you,' she said ambiguously; 'I understand the old one has calved.'

Edward VII's death bed was another occasion of controversy which James Lees Milne in *The Enigmatic Edwardians* and Elizabeth Longford have done much to unravel. The romantic story is that the Queen summoned the King's last mistress, Mrs Keppel, to the King's bedside and 'thereupon fell on her neck and wept with her'. This was the story promoted by Mrs Keppel. However, courtiers reported that Mrs Keppel gained access because she sent the Queen an old letter the King had written nine years earlier during the appendicitis crisis in which, 'he said that if he was dying he felt sure those about him would allow her to come to him'. In the event the Queen shook hands with her and said words to the effect of 'I am sure you always had a good influence on him', and stared out of the window. Mrs Keppel supplied the histrionics.

ELIZABETH I. Elizabeth I, who came to the throne in 1558, was the daughter of Henry VIII and Anne Boleyn. Her early years which formed her character were fraught with danger after her mother's execution. She was a precocious four when her governess Katherine (Kate) Ashley broke the news. Elizabeth was immediately sensitive to her new reduced status saying, 'Why, Governor, how hap it yesterday Lady Princess, and today but Lady Elizabeth?' At one time she lived in Chelsea with her stepmother, her father's widow Katherine Parr, who had secretly married her guardian, Admiral Lord Seymour. Kate Ashley suggested that the Admiral's attentions to the Princess went too far. 'If she were in her bed he would pat open the curtains and bid her good morrow and make as though he would come at her, and she would go further in the bed so that he could not come to her.'

When the Admiral was executed during her brother's reign her verdict was, 'This day died a man with much wit and very little judgement.' When her half-sister Mary became Queen and imprisoned her in the Tower she arrived at the Traitor's Gate saying, 'Here lands as true a subject, being prisoner, as ever landed at these stairs.'

Four years later she was Queen herself and received the news with the words 'This is the Lord's doing and it is marvellous in our eyes.' At Temple Bar on the day before her Coronation on 14 January 1559 she told the people, 'Be ye well assured I will stand your good Queen.' In private she was delighted to get away from the frugalities of her life hitherto, announcing, 'Indeed I like silk stockings so well because they are pleasant and fine and delicate and henceforth I shall wear no more cloth stockings.'

The piracies of Drake; the colonising of Raleigh; his introduction of the potatoe and tobacco and his gesture of spreading his fine cloak so that the Queen could negotiate a puddle as she entered the Inner Temple; the shrewd Stewardship of Burghley and Robert Cecil; the defeat of the Armada; the execution of Mary, Queen of Scots; and above all her famous virginity and her masterly, tantalising political manipulation of the European marriage market are the features of Elizabeth's reign which linger in the popular imagination.

When Raleigh had some hope of the Queen's favours he was observed by her writing on glass; 'Fain would I climb, yet fear to fall'; underneath she inscribed, 'If thy heart fail thee, climb not at all.'

Earlier rumours linked her with Robert Dudley, later Earl of Leicester, whose wife, Amy Robsart, was found conveniently dead, with a broken neck, at the foot of a stone staircase in her house near Oxford. Accident? Suicide? Murder? were the questions posed. 'God's death! My Lord, I will have but one mistress and no master,' is supposed to be her last word to him on the subject.

Burghley had mistrusted the match. When he displeased her she could be brusque with the man who guided her through most of her reign: 'I have been strong enough to lift you out of this dirt and I am still able to cast you down again.' However, when he was complaining of his gout, she said sympathetically, 'My lord, we make use of you, not for your bad legs, but for your good head'; and on his death bed she sent him medicine with the message, 'My comfort hath been in my people's happiness and their happiness in thy discretion.' William was succeeded by his son Robert, Earl of Salisbury, a tiny but influential hunchback. A popular rhyme ran

> Little Cecil trips up and down
> He rules both court and crown.

However, when he said that she *must* go to bed during her final illness she would have no truck with it: 'Little man, little man, the word *must* is not to be used to Princes.'

The Queen used her marriageability as a political advantage, but she answered a parliamentary plea that she should marry with: 'To satisfy you, I have already joined myself in marriage to a husband, namely the Kingdom of England.'

The duc d'Alençon, the heir to the French throne, was one of her suitors and it pleased her to encourage him for a time to the annoyance of the Earl of Leicester, who said that he had won her affection by 'incantation and love potions'. When she wished to end speculation and let him down lightly she gave him her ring very publicly and promised to marry him but meanwhile laid down conditions which the French King could only refuse.

Theatrically Elizabeth I is celebrated for commissioning *The Merry Wives of Windsor*. Legend has it that she expressed a wish to see 'The fat Knight in love'. A more considered suggestion is that she relished Shakespeare's satire on Falstaff's cowardice, greed, fraud and idleness, qualities she recognised in her army captains who in 1587 had been found to have failed to pay over what was owing to their troops.

She was never slow to express displeasure whether the object of her disapproval was a cleric – 'Mr Doctor,' she told a Puritan at Oxford in 1566, 'this loose gown becomes you mighty well; I wonder your notions to be so narrow' – or a military commander.

Her scornful comment on a military escapade in France in 1591 of the Earl of Essex, another favourite, was, 'Rather a jest than a victory.' On Mountjoy's massacres in Ireland: 'I find that I sent wolves not shepherds to govern Ireland.'

and to Leicester on his excuses for failing to subdue Cork she said simply, 'Blarney!'

Her finest hour came when the Spanish Armada threatened in 1588. The prayer she composed at that time has a fine simplicity: 'Oh let Thine enemies know that Thou hast received England . . . into Thine own protection. Set a wall about it, O Lord, and evermore mightily defend it.' Her speech to the troops at Tilbury that same year is more familiar: 'I know I have the body of a weak and feeble woman but I have the heart and stomach of a King and a King of England too . . . I myself will take up arms, I myself will be your general, judge and recorder of everyone of your virtues in the field.'

The cross she bore was her fear of a Catholic plot which might put Mary Stuart, Queen of Scots, on her throne. Mary was the descendant of Henry VII through his daughter Margaret Tudor, whom he married to the Scottish king. Mary's husband was the murdered Henry Stuart, Lord Darnley. When Elizabeth heard of the birth of Mary's son, James VI of Scotland, later James I of England, in 1566 she lamented, 'Alack, the Queen of Scots is lighter of a bonny son, and I am but of barren stock.' Her answer to Parliament, who petitioned for the imprisoned Mary's execution, was a masterpiece of typical temporising: 'If I should say unto you that I meant not to grant your petition, by my faith I should say unto you more than perhaps I mean. And if I should say unto you I mean to grant your petition, I should then tell you more than is fit for you to know. And thus I must deliver you an answer answerless.'

When she died at 70, the Golden Age of Good Queen Bess had become a legend – she did not even neglect to supply one classic anecdote at the expense of Edward de Vere, Earl of Oxford, faithfully recorded by the gossiping John Aubrey. 'This Earl . . . making his low bow of obeisance to Queen Elizabeth, happened to let a fart at which he was so abashed that he went to travel seven years. At his return the Queen welcomed him home and sayd, "My lord, I had forgot the fart."' Some think he spent the seven years writing Shakespeare's plays!

ELIZABETH, Queen, The Queen Mother. The Queen Mother, George VI's widow, has reaped a rich reward in public affection for her devotion to the man she needed so much persuasion to marry. In a moment of more than domestic disaster – when her horse Devon Loch collapsed at the last moment in the run home at Aintree – she dried the jockey's tears and those of the stable boys and patted her trainer, Peter Cazalet, comfortingly on his shoulder. Less benignly, but no less politely, she replied to the captain of a touring ship when he asked if she had been aware that there had been a fire in his boiler room: 'Yes, indeed, Captain,' she replied. 'Every hour someone said there was nothing to worry about, so I knew there was real trouble.'

During the Blitz she was quoted as saying, 'The children won't leave without me; I won't leave without the King; and the King will never leave.'

She has a graceful way of moving down a reception line. Indoors a stylish arc of her left arm and a look upwards with the remark, 'What a lovely ceiling!' can take her five places down. Out of doors it has to be 'what a lovely sky!'

She has a talent for the politely dismissive. To a Boer who said he could never quite forgive the British for having conquered his country she replied, 'I understand perfectly. We feel very much the same in Scotland.'

ELLINGTON, (Edward Kennedy) 'Duke'. Duke Ellington stories which are not specifically musical seem to follow three patterns. They deal with conspicuous consumption of food, stock approaches to women, and mistaken identity.

His chat-up lines were famous. It might be 'I can tell you're an angel: I can see the reflection of your halo shining on the ceiling', or 'My, but you make that dress look lovely'; most notoriously he would ask, 'Whose little girl are you?' He got his comeuppance with this approach when he tried it on the blues singer Big Maybelle, who was as mountainous as her name suggested. In her foghorn voice she replied, 'What the *fuck* you mean, whose little girl am I?'

In the mistaken identity field there was a White House party on Ellington's birthday. In the reception line was Cab Calloway, who assumed President Nixon must be a particular fan of his when the President pumped his hand with special warmth. Then he spoilt it by saying, 'Mr Ellington, it's so good you're here. Happy, happy birthday. Pat and I just love your music.'

At Lime Grove studios Duke Ellington turned up for an interview on the old Cliff Michelmore *Tonight* show a few weeks after a visit by Louis Armstrong. Mrs Grace Wyndham Goldie, the much feared Head of Department, seeing him in the green room advanced graciously. 'How nice to have you back, Mr Armstrong. Did you bring your trumpet this time?'

EPITAPHS. Some of the best epitaphs are penned by their subjects:

Hilaire Belloc –

>When I am dead, I hope it may be said:
>His sins were scarlet, but his books were read.

Dryden was also deeply personal –

>Here lies my wife; here let her lie!
>Now she's at peace and so am I.

G. K. Chesterton inspired two epitaphs by others: E. V. Lucas wrote –

> Poor G.K.C., his day is past –
> Now God will hear the truth at last.

And Humbert Wolfe noted Chesterton's anti-semitism:

> Here lies Mr Chesterton,
> Who to heaven might have gone;
> But didn't when he heard the news
> That the place was run by Jews.

The American poet David McCord's fictional epitaph celebrates a waiter:

> By and by
> God caught his eye.

Even a mother's reported death can be made funny: 'Regret to inform you. Hand that rocked the cradle kicked the bucket.'

EPSTEIN, Jacob. After viewing the avant-garde sculptor Epstein's controversial statue *Christ in Majesty*, an old lady was heard to remark, 'I can never forgive Mr Epstein for his representation of Our Lord. So very un-English!'

EUGÉNIE, Empress of France. The Imperial couple, Napoleon III and Eugénie, invited Queen Victoria to visit France in the 1860s. To impress the English Monarch she decorated the Royal apartments in the Tuileries with masterpieces from the Louvre. Unfortunately the next day Queen Victoria asked to visit the Louvre, and there she found several black spaces with notices announcing 'Removed by order and taken to the Tuileries'.

EYRE, Richard. The director of the Royal National Theatre has managed to write a simple, straightforward and moving memoir. As John Bowen wrote, 'This is a book written by someone who has no time to write a book . . . Nevertherless it is much more pleasurable than most books written by people who do have time.'
  Like many autobiographies Eyre's re-creates his father into the stuff of legend – hard, loud and apparently ignorant, he left the Navy to become a gentleman farmer and concentrate on horses, drink and sex. He tried to seduce all his son's girlfriends, and in one case succeeded. He greeted new arrivals with the refrain,

'Time is short and we must seize/Those pleasures found above the knees.'

However, the epic anecdote which is worthy of Evelyn Waugh concerns his behaviour at Richard's grandfather's funeral. The old boy – immensely cantakerous – lived alone in north Devon but he had a mistress, a widow who lived nearby, a Mrs de Las Casas. The secret was both open and heavily guarded. Unannounced visitors to the dining room might observe her escaping indecorously over the low sill of the window. At the grandpa's funeral service Eyre's father, sitting well to the front of the church, became aware of Mrs de Las Casas leaving her pew with a large shopping bag. Abandoning the obsequies he followed her to his father's house, and eventually into the dining room – drawn by the sound of chinking silver. As Eyre senior entered, Mrs de Las Casas turned, frozen, her hands full of silver cutlery. 'He always wanted me to have this,' she said defiantly. Richard's father had waited long for this denouement. 'It just goes to show there's a God,' he said.

Almost as farsical was Eyre's first appearance in *Henry V* in weekly rep. 'I played Mountjoy, the French Herald, in a costume that made me look like a rather worn playing card. On my first entrance, I faced a somewhat depleted but impish–looking English army. I spoke my first line, "You know me by my habit", only to be greeted by barely concealed gestures of self-abuse under the knitted chain mail . . . I still smart with shame when I think of it.'

— F —

FAULKNER, William. During one of the great Southern novelist's sojourns in Hollywood on the MGM payroll, he found himself in a car with Howard Hawks whom he knew and Clark Gable whom he did not. Hawks and Faulkner talked books. Eventually Gable broke in to ask Faulkner who were the best living writers in America. Faulkner listed Hemingway, Willa Cather, Thomas Mann, John Dos Passos and himself. Gable had learnt something new. 'Oh, do you write, Mr Faulkner?' he said. 'Yes, Mr Gable,' said Faulkner politely. 'What do you do?'

FENWICK, Millicent. Millicent Fenwick was a dynamic American Congresswoman of the 1950s who campaigned for, among other things, mandatory toilets for migrant farm workers, earning her the soubriquet 'Outhouse Millie', and who switched to pipe smoking when her doctor warned her off cigarettes. On her entry into Congress she was called a 'pipe-smoking grandmother'. 'For God's sake,' she suggested. '"Hard-working grandmother" – same number of syllables.' Her most quoted smart reply was provoked by a fellow Congressman attacking a piece of women's rights legislation by saying, 'I've always thought of women as kissable, cuddly, and smelling good.' Millicent Fenwick replied, 'That's what I feel about men. I only hope you haven't been disappointed as often as I have.'

FERRER, José. At the height of his fame in Hollywood and on Broadway in the forties and fifties José Ferrer went to hear Mel Torme, who was playing in Pittsburgh at the Copa Club. At the end of Torme's act Ferrer suggested they go to see Stan Getz with his quartet at the Carousel. Getz invited Torme to sit in on drums and Ferrer – whom Getz did not know (or know of) – pleaded to sit in on piano. He acquitted himself spectacularly in his solo turn and afterwards Getz drew Torme aside saying, 'Hey, man, who's the old cat?' Torme explained that José Ferrer was a big star who got maybe a grand a week on Broadway. Getz was unimpressed. 'If he wants to work with my group he'll have to play for scale!'

It seems to have been Ferrer's fate not to impress musicians. Long before Chubby Jackson had his own band and was a fledgling bass player, he used to bring hungry fellow musicians home to his mother's Long Island house for a meal. When he turned up one night with Ferrer she slammed the door on both of them yelling, 'That's it! No more bums!'

FEYDEAU, Georges. The great French farce writer was born in 1862, the son of Ernest Feydeau, one of whose serious academic works was *The History of the Funeral Rites of the Ancient World*. More in tune with his son's illustrious career was *Fanny*, so severely denounced as 'improper' by the Archbishop of Paris that it sold out its first edition inside a week; all further editions were dedicated to the cleric.

George Feydeau's early overnight success with *La Tailleur pour dames* was followed by a thin period until, having had a play rejected by the director of the Palais Royal he bumped into Micheau, the director of the Théâtre des Nouveautés, who was in the middle of a disastrous season. He asked Feydeau what he had under his arm. 'It's a piece that has just been turned down by the Palais Royal.' He had sent them two plays – *Monsieur Chasse* and *Champignol Malgré Lui*. They had accepted *Chasse* but told him to forget about the other. Micheau asked to read it. 'Not worth the effort,' said Feydeau. 'What have I to lose?' said the director. 'Let me see it.' He was so enchanted by it that when he finished it he ran up to his despairing mother's room and threw it on her eider-down. 'Get up, Maman,' he told her, 'I have brought you a fortune. Here it is.'

It was performed over a thousand times. Three times as often as *Monsieur Chasse*.

Feydeau was a man of rich, rare wit. One day he was talking with Lajeunesse about one of their friends. 'he deserves to be betrayed,' remarked Lajeunesse. 'And even so,' said Feydeau, 'He has to have his wife to help him.'

Dining one evening at Broggi's restaurant in Paris, Feydeau remarked of someone to Edmond de Goncourt, 'I've met his mistress.' 'But that's his wife,' replied Goncourt. 'He introduced her to me as his mistress,' said Feydeau, 'to rehabilitate her.'

There is a cross-Channel echo of the famous Whistler and Wilde 'You will, Oscar, you will' encounter in Feydeau's remark to a third-rate author-imitator who asked him if a *bon mot* of the great farceur's which had been repeated to him was indeed his. 'Yes,' confessed Feydeau, 'But not for long.'

Lucien Guitry, the fashionable actor manager, once asked Feydeau to dinner and invited him to write him a play. 'I would so much like to appear in one of your pieces.' Feydeau replied, 'My dear Lucien, in comedy there are only two main parts.' These words cast a shadow over the distinguished actor's face. 'Two main parts,' Feydeau repeated pitilessly, 'he who slaps and he who gets slapped. It is never the one who slaps who gets the laughs, but the one who receives them. And you, Lucien, could never receive them.'

Feydeau had another rule of farce: 'When in one of my pieces, two characters must not meet,' he said, 'I bring them together as soon as I can.'

He could be scathing about some of the actors who appeared in his plays. 'When I have to deal with a ham actor, of course I advise him to act to the best of his ability.'

The end of his life was unhappy and somewhat depressing. He lived apart from his wife and family, protected by a secretary who collaborated on some of his later work and provoked a royalties controversy after his death.

FIELDS, W. C. Fields, the legendary source of many an anecdote, has been covered so extensively elsewhere that I will satisfy myself with this little gem. A notable misanthrope, he once inserted a display ad in *Variety* wishing 'A Merry Christmas to all my friends except two.'

FIRBANK, Ronald. The early twentieth-century aesthete and exotic novelist Ronald Firbank (*Concerning the Eccentricities of Cardinal Pirelli, Sorrow in Sunlight, Valmouth*, etc.) carried his singular behaviour into his own life. On one occasion he was sitting in one of the Lyon's Corner Houses, which used to be the flagship of the vast catering empire. Waitresses in those days were called 'nippies' and decked out in black bombazine edged with white starched collar and cuffs. One approached him and asked him what he would like. Firbank considered the question, leaning back negligently, and eventually decided on 'Plover's eggs whipped to an amber foam!'

The nippy's reply is not recorded. The next time he ordered, 'Just one tea – I am not hungry today.'

Siegfried Sassoon visited him in Oxford in the house in which he was living opposite All Souls. The rooms were curtained, lit by many candles and festooned with flowers. One table was covered in rich cakes and exotic fruits. The nearest Sassoon got to a coherent remark from Firbank was a screeched 'Blenheim!' and a piercing giggle when he asked where the fruit came from. A few days later he invited Firbank to tea and splashed out on a huge bunch of grapes and a rich chocolate cake. His guest ate one grape as a gesture of politeness, shuddered when faced by a pile of crumpets, and when quizzed on the subject of art and literature managed only 'I adore italics, don't you?'

His quirky wit shines out more vividly in his published work. There is Madame Rinz in *Sorrow in Sunlight* (published in America under the title *Prancing Nigger*): 'A quietly silly woman, Madame Rinz was often obliged to lament the absence of intellect at her door, accounting for it as the consequence of a weakness for negroes, combined with a hopeless passion for the Regius Professor of Greek at Oxford.' I like also, ' "She reads at such a pace," he complained, "and when I asked her where she had learned to read so quickly, she replied 'On the screens at cinemas.' " ' And again, ' "*Basta!*" his master replied, with all the brilliant glibness of the Berlitz school.'

FLYNN, Errol. The larger-than-life Tasmanian film star Errol Flynn shared a beach house in Los Angeles with David Niven in the 1930s. It was nicknamed 'Cirrhosis-on-Sea'. Recalling those days much later in an interview with Barry Norman, Niven remarked of the volatile Flynn, 'One thing about Errol you could always rely upon.'

'What was that?' Norman asked.

Niven grinned. 'He would *always* let you down!'

According to his then very young secretary, Ronnie Shedloe (now a distinguished film producer), Errol Flynn was once filming with the redoubtable Australian actress Dame Judith Anderson. She had never met the great John Barrymore, who was by then drinking himself to death – often in the company of Flynn – and Flynn arranged to bring Barrymore to see her. He duly delivered Barrymore to the apartment in which the actress lived with her aged mother. There was another old dear there and the two veterans giggled and chuckled at Barrymore's risqué conversation, which rather shocked Dame Judith. After a while a huge man – also an actor – entered the room and stood filling the doorway. The second little old lady looked up at him proudly and announced, 'This is Laird Cregar. He's my son!' Barrymore looked at him and then at her. 'My!' he said in amazement. 'What a fuck that must have been!'

FORD, John. John Ford, the great action and Western movie director, abhorred the presence of producers (and screenwriters) on his sets. His greeting if they did risk it was: 'Don't you have an office?' A producer who ventured to remind him that he was three days behind with his shooting schedule was confronted by Ford, who arbitrarily tore ten pages out of the script and said, 'Now we're three days ahead.'

On another Western location a messenger rode up on a horse with a wire from Ford's producer Sol Wurtzel making a similar complaint. Ford called one of his regular cowboy supporters. 'I've got a wire from Wurtzel,' he said, 'I want you to shoot a hole straight through his name.' Then he held the wire up in his right hand and when the cowboy had shot through the producer's name shooting was resumed to applause.

Ford could be superstitious on location, where shooting depended so heavily on the weather. In 1949, making *She Wore a Yellow Ribbon*, he employed an Indian, known as Old Fat, to conjure up a few small clouds for the afternoon shoot. The Indian performed the ritual and sure enough exactly the clouds Ford wanted appeared.

Ford's longest assocation was with John Wayne. Wayne's verdict was 'John Ford isn't exactly a bum, is he? Yet he never gave me any manure about art. He just made movies and that's what I do.' Explaining his success with Wayne to Robert Parrish, Ford said, 'That's how to make 'em good actors. Don't let 'em talk!'

FOWLER, Senator Wyche. The Georgian senator was asked by an interviewer, 'Senator, did you in those permissive sixties smoke a marijuana cigarette?' Wyche Fowler took a deep breath and replied with disdain, 'Only when committing adultery.'

FOX, Charles James. The most famous Fox anecdote tells of the eighteenth-century Whig politician's duel with William Adam, a minister under Lord North who had been the subject of one of Fox's attacks. When Fox refused to declare a good opinion of him Adam insisted on a duel. The two men met in Hyde Park at eight o'clock one morning. Fox's second, Fitzpatrick, suggested that since Adam was a slight figure and Fox bulky, Fox should stand sideways. Fox replied, 'Why, I am as thick one way as the other.' Adam fired and scored a flesh wound in the thigh. Fox fired and missed. Adam again asked for a retraction. Fox again refused. Adam fired again and missed. Fox fired in the air and the matter was over – except for the rumour that Adam had struck Fox's groin and emasculated him. Fox denied it, saying, 'Mr Adam loaded his pistol with government contractor's powder, too weak to penetrate a thick Whig hide.'

Fox was a prodigy, too young at nineteen to make his maiden speech when he was elected to Parliament. When he made his first speech of any significance, in 1769, it was about Wilkes. The 3rd Baron Holland, his nephew, recorded, 'A listener was so impressed that he ripped off part of his shirt and drew a picture of the young orator. It is still preserved in my possession at Holland House, retaining many traits of resemblance to the dark, intelligent and animated features of Mr Fox.'

Fox was born in 1749, the third son of Henry, Lord Holland. He had a charmed early childhood, his father having said, 'Let nothing be done to break his spirit. The world will do that business fast enough.' He followed his own counsel when he came upon the angry child about to smash a watch with a hammer: he shrugged and said, 'Well, if you must, I suppose you must.' Again, he countenanced a loan to his son, then aged just twelve. It reads: 'December 15, 1761. Recev'd, advanced to me by my Father as part of my Fortune, two hundred pounds, C. J. Fox.' When he was on holiday from Eton his father indulged him on a continental tour with a sub of five guineas a night for dice and cards.

His great battles with Pitt were foreseen by his mother, who wrote, 'I have been this morning with Lady Hester Pitt, and there is little William Pitt, *not eight years old* and really the cleverest child I ever saw *and brought up so strictly and so proper in his behaviour that, mark my words*, that boy will be a thorn in Charles's side as long as he lives.'

Lord North made Fox a minister but could not hold his tongue. In 1774 when he could take no more criticism, North wrote a letter of dismissal. 'His Majesty has thought proper to order a new Commission of the Treasury to be made out, in which I do not see your name.'

Many of Fox's nights were spent in gaming and drinking. When he heard a report that he was to be married, Lord Holland said, 'I am glad of it for then he will go to bed at least one night.' In 1774 Lord Holland paid debts on his son's behalf to the tune of one hundred thousand pounds.

Horace Walpole had vividly recorded Fox's nocturnal adventures. He was not, I think, a principal in another reminiscence of Walpole's. It is of a bet, unusual even for White's, a club renowned for betting. A member entering the club fell suddenly to the floor, apparently dead. Several members immediately laid large bets on whether he was really dead or had merely fainted. A doctor was sent for who prepared to bleed the patient but was stopped doing so – it was held to be unfair by those who had wagered most on the fact that he was dead.

FRANKAU, Ronald. Ronald Frankau was a popular cabaret and wireless entertainer in the thirties and forties. He performed solo and in a well-known double act with Tommy Handley. They called themselves Murgatroyd and Winterbottom.

During the thirties, in his solo capacity, Frankau was scheduled to sing songs over the BBC including one, 'Let's go wild', which contained the line 'Let's find Hitler and kick him in the pants'. The BBC executives nervously consulted the Foreign Office. After lengthy discussions Frankau was told that he might sing the song if for 'Hitler' he substituted 'Carnera' (Primo Carnera was a heavyweight boxer of the day). He complained that it neither scanned nor made sense. The BBC was adamant. It refused to upset the German Embassy.

FROST, David. Frost's autobiography is hovering in the wings, but I wonder if he will find room for one of his foreign travel experiences. Arriving in his suite in a New York hotel he called room service and ordered asparagus. A volatile Italian waiter delivered it and to Frost's disappointment it arrived cold with a vinaigrette. Disappointed but determined as always, Frost sent it back and asked for hot asparagus. This duly arrived – but neither butter nor an hollandaise sauce. Back went with a request for butter. Back it came, but the butter was cold and pristine in its slab. By now the waiter was wilting, but he gamely took the plate away and finally returned with freshly steamed asparagus and butter bubbling in a silver salver.

'Well done!' exalted Frost, happy at last.

'*Mamma mia!*' cried the waiter, seizing the tray. 'Now he wants it well done!'

— G —

GAINSBOROUGH, Thomas. Gainsborough, the younger contemporary of Sir Joshua Reynolds and his rival, was a fine painter who loved music. His structured life followed a pattern of rising early and working through the morning, after which he gave his time to music and to his wife and to idly sketching what pleased his eye.

He had his problems as a portraitist, finding the Duchess of Devonshire too lovely to capture and destroying all his efforts but a couple of sketches – both exquisite – and complaining, 'Her Grace is too hard for me.' He refused to paint a pompous alderman who begged him 'not to overlook the dimple on my chin'. 'Confound the dimple on your chin,' said Gainsborough. 'I shall neither paint the one nor the other.' And he put down his brushes not to pick them up again. The chameleon character of actors perplexed him. He tried several times, always unsuccessfully, to paint David Garrick and Samuel Foote. He finally gave up with the words, 'Rot them for a couple of rogues, they have everybody's faces but their own.'

A lawyer once asked him why he talked so often of 'the painter's eye'; 'The painter's eye,' Gainsborough told him, 'is to him what the lawyer's tongue is to you.'

Gainsborough died from cancer. On his death bed in 1788 he sent for Reynolds, who had four more years to live, and they made their peace; 'We are all going to heaven,' said Gainsborough to Reynolds, 'and Van Dyck is of the company.'

GAITSKELL, Hugh. During the fuel crisis of 1947 Hugh Gaitskell was Minister of Fuel and Power. In the campaign to save power Gaitskell spoke at a municipal election meeting in Hastings. He advised the electors to take fewer baths. 'Personally I have never had a great many baths myself and I can assure those who are in the habit of having a great many baths that it does not make a great deal of difference to their health if they have fewer. And as far as appearance [goes] most of that is underneath and nobody sees it.'

Gaitskell later asserted that this was meant to be taken as a joke – which shows the danger of making weak jokes if you are not known for making jokes at all. Churchill took advantage in the House: 'When Ministers of the Crown speak like this . . . [they] have no need to wonder why they are getting increasingly into bad odour.'

Poor Gaitskell continued to be harassed by the story and even got a letter from an old nurse who had not been in touch for 30 years, indignantly denying that he did not wash.

There was a sadly ironic detail when Gaitskell died. On the television programme *That Was The Week That Was* David Frost delivered an attack on the *Sunday Express* political commentator 'Cross Bencher'. Written by Gerald Kaufman, the attack highlighted the inaccuracy of most of 'Cross Bencher's' forecasts. At the end of the programme Frost turned to the Sunday papers and especially to 'Cross Bencher' in the *Express*. Gaitskell was seriously ill at the time but the column prophesied a full and speedy recovery. Frost sighed, looked into the camera and said, 'Sorry, Hugh.'

Sadly Gaitskell died within days.

GALE, Gracie. A stout American madam, Gracie Gale ran Shanghai's most famous brothel, 'The Line', in the 1920s. All drinks and entertainment were paid for on a 'chit' system and were settled monthly – thus 'The Line' was the only brothel in the world where you could get a woman on credit. One local dignitary defaulted on his bill. He also happened to be a vestry man at the city cathedral. The next Sunday Gracie turned up for the service in all her finery and placed the brothel chits firmly in his collection plate.

GAMBON, Michael. Theatrical legends surround Michael Gambon – christened, as in a circus or Music Hall billing, 'The Great Gambon' by Sir Ralph Richardson. There is his conversion from electrical fitter to actor by the experience of passing the open back doors of the Shaftesbury Theatre and glimpsing the magic that lay within; and, not knowing that it was Olivier's set-piece, auditioning for the National with 'Now is the winter of our discontent' . . . .

However, the most endearing story is one he corrected for me. Gambon played Lear for the RSC with Anthony Sher as his very flamboyant Fool. Some time later Anthony Hopkins was to tackle the same Everest of roles at the Royal National. The rumour mill had it that when they met in the labyrinthine corridors of the South Bank Factory Hopkins asked Gambon if he had any advice for him as he embarked on his climb.

'Yes,' rumour has Gambon replying, 'don't have Anthony Sher as your Fool.'

I asked Gambon to verify the exchange. He agreed that Hopkins had asked him if he had any advice.

'What did you actually reply?'

'It's a pisser!'

GANDHI, Mahatma. Richard Attenborough and Ben Kingsley between them have told us most of what there is to know about Gandhi, but they did not include in the film one incident which occurred at the farewell demonstration in Bombay in 1931 before he left for Britain. Gandhi was seen to kiss several women but paid no attention to his wife, who stood aloof.

'Why', someone remarked, 'he is almost a European.'

GASCOIGNE, Jill. The actress Jill Gascoigne once received an abusive letter. It was anonymous but it did boast a postscript - 'If undelivered, please forward to Jenny Agutter.'

GEORGE I. George I, who came to the throne in 1714, was the first of the Hanoverian monarchs. As Elizabeth Longford has observed, 'The best that one can say of them *qua* Royal House is that they improved as they went along, sloughing the boorishness that descended with them on the British throne.' The choice for Parliament was between a British Catholic 'Pretender' who would have been James III and a German Protestant who was happier in Hanover. After the events of the previous hundred years it was not surprising that they plumped for the small, choleric German Prince George, Elector of Hanover and great-grandson of James I. The Act of Settlement in 1701 had pointed the way to the Electress, a gifted woman, but she died two months before Queen Anne, making way for her 'far from gifted son'.

George was an indolent, amorous king. The indolence served conveniently to enable Robert Walpole, a brilliant political manager and a great peacetime statesman, to emerge as the 'prime minister' of a king who could speak no English. His mother, the Electress, who had taken the trouble to learn the language of the people she looked likely to rule, knew it well enough to express her disgust of one of George's mistresses, her lady-in-waiting, to a British visitor: 'Look at that malkin [scarecrow] and think of her being my son's passion.' The visitor was embarrassed until she realised that the other woman had no English.

The Prince was married to his cousin, the beautiful Princess Sophia Dorothea, who had to reconcile herself to her husband's handful of women on the side. Her tragedy was remembered in a film, *Saraband for Dead Lovers*, made at the height of the vogue for costume drama in British cinema. She appears to have been set up by less-than-loyal ladies-in-waiting with a handsome visitor to the court, the Count Königsmark. In the movie Joan Greenwood as the Princess, Stewart Granger as the Count and Peter Bull, the Prince, acted out the mysterious tragedy which was not resolved until George II's time. It appeared that the Princess had been no more than coquettish with the Count while her husband was away: but when her ladies reported this he ordered Königsmark to leave Hanover the next day. The ladies then admitted the Count to the bed-chamber of the Princess to say farewell. He was not seen again until George II's return. He ordered some alterations to his palace in Hanover and in the course of the work Königsmark's strangled corpse was discovered under the floor of the Princess's dressing room. The disgraced Electoral Princess was confined in Ahlden Castle for the rest of her life. She died in 1726, a year before her husband. Just before, he had offered to reinstate and liberate her, but she refused, saying, 'If what I am accused of is true I am unworthy of his bed. If it is untrue he is unworthy of mine.'

Conveniently her husband was able to import his two principal paramours to England, where they soon acquired nicknames. The fat one, Mme Kilmansegge, was created Countess of Darlington by the King but called the 'Elephant and Castle' by the rest of the court. The tall thin one – the woman who had provoked the contempt of the Electress – was the Duchess of Kendal or 'The Maypole' depending on who was making reference to her. Both were greedy. When one was jeered by a mob she called out, 'Why do you abuse us? We come for all your goots!' A heckler shouted back, 'Yes, damn you, and for all our chattels too!' The German arrivals were out for all they could get. One honourable German asked to return to Hanover where people were honest and decent. 'Bah!' said George. 'It is only English money. Steal like the rest!'

'The Fifteen', the rebellion of James, the 'Old Pretender', was put down in 1715. The King was criticised for attending a ball on the day of the execution of two of James's supporters, but the running scandals of the reign set the pattern of Hanoverian monarchs. They were all perpetually at odds with their eldest sons. The Prince of Wales hated all the King's servants and protested when his father insisted that his Lord Chamberlain, Lord Newcastle, stand as godparent at the christening of the Prince's son. The Prince grabbed Newcastle and shouted, 'Rascal, I find you out.' Newcastle thought he heard 'Rascal, I fight you' – so thick was the Prince's accent. As a result the King ordered that his grandchildren should be raised under his care in St James's Palace. The Prince and Princess of Wales went into virtual exile for three and a half years and after a temporary attempt at reconciliation, with the embarrassed Prince kneeling at his enraged father's feet, he left to hear his father grumbling 'Votre conduite! Votre conduite!' It has been suggested that consideration was given to the idea of kid-napping the Prince and transporting him to the plantations and though it came to nothing, after his death the Prince found a letter in his father's papers recommending this course of action. George I referred to his daughter-in-law as 'Cette diablesse, Madame la Princesse.'

George had a passion for agriculture and a loudly trumpeted aversion to the arts. In a rare attempt at the English language he said, 'I hate all Boets and Bainters.' However, when a German congratulated him on his accession to the English throne, he is said to have remarked, 'Congratulate me rather on having Newton for a subject in one country and Leibniz in the other.'

Sophia Dorothea lay unburied for six months after her death. George had been warned by a French woman fortune teller that he would not survive her by a year. Walpole suggests that she may have been put up to this by Sophia Dorothea's parents, the Duke and Duchess of Zell, to scupper any plans the Duchess of Kendal might have had to remove George's wife and occupy that position herself. In spite of this scheming, George I had tactlessly gone to a play at the Haymarket on the day of Sophia Dorothea's death, taking 'the Maypole Duchess' with him.

When he eventually set out for Hanover to bury his wife, the Duchess again accompanied him. On reaching Osnabrück he had doubts and second thoughts, ditched her there and went on alone. It was to no avail as he had a stroke in his coach and, taken on to his palace, died in the room in which he had been born 67 years before.

The Duchess of Kendal swore he had told her he would return and when a big raven invaded her villa at Isleworth she was determined that it held his soul and nurtured it as a pet.

GEORGE II. 'Like his father (George I),' wrote Sir John Plumb, 'George was stupid but complicated.' Unlike his father, he was quite active in affairs of state although easily bullied, first by his intelligent wife Caroline and then by Walpole and William Pitt. He was the last English King to command troops in the field, being present at the battle of Dettingen, where his battle cry was 'Now, boys, now for the honour of England, fire and behave bravely and the French will soon run.' He was on foot, his horse having earlier bolted to the rear. 'I can be sure of my own legs,' he explained. 'They will not run away with me.' The French were defeated.

Twenty years of war did much to boost Britain's economy, and the King's reign closed in a blaze of military glory – victory at Minden, Clive's success in India and Wolfe's in Canada. One courtier complained that General Wolfe was mad. 'Then I wish,' replied George in a rare Hanoverian witticism, 'he would bite some other of my generals.'

On the domestic front he and the Queen spent much time loathing Frederick (Fretz), Prince of Wales. He thought English children were badly brought up. On one occasion Sarah, Duchess of Marlborough, visiting the Princess Caroline, was surprised to find her whipping one of the royal children. 'Ah!' said George, 'You have no good manners in England, because you are not properly brought up when you are young.'

As the Prince of Wales grew so did his parents' disapproval. George II suggested that he might be a *Wechselbalg*, a changeling. Speaking to Lord Hervey about 'Fretz', the Queen said, 'You know as well as I that he is the lowest stinking coward in the world and that there is no way of gaining anything of him but by working on his fear. I know if I was asleep that if he could come behind me he is capable of shooting me through the head or stabbing me in the back.' And on another occasion, 'If I were to see him in Hell I should feel no more for him than I should for any other rogue that ever went there.' Again, 'My God, popularity always makes me sick: but Fretz's popularity makes me vomit!' And: 'Our first-born is the greatest ass, the greatest liar, the greatest canaille and the greatest beast in the world and we heartily wish he was out of it.'

In 1737 when she was on her death bed she was relieved when the King refused to give Frederick access to her. He said, 'He wants to come and insult his poor dying mother but she shall not see him . . . No! No! He shall not come and act his silly plays here, false lying nauseous puppy!' George II's dislike of his son was transferred to his grandson – in Lord Chesterfield's words, 'There is nothing new under the sun, nor under the grandson either.'

George II's other much-quoted remark at his wife's death bed showed less consideration to his wife's feelings. When she urged him to marry again he replied, 'No, I shall have mistresses.'

This was by no means a new development. Although he always appeared to find his wife the most desirable of women, that did not stop him playing elsewhere. For years he lusted after a Miss Mary Bellenden who later married the 4th Duke of Argyll. Always money conscious, he once ostentatiously took out his purse and twice counted the coins in front of her. 'Sire,' she cried, out of patience, 'I cannot bear it! If you count your money any more, I will go out of the room!' When she went out of his life he transferred his interest to Henrietta Howard, who was more ready to fall in with his wishes and who received the title Countess of Suffolk as a reward when he became King. She received £2,000 rising to £3,200. Her husband did not relinquish her without a fight, invading the quadrangle of the palace of St James at night and loudly calling for her and later sending a letter to her via the Archbishop of Canterbury, who passed it to the Queen, who maliciously handed it to her rival. On the whole Caroline was contemptuous of Lady Suffolk, who had to put up with the King's irritating and unimaginative habits. He visited her each night at nine precisely and if early would pace around looking at his watch until the hour struck.

After the affair had run a long course and Lady Suffolk was growing older and profoundly deaf, the Queen began to side with her at the approach of younger, more beautiful rivals. 'I don't know,' the King told his wife, 'why you will not let me part with the old deaf woman of whom I am weary.'

The new threat was Amelia Sophia, Countess von Walmoden and it became real and immediate when George told his wife, 'You must love the Walmoden, for she loves me.' First Caroline tried to persuade Lady Suffolk to stay by her side. Then she changed her tactics and, rather than have her husband spend so much time in Hanover with his mistress, urged him to import her to England.

George could be remarkably coarse. He disapproved of Bishop Headley, the Bishop of Winchester, and told his friend Lord Hervey so in no uncertain terms. 'The Bishop of Winchester . . . as Christ's ambassador, receives £6,000 or £7,000 a year. Pray, what is it that charms you in him? His pretty limping gait or his nasty stinking breath? Or his silly laugh when he grins in your face for nothing and shows his nasty rotten teeth?'

Of his eldest son's marriage to a German princess he was even less enthusiastic. 'I do not think that in grafting my half-witted coxcomb upon a mad woman would mend the breed.'

According to the Duke of Windsor's unpublished reminiscences of 'My Hanoverian Ancestors', during one of the King's absences in Hanover a notice was posted on the gates of St James's Palace which read: 'Lost or strayed out of this house a man who has left a wife and six children on the parish.' A reward of four shillings and sixpence was offered, 'nobody judging him to deserve a crown (five shillings)'. Another poster in the Royal Exchange proclaimed, 'It is reported that his Hanoverian Majesty designs to visit his British Dominion for three months in the spring.' A far cry from his address to Parliament on coming to the throne, 'I have not a drop of blood dot is not English.'

Theatrically, George's preference was for music but he was persuaded to attend a performance by Garrick as Richard III. Unfortunately, the actor who took his fancy was the lowly impersonator of the Lord Mayor of London. Right up to Richard's search for a horse on Bosworth field the King was still asking 'Will dat Lord Mayor not come again?' Garrick must have loved it!

GEORGE III. The grandson of George II, George III was amiable, shy, fussy and conscientious. He came to the throne as a 22-year-old interested in the arts as well as farming. 'George, be a king,' his mother Queen Caroline exhorted him when he ascended the throne. His father Frederick, Prince of Wales, died as a result of a blow from a cricket ball. 'I feel something here,' George said, genuinely moved, 'just as I did when I saw the two workmen fall from the scaffold at Kew.'

Shy or not, he is supposed to have seduced a 'Fair Quaker', Hannah Lightfoot, and to have laid siege to Lady Sarah Lennox. Walpole's account has Lennox making tempting appearances dressed as a shepherdess or haymaker as he rode by. In the tradition of her family he proposed to her through his cousin and when he got her alone asked her what she thought of the proposal; 'Tell me, for my happiness depends on it!' 'Nothing, sir,' she replied; at which George stumped off muttering, 'Nothing will come of nothing.'

In 1761 he married Princess Charlotte Sophia of Mecklenburg-Strelitz. The twice-married Duchess of Devonshire travelled with her to meet the King. 'You may laugh,' complained her charge; 'You have been married twice. But to me it is no joke.' She had cause to worry. When the English crowd first saw her they shouted 'Pug! Pug! Pug!' mocking her upturned nose. 'Vat is dat they do say – poog?' she asked. 'Vat means poog?' The Duchess of Ancaster, who was then attending her, said tactfully, 'It means "God bless your Royal Highness." '

George was the first of the Hanoverians to be typically English and to speak his country's tongue. He was unusually faithful to Queen Charlotte, by whom he had a royal record of fifteen children – most of whom lived, unlike those of Queen Anne.

He wrote to Dr Hurl, who was appointed tutor to the young Princes in 1776, 'We live in unprincipled days and no change can be expected but by an early attention to the rising generation.' He instructed a later tutor, the Bishop of Chester, 'If they deserve it, let them be flogged; do as you used to do at Westminster.' The Duke of Sussex was flogged for having asthma and Princess Sophia recalled that she had 'seen her two eldest brothers, when they were boys of thirteen and fourteen, held by their arms to be flogged like dogs with a long whip'. The King thought it his duty to be present at these punishments.

However well intentioned, George was ill equipped to cope with George Washington, the French Revolution and Napoleon. By the time of Waterloo, George III was popularly supposed to be mad – hence his son's regency – though modern opinion is in favour of the posthumous diagnosis of porphyria. Disconcertingly for his ministers, he talked wildly and believed he was communing with creatures 'not of this world', especially angels. 'Of all the men I have known,' he once said to himself, 'you are the one on whom I have the greatest dependence and you are the most perfect gentleman.'

His cruel treatment is admirably chronicled by Alan Bennett in *The Madness of George III* – especially his sufferings at the hands of the Doctors Willis, a father and two sons – which included a straitjacket, being tied to his bed and other indignities. Defending his profession against the King's strong dislike of doctors, Willis remarked unctuously that 'Our Saviour went about healing the sick.' 'Yes, yes,' agreed the King testily, 'but he had not seven hundred pounds a year for it.'

According to one legend he once got out of his carriage in Windsor Great Park and embraced an oak tree believing it to be Frederick the Great of Prussia.

He always hated London ('I certainly see as little of London as I possibly can, and am never a volunteer there') and bolted to Windsor and the country whenever he could – hence his nickname 'Farmer George'.

He had an interest in 'the new technology' of the eighteenth century: inspecting Sir William Herschel's new telescope at Slough alongside the Archbishop of Canterbury he nudged the churchman towards it saying, 'Come, my Lord Bishop, I will show you the way to Heaven!'

At the theatre his tastes were low-brow. When his father, Prince Frederick, talked of sponsoring a Shakespeare season – a new play a week until he had sponsored the entire canon – George was against the idea. 'Was ever such sad stuff as a great part of Shakespeare?' he protested; 'only one must not say so.' He thought Garrick 'a great fidget who never could stand still'. However, he allowed Mrs Siddons to read to the Princesses and enjoyed theatre as long as scenes of great unhappiness were avoided. He loved low comedy: clowns inspired enthusiasm in him. He even relished the jokes about 'Farmer George' and his interest in agriculture. 'Hee! Hee! Good! They mean my sheep!' he would chuckle when topical references were inserted.

A public row in the foyer of Drury Lane between George and his son is the origin of the tradition that one entrance from foyer to auditorium there is known as 'King's Side' and the other as 'Prince's Side'.

George III was a Drury Lane regular, but in 1800 his arrival in his box for a performance of *She Would and She Wouldn't* was greeted by a would-be assassin's bullet. It missed and landed in a pillow at the side of the box. The culprit, Hatfield, an ex-soldier, was grabbed by the mob. Later a medal was struck to commemorate the King's escape, but on the spot Sheridan ran up an extra verse for the National Anthem which the loyal cast sang for their King – led by one Michael Kelly:

> From every latent foe,
> From the assassin's blow,
> God Save the King!

Four years earlier a woman at the garden door of St James's Palace had appeared to present the King with a petition – which turned out to conceal a knife. She did not harm him, and though he had a momentary concern for a ripped waistcoat, he was calmer than his attendants who might have killed her if he had not called, 'The poor creature is mad! Do not hurt her! She has not hurt me!'

After the loss of the American colonies became a *fait accompli* he was dignified in his reception of John Adams, the first US ambassador to Britain in 1785. 'I was the last to consent to separation, but separation having been made and having become inevitable, I have always said that I would be the first to meet friendship to the United States as an independent power.'

For a simple man he was perceptive on a number of matters, though perhaps not on William Blake's drawings: 'What-what-what? Take them away!' (But for the 'what, what, what' he might have been going through a bad patch.) Wyatt, his architect, was told, 'Six hours' sleep are enough for a man, seven for a woman and eight for a fool.' And he told Eaton, his gardener at Kew, who was packing up a basket of plants for the hated Dr Willis: 'Get another basket, at the same time, and pack up the doctor in it, and send him off at the same time.'

The two crosses he bore were his illness and his prodigious number of offspring. It would seem to be a nice rule for Royal parents to follow a damage limitation exercise – or lack of it – in not producing too many children and, by definition, too much trouble. George III's children did not enjoy being together much either. 'Nothing in my eyes is so terrible as a family party,' said Ernest, Duke of Cumberland, the fifth of his nine sons. Princess Sophia, the fifth of his daughters, complained to her oldest brother, the Prince of Wales, of 'the Windsor nursery' as the girls called themselves. Although oversexed they either married late or failed to net a husband at all. 'Poor old wretches *as we are*,' wrote Sophia, 'four old cats, four old wretches a dead weight *upon you*, old lumber to the country, like old clothes. I wonder you do not vote for putting us in a sack and drowning us in the Thames.' Scandal even suggested that Sophia had a child by her brother Cumberland. In fact her child, passed off as dropsy cured by roast beef, was sired by a courtier, General Garth.

The Duke of Wellington, George IV's executor, summed up the public feeling about his royal siblings: 'They are the damnedest millstones about the necks of any government that can be imagined.'

Perhaps Royal rearrangements in future should stipulate only an heir – or at least, 'an heir and a pair'.

Blind from 1805 and desolated by the death of his youngest and favourite daughter, Princess Amelia, in 1811, the King tottered on at Windsor, scandal free himself, pious, simple and pathetic, until 1820 when, as Byron's epitaph ran,

> He died – but left his subjects still behind,
> One half as mad – and t'other no less blind.

GEORGE IV. King George IV, the eldest son of George III, became Prince Regent during the periods of his father's insanity from 1810 to his own accession in 1820. A voluptuary, irresponsible with money, women and drink, he was also 'The First Gentleman of Europe', 'Prinny' and 'Prince Charming'. Walter Savage Landor, believing him to be the last George, wrote, 'When from the earth the Fourth descended, God be praised, the Georges ended.'

Even as a young man George was gross, his face flushed, his progress portly. However, he had certain drawing room graces. He danced well, sang and could talk wittily. He was an arbiter of taste in art and architecture who provided England with the nucleus of the National Gallery, the Brighton Pavilion, Carlton House, the Nash Terraces in Regent's Park and a much-restored Windsor Castle. At seventeen he romanced the beautiful and profligate 21-year-old actress Mary 'Perdita' Robinson, acquiring the unlikely nickname 'Florizel' for a short time, but the affair was shortlived. Another actress, the Catholic Mrs Maria Fitzherbert, a widow, was his next conquest – as a result of staging a suicide attempt in order to convince her of his passion. They married in secret a year later in 1785. It was an illegal marriage as she was both a Catholic and a subject, and not until 1800 did they set up house together. Mrs Fitzherbert called the next eight years the happiest of her life.

However, George needed to marry again to settle his debts. This he did in 1795. Lord Malmesbury, his emissary to the bride of his choice, Caroline of Brunswick, reported unenthusiastically that her clothes were ill chosen and that cleanliness was not her strong point.

Worse was to come when Caroline was presented to him. As she properly attempted to kneel to him he said to Malmesbury, 'I am not well: pray get me a glass of brandy.' Malmesbury replied, 'Sir, had you not better have a glass of water.' The Prince left the room at a run saying, 'No! I will go directly to the Queen.' Nor was the bride impressed. 'Mon Dieu!' she exclaimed. 'Est-ce que le Prince est toujours comme cela? Je le trouve très gros, et nullement aussi beau que son portrait.'

Matters did not go well on the wedding night. George arrived in Caroline's bedroom dead drunk and collapsed in the fire grate, where he spent the night. However, he may have joined her in bed in the morning. At any rate their child Charlotte was conceived, and Caroline swore that he never slept with her again.

There is a very rum tale of the Prince of Wales being amazed at the size of the penis of one of his brothers. It is alleged that the brother was taken short in their carriage one night and relieved himself out of the window. So great was the flood of water that the coachman mistook it for a rainstorm and urged the horses forward to escape it!

One of Prinny's intimates was the fashion-setter Beau Brummel, who lost his position as favourite when the Prince heard him turn to Lady Worcester and remark, 'Who is your fat friend?' Leigh Hunt was jailed for two years for calling the Prince a 'fat Adonis of fifty'. And Charles Lamb wrote anonymously:

> Not a fatter fish than he
> Flounders round the polar sea
> See his blubber – at his gills
> What a world of drink he swills . . .
> By his bulk and by his size
> By his oily qualities
> This (or else my eyesight fails)
> This should be the Prince of Wales.

Versifiers also had a field day with Princess Caroline. While she was living on Blackheath, her adultery with several men was alleged. An inquiry exonerated her with a warning. When George came to the throne in 1820 she returned from a long sojourn abroad to demand her rightful place beside him as Queen. The King and his Tory government were perplexed as to how to prevent her. She was not popular on her return, but as the Coronation drew nearer public opinion began to swing in her favour. George made an ill-fated attempt to divorce her with a Bill of Pains and Penalties. She attended the debate in the House of Lords and frequently fell asleep. Hence the verse,

> Her conduct at present no censure affords,
> She sins not with courtiers but sleeps with the Lords.

She was accused of adultery on a cruise, sleeping with a major-domo in a lifeboat on board her ship, and bathing in her cabin either with him or in his presence. More verses ensued:

> The Grand Master of St Caroline has found promotion's path;
> He is made both Knight Companion and Commander of the Bath.

Queen Caroline herself held that she only committed adultery on the one occasion when she went to bed with 'Mrs Fitzherbert's husband'.

The bill passed its third reading in the Lords by a slender majority of nine. The diarist Greevy summed up the national feeling with the entry. 'The bill is gone, thank God! to the devil.'

Caroline died on 7 August 1821, nineteen days after her failure to be crowned Queen. After more demonstrations as her coffin was borne to Harwich she was buried in Brunswick. Her hope that her coffin be inscribed 'Caroline of Brunswick, the injured Queen of England' was denied her.

The Prince meanwhile had a number of other mistresses. He was in Ireland when Caroline died. He had arrived there saying, 'My friends! When I arrived in this beautiful country my heart overflowed with joy . . .' The joy was occasioned not at the state visit, but by the prospect of staying with Lady Conyngham at Slane Castle. While he was there the news of Napoleon's death was delivered. Unfortunately the courtier charged with announcing it phrased it misleadingly. 'I have, Sir, to congratulate you,' he said, 'your greatest enemy is dead.' Thinking his Queen was meant, the King said, 'Is *she*, by God?'

He was arbitrary in his judgements. When George Canning, his Foreign Secretary, wanted him to entertain the King and Queen of the Sandwich Islands to dinner he complained to the Duke of Wellington, 'Think of that damned fellow wanting me to have the King and Queen of the Sandwich Islands to dinner as if I would sit at table with such a pair of damned cannibals.'

Going north for a Caledonian Hunt Ball in 1822 he gave firm instructions: 'No foreign dances. I dislike seeing anything in Scotland that is not purely national and characteristic.' The same year he said, 'Either I am mad or Castlereagh is mad.' (As it happened it was Castlereagh who killed himself shortly afterwards.) He was very fussy about uniforms. When Lord Charles Russell appeared incorrectly dressed at a Court Ball he snapped, 'Good evening, sir, I suppose you are the regimental doctor.'

As a young man, George had been frustrated by his father in his wish to have a military career. In later life the frustration led to military fantasies. He would tell visitors that he had led the German charge at Salamanca. He had of course to be incognito and his *nom de guerre* was General Brock. In his own mind he had also led the celebrated attack of the Prince Regent's Own Royal Hussars in 1815 at Waterloo. Wellington, who became an intimate, had a ready and practical answer when George shouted along the dinner table, 'Was that not so?' in a demand for corroboration of his exploits. The tactful reply was invariably, 'I have often heard your Majesty say so.'

This erratic view of events carried through to other areas. After the Catholic Emancipation Act was passed in 1829 on the insistence of Wellington and Peel, but against his wishes and those of the Tory party, he suddenly adopted it as 'his measure'. According to Mrs Arbuthnot's journals he even testified that 'he knew he should carry it at a canter, although the Duke was very nervous.'

Given to lying in bed all day and calling for steaks, pies and choice cuts of joints, washing them down with moselle, champagne, port and brandy, and topping that with laudanum night and morning, his sluggish and self-indulgent lifestyle could not be sustained. 'One night he drank two glasses of hot ale and toast, three glasses of claret, some strawberries!! and a glass of brandy,' noted Mrs Arbuthnot; '. . . it is necessary, I believe,' she added, 'to have a great deal of high food, but the mixture of ale and strawberries is enough to kill a horse. Beware.'

He was not happy about his successor, the 65-year-old Prince William Henry, Duke of Clarence, the third son of George III. 'Look at that idiot!' he said twice to Princess Lieven. In 1826 he added, 'They will remember me if ever he is in my place.' In the year of his death he pointed out William to the Princess again, 'Like a frog's head carved on a Coconut.'

He died on 29 June 1830. Mrs Arbuthnot's verdict was 'a blood vessel in his stomach burst. He put his hand up to his breast, exclaimed, "Good God, what do I feel? This must be death!" ' He had a few minutes to curtains.

GEORGE V. King George V, born in 1865, was the second son of Edward VII and Queen Alexandra. As a second son he seemed destined for the Navy and spent an extremely uncomfortable training period, especially as a Navel Cadet on *Britannia* in 1877. 'They used to make me go up and challenge the bigger boys – I was awfully small then and I'd get a hiding time and again.' Later he was to say to Lord Derby, 'My father was frightened of his mother, I was frightened of my father and I am damned well going to see to it that my children are frightened of me.'

He grew up to be basically shy, albeit quick-tempered, but beneath his gruff salty manner he was a kind and considerate man, more at home in the Royal squirearchies of Sandringham and Balmoral, where he was a matchless shot. He gave short shrift to foreign parts, except the Empire: 'Abroad is awful. I know because I've been there.' He had no wish to visit the USA: 'The nearest I got to the United States was when I walked half across Niagara, took my hat off and walked back again.' And again, 'England is good enough for me. I like my own country best, climate or no, and I'm staying in it. I'm not like my father.' Asked to make a State Visit to Holland he dismissed the idea, 'Amsterdam, Rotterdam, and all the other dams. Damned if I'll do it.'

He had a sailor's penchant for risqué stories and always enjoyed hearing his favourites. One was Lord Louis Mountbatten's account of the visit of his sister, Crown Princess (later Queen) Louise of Sweden to Uppsala Cathedral. The Archbishop was keen to flourish his command of English. He approached a chest of drawers in the sacristy and made the mind-boggling declaration, 'I will now open these trousers and reveal some even more precious treasures to Your Royal Highness.' On being told by the Duke of Westminster that the Duke's brother-in-law, Earl Beauchamp, was a homosexual, he said simply, 'I thought people like that shot themselves.'

In 1893 he married Princess Mary ('May') of Teck. Her family had not been wealthy – 'You see, my parents were always in short street so they had to go abroad to economise.' By her he had six children. On the birth of the fifth he said, 'I shall soon have a regiment not a family.' Princess Mary had previously been engaged to his elder brother, the Duke of Clarence. Their slow courtship, after the sudden death of the unstable Duke, provoked a shove from Princess Louise to Prince George at Sheen Lodge: 'Now, Georgie, don't you think you ought to take May into the garden to look at the frogs in the pond?'

When his father was dying he reported, 'The last thing he understood was when I told him his horse, Witch of Air, had won at Kempton today and he said he was pleased.' The next morning George's eldest son announced that the Royal Standard was flying at half mast, recording that his father 'frowned and muttered, "But that's all wrong," and repeating the old but pregnant saying "The King is dead. Long live the King!" he sent for his equerry and in a peremptory naval manner ordered the mast to be rigged at once on the roof of Marlborough House.'

His attitude to his court and his country was sharp and to the point. When H. G. Wells wrote of an 'alien and uninspiring court', his answer was, 'I may be uninspiring but I'll be damned if I'm an alien.' On another occasion he accurately described it as 'dull perhaps, but constantly respectable'. To his cousin Count Mensdorf he deprecated the British Secret Service: 'Our spies are the worst and clumsiest in the world.'

War was declared on Germany in 1914. His secretary, Lord Stamfordham (of whom he was to say, 'He taught me how to be King'), urged him to display more public geniality. He was dismissive: 'We sailors never smile on duty.' In 1917 he changed the family name to Windsor – setting up the Kaiser's famous jibe that he would like to see that popular opera, 'The Merry Wives of Saxe-Coburg-Gotha'.

Although he read the novels of John Buchan, Gilbert Frankau, A. E. W. Mason, C. S. Forester and even Hemingway, his popular reputation was as a philistine. Asked by Asquith to send a congratulatory telegram to 'Old Hardy' (Thomas Hardy) on his seventieth birthday in 1910, he gave instructions and Mr Hardy of Alnwick (who made the King's fishing rods) received an inexplicable Royal Message. He concurred with Queen Victoria's opinion of Turner – 'I tell you what, Turner was *mad*. My grandmother always said so.' Like his grandmother he preferred Frith, Landseer and Winterhalter. Similarly with music: after hearing the band of the Grenadiers playing a selection from Richard Strauss's *Electra* in the forecourt of Buckingham Palace, he sent the bandmaster a message: 'His Majesty does not know what the band has just played but it is *never* to be played again.' On the other hand, after Kubelik the violinist played at Sandringham he commented, 'He is quite wonderful but I wish he didn't have long hair.' Receiving Lady Diana Cooper after seeing her legendary performance as a silent statue in *The Miracle*, he was somewhat tactless. 'But of course you have no words to say, and talking is three-quarters of acting.' And to an important guest who dropped her hairpin in her soup at Sandringham he joked heavily, 'Did you come here expecting to eat winkles?'

One constant was his devotion to Queen Mary. Rejecting the example of the 'smart set' of his father, Edward VII, he said, 'We have seen enough of the intrigue and meddling of certain ladies. I'm not interested in any wife except my own.' Her passion was antiques. Overhearing her in conversation with her godson, Sir Michael Duff, over dinner at Balmoral he tut-tutted indulgently, 'There you go again, May; furniture, furniture, furniture,' She in her turn indulged him. When he went to sea in a submarine she said whimsically, 'I shall be very disappointed if George doesn't come up again.' Her passion for collection led her to unconventional ways of adding to her treasures. 'May I go back and say goodbye so that dear little cabinet?' was a strong hint to her hosts that she would like to acquire the object in question. When she was told that one of the Royal paintings was a Mercier, not by Nollekens, she was firm: 'We prefer the picture to remain as by Nollekens.'

On one occasion Queen Mary, noticing that her chief detective had been absent for several days, asked what was wrong. The man was in fact suffering from piles, but the embarrassed equerry could only bring himself to confess that he had 'an unfortunate disease'. A couple of days passed and then the King asked, 'What on earth are we going to do about the detective?' This puzzled a second equerry who reassured him, 'Oh, sir, he'll be back soon, he's only got an attack of piles.' The King was instantly relieved. 'Oh,' he said, 'some fool equerry told my wife he had syphilis.'

In 1939 her Daimler was hit by a heavy lorry and although aged 72 and severely bruised, she was casually brave, 'We three were in a heap at the bottom of the car and we got out by the help of two ladders.' On 4 September 1939 at the outbreak of war she evacuated herself to Badminton, the home of the Duke and Duchess of Beaufort (her niece) along with 63 staff and dependants. On her arrival she surprised the Duchess by saying, 'So *that's* what hay looks like!' Adjusting to the country after a life lived entirely in the metropolitan world, she stayed there until 1945.

Both King and Queen were concerned about the succession. George V compared his eldest son (who was to become Edward VIII) unfavourably to the second born. 'You are indeed a lucky man,' he wrote to the Duke of York, 'to have such a charming and delightful wife as Elizabeth . . . You have always been so sensible and easy to work with . . . very different to dear David.' He was remarkably indulgent to the newly married Duchess of York (Elizabeth Bowes-Lyon), even relaxing his strict punctuality standards: 'You are not late, my dear, I think we must have sat down two minutes early.' A few weeks before he died he wrote to Lady Algernon Gordon-Lennox, 'I pray to God that my eldest son will never marry and have children, and that nothing will come between Bertie [George VI] and Lillibet [Queen Elizabeth] and the throne.' To Lord Derby he confided, 'When I am gone the boy will ruin himself in twelve months.' The Prince of Wales had long been a thorn in his side. 'He has not a single friend who is a gentlemen,' he told Mensdorf, and to the Prince he shouted, 'You dress like a cad. You act like a cad. You are a cad. Get Out!' In 1930 when the Prince asked for Fort Belvedere, the Victorian folly in Windsor Great Park, he said, 'What could you possibly want that queer old place for? Those damned week-ends, I suppose.'

He died in 1936 and his eldest son was soon to fulfil his worst expectations: his 'last words' are much bandied about. At some time in the thirties when he was recovering from an illness Bognor Regis was suggested as a suitable place to recuperate. It was then that he said, 'Bugger Bognor!' On the day he died he did say, 'How is the Empire?' but they were not his last words.

GEORGE VI. Born in 1895 and King from 1936 to 1952, Prince Albert was the second son of King George V and Queen Mary. He served in the Royal Navy, 'The Sailor Prince', taking part in the Battle of Jutland before becoming Duke of York whilst at Cambridge in 1920.

In spite of his undistinguished academic record at Osborne (bottom of the class), his stammer and a gastric ulcer he insisted on active service. In a letter to the Prince of Wales after the battle of Jutland in 1916, when he served in the battleship HMS *Collingwood* as a sub-lieutenant, he wrote, 'When I was on top of the turret I never felt any fear of shells or anything else. It seems curious but all sense of danger and everything else goes except the longing of dealing death in every possible way to the enemy.'

His salvation when he was suddenly elevated to King was his extremely happy marriage to Queen Elizabeth – Lady Elizabeth Bowes-Lyon. Their first meeting was in 1905 at a children's party when she gave him crystallised cherries off her sugar cake. Fifteen years later, on 20 May 1920, he danced with her after saying to an equerry, 'That's a lovely girl you've been dancing with. Who is she?' He first proposed to her in 1921 but was not accepted until 1923. There were many rivals. Eventually he announced the great news in a telegram to his parents: 'ALL RIGHT. BERTIE.'

His alarm when he realised that he was to succeed his older brother, the abdicated Edward VIII, as King was hardly reduced by the lessons he had been taking with a speech therapist, Lionel Logue, who gave him tongue twisters like 'Let's go gathering healthy heather with the gay brigade of grand dragoons' and 'She shifted seven thick-stalked thistles through a strong thick sieve'.

He greeted the news that he was to succeed with dutiful dismay: 'I never wanted this to happen: I'm quite unprepared for it. David has been trained for this all his life. I've never seen the state papers. I'm only a naval officer. It's the only thing I know about.' His cousin, Lord Mountbatten, reminded him that when the Duke of Clarence died the future George V had said the same thing to his father Prince Louis of Battenberg, who had said, 'George, you're wrong. There is no more fitting preparation for a king that to have been trained in the Navy.' When a clumsy Bishop stood on his robes at the Coronation, 'I had to tell him to get off it pretty smartly as I nearly fell down.'

Lady Diana Cooper reported favourably on the change of atmosphere under the new regime after knowing life at the Fort: 'That was an operetta, this is an institution.'

At about this time the new Queen was asked if she had seen Chips Channon's extravagant new gold dinner service in his magnificent Belgravia home. 'Oh no,' she joked. 'We're not nearly grand enough to be asked there.'

At Windsor, just before the war, the King met an American boxer, King Levinsky, who was training at Windsor, 'Hey, Majesty,' he said, 'So you're George de Sixth and I'm Levinsky de Foist!'

During the war Gerald Kelly RA took up residence at Windsor Castle to paint the Royal portraits and was not easily dislodged – even when the Royal Princesses lampooned him in a Christmas pantomime as 'Kerald Jelly, the immovable guest'.

Meanwhile the Queen took revolver lessons in case of a parachute attack and rejoiced in the first bomb to fall on Buckingham Palace which enabled her to 'feel I can look the East End in the face'. On a morale-raising visit to Lancashire, a local council entertained her to a lavish meal. She felt that she should point out that strict rationing regulations were observed at Buckingham Palace. The Mayor was unembarrassed; 'Oh well,' he said to her, 'then Your Majesty'll be glad of a proper do!'

According to Field Marshal Lord Carver's autobiography, Carver had an eccentric friend, one 'Looney' Hinde. King George VI was inspecting troops in North Africa in 1943. He put a routine question to Brigadier Hinde. 'Have we met before?'

'I don't think so,' said Hinde.

'You should bl-bloody well know,' said the King tartly.

On a tour before the war the King had noticed that a Canadian mayor did not wear a ceremonial chain. He asked if he had one, 'Oh yes,' said the mayor, 'but I only wear it on special occasions.'

There are many accounts of the attempts of the King and his Prime Minister, Winston Churchill, to take part in the D-Day landings. The simplification I like is this. For safety reasons Eisenhower and the service chiefs were determined to prevent Churchill, whose personal train was already parked in a siding outside Southampton, from joining in. They played a desperate card. That evening Churchill received a message from George VI saying that if it was right for the Prime Minister to take part in the invasion then he himself had an even stronger claim as head of all three fighting services. Churchill gave in.

Both George VI and his Queen had an occasional gift for a sharp remark. Of the Princess Royal's horsiness he said, 'My sister was a horse until she Came Out.' Of John Piper's brooding sketches of Windsor Castle: 'Why is it, Mr Piper, that it always seems to be raining when you do a sketch at Windsor? You've been very unlucky with the weather.' And of the 'Skylon', a very odd exhibit on the South Bank to celebrate the Festival of Britain, 'Like the British economy, it has no visible means of support.'

GETTY, John Paul II. Now that John Paul Getty's troubled early life has led him into the paths of philanthropy he is lavish in his generosity towards the fine arts, the cinema and especially cricket. And concerned in his attitude to those less fortunate: at a dinner in 1993 he was reported to have sympathised to a fellow diner with the plight of the monarch. 'Ah'm sorry your Queen has to pay taxes,' he said. 'She's not a wealthy woman.'

GIBBON, Edward. Gibbon, the great eighteenth-century historian, was permitted by the Duke of Gloucester, King George III's brother, to present him with a copy of Volume I of his *History of the Decline and Fall of the Roman Empire*. Naturally, when Volume II came out Gibbon again turned up to give the Duke a copy. The Duke greeted him genially as he produced his book, 'Another damn'd thick, square book! Always scribble, scribble, scribble! Eh! Mr Gibbon?'

The playwright Sheridan had a similar opinion of Gibbon. Accused of calling him 'the luminous author of *Decline and Fall*', he was challenged on his verdict by a friend. 'Did I say luminous?' he said, 'Oh, I meant voluminous.'

GODDARD, Rayner (Lord Goddard). Lord Goddard is best remembered as a curmudgeonly hanging judge. Some have even suggested that the Lord Chief Justice became sexually excited when donning the black cap and pronouncing the death sentence. However, he was occasionally caught in a lighter context. A woman who appeared before him had fallen off a bus and injured her jaw. Counsel held the conductor responsible for ringing the bell before she had alighted. In his nervousness Counsel blurted out, 'Through this unfortunate accident, caused by the gross negligence of the servant of the Defendant Company, my unfortunate client suffered this most grievous injury to her jaw with the dire result that she could not, for quite a long time afterwards, bite her bottom with her top teeth.'

In 1938 Goddard and Lord Clauson heard an appeal over some property by a Mr Frank Harrison. When they found against him he yelled, 'I want justice!' and pelted them with tomatoes. He was sent to Brixton for six weeks for contempt but was freed after three days because of a written apology in which he explained that he had not gone to court with the intention of throwing the tomatoes at the bench. 'I bought them for my lunch,' he said.

GOGARTY, Oliver St John. Oliver St John Gogarty, the turn-of-the-century Irish politician and writer, deserves to stand as a wit with the rest of the Irish connection – Congreve, Swift, Wilde, Shaw, etc. It is ironic that the Irish joke should be at the expense of a nation that has produced an unusual number of sharp minds. Oliver St John Gogarty is not as widely quoted as his fellow countrymen but I relish his reply on the occasion of a campaign that would have ruined the look of the Liffey. Gogarty had some ministerial responsibility to answer a question about prostitutes who entertained their clients against the trees that lined the river's banks. The motion was to cut them down. Gogarty put a stop to it in one sentence. 'Surely,' he argued, 'the trees are more sinned against than sinning.'

The Liffey brought out the best in him. When a gift of swans was bestowed upon the river he swam across alongside the birds. The Liffey at the time was notorious for the sewage which poured into it. Gogarty was asked if the experience had not been unpleasant. 'Oh no,' he dismissed it. 'It was no more than going through the motions.'

GOLDWYN, Samuel. I see that I did not mention Samuel Goldwyn in an earlier anthology – a man who would have given his name to the language if Sheridan had not got there before him with Mrs Malaprop, or Shakespeare with Dogberry, whose name somehow failed to 'take'.

Goldwyn's career, before he became a movie producer, was as a glove salesman. His partner was called Archie Selwyn. When they parted Goldwyn changed his name from Goldfish. Selwyn is reported to have said, 'Not only did he steal a large part of my money, he also stole half of my name.' There are those who have suggested that young Samuel stole the wrong half – he should have called himself 'selfish'.

Goldwyn was a perfectionist – and prepared to pay for perfection. His Goldwynisms are legendary and often endearing. 'A verbal contract isn't worth the paper it's written on'; 'I can answer you in two words "Im-possible"'; 'I don't care if my pictures don't make a dime as long as people see them.' He spent money on comedies saying, 'Our comedies are not to be laughed at.' He corrected a reporter who referred to 'William Wyler's *Wuthering Heights*', saying 'I made *Wuthering Heights*, Wyler only directed it.' 'Messages are for Western Union' was his. So was 'I was always an independent, even when I had partners' – but perhaps there's more truth than misunderstanding in that. What about 'The trouble with this business is the dearth of bad pictures'? 'Gentlemen, include me out' is famous; as are 'Let's have some new clichés' and 'I'll give you a definite maybe.' He is said to have said, 'I read part of the book right through'; and, to a member of a preview audience, 'Tell me, how did you live the picture?' Then there are: 'In this business it's dog eats dog and nobody eats me'; 'What we need is a story that starts with an earthquake and works its way up to a climax.' Of his wife's hands, which were being modelled, he offered,'Yes, I'm going to have a bust made of them.' Of one of his movies, 'It's more than magnificent, it's mediocre.' Of someone else's, 'If Roosevelt was alive he'd turn in his grave.' Generally, 'Directors are always biting the hand that lays the golden egg'; 'We have all passed a lot of water since then'; 'Anyone who goes to a psychiatrist should have his head examined'; 'I should be sticking my head in a Moose'; 'I had a great idea this morning. I didn't like it.'

There was comeback in his exchange with the writer James Thurber. Goldwyn said, 'I hope you didn't think it was too bloody and thirsty,' to which Thurber replied, 'Not only did I think so but I was horror and struck.' He greeted a synopsis of a story by Maurice Maeterlink, who was insect-happy, with, 'My God! The hero is a bee!' Early on in his movie career as the pace was speeding up he said to his secretary, 'We've got all those files out there, just sitting around. Go out there and throw everything out – but make a copy of everything first.' When the producer Arthur Hornblow told him he was going to name his son Arthur, Goldwyn exploded, 'Why Arthur? Every Tom, Dick and Harry is called Arthur.' Some ascribe the prompting incident to Jesse Lasky's second son, William. for Arthur, read William. Then there is 'You've got to take the bull by the teeth.' To one production assistant who brought him a budget to look over he exploded. The cost would ruin him. 'But, Mr Goldwyn, you said you wanted a spectacle.' 'Yes, but goddam it, I wanted an intimate spectacle!'

He shares with Louis B. Mayer, Harry Cohn, Jack Warner and Adolph Zukor the attribution of the famous sacking sentence 'Never let the bastard back in here – unless we need him.' He was not impressed by stars' demands – of Mary Pickford he said, 'It took longer to make one of Mary's contracts than it took to make one of her pictures.'

How many of these can be definitely ascribed to Goldwyn is problematical. Goldwyn's wife, Frances, said perhaps half. Some have doubtless been grabbed from other phrasemakers, others invented by PR persons building a legend. L. B. Mayer always insisted that when Goldwyn was reported to have said, 'First you have a good story, then a good treatment, and next a first-rate director. After that you hire a competent cast and even then you have only the mucus of a new picture,' he had actually said 'nucleus' but the publicity department was not content to leave it at that.

He got his own back once when his friend Abe Lehn objected to the title of an Eddie Cantor comedy tentatively entitled *Yes, Yes.* 'What's wrong with it?' Goldwyn asked. 'It's too negative.' Goldwyn was amazed. 'And they make out I say funny things!' he chuckled; but he changed the title.

F. Scott Fitzgerald's verdict on Goldwyn was succinct. 'You always knew where you stood with him. Nowhere.'

GOLF. As far as Mark Twain was concerned, 'Golf is a good walk spoiled.' Not so to Bob Hope. 'If you watch a game, it's fun. If you play it, it's recreation. If you work at it, it's golf.' To O. K. Brand, an American sportswriter, it was 'Cow pasture pool.'

To some it is educational – 'I learn English from American pros,' said Robert de Vicenzo; 'that is why I speak it so bad. I call it PGA English.' Another professional on the American circuit, Chi Chi Rodriguez, was also disarmingly frank: 'I'm playing like Tarzan and scoring like Jane.' H. G. Wells was merely an observer: 'The uglier a man's legs are, the better he plays golf – it's almost a law,' he wrote before the days of televised golf, where elegant young men, in immaculately pressed flannels and exotic footwear stroll confidently from tee to green, unruffled by cameras, spectators or the distractions which so disturbed one of P. G. Wodehouse's characters – 'The least thing upset him on the links. He missed short putts because of the uproar of butterflies in the adjoining meadow.'

GOOCH, Graham. Not one to set the table in a roar, the ex-England cricket captain Graham Gooch was born and raised in Leytonstone in Essex and became a professional cricketer after an apprenticeship in tool-making (you can take the man out of Essex but you can't take Essex out of the man). The Mitchell Symons 'One Minute Guide' in the London *Evening Standard* pinpointed his high-pitched voice in listing three things not to say to the then recently separated Graham Gooch if you met him:

'How's the missus?'
'You sound like Julie Burchill.'
'You should have picked that David Gower.'

GOODMAN, Benny. Benny Goodman had all the makings of a good subject for anecdotes. Apart from being a gifted musician and an unusually successful band leader he was eccentric, absent-minded, deadpan and ruthless.

Jazzman Artie Shaw told a Goodman story of the early thirties, before they were both famous. Shaw was deep in a book and Goodman teased him – to his mystification calling him 'J. B.'. Shaw finally asked what he meant by 'J. B.'.

'George Bernard,' said Goodman.

Peggy Lee recalls getting into a cab with Goodman who was deep in thought. He gave no instructions and the cab stayed motionless until the driver asked impatiently, 'Well, buddy?' Goodman came out of his reverie, fished for his wallet and started to get out of the cab saying, 'How much was that?'

André Previn and his trio went to rehearse for a recording with Goodman at his house in Connecticut. They finished playing at a club in New York and were required to be on parade at nine o'clock the next morning. It was a bitterly cold day, rehearsals were sluggish and the vocalist who was to record with them, Helen Wood, finally ventured, 'Benny, you know what the trouble is? It's just horribly cold in here.'

'You're absolutely right,' Goodman said, then pulled on a thick woollen sweater and carried on rehearsing.

The trouble with Goodman stories is that most of them, wrapped up in protestations of affection as they are, leave him looking mean. Jerry Jerome records an incident when he explained that he could not make a two o'clock rehearsal the next day. Goodman asks why. Jerome explains it's his grandfather's funeral. Goodman agrees, 'That's too bad.' Moments later he leans over in the middle of a number and says, 'Can't you get out of that thing?'

Zoot Sims remembered a session when he had bought an apple, a particularly tempting apple, and put it on his stand. 'I had a solo coming up. So Benny grabbed my apple, I stood up and took my solo, and it's the longest solo I ever had with Benny Goodman in my life. He kept signalling "One more" until he finished the apple. Then he said, "That's enough".'

I was always sorry that when Goodman turned up unexpectedly to see *Side by Side by Sondheim* when we were playing to full houses at Wyndham's Theatre, not a single seat could be found for him. On reflection we may have been let off lightly.

GOTTLIEB, Robert. Robert Gottlieb, who preceded Tina Brown as editor of the *New Yorker*, and before that was president and editor-in-chief of the prestigious American publishing house, Alfred Knopf, once passed a wet afternoon in the latter job devising an autumn list for a new publishing house which would be bound to fail. Topping the list was a book called *Canada, Our Good Neighbour to the North*.

GRACE, Dr W. G. Most anecdotes about the legendary nineteenth-century cricketer concern his arrogance towards umpires and opponents on the lines of 'They come to see me bat not to watch you umpire.' However, I am particularly fond of a most touching remark provoked from Grace during his last season when the elderly doctor felt the need to apologise for his inept fielding. 'It is the ground,' he moaned to the bowler he had let down. 'It's too far away.'

GRAINGER, Edmund. A meticulous producer, Edmund Grainger ordered genuine native Americans to supervise the smoke signals for his 1947 movie *The Fabulous Texan*. Before returning them to their reservation he congratulated them on their expertise. 'It was nothing,' one Indian explained. 'We learned how to do it from the movies.'

GRAUNIAD, The. When the *Guardian* newspaper was first faced with an editorial decision on the use of the 'F-word' (there had been race riots in America to report, and 'Fuck you' was a common, abrasive piece of graffiti), the meeting agonised long and hard about whether they should print it. They decided that they would be brave and, appropriately, it emerged in the paper as 'Fcuk'.

GREENE, Graham. In his autobiography the novelist Graham Greene tells how he was once asked by Sam Zimbalist, the American film producer, if he would put some polishing touches to a rewrite of the last part of the screenplay for the film of *Ben Hur*. 'You see,' said Zimbalist, 'we find a kind of anti-climax after the Crucifixion.'

GRENFELL, Joyce. Joyce Grenfell – most English and proper of comedians – sang a song by Michael Flanders and Donald Swann in one of the revues which Laurier Lister staged for her. It was a sort of almanac which started 'January brings the snow', and having rhymed its way through the twelve months moved on from December to 'Back to bloody January again'. Laurier Lister had a profound distaste for expletives and some way into rehearsals asked Grenfell if, 'for him', she would please substitute a less provocative word. She was firm in her refusal, announcing in her most cut-glass tones that having learnt the lyric that way she was afraid that if she changed it at that late stage she might become confused and find herself singing, 'Back to fucking January again.'
     The point was conceded.

GRIFFITH, D. W. (David Wark). The career of D. W. Griffith, the great innovative early auteur of the cinema, spanned the primitive one-reelers and exploded with the racist *Birth of a Nation* in 1915 based on Thomas Dixon's novel and play *The Clansman*, a racist glorification of the Ku-Klux-Klan. The film director marshalled huge crowds and action scenes – Woodrow Wilson called it 'like making history with lightning'. One anecdote has it that Griffith was inclined to pick his nose absent-mindedly in moments of directing stress. On this occasion he ordered a thousand horses in one direction and called for an adjustment in the position of an unruly mob. He was observed by a small child. Noticing the little boy's interest he turned to him patronisingly and asked if he would like to be a director when he grew up. 'No,' said the boy. Griffith, amazed, enquired why. 'My father doesn't let me pick my nose,' the child answered.

Griffith had started in movies as an extra – without much success because his movements were extravagantly jerky. This turned out to be because he had conscientiously researched the new medium and as everybody else's hands in silent films jerked wildly he was doing his best to imitate them.

Griffith was an early opponent of the dismissive word 'flickers', which he felt demeaned a medium which he was convinced would develop into a major art form. He had a nifty technique for outwitting censors – he used to research their special interests and then engage them in an appropriate conversation during suspect sequences. In 1920 in *Way Down East* he got away with a realistic child-bearing scene at a time when you were not even allowed to show scenes of women knitting baby garments in Pennsylvania.

GUITRY, Sacha. Sacha Guitry, the French actor dramatist, son of Lucien Guitry who plied the same trade, produced 130 plays and some 30 film scripts. He was married five times including, on the third occasion, to Yvonne Printemps. His popularity was life-long, except for a brief slip when he was suspected of pro-Nazi sympathies during World War Two. Somehow he survived to continue his history of theatrical success, marriage and many mistresses. It had been suggested that this relentless womanising was for show rather than out of conviction, since when he died in 1957 one of his ex-wives had only one comment – 'stiff at last'.

GURNEY, Sir John. Baron Gurney was a nineteenth-century judge with a reputation for toughness – both with counsel and criminals. So unsentimental was he that the popular supposition was that he had only wept on one occasion – when he went to a theatre to see *The Beggar's Opera*, and heard that Macheath had been reprieved.

— H —

HAAKON, King of Norway. Poor King Haakon had two unfortunate experiences at the hands of the BBC during the war. On one occasion he was to address his beleaguered people and the producer thought it appropriate to introduce his broadcast with a fanfare. Unfortunately the message to the gramophone library got scrambled and the solemn broadcast started with cries of 'Roll up! Roll up!' and 'Allez-Oop!' A record of a fun-fair had been substituted.

Bravely returning to the BBC on another occasion Haakon presented himself at reception and asked for a producer. 'Tell him the King of Norway is here,' he said. Distracted for a moment the unimpressed receptionist checked back as she was about to ring the studio: 'Which King did you say?'

The late King of Sweden, another tall monarch, was similarly discomfited more recently when introduced at a cocktail party by a social climber proud of his connections. Presenting a more modest acquaintance he said proudly, 'I don't think you know my great friend, the King of Norway.'

'Sweden!' snapped the furious King.

HALIFAX, Edward Wood, 3rd Viscount. It was Halifax on whom Neville Chamberlain called when Anthony Eden resigned over appeasement in 1938. I saw him once dining on High Table at Oxford and was struck by his immense height. He was a Yorkshire grandee naturally addicted to shooting. During the Munich crisis a journalist asked him if the late night and the intense business were not taking their toll. 'No,' said Halifax, 'not exactly. But it spoils one's eye for the high birds.'

HALL, Donald. Donald Hall, the poet, has written perhaps the most succinct line of all time. It is called 'Breasts' and it reads:

There is something between us.

In another poem, 'To a Water Fowl', he suggests the social problems of his profession:

> There are the women whose husbands I meet on aeroplanes
> Who close their briefcases and ask, 'What are *you* in?'
> I look in their eyes, I tell them I am in poetry . . .

HALS, Frans. Frans Hals, the seventeenth-century Dutch painter, was a great carouser. It was his habit to get drunk every evening and be put to bed by his pupils, who were privy to his invariable prayer, 'Dear Lord, carry me soon up to your high heaven.' This suggested a practical joke to the liveliest of his pupils, Adriaen Brouwer, who with three co-conspirators rigged up ropes through four holes in the ceiling above Hals's bed and when they had put him into it waited for the prayer, 'Carry me soon up to your high heaven' and proceeded to hoist him heavenwards. Convinced that his prayer had been answered the befuddled Hals added a postscript to his prayer, 'Not so fast, Lord, not so fast, not so fast,' and so on. The pupils lowered him back in place and did not let on for many years, but they had cured Frans Hals of his goodnight bid for heaven.

HAMILTON, William. William Hamilton, MP made a famous maiden speech in the House of Commons in 1755. It lasted for three hours and was described by Horace Walpole as 'perfection'. It transpired that it had been written for him by Dr. Johnson, and he never equalled it in spite of enlisting Burke and others in subsequent attempts. By the time he left the House many years later he was known as 'Single-Speech Hamilton'.

HAMLISCH, Marvin. Marvin Hamlisch, the prolific American popular composer, had his greatest success with the long-running Broadway musical *A Chorus Line*. The morning after the first night, theatrical New York was at his feet. Legend has it that the next day he was shopping in Bloomingdales with his mother, who was suitably impressed by his overnight transformation from working composer to multi-millionaire. Hamlisch spotted a beautiful blue cashmere or Vicuna sweater. He admired it – 'So buy it, Marvin,' his mother encouraged him.

'Oh no, I couldn't,' he protested modestly.

'Treat yourself.'

'No! No! I can't.'

'Marvin, you are the greatest, you're a hit, you are the toast of New York! Buy the sweater!'

'No, Mother, I can't.'

'But you can afford it. You could afford ten of them.'

'No, Mother. It's such a beautiful blue, but I can't!'
'Why not, Marvin?'
'Because then I really *would* have everything.'
I hope it is true. At least it's roughly the way John Guare tells the story.

HARRIS, Sir Percy. Sir Percy Harris was a well-known Liberal MP in the 1930s. His nickname in the Commons was 'the housemaid' because he regularly emptied the Chamber; a sort of forerunner of Paddy Ashdown.

HARRISON, Sir Rex. I have told a few Rex Harrison stories in *Theatrical Anecdotes*, but since his death several more have surfaced in Alexander Walker's biography – mainly emphasising that singleness, indeed selfishness, of purpose with which he pursued his career on stage and film.

In 1971, in New York, when he was dining with his fifth wife, Elizabeth, and some friends at '21, a young man came over to the table and said, 'It really is my day! We've come in on the last flight. You've given me so much pleasure through the years, Mr Harrison, I would like to take this opportunity to thank you.' Harrison smiled an irritated smile and nodded him away. He could not understand why he 'made such a fuss about his last flight. I came in on the last flight from London but I don't go on and on about it.' He hardly thought it made much difference when his wife explained, 'Rex, that was Neil Armstrong. He's just got back from the moon.'

While playing Pirandello's Henry IV in Los Angeles he and Elizabeth employed a camp black butler, 'Tosh', who wore dandified clothes and an obvious curly red wig. Moving to Boston and then to New York they invited him to pack up their things and follow them. On arrival in Boston Rex found that he was missing three favourite Herbert Johnson hats. Tosh was telephoned and told to be sure to bring them with him. A few days later Elizabeth heard that he had been murdered. Rex's reaction was characteristic. 'I suppose I'll never get my hats now.'

As the marriage sailed nearer the rocks, Elizabeth's friend Maria, Lady St Just, told Rex how worried she was about Elizabeth. 'She's so depressed. I have never seen anybody like this.' 'Oh, I have,' Harrison countered. 'All my other wives.'

Soon after, he was completing his autobiography. 'I have to know now. What are your plans?' he asked Elizabeth. 'My plans?' 'Plans for the future.' She was puzzled. 'I'm up to the last chapter of my book. I have to know how to finish the bloody thing. I can't leave us dangling in the air, can I? Are we going to be together when the book is published or aren't we?' In fact he dedicated the book to her but the marriage did not last much longer.

On another occasion Harrison was to sing a number from *My Fair Lady* at a charity show in Drury Lane. He asked the stage manager who was to introduce him and was told that it would be Anthony Quayle. 'Oh well,' he said testily, 'if I can't be introduced by a star, I may as well introduce myself.'

His will decreed that his ashes should be scattered around the hills at Portofino, for long his home. His second son, Carey, carried them there with the casket in the plane's overhead luggage compartment, 'Silently,' he records, 'apologising to my father for making him travel tourist class.'

HAWKINS, Henry (Lord Brampton). Mr Justice Hawkins was considered a good judge in the late nineteenth century, but he had a penchant for making life difficult for barristers appearing before him. He had a sharp tongue for the clergy too. When a chaplain who had preached the Assize sermon fished for a compliment Hawkins was merciless. 'It was a divine sermon,' he said. 'For it was like the peace of God – which passeth all understanding. And, like his mercy, it seemed to endure for ever.'

HEATH, Sir Edward. Ted Heath – the Tory ex-Prime Minister – is not a great source of anecdotes. He was, of course, famously excluded from *Desert Island Discs* for years because he was listed as having already appeared. The mistake occurred because of the band leader who shared his name and was famous far earlier.

John Campbell's 1993 biography revealed few stories but did prompt one from its reviewer, Julian Critchley. It is, perhaps, the best of those which illustrate Heath's lack of small talk.

When he was Prime Minister, an old friend, Sara Morrison, was appointed vice-chairperson of the Conservative party. This was popularly believed to be an attempt to 'turn Ted into a human being'. Soon after her arrival in office she attended the annual party agents' dinner which is held on the eve of the party conference. Heath was placed next to the wife of the chief agent. Ms Morrison, stranded some way away, saw that he seemed to be making little effort to converse.

Knowing why she was there, and possessing a keen sense of duty, she sent over her folded napkin. Inside she had written, 'For God's sake say something.' The Prime Minister opened it, read it and sent it back having written two words: 'I have.'

HECHT, Ben. The Hollywood screenwriter (and co-writer with Charles McArthur of *The Front Page*) claimed that he owed his move to Los Angeles in the 1920s to getting the sack from a Chicago tabloid. His offence? He supplied a headline for a story about a dentist who assaulted a patient in the dental chair: DENTIST FILLS WRONG CAVITY.

Hecht was sceptical of the claims of most Hollywood 'starlets', saying, 'Starlet is the name for any woman under thirty not actively employed in a brothel.'

He was sharp on the subject of David O. Selznick's reading habits too. Selznick loved movies based on books he had enjoyed as a boy, such as *David Copperfield* and *A Tale of Two Cities*. When he mooted the idea of *Little Lord Fauntleroy*, Hecht thought he had gone too far and cabled, THE TROUBLE WITH YOU, DAVID, IS THAT YOU DID ALL YOUR READING BEFORE YOU WERE TWELVE.

HEINE, Heinrich. Heine, the German Jewish poet born in Düsseldorf, left for Paris after the expulsion of Napoleon from Germany and the death of his hopes for any sort of liberal regime in his homeland.

When he lay on his death bed in 1856 his wife, by his side, prayed that God might forgive him. 'Have no fear, darling,' he said. 'He will forgive me – that's his job.'

HELLMAN, Lillian. When Lillian Hellman's play *The Children's Hour* opened to rave notices on Broadway, Samuel Goldwyn considered buying it for the movies. An aide hinted that there might be trouble – 'It's about Lesbians.'

'Don't worry,' said Goldwyn, 'we'll make them Americans.'
(It did get made in 1936 as *These Three* and again, with Shirley MacLaine, after the war.)

HEMINGWAY, Ernest. The celebrated twentieth-century writer and notorious misogynist Ernest Hemingway had an ingenious theory about the ideal, indeed the only, way for writers to work in Hollywood. He suggested a formal approach. 'Attended by their lawyers, the producer and the writer shall stand on either side of the California State Line. Simultaneously the writer shall throw his book to the producer and the producer shall throw across his cheque. Both shall drive off in opposite directions, never to meet or refer to the transaction ever again.'

HENRY I. Henry was the youngest and only English-born son of William the Conqueror. He spent most of his reign fighting the French but also administered great and popular reforms in the law. He was crafty and cruel and yet an able king with something of a reputation as a scholar – hence his nickname, Henry Beauclerc. 'An illiterate king is crowned an ass,' he said.

When he came to the throne at the age of 32 he had fathered 22 acknowledged royal bastards – still a record at the time of writing; but England expects. His father had left him money but no land, advising him to wait. After the death of his brother, William Rufus, he demanded the keys to the Treasury at Winchester. Refused them, he took his case to the people in the streets. promises were never so cheap nor yielded so much.

They included a charter of liberties. Promises of purity and an invitation to Archbishop Anselm to return from Rome banished the spectre of William Rufus's pathic court. Henry's record of 22 lapses was officially relegated to the past as soon as he announced his intention to marry Matilda, a good West Saxon princess conveniently lodged at Romsey. Within four days of William Rufus's death Henry had put his brother's bones beneath a cheap black gravestone, taken the keys of the Treasury and had crowned himself at Westminster by the Bishop of London.

Marrying and crowning his Queen took longer. Aunts do not usually play large parts in English history; but Matilda's aunt, Christina, somehow sensing that there are no small parts, only small actors, stretched her cameo role for three months, centre stage. Matilda and her sister Mary were still languishing in this harridan's care. Christina shared the devotion and determination of her late sister, the Scottish Queen Margaret. Never happier than in the thick, coarse black cloth spun out of horsehair which was the uniform of her order of black Benedictines, she had imprisoned her nieces in the same uncomfortable garb. Matilda wore it under protest and, as soon as she could escape her aunt, did a vicious dance on it.

Despite Henry's wish to marry, the Abbess Christina had no intention of letting the course of earthly love run smooth, and announced to the world that Matilda had already made her vows to God. If this was true she could not marry the King. Henry handed the problem to Archbishop Anselm, who called a council of the church at Lambeth.

Matilda made a passionate and convincing witness under cross-examination. She denied that either she or her parents had wanted a religious life for her. She painted a vivid picture of her forthright father tearing off the hated piece of black cloth with which her mother had once draped her. She admitted wearing the nun's habit at Romsey, but insisted that it was no more than a convenient device to ward off men whom she had no wish to marry. Warming to her theme she described how quickly she got out of it the moment her aunt's back was turned.

The cleric decided that Matilda was free to marry the King; but having got the verdict she wanted, Matilda allowed herself some perverse maidenly prevarication. Suddenly she showed a very feminine reluctance to tie herself to Henry. She can hardly have been unaware of his philandering; nor that across the Welsh border lurked the threat of the seductive Nesta of Pembroke. This Welsh

Princess had established herself as Leading Other Woman and been conveniently married off by Henry to Gerald de Windsor, a pleasant and pliable courtier who allowed his sovereign discreet access to his wife.

For the moment, however, Nesta had to take a back seat as Henry and his court persuaded the reluctant bride to accept his proposal despite, or perhaps because of, a final gesture by the never-say-die Christina, a baleful curse of bride, groom and offspring. To counteract the curse, Henry staged a particularly splendid joint wedding and coronation in Westminster Abbey. Anselm mounted his pulpit and told the congregation firmly that there was neither just cause nor impediment why the two should not be joined in matrimony and dared anyone to bring forward proof to the contrary. The couple embarked on a married life of such decorous respectability that courtiers who preferred William Rufus's dissolute regime sniggered behind their backs and nicknamed them Godric and Godiva, Saxon models of propriety.

Matilda bore Henry two children, William and Alice (who was quickly renamed Matilda). During the latter period of their married life Henry spent much of his time on long campaigns in Normandy, while Matilda remained at home holding court at Westminster, surrounding herself with a cosmopolitan circle of musicians, poets and scholars, but farming her properties rapaciously and rack-renting her tenants with a vigour which would have done her dead brother-in-law credit. She took from the rich to finance the artistic; but that did little to endear her to those whose wealth she was redistributing.

After seventeen years of marriage, Matilda died in May 1118, mourned in her husband's absence by Christina, who retired to a hermitage by a holy water-spring at Kilburn. (The holy status of the site declined as it became first a priory; then, by the nineteenth century, a public house; and finally, in the twentieth, an underground station.) Henry, though reported to be grief-stricken, did not allow his 'corroding melancholy' to interrupt his campaign against Louis, King of France, until he had won.

In November 1120, Henry set sail for England. The mood of victory was still sweetly in the air and the celebrations for Prince William's marriage gave added excuse for partying. The King's entourage, which included the new princess, set sail first. The Prince and his fellow revellers, an entire generation of English aristocrats, including two royal bastards as well as the legitimate heir, were to follow in the *Blanche-Nef*. The 'White Ship', the finest in the Norman navy, was commanded by Fitz-Stephen, son of the man who had captained the Conqueror's ship *Mona*, on the historic voyage to Pevensey in 1066. In a grand gesture, Prince William ordered three casks of wine for the crew so that they might share in the high spirits of his long-drawn-out wedding reception.

The generosity was fatal. It was only after a night of drinking that they got under way, and if the guests were riotous the crew matched their high spirits. Fitz-Stephen was determined to prove that he commanded the fastest ship afloat, a craft which he was convinced could overhaul the King's, which had set sail so much earlier. He crammed on all speed and hit a rock with disastrous precision.

Reports of the tragedy differ. In one account, William bravely goes back to save his drowning illegitimate sister (yet another Matilda) and sacrifices his life for her. In ecclesiastical literature the voyage is dismissed as one more judgement on a boatload of drunken teenage catamites. William is included in the monks' disapproval, as he seems to have been headstrong and arrogant, contemptuous of the English and no great loss.

Only one man survived, a butcher from Rouen who clung to the top of the mast and was rescued in the morning. Even the captain, an exceptionally strong swimmer, stopped trying to save himself when he learned that the King's son was drowned. For three days no one dared tell Henry that his heir was dead. Finally, his nephew, Theobald of Blois, sent in a favourite page to break the news. The King's grief was terrible, and he was popularly supposed never to have smiled again. However, his tears did not blind him to the charms of the young widow's dowry, which he refused to surrender. As she had resolved to become a nun, she had little use for it.

Henry was now 53 and his set ways were thrown into confusion. The hunt for an heir was on and before he could get one, Henry needed a bride. Adeliza of Louvain had all the correct credentials. She was descended from Charlemagne. She was young (under twenty), beautiful (known as 'The Fair Maid of Brabant'), and talented (no one embroidered a standard more neatly); above all, she was available, and a deal was struck.

Adeliza took her wifely duties seriously. She even commissioned a book on zoology so that she might better appreciate her husband's menagerie at Woodstock – but six years passed and she gave the Lion of Justice no cubs.

In 1126 the Emperor of Germany died, making Henry's termagant daughter the Empress Matilda a possible candidate for her father's throne. She remarried, to the young Geoffrey of Anjou, and the birth of Henry I's first grandson brought the old man to Normandy for the last time, more serene now in the pride of grandfatherhood, except at night when dreams of his victims appeared to threaten him, along with the memory of Luke de Barre, a companion of his youth, and later a troubadour knight whose satirical verses had prompted Henry to have his eyes torn out on the scaffold – a form of literary criticism for satirists mercifully discontinued.

On 25 November 1135, Henry went hunting near St Denis le Froment. He overtired himself and, returning at the end of the day, gulped down a dish of stewed lampreys, his favourite food. Of course, his doctor had expressly forbidden him to tax his troublesome stomach with the dish. The 'surfeit' of spiced eels induced acute indigestion; a fever set in and within a week he was dead. His end was more dignified than his father's (his bowels were interred in Rouen), or his brother William's (his embalmed corpse was brought home in state to England); perhaps his remains owed their careful disposition to the fact that he entrusted his obsequies to his oldest bastard.

HENRY II. Henry II was born at Le Mans to the Empress Matilda and her teenage husband, Geoffrey, Count of Anjou. His character gives the lie to the canard that King Stephen was his real father. Both Stephen and Geoffrey were called handsome and Henry was not; but Geoffrey became (like his son) a shrewd and active administrator, and Stephen did not. Henry owed to Matilda some of his restless energy and to Henry I his grasp of public affairs; but in him the Norman legacy of cruelty skipped a generation.

Henry paced and raced through life wearying his courtiers with his demonic energy, ignoring the sores and blisters his restless striding step inflicted on his feet. The family energy took him as eagerly into the study as it did to follow the chase. Physical exercise over for a moment, he would throw himself into the mastery of languages, though he spoke only French and Latin. As he was growing up the fashion for Roman Law was beginning to spread through Europe, and to King Stephen's alarm, 'then were laws and lawyers first brought into England'. Henry lapped up the law with the same thoroughness he devoted to everything.

Though Henry could manipulate the civil law almost unperceived, he could not encroach upon the authority of the church courts without open conflict. He insisted on the King's right to punish criminal clergy who had already had an ecclesiastical hearing. At any period in the Middle Ages his claim would have been disputed, but his timing dealt him two formidable opponents – a vigorous reforming pope, Gregory VII, and an Archbishop of Canterbury, Thomas Becket, who was in one sense to make him famous, and in another to obliterate his achievements.

Romantic, partisan fiction has unleashed a picture of Thomas Becket as a humble, saintly servant of God, resisted and finally murdered by a monstrous tyrant. The hero of this myth was the son of rich Norman merchant parents who settled in London. When his family lost its wealth, he became clerk in the counting house of a relative; and through childhood friends he was admitted into the household of Archbishop Theobald. As Theobald grew older, Becket's influence increased, especially in framing the Archbishop's advice to the King on secular matters. From there it was a short step for this dazzling courtier to become the King's chancellor. He relished the political challenge and was relieved to be rid of his religious responsibilities.

Becket lived magnificently, keeping open house and a lavish table. The chancellor's food and wine was served in gold and silver vessels, in piquant contrast to the King's regular menu of 'half-baked bread, sour wine, stale fish and bad meat'. Henry visited him regularly like a gawping tourist fascinated by the stunning display of which he heard ever more highly coloured reports.

When Becket was dispatched as ambassador to Paris the show he put on dazzled France. As his more-than-royal progress made its way along the northern French roads, men rushed to call their neighbours to stare at the English chancellor's splendour, asking one another, 'If this is the chancellor, what must his master be?' In an attempt at cornering the market in hospitality, Louis forbade the tradesmen of Paris to sell food to his visitors, but Thomas disguised his cooks and sent them under assumed names to stock up from the markets around the capital. For decades, French gourmets were to rhapsodise over a dish of eels (an unfortunate echo of lampreys?) which was prepared by the English and which cost a hundred shillings sterling. It was the most picturesque proof of Becket's prodigality and perhaps the only recorded instance of an English culinary triumph on French soil.

Archbishop Theobald's death in 1162 provoked the critical domestic crisis of Henry's reign. To the King, Becket represented the perfect replacement. He would surely be loyal, understanding and cooperative.

Henry cruelly misjudged his man. Becket picked up the job of church's champion with fanatical devotion. A test case soon presented itself. Philip of Broi, Canon of Bedford, was cleared of a murder charge by the Bishop of Lincoln's court. The King wanted the civil courts to hear the case. He was concerned by the lawlessness of his country, and more especially by the number of crimes committed by the clergy. A simple solution seemed to be that the church should disown its priests who were guilty of violent crimes. Becket refused to yield any of his clerks up to secular justice, fled to the Continent and got the Pope's ear first. King and Archbishop continued to fight their corners with all the ferocity of old friends.

After six years of exile, fulminating from the pulpits of Europe, Becket returned, after an attempt at reconciliation, to preach a hell-fire sermon in Canterbury Cathedral. The news reached Henry in France. 'Will no one rid me of this meddlesome priest?' he is believed to have said: and four knights, accustomed to obeying their master's every whim, rode to slaughter Becket in a corner of his cathedral, despatching him to martyrdom, sainthood and a popular place in history.

Henry's Queen, Eleanor of Aquitaine, eventually tired of her position at the side of the stage while Henry's infidelities were stage centre. Tiring of the enter-tainers with whom she surrounded herself, she devised a new amusement for herself, setting her sons against their father and meddling through them. Fingers were pointed at her when Henry's mistress Rosamund Clifford died; but by then Eleanor was imprisoned in her palace at Winchester, and it is unlikely that she would have had a hand in Rosamund's death in a nunnery. (Wilder rumours suggested that she discovered the affair with Rosamund by following the clue of a ball of silk attached to Henry's spur which led her to a thicket in the grounds of the palace of Woodstock. Concealed in a corner of the park, she came upon Rosamund innocently engaged on embroidery, and in Edward III's reign the place was still known as 'Rosamund's Chamber'.

Rosamund Clifford had two children by Henry and spent her last years in the nunnery of Godstow. After her death St Hugh, Bishop of Lincoln, disapproved of her elaborate memorial, saying that the grave of 'a harlot was not a fit specta-cle for a quire of virgins to contemplate'. His strict reaction may, of course, have been due to the fact that one of Rosamund and Henry's bastards was by now his Archbishop; Geoffrey, the only son of Henry's to tend him at his death.

On his death bed at Chinon, Henry cursed his other offspring and angrily refused the requests of the assembled Bishops to revoke the curses. On the sev-enth day of his fever, Henry seemed better and spoke gently to Geoffrey of how he hoped to see him become Bishop of Winchester or Archbishop of York. 'You alone have proved yourself my lawful and true son, my other sons are really the bastards,' he told him. He took off his jewelled ring and gave it to Geoffrey with his blessing, then was carried into the chapel of the castle and before the altar he confessed his sins and was absolved.

Having overtired himself and the patience of his heirs, he died and promptly suffered the same indignities as his great-grandfather. Servants who should have laid out the body instead stripped and plundered it before William the Marshal arrived to cover it with his own cloak and prepare it for burial. Within 24 hours, Henry was robed and crowned as if for a coronation, borne by his faithful barons down from the rock of Chinon, across a viaduct which he himself had con-structed over the swampy meadows, along the left bank of the winding Vienne river to his burial place. 'He shall be shrouded among the shrouded women' was a whispered prophecy during the last months of his reign and so he was, sur-rounded by the nuns of Fontevrault.

HENRY III. Henry III was King John's eldest son and the first minor to suc-ceed. Henry's long reign (1216–1272) was undistinguished but for his great work – his twenty-year sponsorship of the new church at Westminster. It was dedicated on 13 October 1269 (at a third of the cost of his son Edward I's subsequent expedition to breathe fire and slaughter in the Holy Land).

HENRY IV. Henry IV's position was precarious from the outset. His claims to the throne were dubious, and his suspicious supporters insisted on rewards which straitened his already strained financial circumstances still more. His experience of government consisted almost entirely of opposition to the previous regime.

In contrast to his cousin Richard II, whom he deposed, Henry was not tall, willowy and elegant, but short and stocky, with a thick russet beard. Thirty-two at his accession, he had in his character some of his family's energy, bravery and instinct for adventure, but it was not rounded by any touch of the original or unorthodox. Flashes of Plantagenet temper led him to occasional acts of harshness and cruelty, but his behaviour was more often governed by the reserve and suspicion which every survivor needed to stay alive in dangerous times; by doubts which troubled his conscience more and more as he grew older; and by recurring illnesses which sapped his strength and initiative and made a mockery of the later years of his reign, killing him off by the time he was 47.

Shakespeare's version of the events of Henry's reign concentrates on the Percy rebellion, led by Henry, Earl of Northumberland and his son Harry Hotspur. While inventing Hotspur's death at the hand of the Prince of Wales (he was in fact killed by an unknown archer's arrow), Shakespeare oddly ignored a true anecdote.

Hotspur had been told by a fortune teller that he would die at Berwick, and being a man of the North he assumed this meant Berwick-upon-Tweed. It was not until the eve of the fatal battle that he found he had stationed his troops near the hamlet of Berwick in Shropshire.

Towards the end of his final illness, Henry suffered a stroke as he was praying in Westminster Abbey. He was carried to the Abbot's Lodging, where he was placed in the Jerusalem Chamber. When he was told where he was, Henry (like Hotspur earlier) recognised a prophecy coming home to roost. The King had once been told that he would die in Jerusalem, and had assumed he would die in the Holy City, but now realised that consecrated ground was the most he could hope for. Even there he was not at peace, though – looking for his crown he was told that his son had taken it away. Summoned to his father's side, the future Henry V explained that he had taken the crown believing the King to be dead. 'My fair son,' said the guilt-racked King, 'what right have you to it, for you well know I had none?'

Soon after, Henry IV died, allowing his son to claim the crown without further parental admonition.

HENRY V. Henry V was ambitious to improve on the low standard set by his father. His accession was popular and he presented an identikit picture of a prac-tical, high-minded King. Moved by a piety which bordered on the fanatical, he consulted religious recluses and visited sacred shrines. He spent the first night after his father's death in solitary prayer, and he refused to be interrupted during divine service. It is not surprising that this aura of sanctity should make him seem self-righteous and too good to be true – or at least too good to be attractive.

His first weeks in office had the purposeful optimism of a modern 'first hun-dred days'. He knew himself to be just, thorough, sober, devout and concilia-tory, as well as energetic. He had confidence in his experience as an organiser and as a diplomat. That he was a renowned soldier could only stack the cards still further in his favour.

Shakespeare has chronicled the tennis-ball incident, the breach at Honfleur, Agincourt and the victory on the feasts of St Crispin and Crispinian. He tactfully omits a description of Henry's bride, Catherine of Valois, who although she was known as 'Catherine the Fair' needed all her vivacity to cancel the effect of a long nose which hung down 'almost to her upper lip'.

He was particularly disappointed that his son was born at Windsor while he was campaigning in France, laying his last great siege to the city of Meaux. According to his chamberlain he produced an impromptu quatrain on hearing the news:

> I, Henry, born at Monmouth,
> Shall small time reign and much get;
> But Henry of Windsor shall long reign, and lose all,
> But as God will, so be it.

The cold-blooded discipline of Henry's life was not disturbed by the fever which brought it to a close. His last days were spent conscientiously tying up his affairs. In his last moments he was as eager as ever to proclaim the justice of his claim to the throne of France, and throughout the last night of his life he re-iterated, in the arms of his confessor, his disappointment at not retaking Jerusalem. His last words were an affirmation of his certainty that he was right: barely conscious, he muttered to an imagined antagonist, 'You lie! You lie! My portion is with the Lord Jesus!'

His embalmed corpse was seen off from Paris in a coffin covered by silk and a scarlet cushion. On top sat his effigy – life-size. Four magnificent horses drew the bier. They left the Bois de Vincennes at night escorted by torch-bearers in white. Five hundred men-at-arms mounted on black horses and clad in black armour dipped their lances. Their arrival in London was in solemn contrast to the festivities after Agincourt; but the last rites were the most splendid so far accorded to an English King. His funeral cost £1052. 15s. 7d. Queen Catherine paid for his effigy.

In a macabre postscript Samuel Pepys records that he once kissed her. She died in 1437 at the age of 36, having been subsequently married to Owen Tudor, or at least lived with him and borne him children, and her 'skelleton' was laid beside her husband's in the Confessor's Chapel at Westminster. As a 'special visitor' Pepys, on a day out with his wife and daughters, was allowed to see the 'Bones firmly united and thinly clothed with Flesh, like Scrapings of tanned leather.' Pepys recorded: 'and here we did see, by perticular favour, the body of Queen Katherine of Valois, and had her upper part of her body in my hands. And I did kiss her mouth, reflecting upon it that I did Kiss a Queen, and that this was my birthday, 36 years old, that I did first kiss a Queen.' He had paid an extra twopence for the privilege.

HENRY VI. Henry V's son succeeded to the throne when he was nine months old. Later a feeble and politically inept King, never outgrowing his childish gentleness and naïvety, he inherited the Lancastrian piety of his father's side, together with recurring bouts of madness, perhaps the legacy of his maternal grandfather, Charles VI of France.

Legend has it that even aged two he manifested a religious obsession, refusing to move from Staines to Westminster on a Sunday out of his respect for the Sabbath. Another fable has him attending the trial of Joan of Arc when he was eight. As there are still attempts in progress to have him canonised, there may have been more than one saint in that courtroom. He dressed simply, 'in round-toed shoes and boots like a farmer's. He also customarily wore a long gown with a rolled hood like a townsman, and a full coat reaching below his knees, with shoes, boots and footgear wholly black, rejecting expressly all curious fashion of clothing.' His only lasting memorial is the foundation of Eton and King's College, Cambridge, endowed in great part by £2,000 in gold bequeathed him by his uncle the Bishop of Winchester – an enormous sum in those days, which he would not accept for himself but only for those two seats of learning. 'Forsoothe and forsoothe' was his only method of swearing, and then only to point home that he meant what he said. He was shocked by a Christmas dancing display at Windsor when a courtier arranged a dance of bare-breasted women and equally upset by naked men taking the waters together in Bath.

Henry VI came of age in 1437 and the sixteen-year-old King's authority was soon sabotaged by his slack hand on the reins of government and Jack Cade's revolt, but he had already laid up trouble by his marriage to Margaret of Anjou. A document dating from 1458 suggests that when she arrived in England in 1445 he dressed as a squire and delivered her a note from himself. She was so occupied with the letter that he had ample time to study her. Later the Earl of Suffolk asked what she thought of the messenger and she 'was vexed at not having known it, because she had kept him on his knees'.

Eight years into their marriage Margaret presented him with their only child, Prince Edward: but at that time Henry was undergoing a complete mental breakdown and recognised no one – not even his wife and baby. He recovered at Christmas 1454. The nation rejoiced, and finally seeing his son Henry remarked vaguely that it might be his 'or God's'. Contemporary historians suggest that 'if Henry's insanity had been a tragedy, his recovery was a national disaster'.

By now the dominating force was the Queen, whose maternal instincts drove her to do everything for her son. One anecdote has her and her boy surprised in a forest by a murderous cutthroat; the Queen threw herself at his feet and pleaded for mercy for her son so effectively that the robber burst into tears and vowed that he would mend his ways and serve his prince.

Her talent for special pleading was useless to Queen Margaret as the Lancastrian and Yorkist factions squared up for the Wars of the Roses – a squabble involving seven Kings from Richard II to Richard III, all of whom were descendants of King Edward III.

In the course of this prolonged struggle, the King's heir, Edward, Prince of Wales, was killed – or more probably executed – at the Battle of Tewkesbury in 1471, and the King himself was deposed by Edward IV.

The murder of her son robbed Margaret of Anjou of her last trace of ambition. She could summon up no interest in the claims of any obscure Lancastrian who might come forward to advance them. Now that Henry's heir was dead, Edward had no reason, apart from moral scruples, to keep the Mad King alive, and he was killed at the Tower. According to some Yorkist chroniclers, Henry died of 'pure displeasure and melancholy'. Others suggest a more violent end: 'That night between eleven and twelve o'clock was King Henry, being prisoner in the Tower, put to death, the Duke of Gloucester and divers men being in the Tower.' He probably died in the octagonal room in the Wakefield Tower that had been his prison for so long. Next day his body was exposed at St Paul's, and there 'the silent witness of the blood that welled from his fresh wounds upon the pavement' gave an indication of the manner of his death. That evening his hearse was loaded on to a torch-lit barge, and rowed to the Abbey of Chertsey, where it was interred and 'where it was long pretended that miracles were performed at his tomb.'

It was a bloody end for one of the few medieval monarchs who showed an inclination to oppose the barbarous standards of his day, as this story illustrates: 'Once when he was coming down from St Albans to London through

Cripplegate, he saw over the gate there was the quarter of a man on a tall stake, and asked what it was. And his lords made answer that it was the quarter of a traitor of his, who had been false to the King's majesty, he said, "Take it away, I will not have any Christian man so cruelly handled for my sake." '

HENRY VII. Anecdotally Henry VII does not yield rich pickings except in his careful cost cutting. The King's almoner, Christopher Urswick, offers one story, though. A rash astrologer foretold the King's death and suggested that it would happen inside the year. Summoning the man, the King required him to forecast what he (the astrologer) would be doing on Christmas Day. The astrologer could not tell him so Henry said, 'Then I am a better astrologer than you. I can tell where you will be – in the Tower of London,' to which he then committed him. 'And when he had lain there till his spirit of divination was a little cooled, the King ordered him to be dismissed for a silly fellow.'

Henry's reign was also enlivened by two pretenders to the throne. Lambert Simnel, the son of an Oxford joiner, was taught courtly manners by a priest, Simons, and passed off as the son of the Duke of Clarence. When Simnel's supporters were defeated the King had mercy on him, making him first of all turn the spit and do menial jobs in the royal kitchens and finally promoting him to training the King's hawks.

The second pretender was Perkin Warbeck, who purported to be the younger son of Edward IV, Richard, Duke of York. Warbeck was born in Tournay and made his attempt on the throne in Ireland. He too was defeated, and again the King was merciful. Warbeck and his wife were given freedom at court, but when Warbeck first tried to escape and later plotted against the King, Henry got rid of him and his co-conspirator Edward, Earl of Warwick.

One of the most colourful characters in Henry VII's reign, Gerald FitzGerald, 8th Earl of Kildare, was cleared of alleged treason against the King. A courtier remarked to Henry, 'All England cannot rule yonder gentleman.' Henry said smartly, 'No? Then he is meet to rule all Ireland.'

There is a final irony in Henry's meanness, which manifested itself in his diligently kept account books. According to Francis Bacon, the King had a pet monkey who was encouraged by a courtier to tear up his meticulous accounts – which it did with enormous glee.

HENRY VIII. Henry VIII is probably the best-known monarch in the history of Britain, the Queens Elizabeth and Victoria presenting the nearest challenges. However, he is not the most abundant source of anecdote, from his unusually tall, sturdy and handsome youth to his bloated older age. Mostly, he is familiar for his marital exploits – 'divorced, beheaded, died; divorced, beheaded, survived.'

Sir Thomas More early told his son-in-law Roper that though the King 'doth as singularly favour me as any subject within this realm howbeit . . . I have no cause to be proud thereof, for if my head would win him a castle in France . . . it should not fail to go.' It did go, of course, after the dispute with Rome. Cardinal Wolsey was the first to be dismissed for failing to deliver the dissolution of Henry's marriage to his first wife, Catherine of Aragon, whose hand the King inherited after the death of his older brother, Prince Arthur, who had married her when she was fifteen some five months earlier. On his death bed the disgraced Wolsey said, 'If I had served God as diligently as I have done the King, he would not have given me over in my grey hairs.'

After the birth of his first daughter, Mary, in 1516, Henry wrote to Catherine, 'We are both young. If it is a daughter this time, by the Grace of God the sons will follow.' But they did not and Henry was at odds with the church. Anne Boleyn was not his only mistress during Catherine's life. He also seduced Anne's sister Mary and had a son by one of Catherine's ladies, Bessie Blount. This child, at the age of six, was named Duke of Richmond and St James's Palace was built to be his residence.

The Bishop of Rochester, John Fisher, was the next prelate to incur Henry's wrath – a process speeded when the Pope made him a cardinal, which infuriated Henry. He was beheaded in 1535. According to Jasper Ridley, the King said that 'as Fisher had been given a Cardinal's hat he would cut off Fisher's head and sent it to Rome to have the hat put upon it'. The prophetic More followed two weeks later. He was scathing about the insubstantial structure of the scaffold. 'I pray you, Master lieutenant,' he said to the officer in charge, 'see me safe up, and for my coming down I will shift for myself.'

Anne Boleyn was certainly Henry's great passion – 'I have now been above one whole year stricken with the dart of love,' he wrote to her in 1527. And, in more risqué style, 'Wishing myself (specially of an evening) in my sweetheart's arms, whose pretty dukkys [breasts] I trust shortly to kiss.' She held out for marriage but failed to produce a male heir – only a slip of a girl called Elizabeth.

Jane Seymour, who had been a waiting woman both to Queen Catherine and to Anne Boleyn, married Henry the day after Anne's execution – she was never crowned but she provided her husband with a sickly heir and died as a result of the labour which produced Edward VI. 'Divine Providence hath mingled my joy with the bitterness of her who brought me this happiness.' wrote Henry to Francis, the French king.

Henry continued to romance ladies of the Court. Once, while travelling along the Thames from Westminster to Greenwich to call on a woman he fancied, he is said to have challenged Sir Andrew Flamock to compose an impromptu rhyme in her honour. The King went first:

> Within the tower
> There lieth a flower
> That hath my heart.

A scurrilous version of Sir Andrew's hooray-henryish response has come down as:

> Within this hour
> She pissed full sower
> And let a fart.

The King was not amused.

Much has been made of the plainness and body-odour of 'The Flemish Mare', Anne of Cleves, and of the touched-up miniature which preceded her as a sort of marriage broking advertisement.

When Henry was 55, he died of a fever resulting from an ulcer, and was survived by his sixth wife, Catherine Parr. He was obese and his legs were hugely swollen. According to J. J. Scarisbrick's *Henry VIII*, 'Though he was carried about indoors in a chair and hauled upstairs by machinery, he would still heave his vast, pain-racked body into the saddle to indulge his love of riding and to show himself to his people, driven by an inexorable will to cling to his ebbing life.'

'I never spared men in my anger,' he once said, 'nor women in my lust.'

HERTZ, The Very Revd. Dr J. H. In the summer of 1940 when things were looking pretty black for Britian, the Chief Rabbi, The Very Revd. Dr J. H. Hertz, was lunching with King George VI. According to Chips Channon's diary he assured the monarch that all would finally be well, adding lightly, 'All the same, sir, I would put some of the colonies in your wife's name.'

HILLYER, Lambert. According to Paul F. Beller's book of *Hollywood Anecdotes*, the director Lambert Hillyer, directing *The Shock* in 1923, jumped from a second-storey window during a rehearsal and broke his arm. Irving Thalberg was not amused. 'I told you to hire a double for this stunt,' he shouted examining Hillyer's broken arm. 'I did,' moaned Hillyer, 'but I had to show him how to do it.'

HIRSCHFELD, Al. Al Hirschfeld, the immensely famous American cartoonist, and his wife, Dolly, had a daughter, Nina, who one day expressed a wish to draw. They bought her everything an aspiring artist needs from easel to paints, brushes and paper. They equipped a studio for her. Whenever they visited the studio all they could find were papers littering the studio and entirely blank but for the signature 'By Nina Hirschfeld' at the bottom of each page.

Of course, many less ambitious pictures have been sold to galleries. Was Ms Hirschfeld daunted by her father's skills? And is that why Hirschfeld incorporates 'Nina's' into all his caricatures and lists the number beside his own signature?

HITCHCOCK, Alfred. Recent biographies have emphasised the dark side of Alfred Hitchcock. His attitude to actors summed up in his remark 'Actors are cattle' is represented in a number of anecdotes. During the filming of *Lifeboat* in 1944 a young actress, Mary Anderson, was anxious to impress Hitchcock with her professionalism and to learn how to gain from flattering photography. 'Which do you think is my best side, Mr Hitchcock?' she asked him early in the shooting. Hitchcock did not even give her a look, 'My dear,' he said, 'you're sitting on it.'

Hitchcock further defined his attitude to actors saying, 'My favourite is the actor who can do nothing well. By that I mean one who has presence, authority and can attract attention without actually doing anything. I suppose I really mean control.'

One of his problems was his passion for cool, blonde actresses – his moods ranging from sweetness to sadism. Tippi Hedren described him. 'Emotionally he had all kinds of frustrations and neuroses . . . He thought of himself as looking like Cary Grant. That's tough, to think of yourself one way and look another.'

Tallulah Bankhead was one actress who earned his respect on *Lifeboat* for her endurance and her salty tongue. She was subjected to a variety of ordeals as ocean storm disasters were reproduced in an enormous studio tank. When she gave up wearing underwear and climbed the ladder to enter the tank there were protests – but Hitchcock declined to reprimand her. 'It could be a matter for wardrobe,' he said, 'or perhaps for make-up – or maybe it's even for hairdressing.'

He met his match in the head of studio music when the question of scoring *Lifeboat* arose. Hitchcock wanted no background music because in this ocean epic people would wonder where it was coming from. 'Ask Mr Hitchcock,' responded his opponent, 'where the camera comes from and I'll tell him where the music comes from.'

Psycho is arguably Hitchcock's most famous thriller – especially for the bloodletting scene when Janet Leigh is murdered in the shower. It certainly upset one man, who wrote to Hitchcock to complain that since his wife had seen the movie she could not be persuaded to bathe or shower. What should he do? 'Sir,' replied Hitchcock, 'have you ever considered sending your wife to a dry cleaner?'

I only met the great cockney film director, 'Master of Suspense', on one occasion. Bernard Levin invited me to appear with Hitchcock and Ian Fleming's widow, Anne, on a late-night television interview show and in a sycophantic moment I decided to tell a story that I thought flattered the starriest guest.

An extremely nervous, indeed claustrophobic to boot, friend of mine had gone to the cinema to see a movie – an innocuous movie. Somehow he had got himself into the wrong house. The auditorium was crowded but he was directed to a single, centre seat and settled down for a good laugh. The curtains parted and the Censor's Certificate announced *Psycho* – quite soon the credits revealed that this was an Alfred Hitchcock film. My friend had heard of Hitchcock and would not have gone near one of his scarifying shows given the chance. However, he was trapped centre row so he settled down to behave as beautifully as he could. He held out until the hushed house was watching the shower scene and Janet Leigh's stabbing.

Holding the sides of his seat he tried to stay calm but then the silence was broken by a man sitting next to him who chuckled appreciatively in a low and sinister register. 'Heh-heh-heh!'

My friend forgot politesse and fled the theatre. I offered this as a tribute to the Master.

He looked down his nose. 'You must have very naïve friends, Mr Sherrin,' he sniffed.

No more homage.

HOBSON, Sir Harold. Harold Hobson was the drama critic of the *Sunday Times* for years, succeeding James Agate, whose last years in the job had been jeopardised by a scandal in a male brothel near Gray's Inn Road. Agate had always encouraged his secretary Alan Dent to believe that he would succeed him but betrayed him by recommending Hobson, an appointment which suited his publisher, Lord Kemsley. 'Hobson's all right. Hobson has a daughter, let's have Hobson.'

With his particular passion for French plays and French performers Hobson fulfilled his long tenure honourably – in spite of Penelope Gilliat's crack that Sunday mornings were enlivened by 'the sound of Harold Hobson barking up the wrong tree'.

His passion for France led to a meeting with one of his idols, Jean Genet, in La Coupole. When they were introduced he showered Genet with compliments. Puzzled, Genet asked, 'Alors, monsieur, est-ce que vous êtes pédéraste?' 'Non, monsieur,' Hobson replied. 'Je suis critique.'

Another version has him welcoming Genet at London airport. Hobson's daughter had come with him to drive the car. In answer to Genet's query, 'Est-ce que vous êtes pédéraste?' Hobson's reply was a flurried 'Certainly not, this is my daughter.'

Because of lameness Hobson was always early in his seat at the theatre and left considerably later than the rest of the audience. Unwittingly I once made a cruel jest about his lameness which he instantly forgave. I was writing a diary in the *Sunday Times* about the opening week of the revue *Side by Side by Sondheim* at the Mermaid in 1976 (only seventeen years ago and ticket prices were from 75 pence to £5.95 for combined theatre and dinner). I commented on the various reactions of the critics whom I could spot from the stalls and by an unfortunate printing transposition the phrase 'Harold Hobson was first up the aisle' crept into the text – a description which I had applied to another, able-bodied critic. When the paper arrived on Sunday morning I sped an apology and an explanation round to his flat in Dolphin Square. I got a magnanimous letter back saying that he and his wife had laughed a great deal – especially as she was always chiding him for his tardy exits.

At his memorial service at St Paul's, Covent Garden, in November 1992, the critic John Peter recalled Hobson in mischievous mood. Seeing Kenneth Tynan across a first-night aisle at the height of the Cuban Missile Crisis he hobbled painfully to him to say, 'Kenneth, I gather that we may never see tomorrow, so I thought I would come over and tell you that I never really thought much of Brecht.'

HOLLAND, Lady. The great nineteenth-century hostess was both witty herself and presided over a forum for the wit of others.

When a cross-eyed woman asked the great Frenchman Talleyrand how the confusing political affairs in France were going he replied, 'Comme vous voyez, Madame.' And when Charles Dickens told her ladyship that he was to go all the way to America, she enquired: 'Why do you not go down to Bristol? There are plenty of third- and fourth-class persons there.'

HOME, Baron (Alec Douglas-Home). Lord Home – as Prime Minister one of the few politicians to admit to being hurt by the barbs of *That Was The Week That Was* – is a delightful and eccentric private person. Once mistaken for his own gamekeeper he enjoyed the error, calculating that it would release him from the boring chore of talking to his guests.

Some years later he was discovered watching television. As the image of

Saddam Hussein suddenly appeared on the screen he leant forward and peered at the set, the better to study Saddam's green, purple and magenta striped tie, picked out with gold lines. He then said in some amazement, 'Rum fellow, that Saddam. He's wearing an Eton Ramblers' tie!'

Home's most famous eccentricity was revealed when he explained that he did his higher mathematics with matchsticks. His wife used to try to counter his vagueness when, as Foreign Secretary, he arrived in a foreign country, by repeating the name of the city they were visiting as they descended the steps of their aeroplane. 'Peking! Peking! Peking!' she would mutter to him to prevent him saying to his hosts how happy he was to be back in, for example, Toronto.

During the Tory leadership crisis, after Macmillan's decision to resign, the Conservative whips canvassed Field Marshal Lord Montgomery's views. He said, 'What d'ye want: the best PM or a man to win the election?' The whip said he wanted both. 'You can't have that,' snapped Monty. 'Home'd make the best PM, Hailsham's the best man to win the election.'

Harold Wilson inspired Home's best quip by referring contemptuously to 'the 14th Lord Home'. Home countered neatly by surmising that his opponent must be 'the 14th Mr Wilson'. However, it did not win him the election. Many ascribed his defeat to the way he looked on television. During the campaign he asked a make-up girl if she could make him look better on television. 'No,' she said – and, when pressed, added, 'Because you have a head like a skull.'

'Does not everybody have a head like a skull?'

'No.'

'And', Home added in his memoirs, 'that was that.'

On *That Was the Week That Was* David Frost summed up the contrast between Wilson and Home neatly as 'Dull Alec versus Smart Alec'.

HOME, William Douglas-. William Douglas-Home, who died aged 80 in 1992, was one of the most prolific of British playwrights and one whose quality varied most wildly. His early hits *The Chiltern Hundreds* and *The Manor of Northstead* drew heavily on his own family at the Hirsel in Perthshire, the home of his parents and his brother Alec Douglas-Home. The family had a distinctive eccentricity. the father was known as 'the wee Lordie' and had a habit of praying so loudly in his drawing room before breakfast that a guest congratulated Lady Home on her pet parrot and the uncanny impersonation he gave of her husband.

Family circumstances prompted the two plays mentioned above. In the 1945 landslide Alec Douglas-Home (then Lord Dunglass) lost his Tory seat in South Lanark. The Homes' butler, Collingwood, the most rabid Conservative in the household, was shocked. 'He's lost, my lord,' he spluttered to Lord Home, who was in the middle of *The Times* crossword.

'Who's lost what, Collingwood?'

When Collingwood told him he dismissed the news with, 'Oh, is that all?'

However, the incident gave William an idea for a play about a butler so Tory that he felt the loss of a seat more keenly than his employers. Then he contemplated the son of the house standing for Labour and the butler opposing him. A. E. Matthews as the absent-minded Earl of Lister gave a classic comedy performance.

William Douglas-Home often stood as a parliamentary candidate himself – for various parties. Encountering him at breakfast one morning his brother Alec asked him, 'What party are you in this morning?'

'Wait until I've read the papers,' William replied.

Apart from the string of light comedies – *The Reluctant Debutante* was another hit and so were the star vehicles *The Dame of Sark*, *The Kingfisher* and *Lloyd George Knew My Father* – there were resounding flops like *Aunt Edwina* – in which the author took over Henry Kendall's drag leading role himself for a time – and a string of unproducable plays. But Home's play *Now Barabbas* was a very different matter. It was based on his prison experiences when he was confined in Wormwood Scrubs and Wakefield Prison. He had been court-martialled and jailed for a year for refusing on grounds of conscience to take part in 1944 in the Allies' bombardment of Le Havre, after the Germans had declined to evacuate the French civilian population. Later his other brother, Henry Douglas-Home, asked him, 'Can you give me any advice about prison life?' – on being sentenced for a drink-driving charge in Scotland. William told him to pack a dinner jacket as the governor would be sure to ask him to dine.

HOWARD, Cy (Seymour Horowitz). I am indebted to Dick Vosburgh on this occasion as on many others. In his obituary in the *Independent* he reassigned one of the great show-biz chestnuts. The starting point is Alfred Bloomingdale's production of *Allah Be Praised*, a terrible 1944 musical which was limping to disaster out of town. I have always reported that it was George S. Kaufman who advised Bloomingdale, the store owner, to 'Close the show and keep the store open nights.'

Why is this entry under Cy Howard's name? Well, he was a writer, director, producer, born in Milwaukee, Wisconsin, in 1915. Vosburgh reveals that that piece of counsel was Howard's not Kaufman's. But these stories do attach themselves to famous wits. Vosburgh added two more Cy Howard stories. He married three times. His second bride was Gloria Grahame, who told Vosburgh in an interview (I would not like the reader to think that she knew him well) that she called the writer Howard Teichman, who had been Howard's room-mate in college, on her wedding night and asked him, 'What advice can you give me?' Teichman shouted back, 'Reconsider.' After her divorce from Howard, Vosburgh says, Gloria Grahame married Tony Ray, who was her former step-son. Howard was up to it. 'If Gloria hadn't divorced me,' he said, 'she might never have become her own daughter-in-law.'

HUNT, Holman. When Holman Hunt was painting *Strayed Sheep* (or *Our English Coasts*) he arrived one morning to find fog enveloping the view he was hoping to immortalise. Patiently he took out a book; but he was interrupted by a stranger who revealed himself as another artist and insisted on carrying on a conversation. He launched into an attack on the Pre-Raphaelites, asserting that they never worked directly from nature. Holman Hunt protested mildly that he understood that Millais, Holman Hunt and Collins 'were living together in Surrey last summer and that there they painted the *Ophelia*, *The Huguenot*, and *The Hireling Shepherd*, which were in the Academy this year.'

'Not a word of truth,' countered the other artist. 'You have been entirely imposed upon. I know them as well as I know myself.'

'Personally?' pressed Hunt.

'Yes,' said the stranger, 'And they are all charlatans!'

Holman Hunt let it go at that and never saw the man again but wondered what he would think when he saw the picture of the view they had been contemplating at the Royal Academy Exhibition in May.

— I —

INGE, William Ralph. The Dean of St Paul's and an *Evening Standard* columnist in the 1930s, Dean Inge was known as 'The Gloomy Dean' because of his pessimistic sermons. He is unlikely ever to become the patron saint of feminists, having once tactlessly described women as 'the poor man's men'.

INGRES, Jean-Auguste-Dominique. Ingres, the painter, could veer rapidly from modesty to harsh criticism of his contemporaries. When one sitter complimented him, 'I don't believe Raphael could have painted a finer portrait than that . . .', Ingres jumped in with, 'I will not allow a name such as Raphael's to be used in the presence of one of my own works. I will not allow anyone to compare me with this divine being.' He proceeded to demonstrate how low he was in his own estimation compared to earlier masters . . . 'but as for my contemporaries that is something altogether different.' He then drew himself up to his full – if tiny – height and tapped on the floor boards with his heels to show how he towered over them, 'I am up there on my high horse . . . I am not afraid of them!'

He had a profound contempt for his younger colleague Delacroix. When passing one of Delacroix's paintings he used to cover his eyes and say, 'I've no need to know how not to do it,' and when Delacroix was named a member of the Academy in 1859 he cried, 'They have let the wolf into the sheep fold!'

— J —

JAMES I. King James I was James VI of Scotland, the son of the executed Mary, Queen of Scots and the murdered Darnley. On his accession to the English throne he was 37. Although Elizabeth had once hoped that Almighty God would send a royal heir who would be a 'fit Governor', James was not what she had in mind. Known as 'the wisest fool in Christendom', his obsessions were hunting, learning and young men. He manoeuvred to achieve the subordination of Parliament to the King, and of the Church to the Bishops, though he encouraged the translation of the New Bible.

His boorish habits and quick temper can be judged from his surviving comments. To be Presbyterian Minister he said plainly, 'I give not a turd for your preaching.' Dissolving the 'Addled' Parliament in 1614 he said, 'I am surprised that my ancestors should have permitted such an institution to come into existence.' To his son, the future Charles I, he was prophetic, 'You will live to have your bellyful of Parliament.' On being told that the English people wished occasionally to see his face – difficult as he spent most of the year hunting in the royal forests – 'God's wounds! I will pull down my breeches and they shall also see my arse!' His jibe to unruly courtiers was, 'Go to Hell or Connaught,' considered the most remote and primitive of Irish provinces.

George Villiers, later Duke of Buckingham, who succeeded an earlier favourite, Somerset, was also approved by Prince Charles and the Queen, the extravagant Anne of Denmark. Above all, he appealed to James's sense of humour. He made him laugh. When he was required to defend his infatuation to the Lord of Council in 1617 he said tetchily, 'I, James, am neither God nor an angel but a man like any other. You may be sure that I love the Earl of Buckingham more than anyone else . . . for Jesus Christ did the same, and therefore I cannot be blamed. Christ had his John and I have my George.'

He was tart on the Dean of St Paul's poetry. 'Dr Donne's verses are like the peace of God; they pass all understanding.' But one of his best-known statements is also – today – one of his most politically correct. It is his *A Counterblast to Tobacco* in 1604. 'A custom loathsome to the eye, hateful to the nose, harmful to the brain, dangerous to the lungs and in the black, stinking fume thereof, resembling the horrible Stygian smoke of the pit that is bottomless.'

He died in 1625 twenty years after surviving the Gunpowder Plot. Although the attempt had been scuppered by an informant to the government, James convinced himself that he alone was responsible for uncovering it. According to the Venetian Ambassador he was terrified: 'The King . . . does not appear, nor does he take his meals in public as usual. He lives in the innermost rooms with only Scotsmen about him!'

JAMES II. James II was the younger brother of Charles II, and something of a disaster. Early and late in life he experienced the bitter taste of exile – first to escape Cromwell and later because of his attempts to restore Catholicism to England and to overthrow the Constitution. The Duke of Buckingham summed up his inadequacies and lack of flair compared to his brother: 'The King could see things if he would; the duke would see things if he could.' He married twice – to Anne Hyde when he was Duke of York and later to Mary of Modena. He fathered the future Queens Mary and Anne, and also Prince James Edward, the 'Old Pretender'.

As a young man James escaped from imprisonment in St James's Palace by practising a game of hide and seek with his younger brother and sister for two weeks. His captors grew used to the idea that he might not be found for a half an hour or so. On a pre-arranged night he started the game and then slipped through a door and ran down a side street to the house of some sympathisers by the river, 'One Loe, a surgeon, where he found Mrs Murray who had women's clothes in readiness to disguise the Duke.'

Little else in the Duke's life matched the flair of this ingenious ruse. As King his attitude to Parliament was summed up in two remarks to the Papal Nuncio – it was 'a vast conspiracy of the ill-intentioned'; and he feared 'those in Whitehall more than my foreign enemies'.

On his second marriage, to Mary of Modena, he was forced by the Jesuits to give up his Protestant mistress, Mrs Sidley. He envied the French King's sexual continence saying, 'He is younger than I but I have much less control.'

The birth of James Edward in 1688 occasioned a great deal of rumour, scandal and speculation. It was five years since the Queen had been pregnant and the suspicion was that the Jesuits were arranging a pious fraud. One prophesy – that she would give birth to twins – particularly impressed the Queen, especially when it was suggested that one son would be King of England and the other Pope.

By the time she gave birth to James in St James's Palace, the nation was convinced that the pregnancy was a fiction. The famous rumour was that an infant had been smuggled into the Queen's bedchamber in a warming pan. This is now generally accepted as untrue, but James did not help his case by having few impartial witnesses to the birth. The child arrived a month before he had been expected. Princess Anne, whose position in the succession he would have usurped, had been encouraged to go to Bath and various ruses prevented other credible witnesses from being present. Princess Anne's comment was, 'I should be unfortunate to be out of town when the Queen was brought to bed for I should never now be satisfied whether the child be true or false. It may be it is our brother but God only knows.'

In 1688 James's son-in-law, William of Orange, landed at Torbay in Devon with a Dutch fleet and was quickly joined by English supporters. Earlier, his second daughter, Anne, had fled from London to join her sister Mary with William. 'God help me!' groaned the King, 'even my children have forsaken me!' On 10 December he fled to France. The future Duke of Marlborough had taken his troops over to William. 'If I could have relied upon all my troops I might not have been put to this extremity I am in,' the fleeing King told Lord Feversham. After he settled in France he made the rather dubious boast, 'If I had agreed to live quietly and treat my religion as a private matter . . . I could have been one of the most powerful kings ever to reign in England.'

He made one attempt to regain his throne. With French troops he tried to hold Ireland but was defeated at the Battle of the Boyne on 1 July 1690. He fled to the safety of Dublin, where he complained to Lady Tyrconnel, 'Madame, your countrymen have run away.' Her ladyship was not impressed. 'Sire,' she replied, 'Your Majesty seems to have won the race.'

In a bitter letter to the King of France after his defeat, he wrote, 'I entreat you to interest yourself no more for a prince so unfortunate, but permit me to withdraw with my family to some corner of the world where I may cease to be an interruption to your Majesty's usual course of prosperity and glory.'

JAMES, Henry. Somerset Maugham summed up the pretensions of the American anglophile novelist Henry James most concisely. 'Poor Henry, he's spending eternity wandering round and round a stately park and the fence is just too high for him to peep over and they're having tea just too far away for him to hear what the Countess is saying.' Philip Guedalla wrote: 'The work of Henry James has always seemed divisible by a simple dynastic arrangement into three reigns: James I, James II and James the Old Pretender.' More succinctly William Faulkner wrote him off as 'one of the nicest old ladies I ever met'.

Edith Wharton stresses this side of James in her tales of driving around

England with him. Although her chauffeur had a natural sense of direction James always insisted on sitting beside him, misdirecting him and getting lost. This happened on the simple drive from Folkestone to James's home at Rye – although the town was clearly visible as they meandered around Romney Marsh. When looking for an hotel in the straightforward town of Malvern: 'At each corner he stopped the motor, and we heard a muttering, first confident, then anguished . . . "this is certainly the right corner. But no: stay! A moment longer please – in this light it is so difficult . . . appearances are so misleading . . . It may be . . . yes! I think it *is* the next turn . . . drive on!"' The climax was at Windsor when James was searching for the King's Road and – she catches his rambling circumlocutory style beautifully – asked an ancient local for directions. '"Oh, please," I interrupted, feeling myself utterly unable to sit through another parenthesis, "do ask him where the King's Road is."

' "Ah – ? The King's Road? Just so! Quite right! Can you, as a matter of fact, my good man, tell us where, in relation to our present position, the King's Road exactly is?"

' "Ye're in it," said the aged face at the window." '

When Ellen Terry rejected a play she had asked him to write for her he complained to a friend who suggested mildly that perhaps she did not think the part suited her. 'Think? Think?' was James's response. 'How should the poor, toothless, chattering hag THINK?'

According to G. K. Chesterton, when James moved into his house in Rye he inherited a gallery of gloomy family portraits and went to great pains to track down a surviving member of the family they represented. Eventually he located the sole bearer of the name, 'Far away in some manufacturing town . . . a cheerful and commonplace commercial clerk.' Then he insisted the man should pay him a visit. 'It is also said that the commercial gentleman thought the visit too great a bore and the ancestral home a hell of a place; and probably fidgeted about with a longing to go out for a B and S and the *Pink 'Un*.'

Hugh Walpole recorded that when he was walking with James in the fields beyond Rye he made to give two local urchins a couple of coppers; however, he spent so long explaining to them what sort of sweets they should buy and in which shop, that eventually, 'after listening open-mouthed, their eyes fixed on the pennies, of a sudden they took fright and turned, running and roaring with terror across the fields. James, greatly distressed, could not understand it and harped on it for days.'

As a playwright James was a failure in his lifetime. On the first night of his *Guy Domville*, Sir George Alexander led him on stage for an author's call and left him to face a battery of boos. As a critic, however, he was capable of considerable severity. Of Irving's Mephistopheles in Goethe's *Faust* he wrote, 'That deep note is entirely absent from Mr Irving's rendering . . . though the actor, of course, at moments displays to the eye a remarkably sinister figure. He strikes us, however, as superficial – a terrible fault for an arch-fiend.'

JAY, Sir Antony. Antony Jay has had a distinguished career in broadcasting. He is the son of the actor Ernest Jay, who was once asked over the telephone by a voice he (incredibly) failed to recognise if he would 'like to tour India in *Candida* with Edith Evans'. When he had said the Jay equivalent of 'not bloody likely' the voice revealed itself as belonging to Miss Evans herself.

Tony has been more distinguished in diplomacy and politics, contributing hugely to the old *Tonight* programme, livening up speeches for Nigel Lawson and Margaret Thatcher and selling the TV company he founded with John Cleese for a handsome £15 million.

However, one of his unsung qualities is as a formidable punster. He was producing the *Highlight* programme which preceded *Tonight,* and on one occasion Cliff Michelmore was due to interview a politician when Derek Ibbotson ran a sensational four-minute mile at White City, just around the corner from the studio. Ibbotson was rushed across to join the programme and Jay, seeing a third microphone being hastily placed on the table, remarked, 'One more and we'd have a Formica table.'

It was on this same programme that Michelmore came up against the ultimate conversation stopper – the master question squelcher. He was interviewing the Indian statesman the late Krishna Menon. 'That question is not cast in the mould of my thinking,' said the great man several times. I'd love to try it on Channel 4's teenage romp *The Word.*

JAZZ STORIES. Jazz has spawned literature of put-downs and gags. Wally Stott defined it sceptically: 'If you're in jazz and more than ten people like you, you're labelled commercial.' Louis Armstrong was more downright: 'Hot can be cool and cool can be hot, and each can be both. But hot or cool, man, jazz is jazz.' Unsurprisingly Anthony Burgess used longer words: 'Jazz . . . was illiterate, instinctual, impulsive, aleatoric, unscorable, unprintable – therein lay its charm.' Jazz is religious for Father G. V. Kennars, SJ: 'To swing is to affirm'; or, as Duke Ellington put it in a lyric with Irving Mills, 'It Don't Mean a Thing if it Ain't Got That Swing'. Of 'Bop' Ellington said, 'Playing "Bop" is like scrabble with all the vowels missing.' Paderewski saw jazz as 'a terrible revenge by the culture of the Negroes on that of the Whites'. To Charlie Parker it was 'Your own experience, your thoughts, your wisdom. If you don't live it, it won't come out of your horn.' John Philip Sousa, however, was dubious: 'Jazz will endure, just as long as people hear it through their feet instead of their brains!'

Bill Crow collects some of the most venerable jazz jokes in his *Jazz Anecdotes*: 'How late does the band play?' 'About a half a beat behind the drummer' – 'What's the difference between a bass and a cello?' 'Bass burns longer' – 'How can a jazz musician end up with a million dollars? 'Start out with two million' – 'What sort of people hang around musicians?' 'Drummers'.

Crow cites an amusing incident when Sid Caesar, not yet a star comic, was playing saxophone with Gene Krupa's band. Teddy Napoleon was playing piano and his sister Josephine was the vocalist. The three of them were in a car on the way to a gig in New Jersey when a cop stopped them for speeding. Examining Napoleon's licence he queried the name 'Napoleon?' Caesar started to laugh and said,'Yes, and I'm Caesar!' The cop frowned and pointed to the girl in the back. 'Caesar and Napoleon, eh? And I suppose the girl is Josephine?' 'Yeah, how did you know?'

Drink and drugs feature heavily in the literature of jazz. When the trumpeter Johnny Best saw a sign in a Holiday Inn which read: 'HAPPY HOUR – ALL YOU CAN DRINK FOR A DOLLAR', he made straight for the bartender with: 'Give me two dollars' worth.'

Gene Quill, saxophonist, was playing at Birdland when a picky customer said snidely, 'All you're doing is playing just like Charlie Parker.' Quill made to hand him his saxophone. 'Here!' he said. '*You* play just like Charlie Parker.'

I like the response of Bobby Hackett, a man famous for never saying anything bad about anyone, even Hitler: 'Well, he was the best in his field.'

Bill Crow ends his introduction with a classic shaggy dog story. Red Kelly, a bass player with the Woody Herman band in the fifties, got drunk at a party and spilt ink on a white rug. He panicked, fled the house and collapsed in bed. Next day he returned in remorse to pay for cleaning the rug and accidentally sat on a small dog and killed it. He fled again never to return. As with all good anecdotes it bucketed around. It was elaborated on. It was ascribed to various musicians. Crow checked out the story with Red Kelly at his home in Tacoma, Washington. Kelly explained that he had heard the story in Seattle from a trombone player called Mike Hobi who had read it somewhere. Kelly loved the story and repeated it *ad nauseam* until people assumed it was autobiographical. 'Total strangers would come up and say, "Are you the guy who sat on the dog?" ' Finally he got tired of denying it and went along with the legend.

Ironically, he finally returned to Seattle and bumped into Mike Hobi again who said, 'Listen, tell me that story about you and the dog again?' Full circle.

JERROLD, Douglas. The publisher of *Bentley's Miscellany* said to Douglas Jerrold, the nineteenth-century wit, 'I had some doubts about the name I should

give my magazine. I thought at one time of calling it *The Wits' Miscellany*.'
Jerrold did not hesitate. 'Well,' he said, '. . . but you need not have gone to the
other extremity.'

JOBSON, Richard. My friend Richard Jobson, ex-punk band member, ex-
fashion model, poet, broadcaster and art fancier, recently chaired a Channel 4
programme called *Men Talk*, in which groups of men talked with remarkably
few inhibitions about their sex lives. Unkindly the critic John Naughton
described the cast of one edition as 'two nerds, three exotics and a chairman who
is by Eric Idle out of a lobotomised Scottish Football Manager'. (As vivid a piece
of invective as one could ask for – it reminded me of Clive Anderson's phrase in
the review of a name-dropping media murder mystery novel by John Mortimer.
He suggested that Mortimer must be the result of a romantic encounter between
me and Dame Agatha Christie!)

However, the part of Naughton's review which appealed to me was a limerick I had not heard but which he called venerable. The quotation was
prompted by Jobson's determination to get his panel to discuss the importance
of the sizes of their members.

> There was a young man called MacNabbiter
> Who had an organ of prodigious diameter.
> But it was not the size
> That gave girls the surprise,
> 'Twas his rhythm – Iambic Pentameter.

There is something to be said, Naughton concluded, for a classical education.

JOHN, Augustus. Augustus John, a long-time Chelsea resident in the first part
of this century, was as well-known a womaniser as he was a painter. According
to his biographer, Michael Holroyd, when strolling along the King's Road he
made a habit of patting all the children whom he passed by on the head. 'Just in
case it's one of mine,' he would say.

John's son, Sir Caspar, rose to be First Sea Lord, the professional head of the
Royal Navy. For relaxation he liked to drink in Chelsea pubs where, for the
most part, he went unrecognised. One day a fellow tippler in the Queens Arms
in the Fulham Road asked him what he did for a living. 'Me?' said the First Sea
Lord absently, 'I'm a Jack Tar.'

JOHN, King. John was 21 when his brother Richard I died. His reign, a bewil-
dering mixture of grand guignol and black farce, began and ended in low comedy. Within weeks of King Richard's death, he dropped his lance at his

investiture at Rouen, setting off a fit of giggles among his courtier contemporaries, who could not take their companion's elevation seriously. Seventeen years later he died after mislaying his crown and treasure in the murky waters of the Wash – the event for which, along with the granting of Magna Carta, he is perhaps best known.

This disastrous accident occurred when his journey was interrupted by a whirlpool at the point where the sea tide met the current of the river Welland. Treasure, regalia, the Crown of England and many men were lost in the treacherous sands under the advancing tide. John barely escaped with his life and, shivering in his soaking robes, he watched in impotent rage as the last traces of his pomp and his property were lost beneath the muddy waters. He arrived at Swineshead, a Cistercian Abbey, sick, dispirited and malign. The spiritual atmosphere of the abbey exasperated him and did nothing to raise his spirits. He turned eagerly to food and drink, always a sure source of consolation for him, and finished his meal, liberally accompanied with a new brew of beer, with a dish of peaches.

The fever which broke out could have been due to poison, a surfeit, typhus (not uncommon in the Fens), or to his exhausted mind, sapped by crisis after crisis, and his beleaguered body, assaulted by a lifetime of living too well. As always, after the sudden sickness of a King, rumours abounded. Some said that poisoned pears were the Abbot's way of saving the honour of his sister, on whom John had designs; others claimed that in his ill-temper at dinner he had 'vowed to make the halfpenny loaf cost a shilling before the year was over' and that a Saxon monk, only too aware of John's previous depredations, had decided to nip this villainous plan in the bud.

By morning John suspected that he was dying, but defying fate he mounted his horse and pushed on to Sleaford Castle. Here he was bled, but next day, too sick to ride, he ordered a litter and carried on with his journey north. At Newark he was forced to call a halt and lay doubled up with pain. More for form than from conviction, he asked his physician, the Abbot of Croxton, to hear his confession and give him the sacrament. He was buried in Worcester Cathedral, near the grave of St Wulstan, a Saxon bishop.

JOHNSON, Dame Celia. One of the best-loved and most vividly remembered actresses, Celia Johnson is etched in everybody's memory for her performance in *Brief Encounter*. Her essentially English quality and her 'un-actressy' approach to acting marked her out from many of her colleagues. Her biographer, her daughter Kate Fleming, allows us an uncharacteristic but endearing glimpse of her being catty *sotto voce* at a TV Awards Ceremony when her performance in *Staying On*, again with Trevor Howard, was pipped at the post by Dame Peggy

Ashcroft (for *Caught in a Train* and *Cream in my Coffee*): 'I thought she was just the teeniest bit hammy,' said Dame Celia.

Her career was organised around her family – though she was an incompetent cook and no great manager, while acting came easily and naturally. At one stage Evelyn Waugh wrote testily to Lady Pamela Berry that Peter Fleming's 'wife has had to leave the stage because they have no cook!' Earlier in her career the impresario 'Binkie' Beaumont said of a new play, 'Oh, Celia will only do it if she wants a pair of new curtains.'

Helping to cast *The Reluctant Debutante*, she insisted on Jack Merivale. 'Is he a good actor?' asked E. P. Clift, the producer. 'I wouldn't know about that,' she answered, 'but he can drop me every night at Henley Bridge on the way home.'

She made her only appearance in New York in 1931 as Ophelia to Raymond Massey's disastrous Hamlet. When they arrived in America the producer, Norman Bel Geddes, said ominously, 'I've altered the script a bit.' On the out-of-town opening in Philadelphia the curtain rose to Leon Quatermaine's whis-pered plea in the wings: 'Forgive us, Master Will, for what we are about to perpetrate,' and the *New York Times* later decided that 'Mr Bel Geddes and Shakespeare disagree most violently about the theme of the play.' The English cast members amused themselves looking for hidden characters in the text. They unearthed Marshall Storck, a Scandinavian military man, 'with martial stalk'; an Irish Wolfhound, Pat, 'Now might I do it, pat': and Horatio's girlfriend, Felicity, 'Absent thee from felicity awhile'.

During her later years Dame Celia often played opposite Sir Ralph Richardson. In the partnership, Frith Banbury, the director of *The Flowering Cherry*, found that a good way of getting through to Sir Ralph, 'who was not always amenable to authority', was via her. By the time Lindsay Anderson directed them in William Douglas-Home's *The Kingfisher*, she had refined her own powerful eccentricities and he found both 'pretty well impervious to sug-gestion . . .' One evening at a preview he muttered to Joe Davis, the veteran lighting designer: 'They've got me licked.'

JOYCE, James. At the height of the scandal of the publication by Sylvia Beach of James Joyce's novel *Ulysses* in Paris in 1922, an admirer of Joyce told him that he had hidden a copy among some prayer books and Bibles that were taken into the Vatican and blessed by the Pope!

In 1931, nine years after publication, Harold Nicolson was still forbidden on the orders of Sir John Reith even to mention the name of the book in his regu-lar broadcasts at the BBC.

JOYNSON-HICKS, Sir William ('Jix'). Joynson-Hicks, a celebrated Home Secretary in the 1920s, carried, like Gladstone before him and Neville

Chamberlain after, an umbrella. Like them he became associated with it.

I do not know if it accompanied him on one of his most celebrated outings. An early ecumenist and a devoted Low Churchman he wrote from the Home Office to every church in London suggesting a meeting to discuss a closer rapport. He was discouraged when he received no replies until one arrived from the Vicar of St Mary's, Bourne Street, on the borders of Pimlico and Belgravia, a mixed society of proletarians and socialites. Then, as now, it was a temple of High Anglicanism, an oasis of bells and smells. He accepted the warm invitation to share a Sunday morning service.

'Jix' and Lady Joynson-Hicks arrived to find the welcome warm and the red carpet laid out. They were escorted into the aura of incense and led to a front pew. But when the service began they soon found themselves out of sync. with their fellow worshippers. For a time they tried to keep up with the routine of kneeling, sitting, standing, bowing and crossing, but, in their exposed position to no avail. At last Joynson-Hicks gave in and hissed at his wife, 'Stay standing.' They did so at that point in the ritual when it was most important that they should kneel. Ill-luck had arranged that immediately behind them was a fanatically High Church, horny-handed labourer who was affronted. Slapping his hands on the shoulders of the Home Secretary and his lady he growled, 'Bow, you buggers, bow!'

Hicks was also a favourite target of Lloyd George's invective. He had only added the Joynson to his original Hicks when he married an heiress, Miss Joynson. When Hicks mocked Lloyd George's thundered phrase 'Unearned increment', in the House of Commons, Lloyd George took up the challenge to define it. 'On the spur of the moment I can think of no better example of unearned increment than the hyphen in the Right Honourable Gentleman's name.'

— K —

KATHERINE, Princess of Greece (Lady Katherine Brandram). While I was at Oxford in the very early 1950s, Greece was smitten by a mammoth earthquake. We did a concert and raised a few quid. I remember Alexander Weymouth, now Marquess of Bath, behaving badly in the audience, and Margaret Smith, now Dame Maggie, then an ASM at the Playhouse, mimicking Joan Greenwood in an excerpt from *The Importance*. Some of us bought gallery tickets (about five shillings) for a subsequent gala and I went to a reception earlier in a grand house in Avenue Road to be thanked for my efforts by the committee.

Once there I found that I had lost my puny ticket. Lady Katherine Brandram (Princess Katherine of Greece) was the officiating Royal. 'You must sit in my box,' she said kindly when she heard of my tragedy. And so I found myself, on my first visit to Drury Lane, perched in the Royal Box.

They really had midnight matinées in those days. It started well after eleven with Laurence Olivier tearing off a prologue written by Christopher Fry. Some colourful Brazilians danced, and I recall Christopher Hewitt doing Sandy Wilson's revue sketch about Sir Christopher Wren, 'Hush, Hush, whisper who dares,/Sir Christopher Wren is designing some stairs.'

Lady Katherine and party left around three. I was not going to miss a moment. Alone in the Royal Box at the end I heard the National Anthem strike up. I stood and basked in the spotlight which swung on to me, to the consternation (and envy) of my undergraduate contemporaries in the five-bob gods, who were unaware that I was a temporary member of the Greek Royal Family. The music stopped. I shuffled into my coat. The orchestra embarked on another (unfamiliar) tune. I peered over the box and saw a lot of Greeks at attention. Ramrod stiff I took another call in the wheeling spots. At the end I modestly acknowledged the spatter of applause.

Since, then no matter how terrific the show, Drury Lane has always been something of an anti-climax.

KAVANAGH, P. J. My friend Patrick Kavanagh, the distinguished poet and essayist, was briefly employed as a 'Poly' guide in Switzerland while at Oxford. After a few weeks he became more and more irritated by the stream of plaintive and often idiotic questions by the tourists always prefaced with 'Mr Poly . . .'

He finally forfeited his job when he pointed out the three mountain tops, the Eiger, the Munch and the Jungfrau, It provoked a volley of questions.

'Mr Poly, why is it called the Eiger?'

He translated. 'Mr Poly, why is it called the Munch?'

Again he translated.

'Mr Poly, why is it called the Jungfrau?'

His patience was exhausted.

'Because it's hard to get up!'

He was reported and returned to England.

KEATING, Paul. This is more an example of invective than anecdote.

Paul Keating leapt to international fame soon after becoming Prime Minister of Australia by the simple expedient of putting a guiding arm around the Queen's waist. However, at home he had long been known as a 'wild colonial bowelmouth' in a country where that political skill is much prized.

Born in a working-class suburb of Sydney in 1944 Keating is of Irish descent and grew up under the Irish American code, 'Go to Mass, join the Union, support Labor.' From this background he enjoys teasing Sydney's intellectuals by referring to them as 'the basket weavers of Balmain [Sydney's Hampstead] quaffing wine in good restaurants until 3.30 in the afternoon.'

His early career included managing a rock group, The Ramrods – 'Most of our fans would rather have a fight than a feed.' On one occasion they were supported by an even more obscure band, The Bee Gees, who were booed off stage.

When the Ramrods threatened to break up, Keating said, 'If you carry on I'll stay. if not, I'll do politics.' They broke up and Keating was lost to rock.

Keating's chief political influence was Jack Lang, a Labour Prime Minister of New South Wales in the thirties, and Rex 'Strangler' Connor, an ex-heavyweight wrestler and businessman whom Gough Whitlam made his Minister for Natural Resources. Keating himself became a Minister at 31. One of his most rancorous parliamentary exchanges was provoked by his breaking his engagement to a Sydney girl called Kristine weeks before their wedding, which led to a breach of promise action. In the House Keating referred to the unctuous

KINGTON, Miles   *171*

opposition leader John Howard as 'His Oiliness'. Another MP, Wilson Tuckey, known as 'the Axeman' for his violent destruction of reputations, heckled Keating with cries of, 'What about Kristine?' Keating countered with 'Shut up, you stupid, foul-mouthed grub!' He went on to remind Tuckey of his 1967 conviction for assaulting an aboriginal voter in Western Australia: 'At least,' he thundered, 'I don't get someone to hold somebody against a wall while I belt him with a truncheon . . . You piece of criminal garbage!' he added for good measure. His gracious withdrawal was more like an advance: 'Mr Deputy Speaker, in deference to you I withdraw but . . . all through Question Time those two pansies over there want retractions of things we have said about them. They are a bunch of nobodies going nowhere!'

Another favourite target was Dr John Hewson, born a few miles away from Keating, who scoffed at Keating's lack of formal education: 'Absolutely no economic knowledge, no skill there – and it shows!' Keating took the temperature up a point: 'Hewson has ratted on his class. I'm still representing the working class,' and then seemed to take a leaf out of Denis Healey's book of insults – 'Hewson's speech is like being flogged by a warm lettuce. I have a psychological hold over Hewson . . . He's like a stone statue in the cemetery.' When Hewson complained – 'unparliamentary language' – Keating responded, 'This little flower, this delicate little beauty, this cream puff, is supposed to be beyond personal criticism . . . He is simply a shiver looking for a spine to run up.' (This echoes a Wilson attack on Heath, but Keating is supposed to have a research staff which scans libraries for invective.)

One can't help thinking that the Queen got off lightly with a quick laying on of hands: but isn't there a place on our television for regular excerpts from Question Time down under rather than *Neighbours*?

KERR, Deborah. There is a nice story concerning Deborah Kerr, who was irritated by constant mispronunciation of her name in Hollywood. 'Kerr' always came out 'Cur' not 'Car'. For one of her premières she was asked what special arrangement she would like by an indulgent studio. She asked for an English commissionaire to call for her limo as she left the première for the party. Her wish was granted and the man functioned perfectly getting everyone's name right including hers. 'Miss Kerr's car' came out immaculately with both words sounding exactly the same. Unfortunately he then relaxed, lost concentration and called loudly for 'Mr Alfred Hitchcar's cock!'

KINGTON, Miles. In Miles Kington's long career as a humorist for *Punch, The Times* and the *Independent*, he has produced some absolute gems. On a recent visit to the Edinburgh Festival he collected some wonderful Festival over-heards.

Edinburgh tour guide: 'The average thickness of some Edinburgh walls is more than three feet. The outer foot of that is usually composed of compacted Fringe posters.'

Man in street handing out leaflets: 'Sex and violence! Sex and violence! . . . God, isn't anyone interested in sex and violence any more?'

Two citizens of Bradford-on-Avon: 'We went to see a Spanish puppet group today, doing *Don Quixote* in Spanish. Unfortunately we don't understand Spanish and neither of us knew the story of Don Quixote. But we're sure it was very good.'

Edinburgh tour guide: 'I've brought you here because this is where most of the public beheadings took place and they were a public entertainment in their day – the Fringe of their time, if you like.'

Lady in coffee bar: 'There's a French mime group at the Pleasance called Les Macloma, who do things with a piano I have never seen done before . . .'

Woman phoning Kington's digs by mistake: 'Is Hugh there? Oh. I just wanted to ask him if he could recommend a good basic book on Celtic jewellery . . . I don't suppose *you* can point me towards one, can you?'

Woman with child: 'Some of the children's shows we've been to are a talentless rip-off. I think I'll form a children's theatre group next year and come back with it.'

Overheard in bar: 'I saw him last night in the Gilded Balloon. He wasn't very good. I think I'll go and see him again tonight.'

Perhaps Kington's best overheard is from a woman in another bar: 'Our land-lord asked us if everything was all right. I didn't like to say that it was a grotty flat and that we were being grossly overcharged, so I contented myself by saying that I couldn't find the teapot. He asked if we were from down south, and I said, "Yes," and he said, "Well, that would explain it. We don't have teapots in Scotland. We're quite happy with teabags!" '

KIPLING, Rudyard. Kipling had decided views on honours. Although he was the first English writer to receive the Nobel Prize, he turned down the office of Poet Laureate at least three times and refused all gongs, from the KCB (which he was offered in 1898 when Lord Salisbury was PM) to the OM (from King George V in 1921). In spite of this, he was appointed a Companion of Honour in 1917 without his consent. He wrote a furious letter to the future Prime Minister, Bonar Law, ending: 'How would you like it if you woke up and found yourself Archbishop of Canterbury?'

KIRWIN, Rick. Two actor friends of mine, Rick Kirwin and Terry Sheppard, were appearing for the Thames Television Company in a dramatisation of one of Antonia Fraser's Jemima Shore mysteries – starring the enchanting Patricia Hodge.

I place this anecdote under Rick's name because Terry has since died and will sadly not be able to rush through the alphabet to find his name. As very good friends often do, they became violently bitchy towards one another during the *longueurs* of studio rehearsal. Eyes burned, tongues flashed and the exchange of insults brought their corner of the studio to a standstill. Needless to say the content was ephemeral and a few days after neither could remember what he or the other had said – the clinching line came from one of three elderly male dressers, who, distracted from his stitching turned to the others to say, 'Ooh! Back in the knife box, Miss Sharp!'

KORDA, Alexander. The great Hungarian film mogul signed Orson Welles for *The Third Man* in the role of Harry Lime. He offered him a choice between $100,000 cash or 20 per cent of the picture's profits. The need for urgent cash to finish his own film of *Othello* required that Welles accept the dollar offer. Later *The Third Man* grossed a fortune. 'I could have retired on that,' Welles was to recall regretfully.

— L —

LAEMMLE, Carl. Carl Laemmle was an early motion-picture tycoon who had such a particular concern for his family that he was known throughout Hollywood as 'Uncle Carl'. Ogden Nash celebrated his concern in a couplet which also serves as a useful aid to his name's pronunciation:

> Uncle Carl Laemmle
> Had a very large family.

LANDESMAN, Jay. Jay Landesman, sometime publisher, nightclub manager, writer, Man about Soho and husband of the stylish lyric writer Fran Landesman, retold some amusing anecdotes in his recent memoir *Jaywalking*.

When the Landesmans arrived in England in the early sixties they knew few people here apart from Peter Cook. Needing an agent they considered Cook's, Peter Rawley. 'I'm a terrific lover,' he told Mrs Landesman, 'but a lousy agent.' 'Oh what a pity,' she replied, 'I already have a lousy lover, what I need is a terrific agent.'

The Landesmans brought their own brand of Bohemian living to London and played host to a number of visiting Americans. On one occasion they were with Mel Brooks in the old Pickwick Club. Mrs Landesman invited him to join her in the ladies' loo for a smoke. When she dropped the dope on the floor he bent to pick it up and spotted an intriguing piece of graffiti written in lipstick. 'Terry Cooper is a lousy fuck,' it read. Underneath was the postscript, 'Now you tell me.' Back in the bar the first person they saw was Terence Cooper. Mrs Landesman made the introduction, 'Mel, this is Terry Cooper, whom you've read so much about.'

I like Jay Landesman's memory of tripping on LSD in bucolic Wales. His host, Jeremy Brooks, was beguiled by his intense conversation with a herd of cows. Jay grew expansive, believing that some kind of affinity existed between him and the cows. Ten minutes later Brooks put his hand round his guest's shoulder. 'Jay,' he said, 'I've seen you empty a room but this is the first time I've seen you empty a meadow!' There wasn't a cow to be seen.

The comic actor Chris Langham tells a similar story of tripping with the now sadly deceased dwarf actor David Rappaport in a field in Somerset. Rappaport wandered off and could be seen in the distance earnestly addressing a herd of cows. Returning, he said apologetically, 'It was all right, Chris, the cows did most of the talking.'

LANGTRY, Lillie (Emilie Charlotte). Dining with Somerset Maugham, Lillie Langtry mentioned someone of whom Maugham had not heard. 'But,' replied the Jersey Lily, 'he was famous in two continents.'

'And why was he famous?' asked Maugham.

'I loved him,' she said simply.

LANTZ. Robert. Robert Lantz, the New York-based agent, is one of the wittiest men in that town. He is the son of a Berlin-based film producer, one of whose claims to fame was a life-long feud with a leading critic. For years they cut each other and their wives cut each other. One day they were observed sharing a table in a restaurant. Berlin reeled in shock but the explanation was simple. The restaurant was empty and having no one else to talk to, 'rather than stay silent they had an intermission'.

In Manhattan Robbie has a regular table at the Russian Tea Rooms. One day a new *maître d'hôtel* put him in an identical position but on the opposite side of the room. 'Six people came up to me,' Robbie said, 'and complained of vertigo.'

At various times he has represented Danny Kaye, Burton and Taylor, Marlene Dietrich, Bette Davis, Joe Mankiewicz, Peter Shaffer and a multitude of others. The Lantz office is very big on autobiographies, Elizabeth Taylor's book was a best-seller, so was Michael Jackson's. Lantz had dinner with Jackson but politely declined an invitation to go upstairs after dinner 'to meet the cobra'. Shirley Temple's account of her life followed, 'It's a very thick book and it stops when she is nineteen.'

Back in the period when there seemed to be a new Pope every other week and smoke was regularly puffing out of the Vatican chapel, the actor Frank Langella was having a triumph as Dracula in New York at the Martin Beck Theatre. One day he called the Lantz office in a rage. An actor friend had sent him a screenplay some weeks before and had now phoned to ask if he liked it. As he had not received it he could not comment. The Lantz office had omitted to forward it. Irate, he demanded an explanation from Robbie. 'What can we do, Frank?' said Robbie. 'We have no Pope.' When I pressed him to confirm the story he smiled his Berlin Buddha smile and remained non-committal.

Some years ago he escorted Bette Davis to a Hollywood function where the guests were placed eight to a table. At the next table sat the ancient Mae West with seven men. Miss Davis went across to pay her respects. She bent over Mae West in conversation for a few minutes and returned to announce in a voice that carried, 'She's under ether.'

He once reminded me of a much-loved Gielgud story which I had forgotten. Sir John directed Peter Shaffer's early play *Five Finger Exercise,* in which one character owes not a little to Shaffer's mother. Some years later in Venice, Mrs Shaffer spotted Sir John taking the sun on the Lido. She introduced herself, 'I'm Peter Shaffer's mother.' 'That may very well be true,' said Sir John and moved on. There is no reply to that, but Shaffer woke up in the middle of the night for months afterwards having dreamed that he had thought of the perfect answer. Then he would realise that he had not.

I can use this opportunity to correct a story which I told in *Theatrical Anecdotes.* It was a story of parents who had had a marital crisis. When it was resolved the mother is supposed to have asked their only child who – i.e. which parent – he would have gone to live with if the split had become permanent. The child said, 'Oh, I'd have liked to go and stay with the Richard Avedons.'

When I printed the story I did not know who the couple were supposed to be – however, a letter very soon arrived from Sherlee Lantz. Apparently the story (untrue) has been haunting her for years. In fact there was no rocky patch in their marriage. A friend had posed the question, much to the Lantzs' dismay. 'No child should have to respond to such a foolish inquiry.' *Another* person's divorce was being discussed, and the custody arrangement for their younger daughter. The family friend turned to the Lantzs' seven-year-old, 'and received the response such a disturbing, silly question deserved'.

So now I know.

LATHAM, Sir John. Sir John Latham was an Australian lawyer who rose to be Attorney-General and Chief Justice of the Australian High Court. He was stopped for a traffic offence by a young Irish policeman in Melbourne. Latham gave his name without elaboration. The copper then asked if he was John Latham the barrister. He said he was. 'And would you be the same John Latham who is the Commonwealth Attorney-General?' Latham, who could see himself getting off, agreed that he was. 'Well,' said the policeman, 'you won't be able to plead ignorance of the law, now will you?'

LAWRENCE, T. E. When D. H. Lawrence completed *Lady Chatterley's Lover* he gave a copy of the manuscript to the literary patron Sir Edward ('Eddie') Marsh. Marsh was full of enthusiasm, and dismayed that censorship would prevent immediate publication. He thought that his friend T.E. Lawrence, then serving as Aircraftman Ross, would like to read it. So he wrapped it in brown paper and sent it off. Lawrence returned the manuscript some weeks later, saying how grateful he was to have had the chance to read it but adding that he could not understand the fuss about – 'all this sex business. I never met anyone who cared a biscuit for it!'

Lawrence also inspired one of Noel Coward's better-known quips. He opened a letter to the serving airman with the words, 'Dear 228171338 (may I call you 338?) . . .'

LAWSON, Baron (Nigel). My earliest memory of Nigel Lawson is as a nimble chorus boy in an OUDS pantomime, *Dick Whittington and His Cat,* in which I played the Fairy Queen. He was extremely thin in the early fifties, and seemed to have the longest eyelashes in Oxford. Although he was a precocious undergraduate at Christ Church, there was as yet no hint of the future Chancellor of the Exchequer.

Forty years later, he can be as sharp in his judgements on colleagues as when seeing off his opponents. Jim Prior was an 'affable but short-fused Heathite squire'; David Mellor a 'brash, self-confident, ambitious and not oversensitive lawyer'; and Francis Pym, Thatcher's luckless Foreign Secretary, 'a gloomy Heathite . . . quite the gloomiest politician I have ever met. He would dilate in the watches of the night on how democracy was doomed.'

But Lawson also had a realistic attitude to his opponents. On John Smith (you remember John Smith, readers – nice man, Scottish, neat suit, wears glasses): 'His jokes are invariably better than his speeches, which are entirely predictable. He shows a reluctance to engage in serious economic argument.' There is admiration for Dennis Skinner MP, who had 'a better sense of where the Government was vulnerable than the whole of his party's front bench put together.'

An American academic once suggested to him that life as a minister was too crowded and hectic to allow time to think. 'What you need is a sabbatical,' he added. 'We already have a sabbatical system,' snapped Lawson; 'it's called opposition, and I've had enough of it.'

He wrote of the Commonwealth (of which he had never been a fan), 'It is a largely meaningless relic of Empire – like the smile on the face of the Cheshire Cat which remains when the cat has disappeared.'

In 1987, Lawson went to speak in support of Andrew Mitchell, a former Conservative Party Vice-Chairman and later a Government Whip who was standing for Parliament for the first time. Lawson exhorted the faithful to 're-elect Andrew Mitchell because he has done such a good job in the House during the previous five years'. Mitchell's comment was that his constituents have never believed a Cabinet Minister since.

In his autobiographical memoir *A View from the Wings*, Ronald Millar, play-wright and speechwriter to Heath, Thatcher and Major, spells out the history of Lawson's famous haircut. At the time of the 1987 General Election, Cecil Parkinson drew Margaret Thatcher's attention to Nigel's long hair and Kenneth Clarke's yellow waistcoat, pointing out that they presented a negative image on television. 'Well, *really*,' was her comment, 'I hardly think that hair and coloured waistcoats will mean the difference between victory and defeat. However . . .' And so saying, she raised the phone to the Chancellor and his locks were shorn.

Now they are allowed to luxuriate again in the club-like atmosphere of the Lords.

LEHMANN, Beatrix. On the Radio 4 programme *Loose Ends* the prodigal, but now returned to the fold, actress Helen Burns recalled a story of Beatrix Lehmann – sister of Rosamond and John.

They were playing together in *The Merchant of Venice*, Lehmann as Portia, Burns as Nerissa. Lehmann's great strength was her intelligence, not her embon-point and it was decided that the designer should fit her out with two special breasts. One night, perhaps not the first, as the pair were about to make their entrance Helen Burns noticed that Miss Lehmann was only sporting half a bosom; the left breast had gone missing. She pointed it out to the leading lady who started a feverish search. 'Has anybody seen a tit?' she enquired of the willowy actors who surrounded her in doublet and hose. No one had. 'Surely you know what a tit looks like?' They assured her they did; but no one could find the wanderer.

By now the orchestra had played Portia's entrance music several times and they were going to have to go on. Just before they did Nerissa, appropriately, two paces behind Portia, spotted that she had developed a small hunch back. The 'tit' had gone walkabout. Deftly she dragged it around to its more appropriate position - approximately.

The show was saved but Nerissa spent the rest of the scene wishing she could give just one more tug to complete the effect.

LE SUEUR, Eustache. Le Sueur, the seventeenth-century French painter, was much envied by the better-known but less talented Charles Le Brun, two years his junior and Louis XIV's 'dictator of the arts'. Le Brun's jealousy was tellingly emphasised in his comment on Le Sueur's death: 'I feel now as if I had a thorn just taken out of my foot!'

LICHFIELD, Patrick Anson, 5th Earl of. Patrick Lichfield, prolific photographer, is perhaps best known to the general public for his famous nude or semi-nude calendars. These involve taking very beautiful but not immensely clever girls to exotic parts of the world and snapping them in beguiling, dramatic poses. As the years pass and he continues to photograph, and the models are still around eighteen and Patrick is not, he notices the age-gap mainly in conversation. One girl, overhearing an argument about the monster Central African emperor Bokassa, cocked an ear and joined in defensively. Before they could point out that keeping dead babies in the fridge, trussed and ready for the table, was not an appealing character trait, she had said firmly, 'Surely he wasn't all bad – and I really admire his daughter.' A little interrogation revealed that she was talking of Picasso and Paloma.

Another girl was saddened to be told over breakfast of the news in a daily newspaper that Fred Astaire had died in his eighties. 'But he was so young,' she mourned. She had never heard of Fred Astaire but Freddie Starr was one of her favourites.

It suggests the surreal headline: 'FRED ASTAIRE ATE MY HAMSTER!'

LIDDELL HART, Captain Sir Basil. Sir Basil Liddell Hart, the famous military commentator, recalls in his memoirs that an army manoeuvre on Salisbury Plain in 1931 included some tanks, which were heartily disliked by the cavalry. Not knowing what to do with them, one general decided to use them to guard his own home which was also his HQ. The tank commander reported to the front door and was told by the aggrieved butler to take his tanks round to the servant's entrance.

LILLEE, Dennis. The great Australian fast bowler was playing in a Lancashire league game. The unhappy batsman was hit on the leg and Lillee duly appealed. The umpire gave him out but to Lillee's disgust he did not walk. Lillee insisted in colourful language that he must go. 'I'd love to go, Dennis,' said the batsman, tears of pain in his eyes, 'but I daren't move. I think you've broken my leg.'

LLOYD GEORGE of Dwyfor, David, 1st Earl. It will probably be the fate of the Liberal Prime Minister Lloyd George to go down in history as a notorious womaniser – indeed one who, in the middle of preparing his budget in 1909, had to pressure his wife into accompanying him to the Law Courts and sitting beside him while he denied an affair with a married woman. She knew he was guilty but she agreed to 'stand by him' and saw him win his libel case against the *People* newspaper.

A famous *Private Eye* cartoon showed a Lloyd George look-alike with the caption 'Lloyd George knew my mother.'

His most devoted mistress was Frances Stevenson, also his secretary, who recorded in her diary an occasion when his sexual sophistication came in useful. King George V was not keen on the 1922 Geneva Conference. 'I suppose you will be meeting Lenin and Trotsky,' he said to Lloyd George. 'Unfortunately, sir,' he replied, 'I am not able to choose between the people I am forced to meet in your service.' He went on to explain that a few days earlier he had to meet the Turk Mustapha Kemal's representative Sami Bey – who nearly missed the appointment, having been finally traced 'to a sodomy house in the East End . . . a man who I understand has grown tired of affairs with women and has lately taken up unnatural sexual intercourse.' He went on, 'I do not think there is very much to choose between these persons whom I am forced to meet from time to time in Your Majesty's Service.' Frances Stevenson records that the King roared with laughter.

Lloyd George was a master of the dismissive. He summed up the 1905 Government: 'They died with their drawn salaries in their hands.' Field Marshal Haig was 'brilliant – to the top of his boots'. Churchill 'would make a drum out of the skin of his mother in order to sound his own praises'. Balfour's impact on history was 'no more than the whiff of scent on a lady's pocket handkerchief ' – in spite of the fact that it often had a powerful impact on Lloyd George himself. Curzon was 'worth his weight in brass – sounding brass'.

Perhaps most famous is the judgement he delivered on Sir John Simon: 'He has sat on the fence so long the iron has entered his soul.'

LOUIS XIV (the Sun King). Louis XIV was one of the most consistently successful billiard players of all time. The game was not fashionable until a physician advised the King to take it up as an exercise to cure his severe indigestion. A table (square in those days) was installed at Versailles and Madame de Maintenon, the King's mistress, was required to overcome her reluctance and act as 'marker'. The King's opponents saw to it that he won every game, loudly applauded by his courtiers – hence his impressive record.

LOUIS, Victor. Victor Louis, a mysterious figure who died in 1992, was a Soviet journalist who was popularly suspected of being a KGB colonel. However, he drove his own Bentley around Moscow and augmented his income successfully by writing for several British newspapers. He surprised a British journalist when, at a champagne party at his dacha outside Moscow in the 1970s, he announced that Ted Heath was in the lead in the Fastnet race.

The visitor was amazed that Louis had such early news of Heath's early success with *Morning Cloud*. 'Easy, old man,' Louis reassured him, 'we have a submarine in the area.'

— M —

MACDONALD, James Ramsay. Ramsay MacDonald, the first Labour Prime Minister, was always a prey to climbing snobbery. When the Maxwell of his day, the swindler publisher Horatio Bottomley, fingered him as travelling under a false name 'whose real name is James MacDonald Ramsay' he was more distressed that the news of his illegitimacy was revealed in the presence of the Dowager Countess De La Warr, Lady Sackville, and her maid, who had been carrying the revealing article, than by the revelation itself.

He scandalised his Labour followers by falling deeply in love with the Marchioness of Londonderry. Lady Londonderry, whose nickname was Circe, received an anonymous letter which depicted her as 'an evil woman who tempted the Labour Prime Minister, Ramsay MacDonald, and turned him into a Tory. She is very wicked.' When she showed it to the Prime Minister he was not amused.

MACINNES, Colin. I have a personal memory of Colin MacInnes, author of the novel *Absolute Beginners*, looking like St Peter in a biblical epic as he waited to interview Brendan Behan in Studio G at Lime Grove. Behan was leading the lady producer the length of the studio in earnest conversation. It was 10.30 in the morning. He had one hand round a can of lager, the other tucked under her skirt gently caressing her backside as she continued the conversation pretending nothing untoward was happening . . .

But my favourite sad story of MacInnes concerns his mother, the novelist Angela Thirkell. One day he helped up an old woman who had tripped running for a bus. Suddenly he realised who she was, but sadly his mother no longer recognised him.

MACKENZIE, Kelvin. The editor of the *Sun* has approved many notorious headlines – 'Gotcha!' on the sinking of the *Belgrano*, 'Stick it up your Junta!' also during the Falklands War, and 'Up yours Delors!' spring to mind, though I think my personal favourite is the helpful 'Ten ways to tell if your bride is a bloke'. However, the prize for lapse of taste goes to a headline never published but allegedly suggested by Mackenzie for a story about the machine-gunning of Tamil civilians – 'Tamila Mowdown'.

MACMILLAN, (Maurice) Harold, 1st Earl Stockton. The late John Morgan, the television interviewer and journalist, was discussing TV coverage in the early 1960s with Harold Macmillan, who was then Prime Minister. The PM remarked that he thought it was all too biased. 'In which direction?' enquired Morgan. Macmillan paused and then with a characteristic sweep of his hand replied, 'In all directions.'

The old boy was no fool when manipulating TV. Reminiscing to camera for the BBC he was emotionally recalling the departure of President Kennedy on his last visit to Birch Grove – how he had watched the helicopter disappearing over the summer trees . . . In the middle of this moving description he broke off to comment briskly to the producer, 'You'll need some cutaways here' – perhaps evocative shots of the trees surrounding Birch Grove over which the helicopter had just sunk from view.

In 1959 Macmillan had invited President Eisenhower to Chequers during his State Visit to Britain. Belatedly someone remembered that protocol required that the Lord Lieutenant of a county should be present whenever a Head of State visited his county. After some searching the elderly Earl of Buckinghamshire was located on his estate in Scotland and flown in. Arriving for lunch he was introduced to the President. 'Do you shoot?' asked the Earl. The President said he did. 'Do you shoot grouse?' 'Not particularly,' replied the President. 'Good God!' said the Lord Lieutenant, and remained silent for the rest of lunch, stumped for any other topic of conversation.

Macmillan always preferred Birch Grove to Chequers, where he usually installed his Foreign Secretary, Selwyn Lloyd, possibly because Lady Dorothy didn't hit it off with the butch WAAF sergeant in charge of catering at the time.

MACMILLAN, Sir Kenneth. A prime hunting ground for the anecdotist is the memorial service. Nicholas Hytner spoke at the celebrated choreographer Kenneth MacMillan's farewell in Westminster Abbey on 17 February 1993. Nicholas directed MacMillan's last new work, the dances for *Carousel* at the National Theatre. He had been nervous, he confessed, when he approached the great man to enlist him for the job, and having rattled on, finally blurted out, 'The point is it's all about sex and violence.' At this MacMillan smiled and said quietly, 'That's what I do.'

The last dance which MacMillan made for the show was for the exuberant 'June Is Bustin' Out All Over'. He was unmoved by the fulsome excitement which the first run-through generated, until the dialect coach said, 'It's like an orgy on *speed*.' Kenneth spent the rest of the day happily repeating the phrase.

MANET, Edouard. Victoire, one of Manet's regular models, appealed to the painter to give work to a colonel's daughter, a girl raised in a convent, innocent of life, who was down on her luck. 'But,' insisted Victoire, 'You've got to treat her like a lady. None of your usual filth in front of her.' The impressionist agreed to be on his best behaviour and the next day Victoire arrived with the girl. 'Come on now, darling,' was her way of introducing her, 'show the gent your Twat.'

MANKIEWICZ, Joseph Leo. Joe Mankiewicz, among the most literate of Hollywood writers, faced one of his biggest challenges when he was called upon in his directorial capacity to put some drama into the epic *Cleopatra*. He had to update the script constantly during shooting – spending Sundays and nights writing. Such was the pressure he began compulsively to bite his fingernails. In the end he had to wear gloves to cover the unpleasant effect. But before that Elizabeth Taylor had caught him chewing his nails on the set. 'Joe,' she ordered, 'don't bite your fingernails.' 'I'm not,' he said. 'I'm biting my knuckles. I finished the fingernails months ago.'

Before the nightmare of *Cleopatra* Mankiewicz made a rather good job of Shakespeare's *Julius Caeser*, starring Gielgud, James Mason, Marlon Brando, Edmund O'Brien and Louis Calhern. According to John Gielgud, one of his assistant directors did not match his superior's sensitivity. The man was trying to encourage some uninspired extras into some signs of life before shooting the forum scene: 'All right, kids,' he yelled. 'It's Rome, It's hot and here comes Julius!'

Mankiewicz was a notoriously difficult man – when Katharine Hepburn finished shooting *Suddenly Last Summer* she was so furious with Mankiewicz's treatment of Montgomery Clift, who had been ill throughout shooting, that, having positively assured herself that she had no further commitment to the picture – shooting, retakes, dubbing, voice-over – she spat full in his face and walked out of his office.

Robert Lantz, who was at one time Mankiewicz's agent, was once breakfasted in Hollywood by two producers who wanted a director for a particularly difficult movie project. He suggested Mankiewicz – 'the only possible man for the job'. The two producers were amazed. They pointed out that Lantz no longer represented Mankiewicz. 'No,' Lantz replied. 'It's a rare case of the fan hitting the shit.'

MANSFIELD, Sir James. This eighteenth-century judge ignored religious holidays in running his courts. On one occasion Mansfield sat on Ash Wednesday and got away with it. However, at the end of Lent he went too far when he suggested that the court assemble on Good Friday.

A counsel in the case, Serjeant-at-Law Davy, outwitted him. 'If your Lordship pleases,' he said. 'But your Lordship will be the first judge who has done so since Pontius Pilate.'

He got his day off.

MARGARET, HRH The Princess, Countess of Snowdon. Princess Margaret was born in the days when it was still obligatory for the Home Secretary to be present at the births of those closely in line of succession to the throne. It must have been disconcerting for the Queen Mother to have had Joynson-Hicks at 17 Bruton Street when Sir Henry Simon was delivering the future queen by Caesarean. Princess Margaret provided even more inconvenience. She was due to be delivered at Glamis Castle in late August 1930. The Home Secretary, J. R. Clynes, arrived on 5 August. Lord Strathmore could not bear the idea of having a Socialist politician under his roof, possibly for weeks, and palmed him off on a kindly neighbour, the Dowager Lady Airlie – where he still was when little Margaret Rose arrived sixteen days later.

I also like Princess Margaret's later definition of her own children's status: 'My children are not royal, they just happen to have the Queen as their aunt.'

MARINA, Princess, Duchess of Kent. Queen Mary, meeting Princess Marina of Greece for the first time in 1934 (when she was about to marry her youngest son, Prince George), noticed that she was wearing very red fingernails. She remarked that the King did not like painted nails. 'Your George may not,' smiled the Princess, 'but mine does.'

MARLBOROUGH, John Albert Edward William Spencer-Churchill (Bert), 10th Duke of. During Duke Bert's time an Oxford don was brought out to explain to specialist visitors the treasures of Blenheim Palace. On one occasion he failed to show. Duke Bert said not to worry, he would do it himself. It was not a success. When asked about any priceless piece he muttered dismissively, 'Of the period, of the period,' and moved on.

When it was suggested to the Duke in the 1930s that by way of economy he might get rid of one of several Austrian pastry cooks among the vast domestic staff at Blenheim, he asked plaintively, 'Mayn't a man have a biscuit?'

Inveighing against the taxation and death duties of the Labour Government under Harold Wilson, he reached a climax of anger with the cry 'Damn it all, an Englishman's castle is his home!'

When I last visited Blenheim I closed in behind a guided tour where the guide had more to say than 'of the period' and was much more gushing than the old Duke. Lowering her voice reverently she said, 'Actually the Duke [11th] himself is here today, so if you are *very* lucky you may actually catch a glimpse of His Grace moving about the grounds.'

MARS-JONES, Adam. Adam Mars-Jones – nominated as Best Young British novelist in 1983 before he had written a novel – has a reputation for writing very little. He tells against himself a story of a visit he made to his publishers, Faber and Faber. During the course of it he dropped a shopping list in the lift. It was pounced upon by the poet Craig Raine, who screamed in mock elation the news that Adam Mars-Jones had written something at last.

What he had written was: 'Half a pound of beef.'

MARX, (Leonard) 'Chico'. Chico Marx was a keen backgammon player. Playing Sam Goldwyn, who was less good, he was irritated when Goldwyn's small son knocked over the board three times, forcing them to start again. Losing his patience, he asked Sam senior to send Junior out of the room. However, Junior kept returning until Marx took him by the hand and led him from the room. It was some few minutes before he returned. Amazed, his father asked how Chico had brought it off. 'Simple,' he said proudly. 'I taught him to masturbate.'

MARY TUDOR. Queen Mary was the elder daughter of Henry VIII by Catherine of Aragon. She might well have been a model Tudor sovereign, possessing virtue, courage, learning and intelligence. Her accession at 37 in 1553 was greeted with joy by her people, yet after reigning only five years she died hated and a tragic failure. Her fervent Catholicism – she burned some 300 Protestants – and her marriage to Philip of Spain were the principal causes of her subjects' disenchantment.

Memories of Mary spring mainly from these obsessions. When she was only two she pointed out a Venetian courtier fancy-dressed in a monk's habit saying delightedly, 'Priest! Priest!' As Princess Mary she refused a group of councillors who asked her to conform to the new Prayer Book, saying, 'I am unworthy to suffer death in so good a quarrel. You should show more favour to me for my father's sake who made the more part of you out of nothing.' She dismissed her younger brother the King's support of the Prayer Book with the words 'Can he in these years discern what is fittest in the matter of divinity?' And she dismissed the Protestant Bishop Nicholas Ridley – 'As for your new books, I thank God I never read any of them; I never did nor ever will do. My lord, for your gentleness to come and see me, I thank you; but for your offer to preach before me, I thank you never a whit!' Five years later, when she was Queen, he was burnt at the stake.

Soon after her accession she restored the Mass and banned the Book of Common Prayer, provoking the oddest incident of her reign. A group of Protestants got into her apartments in Whitehall and left a dead dog there. They had shaved its head to look like a priest's, clipped its ears and placed a rope around its neck. Mary was unmoved.

The romantic part of her life did not run smoothly. When she was fourteen she wrote to the 23-year-old Francis Apsley, 'Your humble servant to kiss the ground where you go, to be your dog on a string, your fish in a net, your bird in a cage, your humble trout.' But she was very unworldly in the ways of love. When she overheard her Lord Chamberlain call her lady-in-waiting 'a pretty whore' she called her a pretty whore too, and the lady-in-waiting, Frances Neville, had to explain to her that a whore 'is a wicked, misliving woman'.

At 37 she considered herself too old for the 26-year-old Philip of Spain, but her common sense told her that if she married him she must make herself fall in love with him and bear his children, though by now any idea of sex disgusted her. After the marriage she did her best, but two phantom pregnancies was as much as she could manage. The first was prompted by the papal legate, Cardinal Pole. When he greeted her with the words 'Hail Mary full of Grace!', she said, she 'felt the child leap in her womb'. And in the year of her death she uttered the phrase 'thinking myself to be with child in lawful marriage between my said dearly loved husband and Lord'.

The end of her reign was full of sadness. King Philip neglected her and Calais was lost to France in the year of her death, 'Not that only,' she famously said, 'but when I am dead and opened, you shall find "Calais" lying on my heart.'

MASSEY, Anna. Anna Massey had a great overnight success in the West End in *The Reluctant Debutante* by William Douglas-Home. She was virtually straight from drama school, and Emlyn Williams invented a nightmare story to reflect this astonishing rise. When I told it to Anna at a Foyle's Lunch some twenty-odd years later she said she had always been vaguely aware of it but that not one had ever quite dared to go into its details for her.

Emlyn Williams said that he had dreamed he was a very old actor, forgotten by his profession and living in poverty in a bedsit in Notting Hill Gate. Every day he calls his agent to be told there is no work. Then one day the agent surprises him by saying that he has at last found him a part – not a good part, just a walk-on as a waiter carrying a tray of glasses, but a part none the less, in a new play opening in the West End.

Dutifully the old actor rehearses and as the first night approaches grows more and more nervous. At the actual opening he hears his call, collects his props, throws open the door, trips and sends the tray and contents flying, scattering glass at the feet of the stars.

Dismayed and dejected, he trudges up to his freezing dressing room at the top of five flights of stairs and waits to be told that he has been given the sack. Eventually there is a knock on the door and the ASM enters and says, 'Mr Williams, Dame Anna Massey will see you now.'

At the time that Williams created this story it was a wonderfully witty reflection on the sudden access of fame to a beginner. Now that time has passed and Anna Massey's patient and skilful progress has brought her success in a variety of roles – most notably fine in *Hotel du Lac* on television, and as Lady Utterword in *Heartbreak House* at the National Theatre – there is a sort of double irony in the fact that she might very well qualify for the honour which Emlyn Williams mockingly bestowed on her.

MASSINE, Léonide. Massine was the leading dancer and choreographer for Colonel de Basil's Russian Ballet company in the thirties. According to Massine, the gallant Colonel had never risen above the rank of sergeant. Massine told my friend Michael Hill that on their visit to London one of his more balletic experiences was being chased relentlessly round the furniture of the Royal Suite at Claridges by the King of Egypt. He escaped.

MATTHAU, Carol. Walter Matthau's wife – previously married to William Saroyan – has a sharp line when her husband takes too great an interest in other women. According to Truman Capote in *Answered Prayers*, when a Swedish starlet with a pretty face, an overpowering bosom and unusually heavy legs, took her flirting too far and Walter Matthau asked her age his wife snapped, 'For God's sake, Walter, why don't you chop off her legs and read the rings.'

MAUGHAM, William Somerset. Maugham scattered epigrams and perceptions through his professionally carpentered plays, novels and short stories. 'Impropriety is the soul of wit'; 'To write good prose is an affair of good manners. It is, unlike verse, a civil art . . . poetry is baroque'; 'Women will always write novels to while away their pregnancies; bored noblemen, axed officers, retired civil servants fly to the pen as one might fly to the bottle. There is an impression abroad that everyone has it in him to write one book; but if by this it is implied a good book the impression is false.'

To his notebook he confided, 'At a dinner party one should eat wisely but not too well and talk well but not too wisely.'

He may have regretted this advice when, dining with Lady Tree, he excused himself for leaving early saying, 'I must look after my youth.' Lady Tree was very gracious. 'Next time do bring him. We adore those sort of people.'

Maugham and his elder brother, Viscount Maugham, the Lord Chancellor, hated one another. Robin Maugham, the Chancellor's son, recalled a letter from his father to his famous brother: 'Dear Willie, you may well be right in thinking you write like Shakespeare. Certainly I have noticed during these last few months an adulation of your name in the more vulgar portions of the popular press. And one word of brotherly advice. *Do Not Attempt the Sonnets.*'

Maugham's *Cakes and Ale* was dominated by Alroy Kear, a life-like and satirical portrait of Hugh Walpole. Walpole was dressing for dinner in 1930 when he picked up the book. So horrified was he on recognising himself that he claimed that he read the entire book without shifting the position in which he was standing against the mantelpiece when he had picked it up – an appalled and very stiff author.

Walpole and Maugham had both been educated at King's School, Canterbury. The astute headmaster, Canon Shirley, encouraged competition between them in the making of donations to the school. Walpole left it his remarkable collection of manuscripts – including *Wuthering Heights*. Maugham left the school his entire library, and even asked that, despite his unhappy years at the school – because of his stammer – his ashes should rest in the school grounds.

Just before his death in 1965, in *The Summing Up*, Maugham wrote his farewell to writing: 'Thank God, I can look at a sunset now without having to think how to describe it. I meant then never to write another book.'

MAUPASSANT, Guy de. According to the Goncourt brothers, the nineteenth-century writer Maupassant claimed that 80,000 tarts started work in France, of which only about 40 got to the top in Paris. He pointed out that this top 40 were not women born and bred in Paris – who had a mocking, ironical side which irritated the Parisian customer. Rather the *grande cocottes* were all women born in the provinces 'who had something of the servant about them'.

MAXWELL, Elsa. Elsa Maxwell, the great party-goer, party-giver and freeloader from the thirties onwards, threw one of her most original parties in Paris in 1930. It was called 'As-you-were-when-the-Autobus-called' party. No guest knew when to expect the communal transport. One woman had only half her face made up, several were in their underwear and one man was clad only in shaving soap and a towel.

MCKELLEN, Sir Ian. On one of Ian McKellen's visits to the White House for a theatre fund raiser, Ronald Reagan was the incumbent. With his usual empty artistry Reagan recalled the words of some 'wise old man': 'If only we could understand everything in Shakespeare's plays, the world would be a better place.' McKellen was reluctantly impressed until a few days later, when he heard Reagan on television, addressing a Baptist audience. The President recalled the words of a wise old man: 'If only we could understand everything in the Bible, the world would be a better place.'

McKellen also described the Reagans' running entrance: 'Two septuagenarians telling us they are not old.' He watched from the sofa as they kissed, slapped backs, reached out and touched cheeks, finding an appropriate response for each person. 'It was utterly exhausting and an utter waste of time. He could have signed a cheque and got on with being President!'

MENCKEN, Henry Louis. H. L. Mencken, the great American journalist and essayist, belongs to that select body of people who were so frequently witty and quotable that often when a smart remark is looking for a respectable provenance it is attributed to one of them.

Alistair Cooke swears that it was Mencken whose judgement on Calvin Coolidge is so often quoted. 'Coolidge is dead,' he was told as he sat in the office of the *Baltimore Sun*. 'How did they know?' he asked.

Some ascribe the story to Wilson Mizner. I prefer the most widely quoted source – an exchange between Dorothy Parker and Robert Benchley. To back this up, Peter Benchley (grandson) argues that his aged grandmother, a particularly proper old lady who drifted in and out of senility, sat up suddenly in the course of a drive and lucidly insisted that received versions of the story were incomplete. According to her, her husband brought the news to Dorothy Parker, who asked 'the familiar question, "How did they know?" whereupon Benchley capped it with the missing quip, "He had an erection." '

In any case Mencken has quite enough witty quotations in his name not to need a doubtful attribution.

'The saddest life is that of a political aspirant under democracy. His failure is ignominious and his success disgraceful.'

'There are some politicians who, if their constituents were cannibals, would promise them missionaries for dinner.'

In America it is 'the theory that the common people know what they want and deserve to get it good and hard'.

'A good politician is quite as unthinkable as an honest burglar.'

'Under democracy one party always devotes its energies to trying to prove that the other party is unfit to rule – and both commonly succeed and are right.'

'I hate all sports as rabidly as a person who likes sports hates common sense.'

'Love is man's delusion that one woman differs from another – still, man is better off than women; he marries later and dies sooner.'

MILLAIS, Sir John Everett. Soon after the Victorian painter Millais met John Ruskin, Ruskin became fascinated by the reputation of a phrenologist, Mr Donovan, who practised in King William Street, off the Strand. Ruskin persuaded Millais – a dapper chap looking not in the least like an artist – to go for a consultation. Millais reluctantly agreed after his friend offered to finance the consultation.

Holman Hunt's account of the visit is Dickensian in its enjoyment of the phrenologist's pretensions and the relish with which he showed Millais various 'heads' and death masks – Cromwell, Henry VII, Bacon, Dante. Millais queried the last. 'Who may that old lady be?'

'Which, sir? That? Why, that is Dante Alighieri, the great Italian poet.'

'Not a very cheery sort, I should imagine?'

'No, sir, not often gay, it is true . . . '

By the time he got round to 'reading the bumps' he discovered that Millais had great prospects as a business man. None for the arts. He agreed to produce a written testimony, which Millais arranged to pick up the next day. When he called, Mr Donovan gave it to him with great ceremony explaining that he had added many valuable grace-notes to his character assessment. He then asked Millais to sign his address book. Millais now revealed his name.

'Tell me, sir,' asked 'Professor' Donovan, 'are you the son of the artist who painted a picture last year which excited great attention?' Finally Millais confessed that he was not the son, not the brother, but the artist himself.

Donovan asked to take the report back. Millais refused. He had paid for it. He intended to keep it. Donovan pleaded that there were exceptions to his art and that he wished to make a note of this.

'I would not part with it,' said Millais, 'for a thousand pounds' – and walked out of the shop.

When Holman Hunt introduced Edward Lear to Millais, Lear asked if his rapid fame made him 'disposed to lord it over others?' Hunt said that it was more likely that, subjected to Millais's charm, Lear would end up carrying his bags. Lear vowed he would not. As the three men walked along the cliff between Rye and Winchelsea Millais was enraptured by the shells of a cuttlefish, clean and unbroken. He wished to take them home saying that a painter never knew when they might become useful. He gathered them in a handkerchief and ten minutes later asked Hunt to carry it. Hunt declined and Lear collapsed with laughter. Mystified but pleased, Millais turned to his new friend, 'You carry it for me, King Lear,' he pleaded and Lear took the handkerchief packet happily, chuckling as he often did afterwards, 'He doesn't carry his own cuttlefish!'

In later life Millais assumed a grandeur that amused or offended some. Holman Hunt affectionately remembered walking with him in Bishop's Park, Hammersmith, surrounded by families, when suddenly he launched into a very public reminiscence, 'Bless my soul alive, do you mean to tell me that that's the place where, when I was a child, I used to come fishing for sticklebacks?' Then he raised the tone and announced, 'Only think, and now here am I, a baronet and all that sort of thing, with a fishing of my own of several miles, and land to shoot over.' There is something enchanting about the happy self-endorsement.

At his retrospective at the Grosvenor Gallery, Comyns Carr reports him as touchingly pleased with some pictures and dismayed by others. He had not seen his 1852 picture *The Huguenot* since he had painted it forty-odd years before. It arrived just before the opening and he was nervous. Comyns Carr 'felt his arm tremble on my shoulder during the few moments that prefaced the picture's appearance; and then, when at last it was raised to its place, he said in a voice that was half broken by emotion, "Well, well. Not so damned bad for a youngster." and lighting his little wooden pipe hurried out of the gallery and took his way downstairs into the street.'

MISTINGUETT (Jeanne-Marie Bourgeois). Perhaps we should add Mistinguett to the short list of famous Belgians – she, like Maurice Chevalier, had *some* Belgian blood – though she was born in 1874, in grim circumstances, in Enghien, then a small, rural town outside Paris (now an outer suburb).

She was to go on to be an immense star in France, insuring her legs for 500,000 francs – the 'million-dollar' claim was a publicity gimmick. In her love affairs she rivalled the great courtesans of the day – La Belle Otézo, Emilienne d'Alençon, and Cléo de Mérode, who had a highly publicised affair with King Leopold of the Belgians, becoming known as 'Cleopold'. Mistinguett notched up the 60-year-old King Edward VII when she was 26, and also King Alfonso XIII of Spain. Her first meeting with the latter was not promising. The Spanish King and Queen were expected to attend her performance at the Eldorado Theatre. They did not show up, but sent a courtier to apologise and explain that they had gone to another theatre. He asked Mistinguett to join them for supper. He had kept a carriage waiting. 'Good, then you can drive me straight home,' said Mistinguett.

'But what shall I tell His Majesty?' asked the distraught courtier. 'What will the King say?'

'I imagine he'll use the same word I used when I realised he had stood me up,' said Mistinguett. 'But I imagine he'll say it in Spanish.' Later the affair flourished.

When overtures were made just before the outbreak of World War One on behalf of the German Crown Prince she declined, 'He doesn't need Mistinguett to increase his popularity in France and Mistinguett doesn't need the Crown Prince to help her with her publicity in Germany.'

Chevalier was the great love of her life but the two egos could not sustain a lasting affair.

MITCHELL, Margaret. The one-hit-wonder author of *Gone With the Wind* kept firmly away from participation in the preparation and shooting of the movie. She did, however, agree to attend the Atlanta première in 1939. She was seated next to Gable and was amazed when the camera pulled back from Vivien Leigh tending wounded soldiers to reveal an enormous mass – thousands – of Confederate troops. 'Mah Gawd,' she hissed, digging Gable in the ribs, 'if we'd-ah had as many soldiers as that we'd-ha won the woah!'

According to Howard Deitz, the MGM publicist, it was while Gable was filming in Atlanta that a woman asked to take his hotel room the day he checked out, making it a condition that the sheets should not be changed.

MONET, Claude. The Impressionist painters Monet and Degas had been close friends but quarrelled during the Dreyfus Affair of the 1890s. Years passed and all attempts at reconciling them failed. Then first Monet and then Degas began to have serious trouble with their eyes which nothing cured. At about this time Manzi, a notable collector, made one last effort to bring them together. The two old gentlemen, distinguished figures both, attended an exhibition and 'slowly, with measured steps, they advanced towards one another, with hands held out. Both cried out at the same instant:

"How are your eyes, Monsieur Degas?"

"How are your eyes, Monsieur Monet?" '

MORRISON, Herbert Stanley, Baron. The saddest story of Herbert Morrison, the influential Labour politician and Attlee's Home Secretary, is told of the discovery after his death, in his breast pocket, of his choice of eight records for *Desert Island Discs*. He had always awaited the call to join this exclusive club and, imagining that he might be stopped in the street at any time and be summoned, he had resolved to be prepared. Unhappily the invitation never came.

Morrison is also remembered for a comment of Ernest Bevin's. When Attlee remarked that Morrison was his own worst enemy, Bevin muttered, 'Not while I'm alive he ain't.' Paul Johnson casts some doubt on this one, suggesting that Bevin is reputed to have said it about Dalton, Cripps, Bevan, 'and even Richard Crossman'. He also queries if Bevin was the first to use it.

MORTIMER, John. Although John Mortimer, barrister, playwright and creator of Rumpole of the Bailey, does not claim this legal anecdote, current in chambers and in El Vino's, he has propagated it enthusiastically. The case in question was a complicated commercial affair and the parties involved had gathered in the High Court to hear the verdict. It was a Monday and the embarrassed judge confessed to the court that although he had written his 8,000-word judgement over the weekend he had left it at his home in the country so he could not deliver it till the next day. 'Fax it up, m'lud,' suggested the helpful junior counsel.

The judge considered this and replied, 'Yes, I suppose it rather does.'

MOSER, Sir Claus. Sir Claus Moser, erstwhile aeroplane mechanic, academic at the LSE, statistical adviser to the Committee on Higher Education, head of the Central Statistical Office, Chairman of the Royal Opera House and banker with N. M. Rothschild before becoming Warden of Wadham, was born a German Jew, fled Germany with his parents in the thirties and became a naturalised Englishman in 1947.

He enjoys telling the tale of another German also naturalised in 1947 who finally triumphantly becomes English. However, he emerges from his final hearing looking downcast. His wife takes him to task. 'What's the matter? This is one of the proudest days of your life! Why are you looking so miserable?'

'Terrible news!' he replies. 'We just lost India.'

MUNI, Paul. The great American actor Paul Muni (born in Austria), who graduated from the New York Yiddish theatre and played the leading role of Willy Loman in Arthur Miller's *Death of a Salesman* in London, was a specialist in the biographical films which were particularly fashionable in Hollywood in the thirties and forties. Muni was Louis Pasteur in a 1936 film which celebrated the pasteurisation of milk. In spite of Jack Warner's prediction that the film would flop Muni picked up an Oscar and luckily fought off a suggestion that the movie should end with a voice-over solemnly saying, 'And to this day, housewives all over the world are grateful to this man, because he invented pasteurised milk.'

Later Warner toyed with the idea of a life of Beethoven for Muni, having seen the possibilities of what Hollywood called 'biopics'. Muni was an early method man and as Beethoven was deaf so he was deaf to his neighbour's over-the-garden-wall chatter. As the neighbour was Mrs Mischa Auer, wife of another Hollywood star, she reported the fact that he had ignored her to Mrs Muni. 'Oh,' said Mrs Muni cheerfully, 'he probably didn't even hear you. Today he's Beethoven, so he's deaf as a doorknob!' Later Warner decided against the Beethoven project, telling his producer Hal Wallis to look for a different biographical subject: 'Anything but Beethoven,' he said. 'Nobody wants to see a movie about a blind composer.' At the end of the craze Wallis was quoted as saying, 'Every time Paul Muni parts his beard and looks down a telescope, this company loses two million dollars.'

Muni's obsessive concern for developing his character lay more in his mental preparation than his attention to make-up. On one movie, on a day when he had not expected to be called to the set, an assistant director asked him how long it would take him to get ready, 'Four hours,' said Muni. 'Two hours for the outer man, two hours for the inner man.'

Muni's wife, Bella, kept a vigilant eye on the film set, both to approve his scenes and to make sure his leading ladies did not get too involved. When he shot *The Commandos Strike at Dawn* the director told his co-star, the British actress Anna Lee, not to make physical contact with him – 'Paul doesn't like it.' It was not until they got to shoot some publicity shots and Mrs Muni was not present that Miss Lee found the true reason she had to keep her distance. She was suddenly hauled into a passionate embrace and was so surprised that she found it difficult to respond with enthusiasm. Muni let her go muttering, 'Oh, you English women are so cold!'

With his theatre background Muni brought an old theatrical tradition to the movies. He called it 'The Five Day Test'. He had observed that in newly assembled theatre companies romances broke out quickly between members of the company. 'Boys and girls; girls and boys; boys and boys.' Usually the old character actor falls for the prettiest young chorine. Very exceptionally a youngster falls for a lucky oldster. Muni's advice was to give it five days. 'At the end of that time, if you still want it, *then* do something about it. But usually you don't.' And, with Mrs Muni on the warpath, usually he couldn't.

MURPHY, Eddie. It may be an urban American folk tale – it may be true. I've heard it for some years: but Jean Lamb of The Pleasaunce, Edinburgh, insists that 'friends of a work colleague of mine' (fatal distancing phrase) were visiting New York. They were alone in the hotel elevator until it was summoned by two men on the floor below. The two black men got in and one of them barked out, 'Hit the ground, lady!' The British couple hastily dropped to their knees, and the wife proffered her handbag, hoping that complete compliance would reduce the risk of violence. One of the men was Eddie Murphy. Both laughed heartily. They simply wanted her to press the elevator button for the ground floor. Ms Lamb says her source is reliable: but of course in most New York elevators the ground floor is marked as 'One' or 'L'. I hope it's true. I suppose I'll have to interview Mr Murphy to be sure.

MURRAY, Don. Don Murray played the cowboy opposite Marilyn Monroe in Joshua Logan's 1960 film of William Inge's *Bus Stop*. Ms Monroe had been checking out Freud in the years that lay before – including, in 1954, asking Robert Mitchum when they were filming *River of No Return* to explain an entry in her Freudian textbook. The chapter she was devouring was 'Anal Eroticism'. First she had asked her co-star 'What's eroticism?' and then some time later, 'What's anal?'

She had majored by the time it came to *Bus Stop*, according to Logan, and when Murray spoke a line incorrectly – 'Wake up, *chérie*, it's nine o'clock – the sun's out – no wonder you're so pale and scaly' – and Logan called 'Cut!', she made her informed comment. (The line should have read 'You're so pale and white'.) 'You just made a Freudian slip,' Ms Monroe explained to her co-star. 'You must be feeling right in the scene. That was a Freudian slip about a phallic symbol. Unconsciously you were thinking about a snake. That's why you said "scaly". A snake is a phallic symbol. Do you know what a phallic symbol is, Don?' According to Logan, Mr Murray did. 'Know what it is?' he said. 'I've got one.'

— N —

NIGHTINGALE, Anne. Anne Nightingale has become a very successful popular music journalist and radio disc-jockey. I first came across her in the sixties
when I used to retreat to the Royal Crescent Hotel, Brighton, after performances of *That Was The Week That Was*, in order to avoid the almost inevitable
controversy which seemed to attend on every Saturday night. Working as a
journalist in the town Anne used ingeniously to bribe the hotel night porter to
tell her who was staying in the hotel who might yield an interview.

My favourite Anne Nightingale incident is, however, perhaps not one of
which she is particularly proud. She was interviewing the song writer Paul
Simon, whose initial success was achieved as half a singing duo with Art
Garfunkel. The combination of the two voices is beguiling but the songs are all
written and composed by Simon. Some years ago the singers split up and Simon
went solo. It was at this moment that a sympathetic Anne Nightingale was asked
to interview him for BBC 2. Was it not hard, she asked, for him to carry on
writing without his long-term collaborator. No, he said. But surely they had
been singing together for a very long time? He agreed. So, must it not have been
traumatic to have to write on alone? No. But surely if you have been writing
songs with a partner for all that time and he suddenly splits . . . Eventually Simon
explained coldly but politely to the pop expert that Garfunkel had written none
of the songs – only sung them with him. Simon had written them all himself.

It was here that poor Anne finally buried herself. 'Is this a scoop?' she asked
hopefully. 'No,' said Simon, 'I guess most people know.'

NIXON, Richard Milhous. President Nixon's rehabilitation is a wonder of the
twentieth century. From his persecution of Alger Hiss and his dirty tricks campaign against Helen Gahagen Douglas through his embarrassing television confession in the 'Chequers' speech, to his final disgrace after Watergate, he was

invariably the source of wit in others rather than a wit in his own right. The bitter line 'You won't have me to kick around any more' after one defeat was as near to a memorable quote as he got.

Back in 1970 I. F. Stone wrote, 'The Eichmann trial taught the world the banality of evil. Now Nixon is teaching us the evil of banality.' Harry S. Truman had already shrewdly said, 'I don't think the son-of-a-bitch knows the difference between truth and lying.' Later he elaborated on the theme. 'Richard Nixon is a no-good, lying bastard. He can lie out of both sides of his mouth at the same time, and if he ever caught himself telling the truth, he'd lie just to keep his hand in.'

Lawrence Peter coined the Nixon Political Principle: If two wrongs don't make a right, try three. Art Buchwald found him a convenient target: 'I worship the quicksand he walks in' (later he was to use the same phrase for Jimmy Carter). In the end the bitter Nixon joke exhausted itself. As Gore Vidal said, 'Everyone is so anaesthetised by scandal that if it turned out that Richard Nixon was the illegitimate son of Golda Meir, it wouldn't make the front pages.'

Barbs followed Nixon into exile. The New York politician Bella Abzug neatly tarred Nixon and President Ford in one phrase. 'Richard Nixon impeached himself. He gave us Gerald Ford as his revenge.' Ford, the man who famously 'couldn't walk and chew gum at the same time', was a victim of his own unconscious humour when he intoned, 'President Nixon represents a cross-section of American ethics and morality.'

In his own defence after the 'expletive deleted' tapes, Nixon said, 'People said that my language was bad, but Jesus, you should have heard LBJ!' Lyndon Baines Johnson once gave his frank opinion of a Nixon speech: 'Boys, I may not know much, but I know chicken shit from a chicken salad.'

My favourite Nixon anecdote is contained in a reminiscence of David Frost's. He had secured the right to exclusive interviews with the ex-President and questioned him over several days in California – backed up by an impressive team of advisers as well as a large technical crew.

The taping stretched over a weekend when Nixon and Frost had a rest. When the camera crew returned on the Monday morning Frost was amazed to hear Nixon awkwardly attempting to establish some sort of rapport with the technicians. The stilted phrase sums up his out-of-touch approach to bonhomie. 'Well, you guys,' he asked. 'Done any fornicating this weekend?'

NOLAN, Sir Sidney. Barry Humphries shared artistic roots in Melbourne with Sir Sidney Nolan, the great Australian artist. In his address at Nolan's memorial service Humphries recalled that a stuffed race horse at the Art Gallery drew more spectators than Tiepolo: Ned Kelly's armour, famous from Nolan's pictures, was exhibited at the Aquarium between the sharks and the stingrays. Luna Park was a common feature on their horizons. St Kilda's, where Sir Sidney was raised, had gone down in the world and Humphries' mother thought its inhabitants were 'Common . . . sort of Sydney people.' She suspected white slave traffic, with a tunnel direct to Cairo.

The two men met for the first and last times at the Whitechapel Gallery and at the final meeting Nolan recalled World War Two. Carrying a barely finished canvas by his friend and later his brother-in-law, Arthur Boyd, he was stopped by two suspicious officers. Why, they demanded, was he not in the army? Inspired, Nolan answered, 'I am mentally unfit for military service.' They asked him to open his parcel. He revealed the Boyd. They shook their heads. 'He's a nut case all right,' they agreed.

NOLLEKENS, Joseph. The successful eighteenth-century portrait sculptor is as well remembered for his miserliness as for what he called his 'bustos'. The miserliness was at its peak in Rome, where he lived in filthy lodgings opposite a pork butcher. According to his biographer, J. T. Smith, the butcher 'put out at his door at the end of the week a plateful of what he called cuttings, bits of skin, bits of gristle, and bits of fat, which he sold for twopence, and my old lady (who 'did for' him) dished them up with a little pepper, and a little salt; and with a slice of bread and sometimes a bit of vegetable, I made a very nice dinner.' Whenever good dinners were mentioned he always said, 'Ay, I never tasted a better dish than my Roman cuttings.'

When one John Jackson came to make a drawing of a monument at Nollekens' house the sculptor said, 'I'm afraid you're cold here.' 'I am indeed,' said Jackson. 'Aye,' said Nollekens; 'I don't wonder at it; why, do you know there has not been a fire in this room for these forty years.' His wife was just as mean.

NORMAN, Jessye. The great – in every sense of the word – American soprano Jessye Norman has recently been lumbered with a very old joke. Having difficulty getting her majestic form into a railway carriage, she is supposed to have been advised to 'try sideways' by an attendant and to have replied 'There jes' ain't no sideways.' Not only does the attempt at capturing her speaking voice not ring true, but the joke can be traced to L. Raven Hill's classic 1900 *Punch* cartoon. A stout lady is attempting to clamber into a small horse-drawn bus. The carrier advises 'Try sideways, Mrs Jones, try sideways!' Mrs Jones replies 'Lar bless 'ee, John, I ain't got no sideways!'

Alan Blyth, a more reliable authority, reports Jessye Norman indulging in self-mockery. She entered a studio to record an opera and met her co-star, the generously proportioned Rita Hunter. 'Hi, skinny!' was her greeting.

NORTH, Lord. The eighteenth-century statesman Lord North is best summed up as a prime minister by Dr Johnson's dismissive phrase 'He fills a chair'. But North managed the occasional comeback to criticism. When he was denounced by a whig who used the words 'a criminal' in a debate during which North had fallen asleep he protested, 'It is cruel to deny me the solace which most other criminals enjoy – a good night's sleep before their execution.'

Again, when he received a petition from an Alderman Sawbridge of Billingsgate he said tartly: 'I cannot deny that the Honourable Gentleman speaks not only the sentiments but the very language of his constituents.'

NOTTINGHAM, Max. Max Nottingham of St Faith's Street, Lincoln, is one of those irritating people – like compulsive writers of letters to the newspapers (he is one of those too) – who are compulsive callers of phone-in programmes on radio. He claims records for the number and frequency of his calls. However, he got his comeuppance when a woman from the BBC wrote to him saying, 'We liked your letter and used it on the programme; but unfortunately we said you were a woman who lives in Portsmouth.'

NUREYEV, Rudolf. The anecdote which circulated most plentifully after the great dancer's death told of a boy whom he had picked up at a nightclub but dismissed when he got home, saying, 'Your beauty has faded.'

In a letter to the *Evening Standard* Jim Kelsey suggests that this is a typical bastardisation of a tale which changes its character totally in retelling and mistelling. According to Mr Kelsey, back in the sixties Nureyev was dining in the King's Road with Erling Sunde, then a teacher at the Royal Ballet. They left the restaurant late at night and Nureyev, resplendent in fur hat and coat, tried without success to pick up a young stranger. The boy rejected him and Nureyev, dismayed, turned to Sunde and said: 'My beauty am fading.'

Very soon it became a catch-phrase at the Royal Ballet.

OFFENBACH, Jacques. In his charming book of food and music stories, *Foie Gras and Trumpets*, Charles Neilson Gatley retells a story of the nineteenth-century French composer Offenbach (on a tour of America) and an old waiter at Petry's famous restaurant in Philadelphia. The waiter grimaced at the suggestion of a julienne – 'I don't recommend that. The vegetables they use up – how can they do it?' Offenbach decided to forgo soup and asked if they had salmon. 'Certainly we have. We've had it a long time.' Offenbach suggested a steak. 'The cook will ruin it.' 'Strawberries?' 'Mushy and tasteless.' 'Cheese?' 'I'll ask it to come up,' said the waiter; 'won't need any help. It can walk alone.' Offenbach protested at the man's disloyalty to his employer: 'If I were your employer I would fire you.' To which the waiter said, 'He already has. It's my last night here.' He bowed low and left the table.

Offenbach eventually dined well.

OGILVY, David Mackenzie. The legendary and innovative founder of the advertising agency Ogilvy and Mather, David Ogilvy had a varied career before finding his niche. After leaving Fettes, Edinburgh, and Christ Church, Oxford, and before founding his own company in Manhattan in 1948 he was variously a cook in the kitchens of the Hotel Majestic in Paris, an Aga salesman, an executive in a London advertising agency, an intelligence agent for the British in wartime Washington and a failed farmer in Pennysylvania, deep in Amish country.

His Aga period was one of the most eccentric. Having flooded the grand houses of his native Scotland with cookers, he sold one to the Roman Catholic Archbishop of St Andrews and Edinburgh. As a result he got letters of introduction to every convent in the diocese: 'It took three months to visit them all, but every Mother Superior was waiting for me, pen in hand, to sign on the dotted line.'

At a conference in Bombay he was told that the Indian advertising industry was modelled on that of Madison Avenue. The speaker proceeded to speculate on Madison Avenue's model . . . 'Modesty forbids,' was Ogilvy's answer.

When O&M was taken over after a hostile bid by WPP, the veteran was bitter: 'God, the idea of being taken over by that odious little shit gives me the creeps.'

He lives in grand comfort in France regretting the irony that he once recruited Peter Mayle as a copywriter to save him from a dull job at Shell. Four years later he was hurt when he read an article by Mayle. 'As I'd saved him from hell and Shell you'd think the least he could do if he didn't like me was shut up.' His last words on the subject are beautifully dismissive, 'By the way, are his books on France any good?'

He has not, I hope, seen the television series.

OLIVIER, Lord (Sir Laurence Olivier). Tarquin Olivier's biography of his father throws up a couple of stories about Olivier which have not hitherto had great airing. He was, apparently, so jealous of Vivien Leigh's Oscar for *Gone With the Wind* that he tore it from her hand on their way home from the ceremony. He had lost out for *Wuthering Heights*.

More inventively he dined one night at the Garrick Club with Tarquin and two friends when a club servant was showing off the club's portrait collection to some visitors. 'These,' he indicated, 'are the Zoffanys' – Olivier leapt to his feet. He bowed. 'I am the Poppa Zoffany – and these are my sons, Rocco, Luigi, Paolo . . .'

Many Olivier stories do not demonstrate the same awareness. Another which Tarquin quotes was of Olivier, the naïve young actor, being told by his more sophisticated first wife, the actress Jill Esmond, when they were in Berlin, to meet her at the famous art gallery the Kuntsthalle. His arrival was delayed because, panicking in German, he asked the cab driver to take him to the Fuchshalle.

One Laurence Olivier story turns up in Barry Humphries' autobiography.

At an official reception in Sydney in 1948 for Olivier (not yet knighted) and Vivien Leigh during their theatrical tour of Australia the Lord Mayor introduced them as 'Sir Oliver and Lady Leigh'. In reply to a subsequent correction, he remarked amiably, 'Shit, you can't win 'em all.'

OSBORNE, John. Playwright John Osborne's recently published second volume of autobiography, *Almost a Gentleman*, yields a crop of vivid vignettes. Subjected to the thick charm of 'Binkie' Beaumont's blandishments he 'was made to feel like a mud wrestler being complimented by a Duchess'. He appears to have preferred the 'awesomely unlikeable' American producer David Merrick – 'He liked writers,' said Osborne, 'the way a snake likes live rabbits.' George Devine, his mentor at the Court, is vividly evoked smoking cigars in heavy drag for his transvestite role in Osborne's *A Patriot for Me* and lovingly remembered for his 'fixed bayonet relish' in taking on the philistines. Ex-wives get short shrift but perhaps once again it is his mother, Nellie Beatrice, who provides the most colourful memory. They were at dinner at Stratford-on-Avon during a run of *Othello* with Paul Robeson as the Moor and Mary Ure (the younger Mrs Osborne) as Desdemona. The Osbornes were entertaining Robeson after a performance. 'Oh, Mr Robeson, it's such an honour for us to meet you, especially for my son,' said Mama. 'He's such an admirer of yours. You see, Mr Robeson, he's always been so sorry for you *darkies.*'

OXYMORONS. Sandy Toksvig, the diminutive but unfairly talented writer, actress, director and improviser, has devised a pleasantly diverting game mismatching words – a game for the oxymoronic. 'BBC Enterprises', 'Belgian celebrity', 'poor Andrew Lloyd Webber' and 'Military Intelligence' are four good examples, but her best is 'Channel Television'. This gets in because when Ms Toksvig actually appeared on Channel Television some time ago she found a cameraman in a state of some excitement. 'We're breaking into drama next year,' he boasted. She was sympathetic: 'Are you thrilled?' 'Well, not really; the other cameraman's doing it.' 'Labour Party leadership', 'working lunch' and 'British tennis hopefuls' are three more good candidates.

There used to be a bursar of a public school in Dorset who swore that a sign saying 'Beware, oxymorons abound here' was more effective in keeping out village lads than the usual 'Trespassers will be prosecuted'.

Francis Wheen's biography of Tom Driberg threw up three more new and amusing oxymorons. Tom went to Lancing, said to be a 'liberal' public school. Wheen comments: 'One might as well speak of a comfortable prison or a palatable Liebfraumilch.'

— P —

PAIGE, Elaine. Elaine Paige, star of *Evita*, *Cats*, *Chess* and *Anything Goes*, served a long tough apprenticeship before landing *Evita*, her breakthrough role. She has told how on the first day of rehearsals she was taken out to lunch by the director, Hal Prince. 'He was hugely successful and I was deeply in awe of him.' In the course of conversation Prince said that he was going out that evening to see *Peter Grimes*. Battling bravely and aiming at casual awareness, Miss Paige put her foot in it. 'Of course, I know who he is, but I've never met him.' Prince's reply as he was off to Covent Garden to see Benjamin Britten's opera is not recorded.

PAGET, Reginald, Baron. Reginald Paget was the Labour MP who intervened to rebuke Lord Hailsham in the House of Commons for his holier-than-thou attitude to John Profumo for his part in the Christine Keeler scandal which caused his resignation in 1963. The atmosphere in the country precisely fitted Macaulay's comment in 1843: 'We know no spectacle so ridiculous as the British public in one of its periodical fits of morality.'

'From Lord Hailsham,' said Paget, 'we have had a virtuoso performance in the art of kicking a fallen friend in the guts . . . when self-indulgence has reduced a man to the shape of Lord Hailsham, sexual continence requires no more than a sense of the ridiculous.'

I was in a taxi in New York driving down Fifth Avenue when the news came through that Profumo had confessed to the House of Commons that he had lied earlier. The taxi-driver, opinionated as ever, had got entirely the wrong end of the stick. 'I don't understand all the fuss about this Macmillan guy,' he said. 'At his age it's to his credit.'

PALMERSTON, Henry Temple, 3rd Viscount. Palmerston, the great nine-teenth-century Liberal high priest of Victorian gun-boat diplomacy, was in office for some 48 years. Somehow he managed to combine extraordinarily long working hours – 7 a.m. to midnight - and a full sexual and social life. The social life sometimes suffered: it was said that 'the Palmerstons always miss the soup'; he was three-quarters of an hour late for the Turkish Ambassador – there are echoes of the Duke of Edinburgh's remarks about 'slitty-eyed' Chinese in the way Palmerston brushed aside protests at his lateness at the Ambassador's dinner party: 'a greasy, stupid old Turk . . . one of Bluebeard's attendants'. Talleyrand and Pozzo di Borgo, the Russian Ambassador, were both made to cool their heels –   possibly there was some sexual justification in the latter case, as di Borgo had been the lover of Lady Palmerston when she was Lady Cowper. Even Queen Victoria was a victim of his poor time-keeping. His excuse was abrupt: 'Public business must be attended to, Ma'am.'

Yet for sex there seemed always to be time. He had affairs with three of the seven great hostesses in the early part of the nineteenth century, the *grande dames* who could postpone a Commons debate if it threatened their soirées. He was cited in two divorce actions and also as a co-respondent when he was 79. During an election a rash Conservative wished to expose him as the father of a bastard when he was in his eighties. Disraeli was more prudent. His view was that if the British people found out, Palmerston would 'Sweep the country!'

Lady Palmerston was an invaluable lightning conductor, entertaining lavishly and charmingly at 94 Piccadilly, a great London house now known as 'The In and Out' – the Naval and Military Club.

Palmerston's greatest indiscretion was committed at Windsor Castle. He invaded the bedroom of a lady-in-waiting, a Mrs Brand. She resisted success-fully. The Queen and the Prince Consort were inclined to believe it was an attempted rape. Palmerston claimed that it was a mistake. He insisted that another guest was furious as she had been on tenterhooks waiting for him. It was only the intervention of his brother-in-law Lord Melbourne that got him off the hook.

Lady Stanley neatly characterised his 'brusque impudent' way of approaching a married woman. 'Ha, ha! I see it all – beautiful woman – neglected by her hus-band – allow me, etc . . . '

Speaker Denison recorded a meal which Palmerston downed when he was 81:

He ate two plates of turtle soup; he was then served very amply to cod and oyster sauce; he then took a pâté afterwards he was helped to two very greasy-looking entrées; he then despatched a plate of roast mutton (two slices) . . . there then appeared before him the largest, and to my mind the hardest, slice of ham that ever figured on the table of a nobleman, yet it disappeared just in time to answer the enquiry of the butler, 'Snipe or pheasant, my Lord?' He instantly replied, 'Pheasant', thus completing his ninth dish of meat at that meal.

Palmerston gave his clerks at the Foreign Office a terrible time, though, according to Greville's *Diaries*, they testified that he 'wrote admirably and could express himself perfectly in French, very sufficiently in Italian and understood German'. These virtues were offset by his keeping them working long into the night, stopping their smoking, and eavesdropping on them in the corridors. When he lost his office and was defeated in 1841 they subscribed to floodlight the Foreign Office in celebration.

PARKER, Charlie ('Bird'). Charlie Parker's revolutionary saxophone-playing brilliance and his career of excess figure side by side in the anecdotes of those who remember him. He once pointed out the veins in his arm saying sadly, 'This is my Cadillac . . .' and pointing to another, 'and this is my house'. Towards the end of his life when, according to Bill Crow in his *Jazz Anecdotes* he had 'inhaled, imbibed, ingested and injected monumental quantities of every form of stimulant, euphoric, narcotic, soporific, hypnotic and hallucinogen known to modern man', he was treated by a doctor for what turned out to be his final illness. 'Do you drink?' asked the ill-informed doctor.

'Sometimes,' confessed 'Bird', with a wink at a friend, 'I have a sherry before dinner.'

In Clint Eastwood's film celebrating him, made 33 years after his death, the trumpeter Red Rodney is portrayed. He was telephoned by a reporter on a Nebraska newspaper. He gave her an interview. Before signing off she said, 'Thank you, Mr Rodney. And, by the way, can you give me Charlie Parker's phone number?'

PARKER, Dorothy. Dorothy Parker, the Algonquin wit, was once required to specify the essentials of her trade. She settled for truth. 'There's a hell of a difference between wisecracking and wit. Wit has truth in it. Wisecracking is simply callisthenics with words.' She was not above wisecracking and I have anthologised her theatrical cracks in a previous book. However, her wit was not confined to the theatre. 'This book should not be tossed aside,' she wrote, 'but hurled with great force.' She homed in on women writers: 'As artists they're not – but as providers they're oil wells. They gush!' She aggravated her offence by saying, 'It's a terrible thing, but I can't think of good women writers. Of course, calling themselves women writers is their ruin; they begin to think of themselves that way.'

I see that I left out of my earlier book her devastating generalisation: 'Scratch an actor and you'll find an actress'; and her wire to Robert Sherwood's wife, congratulating her on the arrival of a much-worried-over baby: 'Dear Mary, we all knew you had it in you.' Judged by the available evidence, her favourite straight woman was Claire Booth Luce, who once stood aside for her saying, 'Age before Beauty' – to be countered by 'Pearls before swine'. Later when Ms Parker was told that Miss Luce was always kind to her inferiors she enquired innocently, 'Where does she find them?'

She attempted to conceal a beguiling vulnerability when she married Alan Campbell: 'People who haven't talked to each other for years are on speaking terms today – including the bride and groom.' She was more often sharp than supportive. 'That woman speaks eighteen languages and can't say No in any of them.' (John Gielgud was to say of Ingrid Bergman: 'Poor Ingrid – speaks five languages and can't act in any of them!') I like her put-down to an American actor who had come back from a season in London and had lost some of those hard American consonant sounds ('skedule' for 'schedule' and other betraying mannerisms). 'If you don't mind my saying so,' she said, 'I think you're full of skit.'

She ran off Basil Rathbone as 'two profiles pasted together', and a political witch-hunt with 'the only "ism" in Hollywood is plagiarism'. Into the chestnut class of wisecracks have gone 'And I'll say of Verlaine too: he was always chasing Rimbauds'; more nonsensically, 'There I was, trapped like a trap in a trap', more truthfully, 'Scratch a lover, find a foe'; eventually: 'If all those sweet young things present were laid end to end I wouldn't be at all surprised.'

She was perhaps too keen on the *double-entendre* which the word 'lay' offers. When she was apartment hunting her requirements were simple: 'All I need is room enough to lay a hat and a few friends.' She inspired one of Tallulah Bankhead's confessions by asking her to a particularly wild party: 'The more I behave like Whistler's Mother the night before the more I look like her in the morning,' said Bankhead. Dorothy Parker called her 'Whistler's Mother' ever after.

In another famous party phrase she commented, 'Enjoy it! One more drink and I'd have been under the host.' More soberly she generalised on successful American writers. 'It is our national joy to mistake for the first rate, the fecund rate.' To the American Horticultural Society she announced: 'You can lead a whore to culture but you can't make her think.'

Alexander Woollcott called her 'a mixture of Little Nell and Lady Macbeth'; but she wrote her own epitaph: 'Excuse my dust. This is on me.'

PARKINSON, Cecil, Baron. Enough has been made of ex-Cabinet Minister Cecil Parkinson's misdemeanours: but he did say an extraordinary thing when quizzed on television about his autobiography. He recalled a sergeant who had harangued him on the dangers of sexual pursuit when he joined the army. 'If you want it you'll find it. If you find it you'll get it. If you get it . . . ?'

He went on to compare his failure at the last throw to become Foreign Minister on account of his sexual adventures. He likened it to a professional footballer who breaks his leg 'just when you are about to play for England'.

He did not add the extra risks of playing away from home.

PARKINSON, Michael. Michael Parkinson's addiction to sport is legendary, but as a passionate Yorkshire cricket supporter he was overshadowed by his father. When their first child was about to be born, Parkinson was in London and his wife Mary in Manchester. One day Parkinson got a phone call from his father: 'Job's done,' he said.

Parkinson *fils* asked, 'What job is this?'

'I've shifted Mary to a nursing home in Wakefield.'

'Why?'

'Why! What happens if it's a boy and he's born in Lancashire?'

Giving an after-dinner speech to a drunken and noisy crowd in the outback of Australia, Michael was having a bad time until the man introducing him called for fair play. 'Come on guys, give the Pom a go,' he appealed. 'After all, it'll be better than a poke in the eye with a blunt stick.'

As a boy, Parkinson was desperately keen to play professional cricket and football. His trial for Yorkshire was not successful but as a sixteen-year-old reporter on a local paper he tried a wily ruse to bring himself to the attention of the scouts. Headlines like 'Parkinson on the Goal Trail again' began to appear. They were followed by stories such as 'Ace goal scorer Mike Parkinson took an afternoon off from hitting the back of the net last week but was the brains behind his team's 6-0 win,' and finally, 'Three scouts, believed to be from Barnsley, Wolverhampton Wanderers and Manchester United, were at the game keeping a close eye on goal scoring hot-shot, Mike Parkinson . . . '

Eventually real scouts started turning up. Ruefully Parkinson reports that they left at half-time.

PARSONS, Louella. The two rival Hollywood gossip sisters were Hedda Hopper and Louella Parsons – with space in the papers and time on radio. Can it be possible that, when Ingrid Bergman shocked Hollywood by leaving her husband for Roberto Rossellini and making *Stromboli* in Italy and the news came through that she was pregnant, Ms Parsons when on her radio show and wept into the microphone: 'Oh, Ingrid, Ingrid! Whatever got into you?'

Ms Parsons did have an inside line to the news. She was married to a doctor who specialised in venereal disease and urology. For a long time he was head of the medical department at Twentieth Century-Fox.

Such was Hopper's power that she occasionally called her Beverly Hills home 'The house that fear built'.

PEARL HARBOR. The attack on Pearl Harbor on 7 December 1941 came as a surprise to the American fleet and to the whole world. It now emerges in the official US Naval History that an alert was actually sent to Hawaii about the imminent attack by the Japanese. However, due to the unserviceability of the army radio link between Washington and Honolulu that Sunday morning, the message had to go by Western Union. A telegraph boy on a bicycle delivered the vital telegram to General Short, commanding the defences of the island, several hours after the attack.

PECK, Gregory and Véronique. The Hollywood couple Gregory and Véronique Peck came to see *Side by Side by Sondheim* when we were playing it on Broadway at the Music Box Theatre. I was writing a piece for *New York Magazine* at the time and was delighted to detail how Mrs Peck had struggled valiantly against an overpowering desire to sleep and in spite of every bit of help – nudging and prodding – from her embarrassed husband and daughter sitting on either side, had finally dropped her head and succumbed. I wrote that I assumed that the Pecks had just flown in and excused her lapse as the unjust consequence of jet lag.

It was not until 1992 that I finally met the Pecks at a function organised by Carl Foreman's widow Eve. 'Weren't you the man . . . ?' Mrs Peck opened in friendly fashion. I confessed that I was and they said that *all* their friends had sent the cutting to them. They had laughed rather a lot at it. There was only one thing she wanted to make clear. She did not have jet lag!

PERELMAN, S. J. *Monkey Business* was the first of two films co-written by Sid Perelman for the Marx Brothers. Perelman had to read the script to them in their New York hotel suite. They arrived (late), attended by their wives, producers, agents, accountants, gagwriters and Zeppo's dogs – 27 people in all, plus five dogs.

There was a deathly silence after Perelman finished reading. Finally Chico asked Groucho what he thought of it. Removing his cigar Groucho said, 'It stinks.' At which all the guests including the dogs left the room.

Money Business – rewritten – was to become not only a hit movie but a classic comedy.

One morning in Hollywood Sid Perelman saw John O'Hara's Rolls-Royce parked by the curb. As a mild joke he wrote on a piece of paper 'Dear John, it's no worse than a bad cold' and put the note on the windscreen. Later, in New York, Perelman heard that O'Hara was furious because he thought Perelman was spreading rumours that he, O'Hara, had gonorrhoea. Recalling what he had written, Perelman asked why that should have upset him. 'Well,' said someone, 'because he did have gonorrhoea.' As an English aside, Perelman always claimed that what made him take *The Times* (of London) regularly was reading the account of a man who was arrested for shop lifting when he fainted at the cash desk because he had hidden a frozen chicken under his hat.

PÉTAIN, Henri Philippe Omer, Marshal. Marshal Pétain is remembered, if at all, for the sorry accommodation he reached with the Germans in France in World War Two. Hitherto he had been the hero of World War One.

On the evening of 16 May 1917 two French generals, Nivelle, the Commander-in-Chief, and Pétain, Chief of the General Staff, dined together in the Palace of Compiègne north of Paris. No words were spoken. 'The meal,' Pétain's Chief of Staff recorded, 'was exquisite but *deadly*.' Next day Nivelle had gone and Pétain was Commander-in-Chief.

PHILIP, Prince, Duke of Edinburgh. When Prince Philip was a naval lieutenant back in 1945, he and his cousin Lord Milford Haven crashed a smart party in Melbourne where his ship was visiting. The hostess later complained that some joker in very bad taste had written 'Philip of Greece' in her guest book. Her touchiness was explained by the fact that a mobster in Sydney much in the news at that time was known as 'Phil the Greek'.

His nicknamesake wisely returned to the United Kingdom, married well, and lived happily ever after.

PICASSO, Pablo. Picasso was in Paris during the German occupation. Legend has it that Otto Abetz, Hitler's ambassador in the city, visited him and offered to supply him with coal as his studio was so cold. While he was in the room he spotted a print or photograph of Picasso's great anti-war *Guernica* canvas. 'Oh, it was you, Monsieur Picasso,' said Abetz, 'who did that?'

'No,' said Picasso, 'it was you.'

PINTER, Harold. Justin Mortimer's portrait of playwright Harold Pinter, painted in 1991, caused some comment when it was unveiled at the National Portrait Gallery that August. His father-in-law, Lord Longford, said, 'He looks frightfully sad.' 'Yes,' agreed Lady Antonia Pinter, 'he's thinking about the Kurds and the people of East Timor. It's his human rights face. Terribly appropriate.'

PLAYGOING. Three excuses for not going to the theatre:
Financier Sir James Goldsmith: 'My legs are too long.'
Distinguished film director: 'It's all in wide shot.'
Novelist John Updike: 'I've never enjoyed going to plays. The unreality of painted people standing on a platform saying things they've said to each other for months is more than I can overlook.'

PLOMLEY, Roy. I could never understand my absence from Roy Plomley's isle of sweet musical noises which give delight and hurt not, especially when David Frost, whose ear is twice as cloth-filled as mine, was cast away on at least two occasions. It became a crusade. Every time I launched a play, a book or a film the publicist would ask on which radio shows I had not appeared. Always I said *Desert Island Discs*. 'That won't be difficult,' the publicist would reply. At the end of each campaign I would ask what happened about *Desert Island Discs*. 'Oh, I can't understand it,' would be the lame answer. After countless exercises in this manner – after all I'd been on *Any Questions* under the chairmanship of Freddie Grisewood, there's posh! – I gave up only to get a call some months later from the imaginative PR lady who had chaperoned me around the country on my last plugging exercise. 'I don't suppose,' she asked, 'that you would want to address the first literary luncheon in Eastbourne?'
'Not particularly.'
'. . . Only the other speaker is Roy Plomley . . . '
It was irresistible. We met on the train and seemed to enjoy each other's company. We both went well at the lunch and I thought my *Desert Island Discs* was in the bag.
Roy Plomley died about a week later. I had to wait through the Parkinson interregnum for the advent of Sue Lawley before paying my visit.

POTTER, Dennis. Dennis Potter, the playwright whose credits need not be recited here, sprang a new story on his faithful public during the launch of his television show *Lipstick on Your Collar* – the third instalment in his song-and-dance trilogy.
He recalled an old officer from his days as a National Service other rank. 'Pottah!' the Major bawled. 'Sah!' responded Potter, coming running. 'How do you spell "accelerator"?' asked the old boy. 'I've been through all the blasted "Ex's" in this bloody dictionary.'

POUSSIN, Nicolas. The great seventeenth-century French painter who lived and worked mainly in Rome, and was to provide Anthony Blunt with a special sphere of expertise, simply put the price of his pictures on the back of the canvas – and it was always paid him. Entertaining Bishop Massini in his modest home, the conversation lasted late into the night. Eventually Poussin lit a candle and showed his eminent guest – later a cardinal – down to his coach. 'I very much pity you, Monsieur Poussin,' said the bishop sympathetically, 'that you have not one servant.' 'And I pity you more, my lord,' replied Poussin, 'that you have so many.'

PRICE, Nancy. Nancy Price was one of the most eccentric, opinionated and, in many cases, unpopular actress-managers to hold a place in British theatre.

The designer Anthony Holland recalls working with her in 1936 on her production of Clifford Bax's *The King and Mrs Shore* at the Little Theatre.

The play started with Jane Shore as a wretched old crone and worked backwards to her youth as the beautiful mistress of Edward IV. At the dress rehearsal Miss Price decided that this would not do at all and on the first night the whole thing was suddenly played the other way round – youth to age – which, as Anthony Holland remarks, 'Didn't really help it at all'.

PROUT, Sir Christopher. Sir Christopher Prout's career as a barrister did not yield as neat a nickname as his election as Conservative Member of the European Parliament for Shropshire and Stafford in 1979 and his elevation to Chief Whip, European Democratic Group in 1983. As leader of the Conservative Members of the European Parliament, he was definitively known as 'Brussels Prout'.

PUBLISHERS. The most famous verdict on publishers is the parody – 'Now Barabbas was a publisher' – of St John 18: 40 ('Now Barabbas was a robber'). I once complained to a publisher about his appalling behaviour, reminding him of the phrase, and he wrote back disarmingly, 'I always thought there was a lot to be said for Barabbas.' The judgement is usually ascribed to Byron, who is said to have had his publisher, John Murray, in mind. However, H. L. Mencken suggests that the probable source was Thomas Campbell (1777-1844), which leaves us little the wiser. Edgar Allen Poe wrote, 'K, the publisher, trying to be critical, talks about books pretty much as a washerwoman would about Niagara Falls or a poulterer about a phoenix.' Amanda Ross was no more generous: 'I don't believe in publishers who wish to butter their bannocks on both sides while they'll hardly allow an author to smell treacle. I consider they are too grubby altogether and, like Methodists, they love to keep the Sabbath and everything else they can lay their hands on,'

Arthur Koestler's complaint was of publishers who are also authors, 'A publisher who writes is like a cow in a milk bar.' For the defence Michael Joseph argued, 'Authors are easy to get on with if you are fond of children.' Sir James Barrie used a parable: 'Times have changed since a certain author was executed for murdering his publisher. They say that when the author was on the scaffold he said goodbye to the minister and to the reporters, and then he saw some publishers sitting in the front row below, and to them he did not say goodbye. He said instead, "I'll see you again." '

'Posterity,' George Ade estimated, 'is what you write for after being turned down by publishers.'

Most discouraging of all must surely be the urge to publish a slim volume of verse. Don Marquis said, 'Publishing a volume of verse is like dropping a rose petal down the Grand Canyon and waiting for the echo.'

In the nineteenth century Longmans, the publishers, paid Disraeli the huge advance of £10,000 for his novel *Endymion*. When it failed to sell he offered to return half that amount. Longmans declined to accept the offer but leaked the story to the papers as a publicity stunt to boost sales.

— Q —

QUAGLINO'S. Quaglino's is the restaurant in Bury Street which was famous for its stylish Italian proprietor in the twenties and thirties, when it played host to bright young things, serviced débutante society and particularly pleased the young Barbara Cartland. Its new incarnation – a huge, handsome eating space under the direction of Sir Terence Conran – is the source of a different crop of apocryphal anecdotes because of the difficulty of getting in.

Neil Shand has made two suggestions as to Sir Terence's catering future. One is that he is buying a telephone exchange to convert into a restaurant space on the theory that although it may not be glamorous it will be easier to get through.

An alternative suggestion is that he is negotiating for a furniture factory – also not glamorous but at least you'll be able to get a table.

Another rumour suggests that well-heeled people have lost the habit of putting their sons down for Eton – these days they're putting them down for a table at Quag's.

I used to host a Radio 2 show from the old Quag's. The formula was hijacked from a bygone age. A presenter with guests, sitting among the diners at the side of the dance floor – interviews spaced between cabaret spots and band numbers as the dancing diners swished by. In those days Quag's was nearly always empty and the odd genuine customer didn't mind the BBC presence. However, as Christmas approached office parties took over and the boisterous revellers could not understand why they were being 'shushed' for a broadcast conversation they could not hear. The climax came in the last show before Christmas when I had two septuagenarian guests, Arthur Marshall and Richard Goolden (best known as Mole). It remains, and I hope always will, the only time I have conducted an interview while being pelted with bread rolls.

QUAYLE, J. Danforth. Lest we forget the Vice-President of the United States of America under George Bush, here are a few of his more celebrated statements. A book by Bob Woodward and David S. Broder, *The Man Who Would be President*, suggested that Quayle is a more skilful politician than it would appear. However, the danger of his ambitions being achieved seems for the moment to have passed.

'Republicans understand the importance of bondage between a mother and child.'

'Hawaii has always been a very pivotal role in the Pacific. It is IN the Pacific. It is a part of the United States that is an island that is right here.'

'What a terrible thing to have lost one's mind. Or not to have a mind at all. How true that is.' (Quayle winning friends while speaking to the United Negro College Fund.)

Quayle stumbled in response to a question about his opinion of the Holocaust. He said it was 'an obscene period in our nations's history'. Then, trying to clarify his remark, Quayle said he meant 'this century's history'. 'We all lived in this century'. 'I didn't live in this century,' he said.

'We expect them [Salvadorian officials] to work towards the elimination of human rights.'

'I believe we are on an irreversible trend towards more freedom and democracy – but that could change.'

'If we do not succeed, then we run the risk of failure.' (To the Phoenix Republican Forum, March 1990.)

'I want to be Robin to Bush's Batman.'

'The US has a vital interest in that area of the country.' (Referring to Latin America – it was here that he regretted his inability to communicate . . . as he had never learnt Latin.)

'Japan is an important ally of ours. Japan and the United States of the Western Industrialised capacity, 60 per cent of the GNP, two countries. That's a statement in and of itself.'

'Who would have predicted . . . that Dubček, who brought the tanks in to Czechoslovakia in 1968, is now being proclaimed a hero in Czechoslovakia.' (Actually Dubček was the leader of the 'Prague Spring'; the tanks invaded to quell his liberalisation campaign; he was arrested.)

'May our nation continue to be the beakon of hope to the world' – the Quayles' 1989 Christmas card (not a beacon of literacy, though).

'. . . Getting [cruise missiles] more accurate so that we can have precise precision.'(Referring to his legislative work dealing with cruise missiles.)

'Certainly I know what to do, and when I am Vice-President – and I will be – there will be contingency plans under different sets of situations and I tell you what, I'm not going to go out and hold a news conference about it. I'm going to put it in a safe and keep it there! Does that answer your question?' (Quayle, when asked what he would do if he assumed the Vice-Presidency, 1988.)

Lloyd Benson, Quayle's Democratic rival for the Vice-Presidency, had the last word in their TV debate when Quayle compared himself to Jack Kennedy and Benson said, 'I knew Jack Kennedy – and you're no Jack Kennedy.' (Reagan brilliantly reworked it in knocking Governor Clinton for comparing *himself* to Thomas Jefferson. 'Ah,' said the old communicator, 'I knew Thomas Jefferson . . .')

'Verbosity leads to unclear, inarticulate things.'

'The real question for 1988 is whether we're going to go forward to tomorrow or past to the – to the back!'

'We will invest in our people, quality education, job opportunity, family, neighborhood, and yes, a thing we call America.'

'This election is about who's going to be the next President of the United States!'

'Don't forget about the importance of the family. It begins with the family. We're not going to redefine the family. Everybody knows the definition of the family. [Meaningful pause.] A child. [Meaningful pause.] A mother. [Meaningful pause.] A father. There are other arrangements of the family, but that is a family and family values.'

The final gaffe was perhaps the most sensational – when Quayle, campaigning for re-election, corrected a schoolboy's blackboard spelling of 'potato' – proudly added an 'e'. At least in Congress he had represented Indiana, not Idaho.

QUINTON, Anthony, Lord. At the height of the Falklands War I was hosting a BBC late-night radio interview programme called something like *Extra Dry Sherrin*. The splendid comic Roy Hudd and the comedy-fancying life peer Lord Quinton were discussing the nature of comedy and providing examples of jokes. It is fair to say that the conversation had not caught fire when the programme was broken into by the announcement of a disaster in the South Atlantic. The *Sir Galahad* had been sunk by Argentine forces. Radio 4 went over to the House of Commons. The House was not yet ready for a statement. Would they come back to our studio or would they play 'solemn music'? They played solemn music. Never was music so solemn. As it washed over us Lord Quinton thought for a moment or two. 'Ah yes,' he mused, 'I think I know that tune. It's Sibelius's "You can't win 'em all".'

— R—

RAMSAY, Sir Alf. Sir Alf Ramsay, the last England manager to win the World Cup, was a taciturn, authoritarian man, who allowed no one to feel indispensable. Once when Gordon Banks, by common consent the greatest goalkeeper in the world at the time, bade farewell to Ramsay by saying, 'I'll see you.' Ramsay replied, 'Will you?'

In his lively book of sporting stories, *Sporting Lives*, Michael Parkinson quotes Bobby Charlton on an attempt to sort out a team problem with Ramsay. The England side was due to play a match in a hot climate. Their suits for the trip were uniformly made of a heavy grey material. Charlton was delegated by the players to petition the Manager for permission to wear something lighter. 'The lads thought maybe you could let us wear our blazers and flannels rather than the suits,' he concluded. Ramsay thought a moment and replied, 'I have a completely open mind on the matter . . . tell them to wear the suits.'

RAMSAY, Margaret (Peggy). Margaret Ramsay, the legendary theatrical agent who died in 1991, represented a distinguished gallery of playwrights including at various times Robert Bolt, Alan Aykbourn, Christopher Hampton, Willy Russell, Edward Bond, Peter Nichols, John Mortimer and Joe Orton. She conducted her business from a rabbit warren of offices in Goodwin's Court, off St Martin's Lane – a building which before her tenancy had served as a brothel. She graduated to play agent from being a play reader and chose her plain, straightforward job description because the scripts she read and most admired in her early days came from the agent A. D. Peters who so described himself.

She had a brilliant nose for new talent and never stinted to encourage it. Conversely, she was stridently critical of her authors' work if it fell below the standards she expected of them.

In a supplementary obituary note, one of her old clients, John Holmstrom, recorded her first meeting on English soil with the Romanian playwright Eugène Ionesco. 'Having hastily read the manuscript of (I think) *Rhinoceros* before his arrival at Heathrow, she also swotted up a couple of laudatory French sentences. But the pronunciation of *pièce* eluded her, and the little Surrealist was greeted with 'Cher Maître, vous avez fait une pisse superbe.' Needless to say he was her slave from that day on.

RANDALL, Derek. The old story involving caviar and jam is assuming the proportions of a folk myth – however, the ebullient and undervalued Nottingham and England cricketer Derek Randall gave it true-story status instead of innumerable anonymous attributions. It was on a Test tour of India (1976–77) that Randall was offered caviar and having sampled it complained that 'the blackcurrant jam tastes of fish to me'.

RAPHAEL, Frederic. The novelist, critic and screenplay writer, Freddy Raphael is in dispute with Billy Wilder over a remark prompted by the Academy Awards and the plethora of cloned ceremonies. Who said it? Usually people try to claim a witticism, not renounce it, but according to Raphael, 'I always attribute to Billy Wilder the remark which he, quite unjustly, attributes to me: "Awards are like haemorrhoids – in the end, every asshole gets one." '

RAYMOND, Paul. Paul Raymond, the impresario, striptease king and Soho landlord, might not be considered the most likely product of a convent education ; however he feels that he owes his manners, which he considers exquisite, to the experience. 'I'm a very polite man deep down inside,' he volunteered recently. 'And this is from the nuns.'

REAGAN, Ronald. The phenomenon of Ronald Reagan's presidency produced formula jokes more than genuine anecdotes – apart from the ones that revealed his fallible memory, his artful speechwriters and his resilience in the face of Hinckley's assassination attempt.

There is the classic manufactured anecdote about Reagan at his first summit with Gorbachev. Gorbachev reveals that the previous night he dreamed that he saw the White House with a red banner flying over it complete with hammer and sickle and the words 'Union of Soviet Socialist Republics'. Reagan is dumbfounded and waits for the next summit to reveal that he too has had a dream. Gorbachev asks him to reveal it. 'I dreamed I saw a red banner flying over the Kremlin,' Reagan replies. 'What did it say?' Gorbachev asks. 'People's Republic of China,' says Reagan.

It was Nancy Reagan's biographer Kitty Kelly who alleged that the 70-year-old Frank Sinatra had been spending steamy afternoons in the White House with the 60-year-old Nancy Reagan – leading to the suggestion that Francis Albert was singing to her 'Come Try with Me'.

Nancy's tribute to her husband on her 78th birthday was most touching. 'Everyone should have a Ronald Reagan in their lives,' she intoned – without bothering to consider whether there were enough autocues to go round.

Reagan was the president who kept a pad by his bed in case he woke up and had an idea in the middle of the day.

We missed Reagan on his retirement. He will go down in history as the only president who can't remember what he would like to be remembered for.

REDESDALE, Lord. The father of the Mitford sisters is supposed to have read only one novel – *White Fang* by Jack London – and because it was *so* good never to have read another. However, according to Nancy Mitford, Lady Redesdale once tried to interest him in other literature by reading to him from *Tess of the d'Urbervilles*. It made him weep so much that she had to reassure him that it was only fiction. 'What! Not the truth?' shouted 'Farve'. 'The damned fellow invented all that?'

REID, Helen Ogden Mills. This should really be a Winston Churchill story but there are lots of them and no others involving Mrs Helen Ogden Mills Reid, who was the sister of the fanatically anti-British Colonel McCormick, owner of the *Chicago Tribune*. In 1943 at a lunch with President Roosevelt at the White House she encountered Winston Churchill. She tackled him critically about the treatment of India. 'Before we proceed further, madam,' said Churchill, 'let us get one thing clear. Are we talking about the brown Indians in India who have multiplied alarmingly under the benevolent British rule or are we speaking of the red Indians in America who, I understand, are almost extinct?'

According to Churchill's ADC, Commander Thompson, who recorded the incident in his memoirs, Roosevelt laughed so much that it was feared he might suffer a seizure.

RENOIR, Pierre Auguste. The nineteenth-century painter Renoir used to say that he was the only person to know when one of his pictures was finished. When he'd stopped painting a woman's back and felt he wanted to slap it, he said he knew the picture was done.

RETORTS. The tracking-down to their roots of repeated favourite anecdotes is a pleasing and harmless hobby. Witty or pertinent retorts often make the basis of a good anecdote. I had always heard that the posted reply 'Sir, your letter is before me, and will soon be behind me' had originated with Oscar Hammerstein I in reply to a creditor at the beginning of the century. In a piece in his column in the *Sunday Times*, however, Godfrey Smith traced it to a roughly contemporary English source.

Further research, though, suggests that in the 1780s Lord Auckland wrote to Lord Sandwich explaining why he had switched allegiance from Fox to Pitt. In his reply Lord Sandwich used the formula 'Your letter is before me and will presently be behind me', adding politely, 'I remain, sir, your most humble servant.'

Similarly Howard Dietz, the great lyric writer who also worked as a publicist at MGM, claimed another famous retort when he was accused of arriving late at the office. Now I find a life of Lord Beaverbrook ascribing the same remark to the portly and sybaritic Viscount Castlerose at roughly the same time in the 1930s. He had tried to work in the bank of his uncle, Lord Revelstoke. Rebuked for continually arriving late he replied, 'But think how early I leave' – just as had Dietz.

Dietz is also in dispute with Herman Mankiewicz over a well-known apology to a New York society hostess at the height of fledgling wine snobbery in New York in the thirties. I am inclined to award this one to Mankiewicz as the more conspicuous consumer. Whoever it was rushed from his embarrassed hostess's dinner table and fled to the loo where he was sick. When he returned he said blithely. 'It's all right, the white wine came up with the fish.'

REYNAUD, Paul. Paul Reynaud, during his brief stint as prime minister of France, fell ill at the end of April 1940, a few days before the final German onslaught on France. Whether or not it affected the outcome, the Editor of *Paris Soir* was surprised to arrive at the Cabinet Office and find the beautiful Countesse Hélène de Portes, Reynaud's mistress, sitting behind the Prime Minister's desk issuing orders to generals, ministers and senior civil servants. At a turning point in French history the government of France was in her hands.

REYNOLDS, Sir Joshua. Sir Joshua Reynolds's sitters sometimes gave the eighteenth-century portraitist trouble. Lord Holland felt obliged to say that the portrait he commissioned was hastily executed. In trying to get around to querying the price he asked Reynolds how long he had been painting it. Reynolds fell back on the formula reply in these situations, 'All my life, my lord.'

Dr Johnson did not like Reynolds's version of him. It showed him reading and revealed that he was near-sighted. 'It is not friendly,' he said, 'to hand down to posterity the imperfections of any man.' Sir Joshua suggested that accurate characterisation added to the value. Mrs Thrale, as an intermediary, pointed out that 'he would not be known by posterity, for his defects only, let Sir Joshua do his worst'. She referred to a picture of Reynolds himself with an ear-trumpet – which prompted Johnson to grunt, 'He may paint himself as deaf as he chooses but I will not be *blinking Sam!*'

Reynolds's problem with Haydn – a Royal commission – was different. Haydn showed up twice in great fatigue. Sir Joshua thought he looked stupid and did not want to paint him in that mood. He complained to his princely patron, who supplied an immediate solution – a pretty German girl who, when Haydn slumped for the third time, was revealed behind a curtain and who engaged him in a flirtatious conversation in her native language. Suddenly Sir Joshua had an animated model and was home.

His famous portrait of Mrs Siddons as the Tragic Muse elicited a splendid compliment. He had painted his name on the border of her gown like a piece of embroidery. Mrs Siddons, advancing to examine it, smiled contentedly. Reynolds bowed and said, 'I could not lose this opportunity of sending my name to posterity on the hem of your garment.'

RIBBENTROP, Count Joachim von. Having been the Nazi ambassador to the Court of St James in the 1930s and contributing largely to Hitler's conviction that Britain would not seriously oppose him, von Ribbentrop arrived in Moscow on 23 August 1939 to negotiate the notorious Nazi-Soviet pact. He was extremely surprised in the uncertain diplomatic climate to find the streets decked with hundreds of Swastika banners – unlikely symbols in Communist Russia. In fact they had been borrowed at the last moment from a film set near Moscow where they were shooting an anti-Nazi film.

RICHARD I. Standing six feet five with golden hair and blue eyes, Richard I looked convincing as a king. He was in fact a good news-bad news monarch. He was brave but cruel; an inspired soldier and a disinterested administrator; a hero whose popularity made him a legend, and a King of England who had less interest in his country and spent less time in it than any other; he had strains of generosity and altruism; he was educated and musical. He screwed every penny he could from his people by selling land and honours, then spent the proceeds on fighting in the Crusades; he fought them for the sake of Christianity, but he fought with a ferocity which compounded the bad name which Christianity already enjoyed throughout the Middle East. He was a popular poet and a prolific torturer. More fighter than statesman, he was a muscular homosexual; he was 'a bad son, a bad brother, a bad husband and a bad King', but Kings of England were getting bigger and Richard was the biggest so far. He could look and behave like a convincing hero. *The Dictionary of National Biography* calls him a 'splendid savage', and he lived in an age as savage as any.

Everything in Richard's life before his arrival in the Holy Land was a preparation for his Crusade against the Saracens. Everything that came after his departure was anticlimax. His arrival boosted the morale of the allies besieging Acre, and the 'Griffon-Killer', his ingenious secret weapon, was an immediate success. (This vast tower was drawn up outside the gates of the city, and gave his archers a vantage point from which to shower arrows into the enemy stronghold.) Towards the end of his year in the Holy Land, he would parade before the Saracen ranks and challenge any man to single combat. No one dared accept.

Richard's bravery in action also unleashed the savage side of his nature. When Saladin, his great opponent, failed to appear on cue to discuss the ransom of prisoners – some two thousand taken at Acre – Richard had them butchered with relish, slitting open their stomachs to reveal that many had swallowed their gold in an attempt to keep it safe. Generations of Arab women frightened their young children into obedience by threatening them that King Richard of England would come for them if they did not behave.

Richard's relationship with Saladin was chivalrous as well as savage. Between bouts of fighting each other with wily ferocity, they exchanged gifts of grapes or snow, the caviar of desert luxuries, or Negro slaves or chargers. When Richard's favourite sorrel horse, Flavel, was cut from under him in battle and he had to fight on foot, Saladin, who had observed the mishap from his camp, despatched his finest steed, a gesture which nearly backfired. One of Richard's knights mounted the horse first, and the volatile animal wilfully made straight for the stable from which he had come. Realising that this looked like a crafty infidel trick to capture the English King, Saladin was covered with chivalrous shame and sent another better-behaved beast.

At the beginning of October 1192, Richard, depressed and exhausted by the blazing heat, malaria, the defection of his allies and his failure to liberate the Holy Sepulchre, packed his Queen, Berengaria, and his sister Joan off to Europe and set off on the long journey home himself on 9 October.

It was at this moment that the whole world lost sight of King Richard. The whole world, that is, except his enemies. By a mixture of bad weather, bad navigation, bad geography and bad luck, he found himself in Austria, and proposed to travel, disguised as a Templar, through the territory of an old enemy, Duke Leopold. As rumours of his presence in Austria spread the hunt was on – clues were left in profusion by a proud page whenever he went into town to shop for the King. Eventually Richard was tracked down and discovered sweating in a kitchen, this time disguised in the greasy overalls of a cook, turning a spit, incognito, a monstrous ring still on his fat-splattered finger.

He was hauled before Leopold and thrown into prison. History does not report his discovery but tradition supplies a story too romantic and attractive to be ignored. Blondel, a minstrel friend of Richard's youth, roamed across southern Germany until he reached the castle of Tenebreuse in Styria. Here he learned that a mysterious prisoner was being held in great secrecy. When they were younger, Richard and Blondel had collaborated on a song which 'no one knew save they alone' – plainly it had not made the troubadour's hit parade. Blondel launched into the first verse and was delighted to hear the King pick up the tune and join in. The news was rushed back to England. A year of wrangling followed, complicated by spite, jealousy, greed, fear and pride, before 'the most illustrious living hero in Christendom' could go home.

From then on Richard made war in France. He also carried on the family tradition of designing and building castles. His masterpiece was at Andely on the Seine. He first saw the rocky site when he threw three French prisoners into the ravine below – a reprisal for King Philip's slaughter of some Welsh auxiliaries. In a happier mood, on completion of the castle, he clapped his hands in child-like ecstasy, calling his barons to admire his Château Galliard, his 'saucy castle'.

Richard was not to enjoy his saucy new castle for long. He laid siege to the castle of Chaluz, which was ill prepared to withstand siege by a pack of boy scouts, let alone the legend of the Lionheart. The handful of defenders of the shaky citadel, short of missiles, began dropping stones and beams of wood on the heads of the great King's mercenary engineers who were attempting to undermine them. One of the defenders had only a frying pan with which to ward off the flying bolts of iron. During a lull in the assault, the Knight of the Frying Pan spotted an arrow discharged at him by the King himself some moments earlier. He plucked it from the turret where it had lodged and fitted it to his crossbow. Richard was standing on open ground too confident to bother with armour, apart from a headshield. Noticing the enterprise of the enemy bowman, he clapped his hands and shouted a sporting word of encouragement – a regular intimacy in medieval war-games.

Not since King Harold's death had an arrow struck so importantly and ironically. It grazed Richard's neck and penetrated deep into his side. Richard was a bad patient and gangrene set in. With growing knowledge that death was near, his heroic qualities came back to him. He awaited his end calmly. His orders to hang the garrison of Chaluz were carried out. He made one exception – for the man who had shot him – and he sent for his aged mother, Eleanor of Aquitaine, conveniently nearby among 'the shrouded women' at Fontevrault. Richard had carefully planned the fate of his body; the brain to the abbey of Charroux, the heart in a gold and silver casket to Rouen, the penitent corpse to be laid at his father's feet in Fontevrault. Berengaria was not with her husband. She was distraught in Anjou, mourning a man who did nothing to try to win her love. Possibly she wept because she suspected she would spend the rest of her life trying to wring maintenance out of his relatives. If so, her suspicions were prophetic.

RICHARD II. In June 1381, the fourteen-year-old King Richard II was confronted by a menacing mob of peasants flushed with his uncle's wine and their own success. They came from Essex, sacking houses and manors on the way, and from Kent where castles fell to them and serfs were set free. At Canterbury they broke into the Cathedral during Mass and urged the monks to throw out Archbishop Sudbury and choose a replacement from among themselves. The monks showed little enthusiasm so the rebels elected their own candidate, John Ball, a vagrant priest whom they found conveniently to hand in the Archbishop's prison. Following their leader, Wat Tyler, they marched on Blackheath, where Ball whipped up their enthusiasm with his famous text,

> When Adam delved and Eve span,
> Who was then the gentleman?

Nervous envoys from the King inquired the peasants' purpose. Tyler replied that they came to save the King and destroy his enemies. The King's ministers and the Mayor and Council of the City of London were characteristically slow to respond. At last they collected their wits, placed the boy King in the Royal Barge and set out for Greenwich to talk to the rebels. As they prepared to disembark, they panicked at the sight of the unruly crowd milling on the bank and demanding the head of John of Gaunt (the most unpopular man in the kingdom), as well as the heads of the King's other ministers. Richard would have risked a landing but older counsels prevailed and the frustrated country folk saw the Royal Barge turn tail and withdraw up the Thames to the Tower.

The passions aroused by Ball's eloquence were still running high. The mob pressed on to Southwark, and the citizens of London joined the men from Kent. Their immediate objective was John of Gaunt's impressive palace of the Savoy. Gaunt was conveniently away in Scotland, somewhere between concluding a war and patching up a peace. His son, Henry of Bolingbroke, a few months older than Richard, was inside the Tower with his King.

The yeomen smashed the glazed windows, ruined the painted chambers, and tore down the splendid tapestries. Forbidden by Wat Tyler to loot, they burned and trampled underfoot the jewels, rich ornaments and crowded racks of fine clothes. Moving on, they looked back with satisfaction on a black, smoking ruin as they followed their new route east to meet the rest of the ragged army approaching from Essex.

It was not only the rebels who watched the smoke and flames of the burning Savoy. The boy King had a grandstand view from the Tower; but his panicked counsellors gave him little help. Using his own initiative he issued a general invitation to a meeting at Mile End the next day, and promised a written charter of pardon and sweeping concessions. The crowd were not convinced by the sight of the charter; but they kept the appointment the next morning.

Fires smouldered across the city. To the north one local leader, Jack Straw, set light to the Treasurer's new manor at Highbury. The morning sky was flecked with spirals of smoke, and Richard could see and hear evidence of danger as he rode out from the Tower, at the head of a small band of lords and knights, to reason with several thousand hungry but cocky rebels.

Facing the crowds at Mile End, Richard heard them protest their loyalty to him and their determination to bring traitors to punishment. He encouraged them to hunt down traitors by any means; but to bring them to justice, not to a lynching. Interpreting this as an invitation to anarchy, the mob entered the unguarded Tower. Towards the King's mother, the 'Maid of Kent', their attitude was lasciviously genial. Coming upon the Archbishop at prayer, the mood changed and he and his fellow celebrants were dragged unceremoniously to Tower Hill to be beheaded.

Meanwhile, the King's mother and her ladies slipped through the City to Baynard Castle, where they locked themselves in the royal wardrobe. Through this macabre mixture of murder, clodhopping, amorous dalliance and euphoric confusion, the boy King seems to have wandered unattended and unmenaced, until he too arrived at Baynard Castle, and joined his mother. It had been an inconclusive day, but some of the rebels were satisfied with their exploits and began to think of going home. On the next day, Richard and a small party of Lords went to the shrine of St Edward to pray, unaware that the keeper of the Marshalsea had been dragged from there to Cheapside to be beheaded a few minutes earlier. Richard, attended by the Mayor, rode from his prayers to Southfield where he faced a second crowd. This time the spokesman was Wat Tyler, carried to flights of bombast by a week of undisputed leadership. The devotion of his followers and the craven indecision of his opponents had turned his head and his attitude to the King was dictatorial and insolent. Gracefully and casually, Richard promised to agree to Tyler's demands. Divided between suspicion and a wish to rub in his triumph, Tyler continued to question, hector and insist.

As he overplayed his hand, the King's party grew restless. Losing his temper, the Mayor dragged Tyler from his horse and a squire, Standish, killed him with his sword. For a moment the drama stunned the crowd. Then their mood grew ugly and they advanced. The King dug his spurs into his horse and rode towards them with a brave invitation: 'I am your captain, follow me.' He was lucky in the discipline Tyler had instilled in his followers. Having lost one leader, they followed the new one, created before their eyes. When royalist reinforcements arrived to surround the mob, Richard continued to insist on controlling the occasion. Docile to a degree, the puzzled peasantry heard him pardon them and order them to go peacefully to their homes. Gradually, they lumbered away. Tyler's head replaced the Archbishop's on London Bridge. Richard's closest bodyguards were knighted on Clerkenwell fields and the boy King's certainty that a 'divinity doth hedge a King' received a powerful boost.

Richard's quest for a Queen ended with the selection of Anne of Bohemia, who arrived at Dover in 1382. Anne imported several new fashions to England. The middle-European horned cap, two feet high and two feet wide, built on a framework of wire and pasteboard covered by glittering gauze, caused the biggest stir. Younger ladies at court rushed to adopt the extreme fad; older women dismissed it as the reprehensible 'moony-tire' denounced in the Old Testament by Ezekiel. Anne saved this spectacular fashion coup for her marriage in the newly consecrated Chapel of St Stephen. Richard's own breakthrough was the first handkerchief – an accessory which survived until the arrival of the tissue several hundreds of years later.

Allegations of Richard's supposed homosexuality are hard to substantiate. Little, besides scurrilous and interested contemporary rumour, points to it. Popular history's picture of the sensitive, effeminate, artist King is made up of misleading details. Yes, he read books. He possessed a French Bible and the 'Romance of the Rose', and Froissart presented him with a copy of his love poems, richly bound. Meeting the poet Gower by the river one day, he commissioned him to 'write some newe thing'. Certainly, his warlike father and grandfather would have been unlikely to indulge these interests. Yes, he had a plain wife and delighted in the company of a close circle of handsome young men – but this need not take us too far towards a conclusion.

Clothes are often a giveaway, and Richard's were extravagant and costly, studded with gold and precious stones: but the fashion for jewellery and display was not confined to the King, it was common among the magnates at his court. Sometimes regarded as even more incriminating was the King's passion for baths. The new bath-house he built at King's Langley was a small hall with ten glazed windows built on top of a great oven. At Sheen he commissioned 2,000 painted tiles to decorate his Bath Chamber and brass taps admitted hot and cold water. All this washing must have caused raised eyebrows among the unsympathetic aristocracy, but cleanliness was not automatic proof of ungodliness then any more than now.

When Anne died at Sheen in 1394 Richard's dismay was real and his grief deeply felt. He ordered the palace at Sheen to be burnt to the ground and made a redecorated Windsor his main seat.

Lacking an heir Richard unwisely denied his cousin Henry Bolingbroke his inheritance. Bolingbroke (John of Gaunt's son) eventually confronted and deposed Richard in Wales. The two cousins met inside the walls of Flint Castle, manned by Richard's scrappy remnant. Froissart records that even Richard's favourite greyhound, Math, who had hitherto taken no notice of anyone but the King, promptly transferred his affections to Bolingbroke, privately symbolising for Richard the sudden and final passage of kingship. More public was his humiliating progress to Chester, mounted on a sorry black nag – 'not worth a couple of pounds'.

Richard died in February 1399. The official explanation of his demise was that so disappointed was he by the failure of his supporters that he pined, declined to eat and died of starvation. Unofficial reports said more plainly that he was starved to death.

Subsequent examination of his skull disproved theories that he had met a more violent end at the hands of Sir Piers of Exton, while rumours of his escape, of his survival as a poor half-wit in the Scottish Court and of his burial at Stirling in 1419 are no more than the common conspiracy theories which surround and survive the deaths of kings and presidents and popular singers.

RICHARD III. The question of Richard's physical and mental deformities has been long debated. There is the testimony of 'The Old Countess of Desmond' – this antique phenomenon was supposed to have lived to be 140 and to have recalled late in life how, as a girl, she danced with Richard when he was Duke of Gloucester. She found him 'the handsomest man in the room, except his brother Edward, and was very well made' – which could make her an accurate observer, or just another impressionable royal groupie. A German diplomat who met Richard in 1448 describes him as 'tall and lean with delicate arms and legs'. On the other hand, there is the monster of Sir Thomas More's history and of Shakespeare. John Rous, a rewrite historian ambitious for Tudor patronage, wrote a hardly impartial account: 'At his nativity the scorpion was in the ascendant; he came into the world with teeth, and with a head of hair reaching to his shoulders. He was small of stature with a short face and unequal shoulders, the right being higher than the left.' In an account of a petty street brawl at York, written six years after his death, Richard was described in evidence as 'an hypocrite and a crouchback'.

Contemporary portraits do not reveal the malign features or the misshapen form, but this is hardly surprising. Some deformity must surely have been present to fuel the legend – a God-send to playwrights anxious to contrast Tudor beneficence favourably with the gory Plantagenets whom they had succeeded on such sketchy legal grounds. Modern medical opinion divides over the possibilities.

Over Richard's malign behaviour, there is more controversy. He was possibly involved in the death of Edward, Prince of Wales, at Tewkesbury and probably a party to Henry VI's murder in the Tower. He was almost certainly far away in Scotland at the time of the murder of his brother, the Duke of Clarence, malmsey or no malmsey; but after 1483 the public face of a good soldier, capable administrator and humane arbitrator is washed away in the bloodbath of ambition.

The final struggle of his reign crystallised into a conflict between Richard and his challenger, Henry Tudor, whose claim a few years earlier would have seemed slender; but as it has been calculated that between 1400 and 1485 four kings, twelve princes of the blood and twelve near relatives fell through battle, murder or sudden death it is not, perhaps, surprising that at the end of this epidemic a rank outsider could romp home.

Henry landed at Milford Haven in August 1485, collecting an army as he marched through Wales. He met Richard at Bosworth in Leicestershire. In spite of the King's early record and recent good deeds – he had reverently re-interred the remains of Henry VI at Windsor – a large proportion of the fighting men of the nation sat on their shields and waited to see which way the battle would go. Richard had the larger army, but that advantage was cancelled when Lord Stanley, acting as a weathervane for the whole country, drew up his six thousand men in such a formation at Bosworth that he could swing them into action on the side of whichever general looked like winning.

Richard's last march from Lichfield to Leicester was a grim business. He rode a great white horse, his armour freshly burnished and his crown placed upon his helmet. He frowned in anxious concentration throughout the journey. As he left Leicester in the morning, a blind beggar pronounced a riddling prophecy. He would not return. On the evening of 21 August the King examined the perimeter of his forces, found a sentry asleep and put him to the sword, muttering, 'I found him asleep and leave him so.' The dual chroniclers, Shakespeare and tradition, award him an uncomfortable night, 'most terribly pulled and hauled by divels'. In the morning a leaflet on the Duke of Norfolk's tent proclaimed:

> Jockey of Norfolk, be not too bold,
> For Dickon thy Master is bought and sold.

In spite of this psychological warfare Richard threw himself desperately into battle. Henry Tudor represented the last feasible challenger to his title – kill him and he might still survive. Spurring his horse on with a cry of 'Treason! Treason!' he cut his way towards the challenger. He dealt Henry one blow before he was overpowered, beaten to the ground and slain. As he fell his crown caught in a thorn bush. It was plucked out on his sword by Lord Stanley, who placed it on Henry's head. Richard's body was trussed across the back of a horse and taken to Leicester, where it was buried with little respect.

Richard left at least one bastard son who went to ground in a brickyard after Bosworth, served his apprenticeship there and became a master-builder in Kent where he lived until 1550, ending his days at the age of eighty or more, known as Richard Plantagenet.

RICHARDSON, Sir Ralph. Most of my stories about the great theatrical knight are in *Theatrical Anecdotes*: but I forgot his reply when asked to appear in a charity programme in support of imprisoned writers. 'No,' he said wickedly, 'on the whole I think all writers should be in prison.'

RICHELIEU, Armand Jean du Plessis, Duc de. The French statesman, cardinal and power behind the throne of Louis XIII of France in the seventeenth century is often celebrated in romantic costume drama: but no one seems to have exploited his oddest trait. He had such an overwhelming passion for cats that he left pensions to the fourteen which outlived him.

Could Princess Michael of Kent be a reincarnation of Richelieu?

RIGBY, Harry. Ghostly visitations have always given me a miss so perhaps I am being fanciful in claiming this experience as supernatural. In New York for a couple of days, staying on the West Side in the apartment of my friend Glen Roven, a dazzling composer-lyricist, I lunched at the Russian Tea Rooms on 57th Street, just by Carnegie Hall.

One of the most regular diners there – virtually a fixture – was the whimsical old theatre producer, Harry Rigby. Harry was the man who revived *No, No, Nanette*, *Irene*, and *Good News* and also gave you *Sugar Babies*. At about 12.30 p.m. I watched Harry pass down through the other side of the restaurant. I made a mental note to say hello before I left the room.

Lunch over, I looked around and couldn't find Harry, so, thinking no more of it, I went back up town to be met by a glum Glen. He was a friend of Rigby's and, at a very young age, the conductor of *Sugar Babies*, which had starred Ann Miller and Mickey Rooney.

'Harry died,' he greeted me. 'He had a lunch date at the Russian Tea Rooms and when he didn't make it they phoned his apartment. When they got no reply the janitor went in and found him. He died about 12.30 p.m.'

Did I see Harry keeping his date or some other distinguished-looking Broadway luncher? I like to think I saw Harry.

RIZZUTO, Phil. Phil Rizzuto, the American baseball commentator, gained a certain immortality with his impromptu remark during a baseball commentary which had been interrupted by the news of the Pope's death: 'This puts a damper even on a Yankee win,' he intoned.

ROBERTS, Rachel. Rachel Roberts, the extraordinarily talented Welsh actress who starred in the films *Saturday Night and Sunday Morning* and *This Sporting Life* as well as in many stage successes in the fifties and sixties, had a volatile personality which could not cope with the different lifestyle which she inherited on her marriage to Rex Harrison. Working with him in Paris on the disastrous film version of Feydeau's *A Flea in Her Ear* she confided to her diary, 'Rex grew more and more stiff and distant from me. I suppose I drank more and more.' In her cups she was likely to disappear and make love without taking much care over her choice.

During the filming of *Flea* her part in the shooting schedule finished early and she decided to while away the spare time learning French. One night she did not return to their hotel and when she did turn up the next evening still drunk, she reported proudly, 'Hier soir, j'ai fucké le chauffeur de mon mari.'

In later years she was asked if she missed Rex's way of life – in particular the use of his chauffeur-driven car.

'No,' she said, 'but I miss the use of the chauffeur.'

RODERICK, Stan. Stan Roderick, a splendid session trumpet player who always enlivened the TV show *That Was The Week That Was* by an unmistakable guffaw – usually in the right place – was playing at a recording session for a film score. The distinguished orchestrator and conductor of popular music – a man – had recently decided to change sex, much to the surprise of friends and colleagues. When she returned to work after the operation she was faced with a mammoth score for this expensive movie. She entered to face her orchestra sensibly skirted to conduct the first band call. There was an unsurprising air of tension. She gave the few, formal and precise instructions. The she asked if there were any questions. The band had not yet relaxed and the studio was on edge. With a sentence Stan is alleged to have shattered the nervous atmosphere. 'I suppose,' he enquired, raising his hand, 'a fuck's out of the question?'

ROOSEVELT, Franklin D. When Roosevelt became paralysed by polio in 1921 everyone said his career was finished – except his secretary, Howe, who said, 'Well, this makes it quite certain you'll be President of the USA because a good-looking face on a lame body always gets public sympathy and because you'll be spared all the political nonsense, hand-shaking, platform stumping etc., which ruins a man.'

ROSEBERY, Archibald Philip Primrose, 5th Earl of. The 5th Earl of Rosebery, popularly supposed to be a homosexual, was not a notable success in his job, but managed to achieve the three objectives to which legends said he aspired. He wanted – indeed he needed – to marry the greatest heiress in Britain. He married Hannah Rothschild. He wanted to be Prime Minister. At the collapse of Gladstone's last ministry, when no one would accept Harcourt he became Prime Minister. He wanted to own a horse which won the Derby. He did so three times.

He had a bitchy exchange with Asquith – a later Prime Minister – when they discussed the defection of John Morley, the Irish secretary and a supposed supporter. Asquith said, 'Yes, he's a difficult man to manage. But at least he's a perfect gentleman.' Rosebery replied, 'Yes, but I am not sure he might not best be described as a perfect lady.'

The Rothschild wealth he had acquired did not make him behave entirely properly to his in-laws. When he lived at Mentmore, the great palace which the Rothschilds built, if his wife's relative bored him he would say, 'To your tents, O Israel!'

According to Lloyd George's secretary and mistress, Frances Stevenson, one night, when there was an important debate in the House of Lords Lloyd George overheard Rosebery's valet say to him, 'Your grouse is done to a turn, my lord,' at which Rosebery disappeared, leaving the debate to go its own way.

ROSSETTI, Dante Gabriel. Rossetti was the most charismatic of the Pre-Raphaelites, storming at children who fidgeted when they sat for him; carelessly spilling expensive paints when, along with Burne-Jones and William Morris, he painted the frescos at the Oxford Union, muttering as priceless lapis lazuli ground into real ultramarine, 'Oh, that's nothing. We often do that.'

He invited Fanny Cornforth to pose for him when he came across her cracking nuts with her teeth in the Strand and throwing them at him. She later became his mistress and housekeeper. He met his match in one vivacious servant girl who was 'doing' for him and Burne-Jones. He 'affected the direst madness' and in sepulchral tones recited the lines:

> Shall the hide of a fierce lion
> Be stretched on a couch of wood,
> For a daughter's foot to lie on,
> Stained with a father's blood?

The maid was unimpressed and instead of the soft 'no' which the poem requires in answer simply giggled, 'It shall if you like, sir!'

Rossetti kept an odd menagerie including a wombat and a woodchuck, which he liked to cuddle. Separated from the wombat he fired off this quatrain:

> Oh how the family affections combat
> Within this heart, and each hour flings a bomb at
> My burning soul! Neither from owl or from bat
> Can peace be gained until I clasp my wombat.

There were also a dangerous zebu bull, a racoon which slaughtered a neighbour's chickens – not quite as serious as the marauding wombat, which once destroyed an entire box of cigars. Cigars were eventually to be the death of the wombat. After going missing for days he was found in a cigar box – reduced to a skeleton.

The bull, bought at Cremorne, would chase Rossetti round his garden when not tethered. Then there were a peacock and a gazelle who fought each other.

He was keen on the limerick form and used it to accuse his fellow Pre-Raphaelite J. W. Inchbold, who was inclined to abuse his hospitality.

> There's a troublesome fellow called Inchbold,
> With whom you must be at a pinch bold,
> Or you may as well score
> The brass plate on your door
> With the name of J. W. Inchbold.

ROTHERMERE, Harold Sidney Harmsworth, 1st Viscount. During a dinner party in the thirties attended by the press baron Lord Rothermere and by Brendan Bracken, who owned the *Financial News*, a big news story broke and both men sent out for their own newspapers. Someone brought back one copy of the *Daily Mail* (owned by Rothermere). Someone else brought back a whole bundle of the *Financial News*.

'See what we can do – a copy for everyone,' said Brendan Bracken. 'And only one copy of the *Daily Mail*.'

'Very simple for you, Bracken,' remarked Rothermere. 'Your man brought your whole edition!'

ROTHERMERE, Patricia ('Bubbles'), Lady. Nicknamed 'Bubbles' by *Private Eye* because of her fondness for champagne, Lady Rothermere, who sadly died in 1992, was a devoted grand hostess and an obsessive party-goer. She had been a Rank starlet (Beverley Brooks), her most significant role as Douglas Bader's girlfriend before his accident in Lewis Gilbert's movie *Reach for the Sky*.

After her marriage to Vere Harmsworth, 3rd Viscount Rothermere, she devoted herself to his social life: 'When I married my husband I didn't just marry a man, I married an empire. And, in a way, I think I projected a frivolous image of myself on purpose because I did not want to be the heavy wife of a newspaper publisher.'

Her best-known *mot* predicted the failure of Régine's, the nightclub, on top of the old Derry & Toms building in Kensington High Street. She judged that, because it was situated on the top of an office block a mile from Hyde Park Corner, 'It is too far out of London'.

Ironically she approved the move of Associated Newspapers to Barker's next door because she confused the two stores and thought her husband was acquiring the famous roof garden.

RUSSELL of Killowen, Charles, Baron. Often irascible in chambers, dignified in court, Lord Russell of Killowen, a nineteenth-century judge (and Lord Chief Justice), could relax delightfully in a social setting. When a woman asked him what was the maximum punishment for bigamy he smiled and replied at once, 'Two mothers-in-law.'

— S —

ST JOHN, Adela Rogers. Adela Rogers St John was usually wheeled out in old age to reminisce for TV documentaries about the old Hollywood. Her father, Earl Rogers, an American lawyer who died in 1922, was perhaps an even more interesting subject. Many of his clients were Californian Chinese. As a young woman Adela was sitting in his office when a distinguished, impeccably dressed old Chinaman entered and asked her father how much he would charge to defend him on a murder count. When Rogers told him he paid out the money in gold, bowed and began to leave. 'Hold on!' said Rogers. 'Where are you going?'

'I go kill the man now,' said the Chinaman. 'Then I be back.'

ST JOHN, Henry, 1st Viscount Bolingbroke. An early Tory Party leader in the eighteenth century, when the Tories were profiting from the royal break with the Whig ascendancy, St John seems to have set a pattern for subsequent Tory debauchery – though to be fair he was also celebrated for his oratory, his prose, and his political deviousness. While he was Secretary for War in 1704 he wrote to a fellow MP, Thomas Coke: 'As to whores, dear friend, I am unable to help thee. I have heard of a certain housemaid who is very handsome: if she can be got ready against your arrival, she shall serve for your first meal. Adieu, ever yours most entirely, Harry.'

Bolingbroke himself was apt to boast, before his dismissal on Queen Anne's death, that, 'he was the happiest man alive, got drunk, harangued the Queen, at night was put to bed to a beautiful young lady, and was tucked up by two of the prettiest young Peers in England, Lords Jersey and Bathurst'.

SAND, George (Amandine Aurore Lucile, Baronne Dudevant *née* Dupine). After separating from her husband, the Baron Dudevant, a retired army officer,

George Sand went to Paris and, in 1831, set up life as a writer – particularly as a romantic novelist. She had famous liaisons – with Alfred de Musset and with Chopin – but, according to the Goncourts, in many cases the passion was on their side – especially on the occasion when she slept with Prosper Mérimée. When he climbed out of her bed he picked up a sheet of paper lying nearby. She tried to snatch it out of his hand because it contained a pen portrait of him which she had scribbled while they were making love.

SCHNABEL, Artur. The great pianist and composer Schnabel once interviewed a student who had asked if he could be his pupil. Schnabel tested him and agreed.

'How much are your lessons?' asked the pupil.

'Five guineas each,' replied Schnabel.

'I'm afraid I couldn't afford that.'

'I also give lessons at three guineas, but I don't recommend them.'

SCHWARZENEGGER, Arnold. I once met Arnold Schwarzenegger, the ex-Austrian body-building Charles Atlas of his day, now a film star in violent spectacles and a Kennedy son-in-law. We came together in 1977 in Chicago in a lift or, as they say in that town, an elevator. I don't know why Arnold was in a Chicagoan elevator. I was there to preside over the American regional opening of the musical revue *Side by Side by Sondheim* starring Cyril Ritchard – born 1895 – who was playing the Narrator's role which I had written and originated in London and New York. (Others who followed in my footsteps in America included the Mesdames Hermione Gingold, Arlene Francis, Dorothy Lamour and Peggy Lee.)

Ritchard moved from the West End to Broadway in the fifties. In both places he clashed frequently with Noel Coward. When he played *Private Lives* in New York he proudly drew Coward's attention to his new toupée, demanding approval. 'Oh, my God,' said Coward, 'I thought it was a yachting cap!' Back in England, they had differed over a Coward lyric in the revue *Sigh No More* (1946). The song referred indelicately to three nuns. Ritchard, a devout Catholic convert, protested, 'My aunt was a nun.'

'Very well,' replied Coward. 'Make it *four* nuns.'

Unfortunately Ritchard died on stage in the middle of a matinée of *Side by Side* and the company manager, an ex-dancer in his mid-sixties, couldn't wait to clear away the corpse, grap the script, dash on and finish the show – which must, of course, go on.

There was, however, a regular understudy, a charming actress based in Chicago, Brenda Forbes – who had no time to get to the theatre. Her birth date is unrecorded but she is of a similar generation, made her first stage appearance at the Lyric Theatre, Hammersmith, in 1927 and supported Katherine Cornell with distinction on Broadway in the 1930s. She had also given her Lady Montague (an unrewarding role) and understudied Edith Evans's Nurse in the Cornell *Romeo and Juliet*.

For the Chicago production Cyril Ritchard had insisted on adding two songs to the Narrator's role – singing is not one of my accomplishments but he considered it one of his. When we arrived Miss Forbes was in a tizzy. She had been sent neither script nor song copies from which to learn her part. I rushed off to the top of the hotel (the theatre was in its basement) where there was a photocopying machine. Having produced a complete score and script I brought them back to a delighted Miss Forbes. 'Oh! What a relief,' she cried. 'Now I can study the script *and* the songs. I'm so glad about the songs,' she trilled with all the secure pity of an old pro, 'I'm told that the poor boy who played it in New York wasn't allowed to sing them!'

It was on the way down in the elevator with the script that I met Mr Schwarzenegger. As I got out I said, 'Good morning,' to which he replied, 'Have a nice day.'

SCOTT, George C. The powerful American actor and film star George C. Scott was the principal player in an anecdote which David Susskind used to tell. It may be apocryphal – if it is, apologies to Mr Scott – but it perfectly illustrates the self-absorption of some great actors.

Scott was starring in a New York cop series produced by Susskind. During the filming of one episode a disagreement between Scott and the director escalated to reach an impasse and threatened to bring the production to a halt. Susskind called the opponents for a meeting at the close of shooting. The discussion began around six and ended inconclusively and acrimoniously. In the early hours Susskind was awoken to be told that the director had just had a heart attack and was dead.

Waiting until six, when he knew Scott would be preparing for shooting, he called the actor and broke the news to him.

'Ya,' said Scott. 'I don't feel too good myself.'

SHANKLY, Bill. The great Liverpool manager was also the most memorable soccer phrase-maker. He did it in one with 'Some people think football is a matter of life and death. I don't like that attitude. I can assure them it's much more serious than that.' On particular matches he was just as definite – asked about his team line-up: 'I'm not giving away secrets like that to Milan. If I had my way I wouldn't even tell them the time of the kick-off.'

Football crowds have been known to re-write popular songs with folk poetry to be bawled from the terraces. My favourite is the Chelsea fans' version of 'My Bonny Lies Over the Ocean'.

> If I had the wings of a sparrow
> If I had the ass of a crow
> I'd fly over Tottenham tomorrow
> And shit on the bastards below.

SHARWOOD, James Allen. Old James Allen Sharwood, of the famous spice firm, started his life romantically and ended it in black farce. Having opened a wine department in a grocer's shop, he expanded by shipping 'French comestibles' to the Viceroy of India. Lord Dufferin's French chef introduced him to oriental spices and he shipped them back to England. In 1889 he went solo, and retired in 1927. For the rest of his life he travelled the world, always accompanied by an embalming kit because he didn't trust foreign undertakers. He died in South Africa in 1939, and not before the 1950s could his wish to be buried beside his wife in Wimbledon be honoured. By now the embalming kit had been forgotten and his ashes were shipped to Southampton. En route to Wimbledon the lorry was hijacked and presumably the villains, finding no use for his ashes, scattered them among the Hampshire hedgerows. So somewhere in that rich earth there lies a richer dust concealed, a dust that gave us curry powder, chutney, Bombay Ducks, Chinese figs and poppadoms, and is forever Sharwoods.

SHAW, Dennis. Between them, Jeffrey Bernard and Keith Waterhouse have immortalised the late Dennis Shaw in the play *Jeffrey Bernard Is Unwell*. Shaw, known as 'Den-Den', was a sometime agent (in an office which was furnished with a desk, a chair and a gin bottle) and an actor who, to quote the script, 'was 20 stone and encrusted in warts and played B-picture villains and Gestapo officers back in the fifties'. He was notorious for his bad behaviour, 'banned from every pub within a square mile of Piccadilly Circus'.

Waterhouse missed out one of his favourite 'Den-Den' sagas in the play. They were dining in a Soho restaurant and Shaw ordered *duck à l'orange*. When the dish arrived he prodded his fork into the rather dry petit pois and asked the waiter what they were. 'They are peas, Mr Shaw,' said the waiter. 'These aren't peas,' rasped Den-Den. 'These are the pellets you shot the fucking duck with.'

'Mr Shaw, I have been a waiter here for thirty-five years, and never has a customer spoken to me in that fashion.'

'You've been a waiter in the same place for thirty-five years? I'm not surprised, when you serve used ammunition as a vegetable!'

A woman once approached Shaw in Shaftesbury Avenue and stuttered, 'Excuse me. Could it be . . . ? Are you . . .?'

Shaw: 'Well, come on, out with it. I'm in a hurry. What do you want?'

Woman: 'Are you Dennis Shaw?'

Shaw: 'Of course I am. Why the hesitation?'

Woman: 'Well, it's such an awful thing to ask anybody.'

SHELBURNE, William Petty, 2nd Earl of. Lord Shelburne, an eighteenth-century politician, once fought a duel with a Scottish MP, Colonel William Fullerton, who had accused him of treachery with the enemy. They met in Hyde Park and Fullerton wounded Shelburne in the groin. In a letter to a friend the injured peer wrote modestly, 'I don't think Lady Shelburne will be any the worse for it!'

SHELLEY, Percy Bysshe. The poet Shelley, an extraordinarily egotistical man, was born heir to a baronetcy and a fortune. He preached equality and hated fox-hunting. A vegetarian, he also refused to eat sugar as it was produced by slave labour. At school he was called 'the Eton Atheist'. At Oxford he advocated pacifism, revolution, free love, wife swapping and equality for women. His indulgent father paid for 1,500 copies of his Eton poems to be printed so he arrived in Oxford a published poet. He was introduced to Slatters, the printer and bookseller, by his father with the words, 'My son here has a literary turn. He is already an author and do please indulge him in his literary freaks.'

He eloped with Harriet Westbrook, a sixteen-year-old school-fellow of his sister Elizabeth, denounced his family and dismissed a mild reproof from the family solicitor, William Whitton, with the words 'Mr S. commends Mr W. when he deals with gentlemen (which opportunity may not often occur) to refrain from opening private letters or impudence may draw down chastisement on contemptibility.'

When Harriet refused to join his travelling European harem with Mary Godwin and Claire Clairmont he so abused her that she drowned herself in despair. In spite of his inherited wealth he proved an inverterate conman to tradesmen, and many people were still trying to retrieve debts or loans, ranging from a few pounds to thousands, twenty years after his death by drowning off Livorno on 8 July 1822.

By then he was planning to abandon Mary (whom he had married after Harriet's suicide) for Jane, the beautiful common-law wife of Edward Williams, a half-pay lieutenant of the East India Company.

After this extraordinary and indulgent life it is perhaps not surprising that Matthew Arnold should report Fanny Kemble's memory of Mary Shelley. The actress told him that Mrs Shelley had asked her advice in choosing a school for her son. She replied with 'Just the sort of banality, you know, one does come out with: oh send him somewhere where they will teach him to think for himself.'

Mrs Shelley replied, 'Teach him to think for himself? Oh my God, teach him rather to think like other people.'

The widow Shelley, while building Shelley's literary monument after his death, certainly made her feelings plain about the left-wing Bohemia, 'its excitements, falsities and cruel disasters', through which her husband had roamed. As her son Percy was growing up a friend watching him read said, 'I am sure he will live to be an extraordinary person.' Mary was unimpressed by the prospect. 'I hope to God,' she erupted, 'he grows up to be an ordinary one!'

Shelley's college at Oxford was livid when in 1992 a Shelley Ball was held there. Members of the anarchist group Class War invaded the quad, spitting and jeering at the dancers, damaging cars and lighting fires outside the college. One undergraduate was puzzled. 'I can't understand it,' he lamented. 'Unless some-one took a severe dislike to Shelley's poetry there can be no explanation.'

In all the excitement over Shelley's bicentenary in 1993 no verdict touched the eloquent simplicity of the reflection of Dr Hornby, the nineteenth-century headmaster of Eton, who said, 'I rather wish he had been at Harrow.'

SHULMAN, Milton. Milton Shulman, critic and columnist of the London *Evening Standard*, recently revealed a fascinating connection with the Lady Chatterley trial some 30-odd years ago. Lawrence's novel, or rather its publisher, was being charged with being liable to deprave and corrupt. Penguin Books thought Shulman's reputation as a critic might help their case. In the end they decided that they had heavier guns which they could fire in their defence – but not before he had been asked by counsel about the plentiful use of the word 'fuck'. 'If the word "fuck" is deemed to corrupt,' he said, 'then the British army is corrupt beyond redemption.' In summing up to the jury, Gerald Gardner, Penguin's barrister, modified Shulman's words slightly. 'If the word "fuck" is deemed to corrupt,' he said, 'then ninety-five per cent of the British Armed Forces are corrupt beyond redemption.'

SHURLOCK, Harold. Harold Shurlock was a censor on the staff of the Breen Office in America in the fifties and sixties. Acting on the advice of the Twentieth Century-Fox censorship consultant, Frank McCarthy, George Cukor, the director of *Let's Make Love*, a movie starring Marilyn Monroe, Yves Montand and Frankie Vaughan, invited Shurlock to visit the set to witness the shooting of a scene which he thought might raise problems. It was a romantic encounter between Monroe and Montand. Monroe turned her formidable little-girl charm on Shurlock: 'This is the first time I've ever met a censor,' she breathed before playing the scene. Shurlock was shocked by the scene and objected to it. Open-eyed she asked why. He told her he could not allow her 'wriggling and rolling in a horizontal position'. Monroe affected not to understand. 'It's horizontal,' repeated Shurlock; 'It's as though you were getting ready for the sex act.' 'Oh, that!' smiled Monroe. 'You can do that standing up.' She kept her scene.

SIMS, Zoot. Zoot Sims was another star saxophone player who was a conspicuous consumer. Asked by a fan how he could play so well when he was loaded, his reply was at least logical: 'I practise when I'm loaded.' Driven home by two fellow musicians, one of whom had a cast in one eye and the other a false eye, he leant forward in the car and examined them. 'What's the matter, Zoot?' asked one. 'I just wanted to make sure you two guys were keeping both eyes on the road,' he replied before sinking into a contented sleep.

Another fan was determined to show his mastery of the hipster jazz vocabulary. 'Hey man!' he said, pointing to a girl. 'Hip that crazy chick at the bar!' Sims replied, 'Yeah, I'm dig!'

Appearing snappily dressed in a bar at noon he caused a ripple of interest by being so elegant so early in the day. 'I don't know,' he excused himself, 'I woke up this way.'

SKEFFINGTON, John Clothworthy Talbot Foster Whyte-Melville, 13th Viscount Masserene and 16th Viscount Ferrard.

It may not be quite fair to include the 13th Viscount in a book of anecdotes but his eccentricities were so redolent of a previous age that they should be recorded. In his foreword to the 13th Viscount's book, *The Lords*, Lord Hailsham, then Lord Chancellor, wrote 'One hopes that Viscount Masserene and Ferrard will never be reformed.'

I first became aware of Lord 'Mass of Cream and Feather' in the 1960s when he said in the Lords, 'I have never actually been to [I think it was Rhodesia] but I have been *extremely* near.' True to form, in the 1980s he addressed his peers on the Brixton riots. He suggested that he was 'the only member who has spoken today who has had agricultural estates in Jamaica'. He said the only riots he had witnessed there were 'riots of joy, because when I arrived I always gave a big barbecue for all the people'.

He was born in 1914 and died in 1993. Brought up at the family seat of Antrim Castle (built in 1613 by Sir Hugh Clothworthy, 1st Viscount Ferrard), his official career is summed up as Eton, Black Watch, Monday Club, Scottish

Estates, Field Sports, Carlton, Turf, Pratts etc. He drove the leading British car at Le Mans in 1937; presented *Countess Maritza* at the Palace Theatre; and at his principal seat, Chilham Castle, kept falcons and an Imperial eagle.

But it was his contribution to the debates in the Lords which fuelled the legend. On unemployment, he suggested that the situation was not as bad as people were saying. He had been trying for months to find an undergardener for Chilham. Moreover, he pointed out, British Rail were complaining of shortage of staff and he couldn't understand why trains were overcrowded when work could be provided for people available to build more.

He made many speeches about bulls (there were six in his coat of arms). In the course of one, he remembered firing his catapult at a sparrow and hitting on the head an old man who was taking a bath. 'My father got the blame.'

Twice he tried unsuccessfully to restore the right of Irish Peers to claim their seats in the Lords.

On one occasion he confessed, 'It might have taken me a long time to become a Conservative if I had been born in a Liverpool slum.'

All his speeches in the Lords had marked characteristics. There were phrases like 'I am rather ignorant on the matter . . . it is not quite my line of country . . . I have not read the bill properly'; but the self-deprecation was mixed with Boys' Own stuff. 'We are on a one hundred per cent wicket here . . . I shall change the bowling for three or four minutes and speak on . . . I shall now change horses and speak for a few minutes on . . .' He had a monstrous stammer – 'actually' was the word which signalled that he was in trouble and Hansard had strict orders to omit it.

However, it was the wealth of anecdotal detail that really distinguished his speeches and perhaps make him a proper candidate for this book. Returning to bulls during the Committee Stage of the Wildlife and Countryside Bill in 1981 he was in fine form. 'The only annoying thing which has happened to me was when one shorthorn of mine went to investigate a hiker's tent. They were not there, and he got tangled up in the guy ropes and somehow unfortunately got a frying pan attached to his horn. This was extremely annoying for the cows because whenever he tried to get near them they heard this thing banging and fled. It was also very annoying for me, because I could not get a cow served, and in the end the poor bull had to be shot.'

Another bull of his 'wandered into a wedding reception in Kent, causing a bit of a panic and demolishing a wedding cake'. His sage advice to their Lordships was not to put up 'Beware of the Bull' signs: 'It is not good . . . because very rude things are sometimes written on them! I have found that one of the most effective notices is "Beware of the Agapanthus." '

He acquired a plastics factory in Deal, 'sort of by mistake,' which qualified him to speak in any debate on industry. His arcane expertise on alcohol was gained during his army experience in the Gorbals: 'The drunkenness there was appalling. What some people used to do was to put gas into a milk bottle. That makes you roaring drunk in a very short time.'

As late as 1986 he told fellow peers, 'I would say that the great majority of the people in our former empire would be very pleased to come back under the administration of Britain.'

He delighted in the acquisition of goods by his employees; 'their children have toys which I never did . . . they have a nice motor boat . . . they stole the propeller of my motor boat and they have it on theirs. But there you are; it is difficult to prove.'

Towards the end he deplored the quality of those in Government. Lady Trumpington – Agriculture – 'did not know the difference between a dough-nut and a turnip . . . and there's that fat-faced fellow . . . Taylor.'

'Mellor?'

'Yes, Mellor, that's the one. Don't think much of him. Doesn't know how to behave.'

His heir is his son John David Clothworthy Whyte-Melville Foster Skeffington. He has a great deal to live up to.

SMITH, Adam. The great eighteenth-century economist and Professor of Logic at Glasgow University, Adam Smith was a caricature of the absent-minded professor.

Inspecting a tanning works in Glasgow, he was talking with such absorption of his subject while standing on a plank across the tanning pit that he stepped off and 'plunged headlong into the nauseous pool. He was dragged out, stripped, and, covered with blankets, conveyed home in a sedan chair where, having recovered from the shock of this unexpected cold bath, he complained bitterly that he must leave life with all his affairs in the greatest disorder.'

On another occasion he chattered on while absent-mindedly rolling a piece of bread and butter in his fingers and then putting it into the teapot. On tasting the tea he complained that it was the worst he had ever come across.

One Sunday morning in Kirkaldy he was strolling in his garden in his night-clothes when his concentration prevented him realising that he had strayed onto a path leading to the turnpike road, and then the main road. He did not come out of the reverie until he had walked fifteen miles to Dunfermline, where the bells of the church broke the mood for him.

SMITH, F. E., 1st Earl of Birkenhead. After a successful career at the bar beginning as a barrister on the Northern Circuit in Liverpool, Smith entered

Parliament as Tory MP for Birkenhead and on 12 May 1906 made perhaps the most famous maiden speech in parliamentary history. Tim Healey, a past master at impressing the House, passed him a note as he sat down. It read: 'I am old, and you are young, but you have beaten me at my own game.' The next evening an old lady at dinner enquired, 'Who is this Effie Smith? She can't be a modest girl to be talked about so much.'

He had already made a reputation for wit in court. Defending a tramway company sued over an accident to a small boy who claimed that it had led to blindness, he faced Judge Willis, a patronising, sanctimonious County Court judge who appeared much moved by the plaintiff's plight. 'Poor boy, poor boy,' he said, 'blind. Put him on a chair so that the jury can see him.' Smith was having none of this: 'Perhaps Your Honour would like to have him passed round the jury box.' 'That is a most improper remark,' rounded the judge. 'It was provoked,' said Smith, 'by a most improper suggestion.'

Judge Willis would not leave it there. 'Mr Smith, have you ever heard of a saying by Bacon – the great Bacon – that youth and discretion are ill-wed companions?' 'Indeed I have, Your Honour; and has Your Honour ever heard of a saying by Bacon – the great Bacon – that a much talking judge is like an ill-tuned cymbal?' Willis was roused. 'You are extremely offensive, young man.' Smith was determined to have the last word. 'As a matter of fact we both are: the only difference between us is that I'm trying to be and you can't help it. I have been listened to with respect by the highest tribunal in the land and I have not come here to be browbeaten.'

Another judge got similarly short shrift when he told Smith that he had read his case and thought little of it. 'I have read your case, Mr Smith, and I am no wiser now than I was when I started.' 'Possibly not, my Lord, but far better informed.'

Winston Churchill summed up F. E. Smith's strength. 'For all the purposes of discussion, argument, exposition, appeal or altercation, F.E. had a complete armoury. The bludgeon for the platform; the rapier for personal dispute; the entangling net and unexpected trident for the Courts of Law; and a jug of clear spring water for an anxious, perplexed conclave.'

Smith was Carson's right-hand man from 1909 to 1914 in persuading Ulster not to accept Home Rule. Seven years later he was Lord Chancellor and so led the process of ratifying the Irish Treaty of 1921. This produced two memorable exchanges. When he told Michael Collins, the Irish leader, 'I may have signed my political death warrant tonight', Collins replied with prophetic accuracy, 'I may have signed my actual death sentence.'

More frivolously, Smith answered Woodrow Wilson's solemn enquiry – 'And what in your opinion is the trend of the modern English undergraduate?' – 'steadily towards drink and women, Mr President.'

Much of F. E. Smith's wit acknowledges him as an apostle of Aristotle in his 'cultured insolence'. To the Labour politician J. H. Thomas, who, as a new MP, asked the way to the House of Commons loo, Smith's directions were succinct: 'First left, go along the corridor. You'll see a door marked Gentlemen. Do not let that deter you.' Somehow they stayed friends and when Thomas complained of 'an 'ell of an 'eadache', Smith prescribed 'a couple of aspirates'.

Paul Johnson has gone to great trouble to authenticate one of the most notorious F. E. Smith stories. I always heard that having lunched at the Café Royal he called in at the Athenaeum, of which he was not a member, on his way to the Houses of Parliament and used the lavatory. When a member said that this was a club and not a public lavatory he replied, 'Oh it's a club as well, is it?'

Paul Johnson thought – in his invaluable (to me at least) collection of political anecdotes for OUP – that the club was the Royal Automobile Club in Pall Mall, which has a gents immediately opposite the entrance which he had himself used on occasion. Club members noticed Birkenhead's frequent use of it and got a club servant to watch out for the Lord Chancellor and remonstrate, only to be told, 'Oh, this is a club, is it? I always thought it was a public lavatory.' Which is more brutal and, I think, less funny. However, Johnson points out that John Campbell, Birkenhead's most recent biographer, by using street plans and deducing the likely route he took, has 'proved' that it was the National Liberal Club. In Johnson's view the location of its gents – right across the inner hall and down the steps – makes it an unlikely contender. He believes that the issue is still open.

I'm staying with my route, my club, my loo and my punch line.

SMITH, Dame Maggie. Michael Coveney's excellent biography of Dame Maggie, *A Bright Particular Star*, has been published since my *Theatrical Anecdotes* and puts on record a few more Maggie Smith stories.

Playing in Ronald Harwood's *Interpreters* she took violent exception to the bilious green set and the acid green carpet which matched it. 'Invoking the name of one of the outstanding snooker champions of the day she would complain . . . "When I get out on that stage I feel like Hurricane Higgins." '

She also disliked the factory aspect of the National Theatre building in which she could easily lose her way between dressing room and stage. She always carried a poem sent to her by John Moffat which read, 'Fuck and bloody arsehole, shit, bugger, damn; I don't know where the fuck I am.'

The only story I know of Maggie Smith and Coral Browne in conversation took place when Maggie was about to play Lady Macbeth for Robin Phillips in Stratford, Ontario. Meeting Coral in Hollywood before rehearsals, Maggie asked for advice. 'It's a fucker, darling,' Miss Browne told her encouragingly, 'and all I can say is keep your eyes open in the sleepwalking scene. For some reason it rivets the fuckers.' She was riveting.

Filming *Sister Act* with Whoopi Goldberg, a film she did much to lift into fitful laughter, there was a script problem on location in Reno. Maggie was playing a Mother Superior; Ms Goldberg a night-club singer on the run and disguised as a nun. On the set actors were querying a message supposedly sent by the Pope to his subordinates. There was no plausible means by which he could have sent it. Looking up from her chair on the sidelines Maggie offered, 'By fax vobiscum, I presume.'

Coveney supplies another Smith story but omits the punch line. Some months into the run of the famous National production of *Othello*, Olivier was trying to persuade Maggie to play Vivien Leigh's old role in Thornton Wilder's *The Skin of Our Teeth*. She was resisting the idea and all the other suggestions he was making.

So incensed was Olivier that during the performance that followed her rejection of the part, in the scene where he should have hit her with Lodovico's proclamation, he slapped her with particular force across the face with his hand. Maggie was knocked out cold. Edward Petherbridge, who was playing a small part, let out an involuntary cry, 'Oh, Mag!' Frank Finlay had to improvise a new piece of business for Iago: carrying an unconscious Desdemona from the Senate House.

What Coveney does not record is that as she came to on her way to the wings, she muttered laconically, 'First time I've seen stars at the National.'

SOAMES, Nicholas, MP. Nicholas Soames has a reputation as a gourmand, a gourmet (up to a point) and something of a wit. The first two qualities must have helped his elevation to a junior ministerial job in Food, while the latter was best exemplified when the trendy Labour MP Paul Boateng proudly strode into the House of Commons showing off his fashionable new unstructured suit.

'One more fitting, I think, Paul,' sang out Soames.

SOUTH, Robert. Dr South was a fashionable parson who once found himself preaching before King Charles II and a row of noblemen who were all nodding off to sleep. He found the perfect antidote, breaking off his sermon to say: 'Lord Lauderdale, rouse yourself; you snore so loudly that you will wake the King.'

SPENDER, Stephen. Spender met T. S. Eliot when he was a young man and gushingly announced that he wanted to be a poet.

'Wanting to write poetry I understand,' mused Eliot, 'but wanting to be a poet...'
He left the remark eloquently unfinished.

STALKER, John. Although John Stalker is famous for his high-level police work in Manchester and in Northern Ireland, I was delighted to hear of his unconventional rush into matrimony. As a young copper of three weeks' experience he was on the beat in Manchester's Moss Side, when he approached a suspicious character in a donkey-jacket standing at a bus stop with a parcel on the pavement at his feet. As Stalker stooped to examine it he smashed his head into a lamppost.

Stalker's face was a mess – as he says, 'In Cooper terms, more Henry than Gary.' He had to go to hospital to have it put back in place. When he woke up after the operation his girlfriend, Stella, visited and, though shocked by his appearance, she proudly told him that she had won a beauty contest and was Miss Prestatyn. Part of the prize was a two-week holdiay for one at Prestatyn Holiday Camp. Through the anaesthetic haze Stalker managed to suggest that she should convert it to a one-week holiday for two – and they should use it as a honeymoon.

'Is that a proposal?' she enquired.

He nodded.

'Do you know what you're saying or is it the anaesthetic?'

And so they were married on 4 August 1962 and as a married woman Mrs Stalker's career as Beauty Queen came to an end.

STAMP, Terence. There is a Terence Stamp anecdote I have been longing to authenticate since the 1960s but which I was unable to prove until I interviewed him on *Loose Ends* in April 1993. Stamp was in the first full flush of cinematic beauty when he stayed overnight with an actress who was filming a Crippen movie. She had to leave early for the studio. She crept out leaving him asleep. Some hours later he awoke to hear the maid banging about in the next room. Then she came into the bedroom. Terence's aureole of Billy Budd curls appeared over the coverlet. 'Don't worry,' she said, unimpressed; 'we've 'ad Albert Finney 'ere.'

It is only fair to say that Terence insists that, after the maid had barged in, the conversation went, 'Morning, Albert.' Terence, blearily: 'It's not Albert; it's Terence!'

STEPHEN, King. Stephen was the grandson of William the Conqueror. He usurped the throne and in his struggle to retain power allowed the kingdom to fall into anarchy with his barons plundering at their pleasure. In the words of the historian G. M. Trevelyan he was 'wholly unfit to be king'.

Stephen's immediate rival for the crown was an old mistress (and also his first cousin), Empress Matilda, Henry I's daughter. If she was haughty, grasping and hated, Stephen of Blois, Count of Boulogne, was brave, handsome and popular. Stephen, who had been the first layman to swear loyalty to Matilda, was the first to forget his oath. If he could not forget his affair with the Empress, carried on fitfully during her young widowhood and restoked during the uneasy early years of her second marriage, he had to put it to one side. He owed *his* title to his marriage to Empress Matilda's first cousin, Matilda of Boulogne. (Conveniently, if he talked indiscreetly in his sleep, drowsy murmurs of 'Maltilda' could never compromise him.)

After nearly twenty years of fighting Matilda's armies, Stephen found himself facing her son Henry. When the hardened warrior finally met his twenty-year-old adversary, the two men discovered that they were probably the only ones in the kingdom who still wanted to fight. The compromise was simple: Stephen would reign over England undisturbed by Henry until his death. On his passing, Henry was solemnly guaranteed the succession. With some reluctance they embraced at the end of the interview. Henry called Stephen 'king' and 'father'. Stephen's son Eustace, the man who stood to lose from this agreement, rode away from his father's court in disgust to ravage the countryside of Cambridgeshire.

In 1153 Eustace died suddenly – religious historians insist that he choked on the first piece of meat he ate after plundering the monks of Bury St Edmunds. Others, less sure of divine retribution, put it down to brain fever. At any rate he left no heir by his wife, Constance of France, nor was his younger brother, William, anxious to contest the succession.

The last seven months of Stephen's reign were the happiest. He had never been able to face critical decisions and suddenly there were none for him to make. Suspense removed, he made a solemn progress through the north of England, an empty ritual which convinced no one except the leading actor – the old matinee idol 'showing himself off as if he were a new king', confident at last that with no rival to challenge him, his performance would be convincing.

He died on 25 October 1145, having ruled England for nineteen years. The *Anglo-Saxon Chronicle*'s verdict on his reign was succinct: 'Men said openly that Christ and His saints slept.'

STEVENSON, Adlai. Twice the unsuccessful US Presidential candidate, Adlai Stevenson lives more in the public memory for wit than for anecdotes – apart from the photograph which revealed a more human side when it showed a hole in the sole of his shoe.

He was sharp on the press. 'Man does not live by words alone, despite the fact that he sometimes has to eat them.'

'An editor is a person employed on a newspaper whose business is to separate the wheat from the chaff and to see that the chaff is printed.'

'Writing good editorials is chiefly telling people what they think – not what you think.'

'Accuracy to a newspaper is what virtue is to a lady; but a newspaper can always print a retraction.'

Stevenson had an attractive habit of keeping anecdotal notebooks which he filled with 'good things'. For example: 'Alcibiades was telling Pericles how Athens should be governed, and Pericles, annoyed with the young man's manner, said, "Alcibiades, when I was your age I talked just the way you are talking." Alcibiades looked him in the face and rejoined, "How I should like to have known you, Pericles, when you were at your best." '

And 'When Eva Perón was in Barcelona, she complained that she had been called "puta" [prostitute] as she drove through the streets. An old general apologised saying, "Why, I've been retired for twelve years and they still call me General." '

Stevenson's own most quoted political epigrams include: 'An independent is a guy who wants to take the politics out of politics'; 'Someone must fill the gap between platitudes and bayonets'; 'Any boy may become President and I suppose it's just one of the risks he takes.' When he was given a thankless supporting role in 1960 he used a parable to comment on the Kennedy phenomenon. He told a story of 'Jimmy, aged eight, who went over to play with his friend , Bill. "Let's play cops and robbers," he proposed. "I'll be the good guy and you can be the bad guy." Bill's little brother, Tommy, aged four, said eagerly, "Can I be the commercial?" '

But he reserved his big guns for the Republicans. 'I like Republicans . . . I would trust them with anything in the world except public office'; and 'Whenever Republicans talk of cutting taxes first and discussing national security second, they remind me of the very tired, rich man who said to his chauffeur, "Drive off that cliff, James. I want to commit suicide." '

Of Eisenhower's political crusade he said, 'The General has dedicated himself so many times he must fee like the cornerstone of a public building.'

On Nixon: 'Nixon is the kind of politician who would cut down a redwood tree, then mount the stump for a speech on conservation'; and: 'Nixon's farm policy is vague, but he is going a long way towards slowing the corn surplus by his speeches.'

But he was speaking before Nixon retired to California in disgrace, taking only one walk a day . . . 'to go and launder his money'.

STEWART, Michael. The passing of Michael Stewart from the role of England's Test team manager will hardly be regretted by the Cavaliers of English cricket. One anonymous English cricketer defined him as 'an inflexible, robotic character, who would prefer his players to have a brain implant programmed to his own outlook and attitudes'.

I once asked Peter Roebuck if it was true that he had said Stewart mistrusted any cricketer who read past the sports pages of a newspaper. 'He mistrusts anyone who reads past the sports pages of the tabloids,' corrected Roebuck.

Some of Stewart's statements to the press are masterpieces of robot-speak. When Michael Atherton was dropped from a one-day international, 'He is not on the best terms with himself batting wise, obviously, and we wanted, on the tempo we were looking for in this particular game, for him not to force things outside his natural game. And therefore he's not playing in this one.'

Martin Johnson of the *Independent* translated this as 'We've dropped him for slow scoring.' Two other gems: 'It was understandable disappointment' – batsman scythes down his stumps after dismissal. And 'If we'd been playing well we'd have been more successful' (of the disastrous Ashes tour 1990–91).

STOKES, Richard. Richard Stokes was the Labour Minister of Works during the building of the Battersea Garden development as part of the 1951 Festival of Britain. The enterprise was sabotaged by a series of strikes. Finally, Stokes visited the troubled site to discover the cause of the latest stoppage. He was told it was a shortage of shovels. 'Well,' said Stokes, 'tell the men they'll just have to lean against each other.'

STOPES, Dr Marie. I only met Marie Stopes on one occasion, when Nigel Lawson and I drove to London from Oxford, where we were both undergraduates in the fifties, to hear a debate between Stopes and Norman St John Stevas (as he then was) on, inevitably, birth control. As I remember, Norman won in every debating sense but Dr Stopes won the vote.

Her doctorate was in science not medicine, and from the 1920s she had been fighting a long battle to legitimise and popularise birth control. There was even a Birth Control Ball at the Hammersmith Palais de Dance. Some wag, reversing the cry of contemporary ice-cream sellers ('Stop me and buy one') suggested that *her* slogan should be 'Buy me and stop one'!

Marie Stopes's zeal in promoting birth control overshadowed her enthusiastic efforts at playwriting. She submitted two plays to Sir Barry Jackson during the time that he ran the Birmingham Repertory company. According to Tom English, his long-time friend and assistant, Sir Barry considered both to be 'impossible and unacceptable'. One was called *Venus and Methuselah*, the other *The Staff*. It was *The Staff* which contained the stage direction, 'A pregnant pause'.

STRACHEY, Lytton. When the Hon. Lytton Strachey, author of *Eminent Victorians* and much more, was summoned before a military tribunal during World War One he chose to appear as a conscientious objector, not as one unfit for service on grounds of ill-health – though he would certainly have qualified on those grounds.

The examining chairman had two stock questions. To the first – 'I understand, Mr Strachey, that you have a conscientious objection to war?' – he replied in his extraordinary and characteristic voice, 'Oh no, not at all, only to *this* war.' The chairman moved on to his second question, guaranteed in his experience to discomfit any witness: 'What would you do if you saw a German soldier trying to violate your sister?' Strachey struck an attitude of heroic virtue and replied, 'I would try to get between them.'

The high fluting voice provides a nimble pay-off in most Strachey stories. On a visit to Rome he was entertained by Princess San Faustino (a favourite character in Cole Porter lyrics). At the time she was espousing a mad scheme for making everything – 'Factories, synthetic chocolates, motor cars, building materials and bath salts' – out of soya beans. Having trilled on about her idiotic scheme, she sought the approval of her guest of honour. What did he think of her plan? The voice shot up an octave in horror at the idea: 'I'm afraid I don't like beans.'

An anecdote which Sir Alec Guinness tells about Strachey requires exact pitch because it concerns not only Strachey but also Sir Edward Marsh (the dilettante, inveterate first-nighter, poetry patron and sometime private secretary to Winston Churchill) who had a similarly high-pitched voice.

On the morning that Eddie Marsh received the first batch of poems sent to him by Rupert Brooke, then a Cambridge undergraduate, he rushed from his rooms in Gray's Inn to a bookshop in Bloomsbury where sympathetic souls gathered. He was in a state of high excitement. Coming upon Lytton Strachey he unburdened himself of the news of his great discovery, his voice rising perilously high in his enthusiasm. He told him of the poems and said that they were 'Steeped in Beauty! Steeped in Beauty!' Catching his excitement Lytton Strachey went even higher, echoing the single word, 'Steeped?!'

STRITCH, Elaine. On the radio programme *Loose Ends* Elaine Stritch told a story of the West End first night of Noel Coward's musical *Sail Away* in which she starred. Aware of her sometimes exuberant behaviour Coward warned her to behave herself at the post-play party at the Savoy. She dressed conservatively and was surprised to find herself going up in the lift with Coward and a very intoxicated Vivien Leigh and Kenneth More. Still on her best behaviour, she was admonished by Coward's wagging finger, and heard him say, 'I told you to behave properly, Elaine; I didn't tell you to come as a fucking nun!'

Having told the story, she turned to me and said, 'You can edit that out on the tape, can't you?'

'No,' I said, 'this is live.'

'Oh my God! Live television!'

'No Elaine, live radio.'

'Radio? You mean I didn't need to put on my face?'

SUTHERLAND, Anne Hay-Mackenzie, Duchess of. The Dukes of Sutherland (the title, created in 1833, of the Egerton family) were living in particular splendour during the later part of Queen Victoria's reign. The 3rd Duke owned four stately homes, half a dozen smaller houses and two yachts. He resided in such grandeur at Stafford House (now Lancaster House) in London that when Queen Victoria left after a visit she remarked to the Duchess, 'I am returning from your palace to my house.'

SWIFT, Jonathan. Dean Swift's delight in the praise which greeted the publication of *Gulliver's Travels* was only increased by the report – perhaps apocryphal – that an Irish bishop had denounced it. 'That book was full of improbable lies, and for his part he hardly believed a word of it.'

In matters of poetry Swift preferred poets to hide their verses under a bushel. He wrote that a copy of verse, kept in a cabinet and only shown to a few friends, is like a virgin, much sought after and admired: but when printed and published is like a common whore whom anybody may purchase for half a crown.

According to George Coleman in a book of anecdotes and reminiscences published in 1823, Swift was walking from London to Chester when a violent summer storm caused him to take refuge under a great oak tree outside Lichfield. He was soon joined by a man and a pregnant woman who were on their way to Lichfield where they were to be married. As the woman was many months gone and there seemed no time to be lost Swift offered to marry them there and then. He performed the ceremony and as the sky brightened the newly weds prepared to depart. Suddenly the bridegroom remembered that he had no certificate to witness the validity of the cermony. Swift wrote out one for them in verse:

> Under an oak in stormy weather
> I joined this rogue and whore together;
> And none but he who rules the thunder
> Can put this rogue and whore asunder.

SWIFT, Sir Rigby. F. E. Pritchard, in his biography of Mr Justice Swift, the early twentieth-century judge, highlights Swift's occasional impatience with counsel who were due to be in two courts at once. On one occasion at Northampton Assizes, when Swift was hearing a case in which a woman was asking for damages on account of an accident which gave her double vision, he saw her counsel's clerk, Arthur Ward, enter the court. He enquired of the plaintiff: 'Tell me more about this double vision. Does it mean you see two of everything?'

'Yes, my lord.'

'Do you see two of me?'

'Yes, my lord.'

'Do you see two of the usher there?'

'Yes, my lord.'

'Do you see two of Mr Arthur Ward?'

'Yes, my lord.'

To which Swift replied, 'Well, that's very fortunate, because one of him is wanted in the other court.'

Another biography of Swift (by E. S. Fay) recounts the classic case in a Manchester court when a young barrister appearing before Swift was doggedly hammering away at his case, he alone oblivious to the fact that he was streets ahead and that the judge was on his side. A KC, J. C. Jackson, whose case came next on the list, passed him a note saying, 'Sit down, you bloody fool. Can't you see the old bastard is with you?' Swift asked if he might see the note. The young counsel hedged, saying that it was a personal note from Mr Jackson. Swift then asked Jackson if he minded. Jackson said, 'Not at all, my lord.' The note was handed to Swift who read it and gave it back with the words, 'A very proper note. I quite agree with it.'

— T —

TALLEYRAND-PÉRIGORD, Charles Maurice de. The great, devious, French Revolutionary statesman and Foreign Minister was so obsessively suspicious of world events that when the Turkish Ambassador to France died, his only question was, 'What does he mean by that?'

TELEGRAMS. The short sharp prose of telegrams often brings an anecdote into sharp focus.

Evelyn Waugh scored heavily over his editor when told to investigate the alleged death of an American nurse in Abyssinia. The message he received was REQUIRE EARLIEST NAME LIFE STORY PHOTOGRAPH AMERICAN NURSE UPBLOWN ADOWA. Waugh checked the facts and his reply was considerably shorter: NURSE UNUPBLOWN.

Cary Grant's reply to a magazine's query – HOW OLD CARY GRANT – is justly famous. He wired OLD CARY GRANT FINE HOW YOU?

There was a classic exchange in 1898 between the war artist Frederic Remington and the newspaper magnate William Randolph Hearst. Remington cabled EVERYTHING IS QUIET. THERE IS NO TROUBLE HERE. THERE WILL BE NO WAR. WISH TO RETURN. REMINGTON. It is Hearst's reply which sticks in the mind. PLEASE REMAIN. YOU FURNISH PICTURES AND I'LL FURNISH THE WAR. HEARST.

In 1844 a telegram sent from Paddington to Slough led to the arrest of two pickpockets, Oliver Martin and Fiddler Dick, who had been working the train between the two stations. Later the same year the police were alerted by telegraph to the presence of a murderer, John Tarwell, on the Great Western Railway. The wire ended: . . . HE IS IN THE LAST COMPARTMENT OF THE SECOND FIRST CLASS CARRIAGE. He was arrested for killing his mistress when he arrived at Paddington. It was 66 years before a wire led to the arrest of Dr Crippen and Ethel Le Neve fleeing to Canada on the *Montrose*.

It is difficult to authenticate the couplet which Alfred Austin is supposed to have written in 1871 on hearing that the news of the Prince of Wales's illness had been flashed around the world.

> Across the wires the electric message came
> He is no better, he is much the same.

The outbreak of the 1914–18 war inspired a very British telegram handed in at Exford on 4 August. It went to Rumwell Hall, Taunton, and ran: NO HUNTING IF ENGLAND DECLARES WAR. TUCKER, HUNTSMAN.

Noel Coward was a great telegram sender and the outbreak of World War Two inspired one to Jack Wilson, his partner: GRAVE POSSIBILITY WAR WITHIN FEW WEEKS OR DAYS IF THIS HAPPENS POSTPONEMENT REVUE INEVITABLE AND ANNIHILATION OF ALL OF US PROBABLE. When the revue *Set to Music* went ahead Coward followed up with SUGGEST YOU ENGAGE EIGHT REALLY BEAUTIFUL SHOW GIRLS MORE OR LESS SAME HEIGHT NO PARTICULAR TALENT REQUIRED.

Coward also sent whimsical wires to his staff: From Florence he cabled HAVE MOVED HOTEL EXCELSIOR COUGHING MYSELF INTO A FIRENZE; and again AM BACK FROM ISTANBUL WHERE I WAS KNOWN AS ENGLISH DELIGHT.

Gertrude Lawrence caught the habit. When an estate agent in Bermuda said the house she was considering there came with a maid, a secretary and a chauffeur, she telegraphed AIRMAIL PHOTOGRAPH OF CHAUFFEUR.

Florenz Ziegfeld, the American impressario, sent the most and the longest telegrams – however, they mostly lacked wit and therefore have no place here. The theatre was the natural home for the compulsive wirer and the first-night fax has hardly replaced it. George S. Kaufman used it to give notes to actors like Billy Gaxton (see *Theatrical Anecdotes*). (They would not arrive for two days under the new arrangements which would destroy the joke.) Kaufman was on the receiving end of a wire from Alexander Woollcott on the occasion of his fifth wedding anniversary: I HAVE BEEN LOOKING ROUND FOR AN APPROPRIATE WOODEN GIFT AND AM PLEASED HEREBY TO PRESENT YOU WITH ELSIE FERGUSON'S PERFORMANCE IN HER NEW PLAY.

The impresario Billy Rose cabled Stravinsky, who had contributed to a dance interlude for Markova and Dolin for a Broadway revue. He suggested that although the ballet was 'a great success' re-orchestration by the Broadway master Robert Russell Bennett might make it even better. Stravinsky replied: SATISFIED GREAT SUCCESS.

The Queen, of course, sends telegrams to centenarians. However, a consultant doctor who was announced as Honorary Physician to Her Majesty got this (not from her): CONGRATULATIONS. GOD SAVE THE QUEEN.

Babies produce wires. (See Dorothy Parker.) Eddie Cantor to Norma Shearer, whose husband was the movie producer Irving Thalberg: CONGRATULATIONS ON YOUR LATEST PRODUCTION STOP SURE IT WILL LOOK BETTER AFTER IT'S BEEN CUT.

The painter Whistler missed Oscar Wilde's wedding with this apology: AM DETAINED. DON'T WAIT. G. K. Chesterton's wire to his wife has passed into legend: AM IN MARKET HARBOROUGH. WHERE OUGHT I TO BE? A one-word reply was enough: HOME. Best of the self-conscious wires was Robert Benchley's from Venice to the New Yorker: STREETS FULL OF WATER. PLEASE ADVISE.

I had not come across one of the ruder wires until I read Angus McGill and Kenneth Thomson's book *Live Wires*, which celebrates this branch of literature. Another film figure, Carl Laemmle Junior, cabled his father who had founded Universal Pictures: PLEASE WIRE MORE MONEY AM TALKING TO FRENCH COUNT RE MOVIE. Daddy got back to him quickly: NO MONEY TILL YOU LEARN TO SPELL.

In 1916 Norman Douglas, the novelist, slipped bail when charges were pending over an indecent offence with a young man. Twenty-five years later he came back, cabling a friend FEEL LIKE A BOY AGAIN.

The final wire is probably a fiction. It is an exchange between a Foreign Editor and his reporter.

WHY UNNEWS?

UNNEWS GOOD NEWS.

UNNEWS UNJOB.

TENNYSON, Alfred, Lord. The hundredth anniversary in 1992 of the death of Alfred, Lord Tennyson inspired an outburst of biographies, including one by Michael Thorn which made the curious claim to be 'the first biography of Tennyson to refer to the television soap opera *Neighbours*'.

In old age the Poet Laureate was inclined to rail against tourists and trippers who invaded his estate, condemning them indiscriminately as 'cockneys'; and he made a habit of shortsightedly mistaking old friends for autograph hunters. 'I have not the least idea who you are,' he snapped at George Eliot, arriving at a service in Westminster Abbey.

However, my favourite Tennyson anecdote has him experiencing his first railway journey. He was bowled over by the talent of the driver: 'Such a good steerer, we had. We approached a dark tunnel and I was terrified; but so great was his skill that he drove the engine straight at the centre of the aperture. He touched neither one side of it nor the other before we emerged.'

As a boy of fifteen he had been profoundly affected by the death of Byron.

'Byron was dead! I thought the whole world was at an end. I thought everything was over and finished for everyone – that nothing else mattered. I remember I walked out alone, and carved "Byron is dead" in the sandstone.'

In the 1840s one of Tennyson's watering holes was the Cock chophouse in Fleet Street. To one set of verses he added the words, 'Made at the Cock' and addressed the opening lines to the head waiter:

> Oh plump head-waiter at the Cock,
> To which I most resort,
> How goes the time? 'Tis five o'clock
> Go fetch a pint of port.

William Allingham, ambitious to be Tennyson's Boswell, sought out the 'plump head-waiter' and identified him as one 'William'. Sadly, although Tennyson had a clear picture of William, the waiter had no idea of Tennyson. 'I don't know his appearance at all, sir. A gen'elman might be coming here twenty years without me knowing his name.'

Tennyson's farouche appearance often caused comment. Receiving his honorary DCL at the Sheldonian, his hair hanging to his shoulders in poetic disorder, he was greeted by a voice from the gallery calling, 'Did your mother call you early, dear?' Once on one of his frequent walks through London with a little girl, Elspeth Thompson, he was unaware that it was his great Spanish cloak and huge sombrero which caused people to stop and stare at the odd couple. Turning to his small companion he said, 'Child, your mother should dress you less conspicuously: people are staring at us.'

In Covent Garden he met a man who claimed to have been drunk for three days and swore he would never drink again if Tennyson would hear his solemn oath. It is not recorded if this early bid for AA worked.

An eccentric piece of pedantic criticism was offered to Tennyson by Charles Babbage, a Cambridge don who occupied the Lucasian chair of mathematics and who deplored the lines,

> Every minute dies a man,
> Every minute one is born . . .

Babbage held that the world's population was constantly increasing: 'I would therefore take the opportunity of suggesting that in the next edition of your excellent poem the erroneous calculation to which I refer should be corrected as follows: Every moment dies a man/And one and a sixteenth is born.' Even so Babbage had made a concession to Tennyson's metre: 'The actual ratio is 1.167.' Tennyson did finally modify his couplet to the extent of rewriting 'every minute' to 'every moment'.

Tennyson was once introduced to an elderly lady who praised his poetry extravagantly. The old boy merely grunted, 'Madam, your stays creak disgustingly.' Later he returned to her. Naturally she expected an apology. She hardly got it. Instead the Laureate muttered, 'Beg your pardon, ma'am. It was not your stays but my braces.'

Tennyson was not keen on washing. His wife insisted on inspecting his hands when he sat down to a meal. Once he absent-mindedly showed them to a strange woman who promptly sent him off to wash them.

He came from a troubled, gloomy family. When Dante Gabriel Rossetti met one of his younger brothers he was surprised to be told, 'I am Septimus, the most morbid of the Tennysons.'

When Margot Tennant suggested that Carlyle and his wife would have been perfectly happy if they had never married, Tennyson poo-poohed the idea – 'By any other arrangement four people would have been unhappy instead of two.'

It was Carlyle who lobbied Monckton Milnes (Lord Houghton) for Tennyson's pension. Milnes protested that his uncaring and unknowing constituents might think he was soliciting a pension for one of his poor relations. Carlyle's rebuke was formidable: 'Richard Milnes, on the Day of Judgement, when the Lord asks you why you didn't get that pension for Alfred Tennyson, it will not do to lay the blame on your constituents. It is you that will be damned.' Tennyson got a civil list pension of £200.

Poor old Tennyson, he could turn a nasty phrase on occasions. Perhaps his most violent metaphor was a comment on the nineteenth-century critic Chirton Collins. He dismissed him to Edmund Gosse – 'I think,' said Tennyson, 'that he is a louse on the Locks of Literature.'

THATCHER, Baroness (Margaret Hilda). I have mentioned in my introduction Baroness Thatcher's problems in lightening her memoirs with anecdotes, but I have collected one which may come as news to her. Soon after Mrs Thatcher – as she then was – became Prime Minister she lunched at Birchgrove with Harold Macmillan – as he then was – and his grandson Alexander Macmillan – as *he* then was. Luncheon conversation was mainly a monologue, and she was still talking as she stepped into her car to drive away. As the two Macmillans waved her goodbye, Harold turned to his grandson and muttered, 'Alex, do you remember how you felt at school when you failed in Geography?'

There is also a fascinating theory (which the Baroness might care to disprove in her second volume of memoirs) that she is a second cousin once or twice removed of the late Lady Diana Cooper. Few people doubt that Diana was the child of Harry Cust, nephew of the third and last Earl of Brownlow, and not of the Duke of Rutland. There was a time when Mrs Thatcher's grandmother was in service at Belton where the overly romantic Harry was a visitor, and since he fathered most of the children around the Brownlow family seat at the time he may well have exercised his *droit de seigneur* in this direction also. The Eton master who taught the brilliant Cust reckoned that he had a better prospect of being Prime Minister than his contemporaries, the Lords Rosebery and Curzon; how ironic if his early promise bore fruit three generations later. Since the DNA tests on the murdered Romanovs have proved so successful, it should be a simple matter to compare the genetic strains of the Custs and the Thatchers. When confronted by the suggestion, Lady Diana would only say that the data would have to be carefully checked – but it was an interesting coincidence that the Belton silver was on loan to 10 Downing Street during Mrs Thatcher's tenure of office.

A few other memories might leaven her memoirs. Nigel Lawson for one was stark on her handling of the European Community. 'On most issues her approach was foolish. Her style and tone of voice came to irk the others so much that they instinctively sank their differences and joined forces against her.' Lawson found her Cabinets a simple joy. 'The Cabinet's customary role was to rubber-stamp decisions that had already been taken. I used to look forward to Cabinet meetings as the most restful and relaxing event of the week.' However, he was on her side against those who pressured her to make a U-turn. 'What they offered was cold feet dressed up as high principle.'

More leavening might come from Denis Healey's colourful descriptions of her. He has called her 'The parrot on Ronald Reagan's shoulder', 'Winston Churchill in drag', 'Calamity Jane' and a 'bargain-basement Boadicea'. He capped the label 'The Iron Lady' with 'She's got metal fatigue'. To Dennis Skinner she was 'The Westminster Ripper' – a suitable opponent for 'The Beast of Bolsover'.

From the Tory benches, Julian Critchley's verdict was more sophisticated and considered. 'If she has a weakness, it is for shopkeepers, which probably accounts for the fact that she cannot pass a branch of Marks and Spencer without inviting the manager to join her private office. In the Party, the Military Cross has given way to Rotary Club badges. The knights of the shires have given way to estate agents and accountants.'

My first meeting with Margaret Thatcher was in 1970 when she was on a pilot programme for the subsequently successful *Quiz of the Week* – the news quiz formula revived in the 1990s as *Have I Got News for You*. A *Private Eye* team faced Antonia Fraser, Lena Jeger and Margaret Thatcher, then at the height of her 'Milk Snatcher' period as the Shadow Minister for Education. As I recall, she got every answer right and made no jokes. (Twenty-two years later, she could still remember one of the questions in detail.)

Famous for not getting the joke, she did not understand Sir Ronald Millar's reference to 'Give 'em the old one-two, Maggie,' in his parody of Jerry Herman's 'Hello Dolly' as a campaign song; or his crack about 'keep taking the tablets' for a speech. She was exasperated during the 1979 election campaign when Ken Dodd was wheeled on to warm up the audience for her in Bolton. At the hall, Doddy, finding that he was as usual going well, exceeded the planned five minutes and went on for over half an hour. Mrs Thatcher was waiting impatiently in an anteroom. 'I should have done the warm-up and let him do the speech,' was her only comment. The Bolton marginals went back to Labour.

A last word from the lady herself. Some years after she left No. 10, the Baroness, in mellow mood, was asked by a group of intimates why she had favoured John Major as her successor. 'Because he always did what I told him to do,' was her instant reply.

THESIGER, Ernest. Three Thesiger stories escaped *Theatrical Anecdotes*. Visiting his old school, Marlborough, the wizened, cadaverous, mincing-mannered old needle-worker spotted a particularly well-built sixth former. To his host, the Senior Master, he confided, 'I'd give anything to be that boy's mother.'

Uncharacteristically running for a bus, laden down with parcels, he was caught with one foot on and one foot off, 'Stop! Stop!' he shrieked. 'You're killing a genius!' Fortunately the conductor heard him and his genius remained intact.

During the war he was reported as hurrying down a side street and muttering, 'I'm off to see if X Mansions is really razed to the ground, as I have an uncle who lives there and I know I'm in his will!'

THOMAS, Dylan. Rayner Heppenstall recalls a visit to Mousehole in Cornwall with the bucolic poet Dylan Thomas and his wife Caitlin. They stayed at a guesthouse called The Lobster Pot and after one evening of heavy drinking when Thomas had railed against a classically beautiful sunset making 'savage remarks about picture postcards and visual *clichés*' and continuing to talk and drink copiously, he stopped suddenly and said, 'Somebody's boring me, and I think it's me.'

THOMAS, James Henry. J. H. Thomas, the Labour Cabinet Minister in the 1920s, once began to address the Cabinet about the 'addock committee. Ministers, aware that he had trouble with his 'h's, assumed he was mistakenly referring to the herring committee – a current cause for concern. After much hot air at cross purposes it turned out that he was talking about the 'ad hoc' committee.

He was a frequent target of F. E. Smith, under whose name two other Thomas stories appear.

THORNDIKE, Dame Sybil. I have never heard the concern for good works demonstrated throughout their lives by eminent actors Dame Sybil Thorndike and Sir Lewis Casson better summed up than by their daughter, who, Emlyn Williams reported, one day answered the telephone by saying, 'They are neither of them in. Daddy is reading Shakespeare Sonnets to the blind and Mummy's playing Shakespeare to the lepers.'

THYSSEN, Heini, Baron. Heini Thyssen combined his collection of beautiful wives with acquiring even more beautiful works of art. Many of the greatest (of the latter) are committed to galleries in Spain, but the favourites among his priceless paintings hang in his home, the Villa Favorita, on Lake Lugano in Switzerland. When a visitor asked why he hung a Sisley above his television he said, 'My wife likes to watch the television. I like to watch the Sisley.'
    The Baroness was once married to Lex Barker, a screen Tarzan.

TIEGS, Cheryl. Cheryl Tiegs, the American model, was paid a ludicrous $70,000 for putting her name to a book she had not written entirely herself. 'The problem with writing,' she complained, 'is that there's not much money in it.'

TIOMKIN, Dmitri. Tiomkin, the Russian-born Hollywood composer, will always be remembered for his Oscar acceptance speech for Best Musical Score in 1955. 'I would like to thank Beethoven, Brahms, Wagner, Strauss, Rimsky-Korsakov . . .'
    Nine years earlier David O. Selznick had engaged Tiomkin to compose the score for *Duel in the Sun* – a picture which was soon known be its nickname, *Lust in the Dust*. Selznick peppered him with the characteristic memos asking for a Spanish theme, a ranch theme, a love theme, a desire theme, and an orgasm theme. Tiomkin was sanguine about the love theme and the desire theme: 'That I can write; but how do you score an orgasm?' Selznick demanded that he try. Tiomkin worked hopefully on an interesting dramatic crescendo and proceeded to orchestrate it with Selznick's permission. When Selznick heard it, after praising the other themes he begged Tiomkin to work on the orgasm theme again. The composer agreed and eventually his final version was married to the print of Gregory Peck making passionate love to Jennifer Jones. Selznick gave it a thumbs down. It was, he said, too beautiful. 'It isn't orgasm music. That's not the way I fuck!' 'Mr Selznick,' yelled Tiomkin, his patience finally exhausted,

'you fuck your way! I fuck my way! To me, *that* is fucking music!' Disarmed by Tiomkin's outburst Selznick finally agreed the orgasm theme.

Another old legacy that Tiomkin has left the world is the Russian Tea Room in New York which he founded with his wife, the Broadway choreographer Albertina Rasch.

TOSCANINI, Arturo. The legendary temperamental conductor Toscanini could be severe with his musicians. During one dressing-down he hit them where he knew it would hurt them most: 'After I die I shall return to earth as keeper of a bordello; but I won't let one of you in.'

TREE, Maud, Lady. On her death bed Lady Tree, Herbert Beerbohm Tree's widow, was visited by her solicitor to put her affairs in order. Her daughter Viola asked if the interview had been distressing for her. 'Not at all,' she said. 'He was just teaching me my death duties.'

Viola was herself something of a wit. At the age of two her home was visited by W. S. Gilbert. (A kind invitation by Beerbohm Tree whom Gilbert had told after one performance, as he contemplated rivulets of sweat running down the actor, 'Your skin has been acting at any rate.') The two-year-old Viola was encouraged to kiss Gilbert. When she refused her father pleaded, 'Oh, kiss Gillie. Daddy loves Gillie.' 'Then Daddy kiss Gillie!' she said smartly.

When she was older she asked her father to buy her a pony. He told her he could not afford one. She said if he could afford to put on *Hamlet* he could afford to buy her a pony – indeed, if he acted Hamlet a bit better he would be able to afford to buy her a superior animal.

TROLLOPE, Anthony. The most charming – and perhaps saddest – literary anecdote in Trollope's *Autobiography* concerns the death of his immortal character Mrs Proudie. When he was writing *The Last Chronicle of Barset* he often stayed overnight at the Athenaeum and worked in the morning at one end of the long drawing room. One day he overheard a couple of clergymen abusing him and complaining that he reintroduced his characters so regularly – Archdeacon Grantly, The Duke of Omnium . . . 'if I could not invent new characters,' said one, 'I would not write novels at all.' They moved on to condemn Mrs Proudie. Trollope could resist no longer. He stood between them, confessed who he was and said, 'As to Mrs Proudie, I will go home and kill her before the week is over.' And so he did, in spite of their protestation that their comments had been frivolous.

'I have sometimes regretted the deed, so great was my delight in writing about Mrs Proudie, so thorough was my knowledge of all the little shades of her character. I have never severed myself from Mrs Proudie, and still live much in company with her ghost.'

Most memories of Anthony Trollope detail his unhappy childhood, his determinedly money-making mother, and his own industry and relentless output. Victoria Glendinning's recent biography spotlights two amusing aspects of his wife, Rose Heseltine, the daughter of a crooked Yorkshire bank manager, whom he met and married in Ireland.

By Trollope's own account in proposing to her he said she could take him or leave him. Her equally unromantic reply was, 'Well, I don't exactly want to leave you.'

Her view of her husband's industry was also matter-of-fact. She complained to Nathaniel Hawthorne's son, 'He never leaves off; and he always has two packages of manuscript on his desk, besides the one he's working on and the one that's being published.'

TRUEMAN, Frederick Sewards. The Yorkshire and England ex-fast bowler and raconteur bids fair to be the Oscar Wilde of cricket anecdotage. Proposing a toast to sportswriters at an annual dinner he glowered: 'I'm here to propose the toast to sportswriters,' he said looking around the room. 'It's up to you if you want to stand up.'

Trueman is a magnet for apocrypha, a creator of chestnuts and a skilled reteller of other cricketers' wit. Batting with Cowan, a fine quick bowler and appalling batsman, for Yorkshire against the West Indies, they were facing a fast bowling onslaught. Wes Hall sailed in to Cowan. Cowan's bat prodded to leg. The ball rocketed past the off stump. 'I think this fella has found my weakness, Fred,' said Cowan. The next delivery encouraged Cowan to play to the off side. The errant ball shot over the leg stump. 'It looks to me he's found both of 'em now,' said Trueman.

Reporting Emmott Robinson, Trueman evokes the era of Amateur and Professional when the two classes were required to converge onto the pitch from the pavilion through different entrances. The occasion was an early appearance by A. E. R. Gilligan, future amateur Captain of England – done up to the nines. As he approached the wicket a fellow-professional came up to Robinson – 'What's this fella doin' then?' he asked. 'I don't know,' said Emmott, 'but he smells nice.' He proceeded to bowl Gilligan comprehensively first ball. Gracious, gentlemanly and condescending, Gilligan deigned to speak to him on the way back to the pavilion. 'Well bowled, indeed, Robinson. That was a great ball.' 'Aye,' said Robinson, 'but it were wasted on thee.'

Trueman also tells of the time when Washbrook and Wharton were opening for Lancashire, with Washbrook on 90 and Wharton on 99, when Washbrook called a quick single. Wharton refused to move and Washbrook barely regained his ground in time. 'It is a well-known fact,' he snarled the next time they met in the middle of the wicket, 'that I am the best judge of a single in all England.' 'Yes,' Wharton concurred, 'and it's a well-known fact that when I'm on 99, I'm the best judge of a run in all the bloody world.'

On one occasion Trueman entered an opposing team's dressing room breathing fire and slaughter. 'I need nine wickets from this match,' he announced, 'and you buggers had better start drawing straws to see who I don't get.'

Reproving Raman Subba Row in the West Indies, after Subba Row had dropped a slip catch that led to four runs off his bowling, Trueman received the apology ungracefully and asked what about the four runs. 'I'm sorry about that,' said the hapless Subba Row, 'it might have been better if I'd kept my legs together.' 'Yes,' Trueman agreed, 'it's a pity your mother didn't!'

TRUMAN, Harry S. Memories of Harry Truman – who succeeded Franklin Roosevelt as President and then confounded expectation by beating Thomas Dewey (the dapper Republican magnificently dismissed as 'the man on the wedding cake'), after newspaper headlines had hit the streets prematurely announcing his triumph – were revived during the 1992 Presidential campaign when both George Bush and Bill Clinton claimed a Truman inheritance. As Truman had come from behind, so George Bush sought to prophesy the same election pattern in his acceptance speech for the Republican Party nomination – even using one of Truman's battle cries, 'Give 'em hell!' Margaret Truman (Harry S.'s daughter) attacked Bush as 'a hypocrite' and said that, although she found him personally pleasant, she had not expected him to be 'a political plagiarist'.

Margaret had good cause to cherish her father's memory. When he was President she was an aspiring soprano, emboldened to give a concert. Hulme, the critic of the *Washington Post*, gave her a lousy notice. Harry 'gave him hell'.

Mr Hulme,
I've just read your lousy review of Margaret's concert. I've come to the conclusion that you are an 'eight ulcer man on four ulcer pay'.

It seems to me that you are a frustrated old man who wishes he could have been successful. When you write such poppycock as was in the back section of the paper you work for, it shows conclusively that you're off the beam and at best four of your ulcers are at work.

Some day I hope to meet you. When that happens you'll need a new nose, a lot of beefsteak for black eyes, and perhaps a supporter below!

[Westbrook] Pegler, a guttersnipe, is a gentleman alongside you. I hope you'll accept that statement as a worse insult than a reflection on your ancestry.

Harry S. Truman

In the words of his other famous phrase which graced the desk of the Oval office, 'The buck stops here!'

TURNER, Joseph Mallord William. The nineteenth-century painter Turner had no great reputation when he was in Rome – indeed there was a British sales-man whose technique in selling was so flamboyant that he was the better known. Roman wits who *did* know, and were critical of Turner, used to say 'One Englishman sells mustard, the other paints it.'

He was secretive about his working methods and generally painted behind a locked door. His obstinacy in argument is illustrated by an encounter with Lord Egremont at Petworth. Turner had introduced a floating carrot into a painting and Egremont insisted carrots do not float. Turner called for a carrot and a bucket of water and proved his point.

Whenever possible he bought in his own works when they came up at auc-tion – if he could not get to the sale himself he sent a representative. When the pictures of a Mr Green, a Blackheath collector, came up for sale, including two Turners, he sent 'a clean ruddy-cheeked butcher's boy in the usual costume of his vocation'. James Christie the auctioneer interrupted him in mid-bid for his impertinence; but when the lad produced a greasy note from Turner authoris-ing him, 'the auctioneer smiled, and the bidding proceeded'. Both pictures brought high prices as the painter had hoped they would.

There was a rivalry between Turner and Constable illustrated in 1822 when Constable exhibited his colourful *Opening of Waterloo Bridge* in Somerset House. Turner finding one of his grey sea pieces beside it added 'a round daub of red lead, somewhat bigger than a shilling, on his grey sea and went away without a word'. The effect was to upstage Constable's picture and when Constable entered the room he took one look and said, 'He has been here.' A day and a half later Turner returned to convert his scarlet seal into a buoy.

On another occasion, when Constable could not fathom the tiny but vitally important element lacking in one of his paintings he asked Turner's advice. 'I say, Turner,' W. M. Thornbury has him saying in his *Life of J. M. W. Turner*, 'there is something wrong in this picture, and I cannot for the life of me tell what it is.' Turner considered it, took a brush and 'struck a ripple in the fore-ground'. At a glance he had seen what was needed to perfect the painting.

As a member of the Royal Academy 'hanging committee' Turner espoused the cause of a young artist, Edward Bird, whose painting his colleagues admired but said they could find no room for. 'We must find a good place for this young man's picture,' Turner insisted. 'Impossible – impossible,' the others cried. 'Turner said no more, but quietly removed one of his own pictures and hung up Bird's.'

A visitor to Burlington House once insisted that Dante Gabriel Rossetti should go and see the new Turner – called *Girls Surprised while Bathing*.

'Umph!' was Rossetti's answer. 'Yes, I should think devilish surprised to see what Turner had made of them!'

TYNDALE, William. William Tyndale's translation of the New Testament into English in the sixteenth century was a prime object of disapproval by the Bishop of London, Cuthbert Tunstall, who sought to buy up all the copies through the agency of a London merchant, Augustine Packington. Packington approached Tyndale with an offer. When Tyndale was told the name of the principal he remarked that the Bishop would surely burn and suppress the edition. Packington agreed. 'I am the gladder,' said Tyndale. 'I shall get money to get out of debt, the profit I shall use to correct the first edition and reprint.' The Bishop burnt his books, Packington had his thanks and Tyndale had the money for more and better editions.

— U —

ULYSSES. At the height of the scandal of the publication by Sylvia Beach of James Joyce's novel *Ulysses* in Paris in 1922, an admirer of Joyce told him that he had hidden a copy among some prayer books and Bibles that were taken into the Vatican and blessed by the Pope!

In 1931, nine years after publication, Harold Nicolson was still forbidden on the orders of Sir John Reith ever to mention the name of the book in his regular broadcasts at the BBC.

UMBERTO, Crown Prince of Sicily. Chips Channon, the celebrated millionaire MP, socialite and diarist, was not above laughing at himself. One diary entry reads: 'The Crown Prince Umberto is charm itself but has no great intelligence. He reminds me of myself.'

UNCLE NED. Nineteenth-century rhyming slang for bed. 'Upright' was nineteenth-century slang for the sexual act performed standing up; it was also known as 'perpendicular', and a 'threepenny bit' derived from the rhyming slang for 'tit'.

URBAN. Urban is the name adopted by eight popes. The least enlightened was Urban VIII, who condemned Galileo for demonstrating that Copernicus's assertion that the earth went round the sun must be right. Pope Urban was convinced that the opposite was true and it took until 1993 for the Vatican to admit that Galileo got it right.

URSULA, Saint. Ursula was a legendary English princess who went on pilgrimage to Rome in the fourth century, at the head of 11,000 virgins. All were ravished by the Huns on the return journey.

USTINOV, Peter. Peter Ustinov is so much the definitive anecdotalist that it is perhaps impertinent to offer Ustinov stories. However, I believe these are worthy of wider currency.

Ustinov was at a reception at 10 Downing Street for the President of Iceland – an actress. He owed his invitation to the fact that his play *Half Way Up the Tree* had just been a great success in Reykjavik. Mrs Thatcher said innocently to him, 'We don't see you here very often,' to which he snappily replied, 'The President of Iceland doesn't come here very often!'

He played his own *Beethoven's Tenth* in Berlin, in German. He enjoyed the discipline of acting in a language he knows well, but not well enough to allow him the luxury of forgetting his lines. He found it exciting to be kept on his toes every night and not to be able to talk his inimitable way out of it if he dried. He also appreciated the way the German audience received a witty line with a sound which is not quite a laugh. 'There is a short, sharp intake of breath. I call it a wine-tasting noise.'

He does a brilliant impersonation of King Hussein of Jordan – not many people *do* King Hussein but I assume it is brilliant. 'He speaks so quietly you have to lip read him,' says Ustinov. He also once visited a Bedouin in a palatial desert tent. The hospitality was generous but the host had a preoccupied air. 'You visit us on a bad day,' he told Ustinov. 'One of our young men has eloped with a girl from another tribe and they are asking for twenty thousand dollars American for her virginity. We have offered eight thousand dollars American and we are awaiting their reaction.' Outside, said Ustinov, a wife sat weaving a length of tent cloth with her feet and a gleaming Mercedes waited to take the children to school.

Ustinov is a book-signing buff. At Hatchard's on one occasion a friendly American in large, dark glasses and a green golfing hat pulled well down came up and asked him to sign a book. 'To whom shall I make it out?' 'Don't you remember me, Peter?' said the purchaser. 'Remember you? I can't see you!' 'It's Bing Crosby.'

Crosby was followed by a lady who asked, 'Would you sign this for Rosalind, please?' Ustinov started to sign ROS when she stopped him. 'No! No! It's ROZALYNDE – you see I'm from New Zealand.'

Once in Glasgow a young man flung a book down in front of Ustinov the author and said abruptly, 'Would you sign it to "The Auld Fools," it's for my parents.'

On an early visit to America Ustinov was trying out a play in Boston when he was interviewed by the formidable gossip columnist Louella Parsons. 'You must spend a lot of time on your feet in this play, Peeder?' she said abruptly at one point. 'Yes, well, I walk about quite a lot in the first act,' he replied innocently.

'And what about the second act?' she pressed. 'Oh, I do get to sit down a bit in act two,' he countered, puzzled. She pounced: 'What about the third act?' 'I stand all through act three.' 'There!' she said, swinging round triumphantly to the camera: 'That is the problem for so many American housewives. You are on your feet all day, but get Preparation SE39 and soothe your aches and pains away.'

In Canada he made a commercial himself for American Express. A Canadian journalist asked him why he did it. 'To pay for my American Express,' was the neat explanation.

UTRILLO, Maurice. Ambrose Vollard, the French art critic, tells an anecdote of a woman whose son was feeble-minded. Her friend said, 'If he falls in love he may recover his reason.' So she gave tea parties and invited nice girls, but the son threw the cakes on the floor and remained idiotic from drink. 'Turn him into a painter,' was the next piece of advice she received; 'he'll be just the thing and will probably make you a fortune.' She took the advice and he did just that.

Later Utrillo (for it was he) brought a successful suit against James Bolivar Manson, the Director of the Tate Gallery in 1932, who had listed him in a Tate Catalogue as dead from alcoholism when he was in fact alive and, for once, sober.

— V —

VANBRUGH, Sir John. Vanbrugh, architect of Blenheim and much of Greenwich (as well as an amusing playwright), waited for a posthumous anecdote – his epitaph by Abel Evans:

> Under this stone, Reader, survey
> Dear Sir John Vanbrugh's house of clay.
> Lie heavy on him earth! for he
> Laid many heavy loads on thee.

VAN DRUTEN, John. John Van Druten's early problem play, *Young Woodley*, a calf-love play in which a schoolboy falls in love with his housemaster's wife, caused some concern when it was submitted to the Lord Chamberlain in 1925. After much discussion it was refused a licence and Basil Dean, the director, arranged for it to be presented for a private performance on a Sunday night. Lord Cromer, the censor, saw it and sent the play to the President of the Board of Education who thought more harm might be done if it became known that a play about public school life had been banned. It was then presented at the Arts Theatre. Cromer came again and sanctioned everything except a remark of one of the schoolboys that he 'wouldn't mind being boots in the girls' school'. This was a reference to a recent scandal at a well-known girls' school where a German boot boy had enticed girls into his large boot cupboard the better to deflower them.

VAN DYCK, Sir Anthony. Van Dyck, The Dutch artist who had such a success as a court painter to King Charles I, played a neat trick on Frans Hals, a younger painter who revered him but did not know him before he left Holland for England. Having heard of the growing reputation of Hals, Van Dyck visited him incognito in Haarlem and, when Hals, a great drinker, had been prised from his favourite tavern, asked him to paint him. Hals agreed and when the portrait was complete Van Dyck admired it and asked if he might try to paint Hals – now he had seen how it was done. Hals agreed and soon realised from the way he held brush and palette that this was no novice. When Van Dyck had completed the portrait Hals took one look at it and embraced the artist saying, 'You are Van Dyck: no one but he could do this.'

As a pupil of Rubens, Van Dyck once retouched a Rubens which fellow pupils had smeared during studio horseplay. Examining it in the morning Rubens found that he liked it better than he had the night before.

In England Van Dyck enjoyed the favour of the great nobles and of King Charles and Queen Henrietta Maria. Initially he was meticulous but after he had painted a great number of portraits he worked more hastily, telling a friend, 'I worked a long time for my reputation, and I do it now for my kitchen.' He said to Charles, 'An artist who keeps open house for all his friends, and opens his purse to his mistresses, only too often experiences the problem of empty coffers.' He enjoyed painting the Queen and in particular her exquisite hands. When she asked why he took more trouble with her hands than her head he replied, 'Ah, Madame, it is that I expect from those hands a reward worthy of their owner.'

VASARI, Giorgio. Giorgio Vasari is the supreme example of an anecdotalist working exclusively on the *Lives of the Most Excellent Italian Architects, Painters and Sculptors* who had lived and drawn and painted and sculpted before 1550 when he published his book.

Well-behaved artists are less likely to achieve notoriety than their rowdy colleagues, and Vasari did as much as anyone to establish the cult of the artist as 'anti-hero' and a sense of the 'otherness' of the creative nature.

Without Vasari we would probably not know that Leonardo threatened to paint an officious prior as Judas in his *Last Supper*. Or that Donatello opted for breaking a bust with his own hands rather than permit delivery to a client who was unappreciative, or that Michelangelo only carved his own name into his St Peter's *Pietà* when he heard a stranger insisting that it was the work of a rival sculptor.

VAUGHAN, Father Bernard. Before World War One Father Bernard was renowned for his fashionable Mayfair sermons on the theme of 'The Sins of Society'. His favourite off-duty joke was to lean out of a railway carriage window and shout to a departing fellow traveller, 'You've left something behind!' When the man came back to collect 'it' he would be told, 'You've left behind a very bad impression!'

VELASQUEZ, Don Diego Rodriguez de Silva y Velasquez was loaded with honours by Philip IV of Spain, made a Gentleman of the Wardrobe and finally a Gentleman of the Bedchamber. So great was the favour in which he was held by his king that when the young son of one great nobleman told his father proudly how he had treated the painter casually, even rudely, his father sent him to apologise immediately, refusing to see him until he had done so.

However, where anecdotes are concerned, Velasquez's greatest triumph was perhaps his portrait of Don Adriano Palido Paresa, Admiral of the King's Fleet in New Spain. After the King had ordered the Admiral to leave Madrid on a mission, he entered Velasquez's chamber where the painter was working on the picture which he had nearly finished. Philip immediately berated the Admiral for staying in the capital after he had been ordered to leave. It took some time and Velasquez's explanation before the King realised that he had harangued the portrait not the Admiral, who had long gone to do his duty.

VENUTI, Joe. Joe Venuti, the jazz violinist, had a tiresome penchant for practical jokes, which dominates most of the stories recorded about him. However, during a resurgence of interest late in his career in the late seventies he was playing in a club in Schenectady. Pleased with the interest a new generation was taking in him he announced: 'Ladies and gentlemen, I'm gonna do something I don't usually do. I'm gonna take a few requests.' A punter asked for 'Feelings'.

' "Feelin's",' said Venuti, ' "Feelin's!" Why, that's the worst goddam song I ever heard! That's it, no more requests. You had your chance.'

He played 'Sweet Georgia Brown'.

VICTORIA, Queen. Daughter of the exceedingly bald Duke of Kent (Sheridan said that this was because grass did not grow on deserts), Victoria ascended the throne at the age of eighteen. Her father was impressed by her infant energy: 'This is rather a pocket Hercules than a pocket Venus.' As she grew to realise how near she was to the succession she told Baroness Lehzen, 'I am nearer to the throne than I thought'; and added, 'I will be good.' In 1833 she recorded in her diary, 'I am fourteen years old! How very old!' Soon she was old enough to fight off the efforts of her widowed mother and Sir John Conroy, who was rumoured to be her lover, to dominate her. When the Archbishop of Canterbury and Lord Conyngham came to tell her she was Queen her hand shot out to be kissed almost before the words were out of Conyngham's mouth. Her first order was to have her bed moved into a room of her own.

Her Whig Prime Minister, Lord Melbourne, quickly exerted a powerful influence on her, to the dismay of the Tories. The Whig defeat in 1839 panicked her. She fought to keep her Ladies of the Bedchamber and not have them replaced by Tories. The diarist Charles Greville reckoned that her feelings for Melbourne 'are sexual though she does not know it'.

Her engagement to Prince Albert of Saxe-Coburg and Gotha, three months her junior, was announced in 1839. At seventeen she had rejected two sons of the Prince of Orange as possible suitors, writing to her uncle, King Leopold of the Belgians: 'The boys are both very plain and have a mixture of Kalmuck and Dutch in their faces, moreover they look heavy, dull and frightened and are not at all prepossessing. So much for the *Oranges*, dear uncle.' Albert was different. 'It was with some emotion that I beheld Albert who is beautiful!' she wrote.

Etiquette demanded that she propose to Albert, which she did nervously but enthusiastically. The night before their marriage in 1840 she wrote in her Journal, 'The last time I slept alone.' The marriage was passionate, devoted and productive of innumerable offspring. Not a prude to begin with, under Albert's influence she more and more embraced the 'Victorian' attitudes of the century. Although their life together was happy and exemplary, the familiar Hanoverian cycle of discord with the Prince of Wales began early. Edward was her second child. She had eight out of her nine children before she discovered 'That blessed chloroform . . . the effect was soothing, quieting and delightful beyond measure.'

Her reign was strewn with semi-farcical assassination attempts, the first in 1840; and with attempts by small boys to get into Buckingham Palace. The first was 'the boy Jones' who had three goes. The first time he was declared insane. The second time he was put on the treadmill; the third time, the treadmill was repeated and then he was sent away to sea.

Gwen Raverat in *Period Piece: A Cambridge Childhood* tells the story of the Queen visiting the university when Albert received an honorary degree. Shown over Trinity by Dr Whewell, the Master, she looked down over the bridge and saw the signs of loo paper bobbing along. 'What are those pieces of paper floating down the river?' she enquired. 'Those, ma'am,' he replied with great presence of mind, 'are notices that bathing is forbidden.'

Victoria's relationships with her Prime Ministers were critical. With Palmerston she and Albert clashed over foreign policy, especially his 'gunboat diplomacy', and there was the case of his entering a lady-in-waiting's bedroom at Windsor uninvited, but when he died she told her Journal, 'He had often worried and distressed us, though as Pr. Minister he had behaved *very well*.'

Prince Albert's death in 1861 after his triumph with the Great Exhibition and the end of the Crimean War poleaxed her and she was determined to blame it on a recent scandal involving the heir to the throne. Her widowed seclusion became a public scandal until Disraeli helped her partially to recover from it. When he received a copy of her *Highland Diaries* he managed his most fulsome compliment, 'We authors, Ma'am.' But, as he told Matthew Arnold, 'You have heard me called a flatterer, and it is true. Everyone likes flattery and when you come to royalty, you should lay it on with a trowel.' In 1875 with the co-operation of the Rothchilds he delivered the Suez Canal to her, 'presenting' it with the words, 'It is just settled; you have it, Ma'am.'

The title Empress of India was another well-judged present. Comparing himself to his great rival he pointed out, 'Gladstone treats the Queen like a public department; I treat her like a woman.' Not far from the Queen's protests that Gladstone addressed her 'like a public meeting'.

The great mystery of the Queen's declining years was her relationship with John Brown, the royal couple's favourite ghillie, who came south to attend Victoria four years after Albert's death, which had sent her into deep mourning. 'He *would* die,' she said, 'he seemed not to care to live.' Her private secretary, Sir Henry Ponsonby, assessed Brown simply as 'a first-class servant'. But scandal, particularly in America, attached to him, and *Punch* published an imaginary Court Circular instancing his 'day'. Certainly he was autocratic. Another private secretary, later Lord Stamfordham, was told curtly at Balmoral, 'Ye'll no be going fishing. Her majesty thinks its about time ye did some work.' The Queen hated tea. When she once congratulated Brown on the best cup she had ever drunk, he replied, 'Well, it should be, Ma'am, I put a grand nip o' whisky in it.'

He died of delirium tremens and erysipelas, as had another of the Brown family while in her service. Elizabeth Longford notes that she had it hushed up, 'believing that stimulants were necessary to hard-working servants – though not to the upper classes!'

He was succeeded in her approbation by Abdul Karim, the Munshi (secretary), an ignorant Muslim who gave himself fantastic airs, lorded it particularly over the royal under-servants, and induced 'Munshimania' in the Queen and rebellion in the Royal Household.

Elizabeth Longford makes the point that there is no documented record of the Queen's most famous phrase 'We are not amused' – though her journals are full of 'I was very much amused'. Indeed, she seems at times to have been an uncontrollable laugher, going purple in the face in Crathie church at Balmoral in her attempts not to laugh when wee Dr Magregor prayed 'That the Almighty would send down His wisdom on the Queen's Ministers, who sorely need it.' She was also fond of telling the story of a sentimental address by a regimental sentry when she was leaning out of her window at Windsor in the moonlight. Bursting with laughter, she would explain, 'He took me for a housemaid!'

When she asked a member of the household in which limb a maid-of-honour had rheumatic pains he told her that they were in the lady's legs. She observed with a smile that when she came to the throne 'young ladies did not use to have legs.'

She would often be tart. Driving at Osborne towards the end of her life with the equally elderly Lady Erroll she was very silent. Loelia Erroll sought to draw her out. 'Oh, Your Majesty,' she offered, 'think of when we shall see our dear ones again in Heaven!' The Queen failed to brighten. 'Yes,' she said glumly. 'We will all meet in Abraham's bosom,' tried Lady Erroll gamely. 'I will not meet Abraham!' said the Queen firmly, noting in her Journal that night, 'Dear Loelia, not at all consolatory in moments of trouble!'

When she was to be painted by von Angeli she grunted, 'It better be done before I get too hideous to behold.' When she visited the Black Country she was dismayed. 'It is like another world. In the midst of so much wealth, there seems to be nothing but ruin.' On Florence Nightingale, whom she admired, 'I wish we had her at the War Office.'

Her death bed was attended by hordes of Royals and courtiers. Princess Louise's husband, the Duke of Argyll, said that she went down 'like a great three-decker ship'. The Kaiser was in attendance – although, in spite of her affection for her first grandson, she had often complained of his adopting 'imperial airs' in the family circle as well as in public. Her doctor, Sir James Reid, asked the Prince of Wales if he should tell her. 'No', said Edward, 'it would excite her too much.' However, when she rallied he visited her alone. After the usual bulletin – 'The Queen is sinking' – she died at 6.30 on 22 January 1901. The doctor had never seen her in bed until six days before her death and was amazed to find out after it that she had suffered a prolapse and ventral hernia. She was buried with various effects and photographs of Albert, and Queen Alexandra's flowers which concealed a photograph of John Brown from her relatives and which she had insisted should be in the coffin.

VILLIERS, James. James Villiers, the actor (and somewhere in the 120s in line of succession to the throne), not only possesses one of the most distinctive presences on the stage, but has a voice to match. He was a late choice of William Gaskill for one of the fops in his production of The Way of the World at Chichester which later transferred to the Haymarket. The stars were Joan Plowright as Lady Wishfort and Maggie Smith as Millamant. She had played with him before when he was Victor to her Amanda in Private Lives. In fact rehearsals had already started when Gaskill announced to the cast that he had at last found an actor.

'Who?' asked Dame Maggie.

'He's called James Villiers.'

'Oh God,' she said to Joan Plowright, 'he's going to make the rest of us sound pretty common.'

W ALLACE, Edgar. In the last six years of his life Edgar Wallace, who died in 1932, wrote 28 novels. It was a current jibe to asked for the 'midday Wallace'. In 1930 he stood as a Liberal candidate for Parliament, saying that he wished to enter the House of Commons because 'a writer of crook stories ought never to stop seeking new material'.

W ALPOLE, Horace, 4th Earl of Orford. Queen Charlotte, the wife of George III, was no beauty but someone at court remarked that in her later years she had become somewhat better looking. 'Yes,' said Horace Walpole, 'I do think the *bloom* of her ugliness is going off.'

W ALPOLE, Sir Robert, 1st Earl of Orford. First Lord of the Treasury and virtually the first Prime Minister from 1721 to 1742, Walpole would not prolong his Councils if he lost his temper, saying, 'No man is fit for business with a ruffled temper.' One of his skills was playing cleverly with parliamentary procedure and, above all, patronage of bishops whom he wished to persuade to his side. He would ask 'Is he mortal?', meaning could he be bribed? He believed that everything could be managed in this way, 'There is enough pasture for all the sheep.'

W ALTERS, John. These stories are not primarily about John Walters – the ex-BBC Radio 1 producer who was responsible for John Peel's shows for more years than he cares to remember – but Walters is a compulsive raconteur and he is my only source of these two tales.

The American poet-singer Bob Dylan was a close friend of Dave Stewart of the Eurythmics who, as is increasingly the custom, had his own recording studio. He invited Dylan to use it any time he was in England. The address was, let us say, No. 11 Something Street. Dylan feeling inspiration strike set off for his friend's studio. Unfortunately he finished up outside No.11 Something *Close*. Unaware of his mistake he rang the bell and the woman of the household came to the door and asked his business. He said his name was Bob Dylan and 'Dave' had said he could come round. Since by a happy coincidence the woman's husband was also called Dave she asked him in saying Dave would be back soon, and installed him in the sitting room with a cup of tea. On hearing her husband come in she called out gaily, 'Bob Dylan's here for you, Dave.' His reply is not recorded.

Walters' other story harks back to the days when he was in a band called the Animals, with Alan Price. On tour in Aberdeen, they were drinking happily in a pub. Upstairs a wedding breakfast was in noisy progress. Hearing that Alan Price was downstairs the bridegroom rushed down and asked Price to play for his wife, 'your biggest fan'; and added that it would make her wedding day. Price agreed graciously but no sooner had he started thumping out a tune than the bride's father ordered him off, pointing to a local lady pianist with the words, 'I've paid 'er to play, so get off!'

WARNER, Jack. Originally there were four Warner Brothers, Albert, Sam, Harry and Jack, who ran the Burbank studios with a contempt for critics which matched Harry Cohn's. 'Don't pay attention to bad reviews,' was Jack's advice. 'Today's newspaper is tomorrow's toilet paper.'

Like most Hollywood moguls Jack Warner preferred to decide on a movie after reading a synopsis rather than after working his way through a novel. In 1933 when Mervyn Le Roy cabled him: 'PLEASE READ ANTHONY ADVERSE. WOULD MAKE GREAT PICTURE FOR US', Warner wired back: 'READ IT? I CAN'T EVEN LIFT IT.'

Encountering Albert Einstein, who was on a tour of the Warner studio, he boasted that he too had a theory of relatives which matched Einstein's theory of relativity. 'Really?' said Einstein. 'What is your theory?' 'Don't hire 'em.' This, of course, was a precept not followed by Louis B. Mayer who promoted his daughter's husband, David O. Selznick, prompting an unidentified Hollywood wit to say, 'The son-in-law also rises.'

Another distinguished visitor to Warner studios during World War Two was Madame Chiang Kai-shek. She made a generous speech thanking Hollywood for its fund-raising aid to China. In replying, Warner lost his thread and looking straight into her eyes said, 'Holy cow, that reminds me. I forgot to pick up my laundry.'

He could be acute as well as frank in his assessments of directors. Once he remarked, 'To Raoul Walsh a tender love scene is burning down a whorehouse.'

He was dictatorial to his writers. They were required to observe a nine-to-five-thirty schedule, limit lunch to half an hour, and wear their pencils down a set length every day. If a picture they had worked on got bad reviews they would say, 'We can't think why, because we were there at nine o'clock, we took a half an hour for lunch and our pencils were down to here. So it couldn't be our fault.'

When Norman Krasna was clashing with Jack Warner over his script for *Princess O'Rourke*, starring Olivia de Havilland, Warner accused him of holding up production by leaving early. He demanded an ending to the script. Krasna looked at his watch and said that he had a solution – and the perfect ending. Warner, excited, wanted to know what it was; 'I can't tell you,' said Krasna. 'Why?' demanded Warner. 'Because,' said Krasna, 'I thought of the answer after 5.30.'

Warner bent the rules for William Faulkner and allowed him to work from home – to his surprise he later found out that 'home' was not somewhere in the Hollywood Hills but in Oxford, Mississippi.

Song writers got short shrift too. When Harry Warren told Warner that it could take three weeks to write a song he exploded, 'Three weeks to write one lousy song!' Warren corrected him, 'No! Three weeks to write one good song!'

When Warner went to the races with Mervyn Le Roy – who reckoned himself an insider – he was sworn to secrecy before, during and after the race which featured Le Roy's hot tip. It came in last. From home Warner wired Le Roy: 'NOW CAN I TELL?'

He had a passionate hatred of television, which enabled a screenwriter, Mel Shavelson, who knew about it, to win a bet from two song writers, Sammy Fain and Paul Francis Webster (who didn't). They played Shavelson their new song for a Warner picture. He told them it would never be in the movie. The bet was $10. The next day they played it to Warner, unaware that he would not even let a TV set appear on the screen. The next day again they came to pay Shavelson his money. The song was called, 'I'm in Love with a Girl on Channel 9'.

When Wilson Mizener was hired to write scripts for Warner he entered his new employer's office bearing an LA telephone book. He dropped it on Warner's desk saying , 'This might have been good for a picture, but there are too many characters in it.'

Warner's ironic epitaph should be his verdict on hearing that Ronald Reagan was seeking nomination for Governor of California – 'No, No! Jimmy Stewart for Governor – Reagan for Best Friend.' He did not live to see Reagan elected President – twice!

Wilson Mizener's verdict on working at Warner's was frank, 'Working for Warners is like fucking a porcupine. It's one hundred pricks against one.'

Mizener also said perhaps the hardest thing about Warner: 'He has oilcloth pockets so he can steal soup.'

WATERHOUSE, Keith. Longstanding *Daily Mirror* and latterly *Daily Mail* columnist Keith Waterhouse has the great distinction of having turned down the late Robert Maxwell when the Bouncing Czech said to him, 'Put your pension in my hands, Keith, and I will enhance it.' He had invited Maxwell to lunch at the Connaught only to find that no reservation had been made. He solved that problem by giving the maître d'hôtel £20 and employing the bravura lie that he was 'lunching the man who has just bought this hotel'. A few minutes later he was amused to see two Americans being politely escorted from the dining room with the words, 'If sir wants a steak I think he'll be much happier in the Grill Room.'

Less impressive was Waterhouse's return to Leeds for a family funeral. He enquired of one of his sisters who an old man was who was nursing a drink across the room: 'You daft bugger,' she said, 'that's your brother.'

He insists that Yorkshire taxi-drivers eclipse their cockney colleagues as idiosyncratic conversationalists. He once had a silent pilot whose only words were: 'On the way I'll have to drop off a red cabbage for a friend of the wife's.' I once had a taxi driver in Leeds who had an opinion on everything. On the ruins of Kirkstall Abbey, 'American women say to me, "was it bombed in the war?" I say, "Aye, t'war between Henry VIII and t'Pope." ' On the information that the new owners of Harry Ramsden's famous shop might franchise their produce world wide, 'Kentucky Fried Chicken and Chips.' And on Yorkshire's idea of introducing non-natives into their cricket team: 'They 'ad fifty new bowlers at nets t'other day. Thirty were Asian.' I suggested they might find some slow bowlers in there. 'Need a few fast ones. 'Aven't 'ad one since Fred turned pundit.'

WATERSTONE, Timothy. The creator of the Waterstone's bookshop chain was sacked by W. H. Smith in 1981. His chairman's final words were 'I don't mind what you do as long as you don't open any bookshops.' W. H. Smith's bought Waterstone's eight years later for £42.2 million.

On his first day as a book seller under his own name Waterstone sold his first book – The Koran – for £25 and made an encouraging total of £924. Then he left the bag with the entire day's takings in a carriage on the Circle Line.

I always hoped that my favourite Christina Foyle story concerned Waterstone. Miss Foyle had long meditated on who should be her successor. Discussing it with Ronald, her husband, they eventually settled on a particularly promising young employee. One weekend they decided to break the news to him on the following Monday. When she arrived at the office she found that he had already requested an interview. When he turned up, before she could give him the good news, he explained that he had got a better job and regretfully handed in his notice. He left amicably never learning that he had abdicated an empire.

It would have been nicely symmetrical if he had been called Tim Waterstone – but sadly he was not.

WATERTON, Charles. Charles Waterton was a wealthy nineteenth-century northern squire and explorer who practised an ultra conservatism and eccentricity, like many Catholics turned inward and isolated by the anti-Catholic feeling of the late eighteenth century. He was painted capturing a 10-foot crocodile or cayman by sitting astride it. Asked how he kept his seat, he replied: 'I hunted some years with Lord Darlington's fox-hounds.'

WAUGH, Evelyn. Waugh crops up elsewhere in this book, but more than deserves his own entry. According to Waugh in a letter he wrote to Harold Acton in April 1952, he stayed two nights at the Villa Mauresque, the Cap Ferrat home of Somerset Maugham. On the first evening Maugham asked Waugh what someone was like. Presumably without thinking Waugh replied: 'A pansy with a stammer.' He added in the letter, 'All the Picassos on the wall blanched.'

Waugh's son Auberon has memorably recorded the occasion when his father commandeered his children's entire ration of bananas especially doled out by the government after the war. His autobiography, *Will That Do?*, makes the most of the greedy parent who ate them before his children's envious eyes, liberally dousing them with cream.

His novels are crammed with aphorisms. From *Decline and Fall*: 'I expect you'll be becoming a schoolmaster, sir. That's what most of the gentlemen does, sir, that gets sent down for indecent behaviour.'

From *The Loved One*: 'You never find an Englishman among the underdogs – except in England of course.'

From *Vile Bodies*: 'All this fuss about sleeping together. For physical pleasure I'd sooner go to my dentist any day.'

From *A Little Learning*: 'Assistant masters came and went. Some liked little boys too little and some too much.'

From *Scoop*: 'Personally I can't see that foreign stories are even news – not real news.'

Oh, back to the books!

WAYNE, John. Stanley Baker, the Welsh movie actor who died too young, once asked John Wayne's advice on how he should play a certain part in a movie. 'The Duke' listened to Baker's questions and then said laconically, 'Just get out there and clank.'

WELDON, Duncan. Duncan Weldon really belongs in *Theatrical Anecdotes* but his testimony came too late for that. He is one of the most prolific British producers. His career followed the traditional pattern built initially on touring productions of West End hits, pantomimes – quantity rather than quality, initially. However, he was always ambitious for greater things and progressed rapidly to smart offices above the Strand Theatre in Ivor Novello's famous old flat. Here he had a first meeting with two stars whom he hoped would agree to appear in a play for him. They were John Gielgud and Ralph Richardson. After lunch he took them back to the office to finalise arrangements for the play. It was a pre-Christmas meeting and somewhat to his embarrassment he found that the stairs leading up to the inner sanctum were festooned with dwarfs who had answered his partner's casting call for *Snow White*. Neither Gielgud nor Richardson remarked on the phenomenon and by the time the meeting was over the dwarfs had gone.

The play was presented and some years later Gielgud appeared in another (Julian Mitchell's *Half a Life*) under Weldon's banner. The tour took the play to Toronto where Gielgud was given some honour at a formal luncheon. Weldon went along to give him moral support and was amazed as Gielgud launched into his speech of thanks. He expressed his gratitude for the award and then praised the enterprise of his producer in presenting the play and bringing it to Toronto. 'Extraordinary fellow, Weldon,' he said; adding out of the blue, 'Extraordinary. He employs dwarfs, you know.'

For a long time Duncan Weldon was in partnership with Louis Michaels, who became involved in theatre late in life both as a co-producer and a bricks-and-mortar man. Early in their partnership Weldon took him to see Peter Coe's production of *Macbeth* at Leatherhead, with a view to transferring it to the West End. After about ten minutes Louis, apparently unaware of the play or its author, turned to his partner in a fury saying, 'Duncan, where did you dig up this load of rubbish?' In Billingham to view a specially expensive stage set by Ralph Koltai, Weldon and Michaels were dismayed when the curtain rose on their private view of a simple disc.

'But it cost fifty thousand pounds!' Michaels exploded.

'Yes,' said Koltai. 'And you'd never think it!'

Despatched to New York to woo Katharine Hepburn back to the West End, Louis Michaels couldn't come up with a play on his shopping list which appealed to her. Stalling, he called Weldon in London for more suggestions. He came up with a brainwave, *The Cherry Orchard*. Michaels asked him briefly to outline the plot. Weldon did his best. Michaels was dismayed. 'Duncan, I can't offer America's greatest actress a play about choppin' trees down!'

Weldon himself does not avoid the occasional near-Goldwynism. Bemoaning the fact that his production of Alan Bennett's *Talking Heads* at the Comedy Theatre had to close while playing to capacity he lamented, 'Alan won't go on and Pat Routledge is going to Greenwich to do *The Corn is Green*.' 'Who's presenting that?' he was asked. 'I am. That's the trouble with me, my successes stop too soon and my failures run for ever.'

Meeting Richard Nelson at the Barbican after the first night of his extremely long – some four hours – play about Columbus and the discovery of America Weldon complained, 'What took you so long? I can do it in three hours on Concorde.'

WELLES, Orson. One of the women who repulsed the multi-faceted actor, director, magician and raconteur Orson Welles was, oddly enough, 'a homely Italian actress with a face like a spoon'. Apparently she had a great, if mysterious, allure for men, and Welles became besotted. He confided his love to his friend Charles Lederer, who wrote telling him to try to visualise her sitting on the lavatory picking her nose. Welles wrote back, 'It's the most enchanting vision I've ever thought of!'

Asked to name the three best directors whose work he had seen in Hollywood, Wells modestly replied, 'I like the Old Masters; by which I mean John Ford, John Ford and John Ford.'

In 1948 when he was directing *The Lady from Shanghai*, Welles overran his schedule at great expense. The production manager, Jack Fier, was supposed to prevent this. He tried and Welles began to hate him. Towards the end of shooting he put up a sign reading 'The only thing we have to Fier is Fier itself.' Fier made his own sign in reply: 'All's well that ends Welles.'

WELLINGTON, Arthur Wellesley, 1st Duke of. The Duke of Wellington, England's most famous soldier, was a memorable phrase maker – particularly for a military man. However, his most famous phrase, 'The Battle of Waterloo was won on the playing fields of Eton', is apocryphal. What he actually said was, 'I really believe I owe my spirit of enterprise to the trick I used to play in the garden,' referring to the garden of his Eton boarding house. To his officers at Waterloo he said, 'Hard pounding, this, gentlemen. Try who can pound the hardest.' Of his men he said – pointing to one – 'There, it all depends upon that article whether we do the business or not. Give me enough of it, and I am sure.'

After Waterloo he said, 'By God! I don't think it would have done if I had not been there.'

More generally, he urged preparedness for Britian: 'There is no such thing as a little War for a great Nation,' and more philosophically, 'Next to a battle lost, the greatest misery is a battle gained.'

Of his origin – he was born in Ireland but was English – he said, 'Because a man is born in a stable, that does not make him a horse.' When his ex-mistress, Harriette Wilson, wrote her *Memoirs*, her publisher, Joseph Stockdale, sought to blackmail Wellington with the words, 'I have stopped the press for the moment: but as the publication will take place next week, little delay can necessarily take place.' Wellington was forthright: 'Publish and be damned.' When he was told that a certain Lady Frances Shelley had rejected the advances of a fat Austrian baron with the explanation that she could not have surrendered, as, 'I have even resisted the Duke of Wellington', he said to his niece, 'In my own justification . . . I was never aware of this resistance.' When a mob forced him to cheer George IV's Queen Caroline he muttered, 'God Save the Queen, and may all your wives be like her!'

Entering politics, he was dismayed by the results of the Reform Bill. Looking down on the new Members from the Peers' Gallery and asked what he thought he said, 'I have never seen so many bad hats in my life.' Much later in life the list of names in Palmerston's 1851 Cabinet provoked such a stream of 'Who? Who?'s that it was known as the 'Who? Who? Ministry'. At the time of the Great Exhibition Queen Victoria called him in to advise her on how to get rid of the sparrows who were fouling the Crystal Palace and obviously could not be shot. Severely practical he said simply, 'Sparrowhawks, Ma'am.'

W. P. Frith's *Autobiography*, published in 1888, recalls the delight the painter and secretary of the Royal Academy, one Jones, took in being mistaken for the the Duke. When Wellington heard this he said, 'Mistaken for me, is he? That is strange, for no one ever mistakes me for Mr Jones.' Not long after, as he walked in Pall Mall, a minor civil servant raised his hat to him saying, 'Mr Jones, I believe.' To which he replied, 'Sir, if you believe that, you will believe anything.'

WEST, Benjamin. Benjamin West (1738–1830) takes the palm as the most vain of artists. Of a visit to Paris, where he believed himself to have been the centre of attention, he said, 'Wherever I went, men looked at me and ministers and people of influence in the state were constantly in my company. I was one day in the Louvre – all eyes were upon me: and I could not help observing to Charles Fox, *who happened to be walking with me*, how strong was the love of art, and admiration of its professors, in France.'

However, perhaps his most grandiloquent claim was, 'When my pictures come into the exhibition, every other painter takes his place as if a Sovereign had come in.'

WEST, Mae. Mae West, the famous screen and stage vamp, so curvaceous that an inflatable life-jacket was named after her during World War Two, lived to a great age and differed from many contemporaries in that her on-screen and off-screen witticisms were usually her own work and did not depend on scriptwriters or studio publicists.

I have dealt with her stage career in *Theatrical Anecdotes* – though I did omit her impromptu exchange with a very good character actress, Alison Skipworth, who suspected correctly that Miss West was stealing a scene from her. 'I'll have you know I am an actress,' intoned Miss Skipworth. 'It's alright, dearie,' replied Mae, 'I'll keep your secret.'

Her arrival in Hollywood bothered the guardians of morals. Her first starring role in 1933 was opposite the young Cary Grant in *She Done Him Wrong*. She opened with 'Why don't you come up sometime 'n' see me?' When Grant looks at her quizzically she says, 'Aw, you can be had.' Another gem from the same script: 'When women go wrong, men go right after them.' To the compliment that she is 'a fine woman' she replies, 'One of the finest women who ever walked the streets.'

She hipped and swaggered and tossed off lines like 'It's not what I do, but the way I do it,' or 'It's not what I say, but the way I say it'; 'It's better to be looked over than overlooked'; 'It's not the men in my life that count but the life in my men'; and 'I'm a girl who lost her reputation and never missed it.'

Linked with W. C. Fields the chemistry was even stronger. When she tells him her name in *Hooverbelle* he responds, 'What a euphonious appellation!' When he asks if he can kiss 'her symmetrical digits' her reply is 'Sure, help yourself.'

She was on the ball with interviewers too. Hedda Hopper, the Hollywood gossip columnist, asked her how she came to know so much about men. 'Baby,' said Miss West, 'I went to night school.'

She was proud of her writing skills: 'When you think about it, what other playwrights are there besides O'Neill, Tennessee and me?' And she clashed with Lubitsch over her habit of taking all the good lines: 'I'm writin' the story,' she said, 'and I'm the star.' Lubitsch advanced the case of two-character drama: 'Look at Romeo and Juliet.' 'Let Shakespeare do it his way, I'll do it mine,' was her reply. 'We'll see who comes out better.'

She boasted that she had mirrors in her bedroom because: 'I like to see how I'm doin'. When I'm good, I'm very good; but when I'm bad, I'm better.'

WHISTLER, James Abbott McNeill. The life of the painter was strewn with conflict, especially with critics – though he is also vividly remembered for his exchange with Oscar Wilde at the Café Royal. To a witticism of Whistler's Wilde murmured, 'Oh James, I wish I had said that' – Whistler's reply was: 'You will, Oscar, you will.' In his letters Whistler castigates his critics: 'Can anything be more amazing than the stultified prattle of this poor person . . . Good God, did this ass in his astounding wisdom believe that a Symphony in F contains no other note but . . . a continued repetition of FFF. Fool.'

The critical hurts reached a climax when Ruskin described Whistler's painting *The Falling Rocket* as 'flinging a pot of paint in the public's face'. He called the asking price of 200 guineas an outrage. Whistler sued in one of the most lively libel trials in art history. He was flamboyant and assured in court, especially when giving evidence. Ruskin's counsel asked how he could charge 200 guineas for a painting which took only two days to 'knock off'. Whistler's reply was 'I ask it for the knowledge of a lifetime.'

It was an expensive victory for Whistler, who won the case and was awarded damages of one farthing. The costs bankrupted him, but years later he was able to write to his wife explaining his joy at staying in the room Ruskin had occupied during the trial: 'I understand that he was in a most beautiful state of exasperation – tearing up paper and tossing pans about all over the place! Delightful, isn't it?'

A softer side of Whistler is revealed by a Mr Harper Pennington who recorded that he once stood beside the painter in Whistler's studio in Tite Street, contemplating the famous picture of Whistler's Mother – and made a fulsome compliment about the beauty of the face and figure. For a moment Whistler dropped his guard and nervously stroked his chin. After a long pause he volunteered, 'Yes – one does like to make one's mummy look as nice as possible!'

More sharply, when someone objected that the good manners of the French were all on the surface Whistler snapped, 'Well, you know, a very good place to have them.'

When Carlyle was painted by Whistler he gave him an account of his previous experience of being painted by G. F. Watts, 'A mon of note!' The process was very elaborate and the painter highly secretive until he finally revealed the finished portrait to his sitter with a flourish. 'At last the screens were put aside and there I was. And I looked. And Mr Watts, a great man, he said to me "How do ye like it?" And I turned to Mr Watts, and I said, "Mon. I would have ye know I am in the hobit of wurin' clean lunen!"'

He found an oblique way to damn Lord Leighton to a group of adoring ladies: 'He is such a wonderful musician! – such a gallant colonel! – such a brilliant orator! – such a dignified president! – such a charming host! – such an amazing linguist! – H'm, paints too, don't he, among his other accomplishments?'

WHITE, James. Jimmy White was one of the most colourful self-made northern millionaires of the 1920s, owning race horses and a yacht and funding the
arts. Sir Thomas Beecham was a leading beneficiary – waiting outside White's
inner office one day he was confronted by an agonised caller who insisted on
seeing the great man. Stalling him, Beecham asked the visitor what was the reason for his urgency. 'He owes me a hundred thousand pounds.' White was
being shaved in the other room. 'Jimmy,' Beecham called, 'it's a matter of petty
cash!'

On one occasion when White had backed a play in London he hired a private
train to take himself and a single companion to London for the opening night.
He was seen handing out five-pound notes to the station staff. Three years later,
in 1927, he went bust for £600,000 and committed suicide.

WILDE, Oscar Fingal O'Flahertie Wills. So much of Oscar Wilde's wit is studied and considered in his plays that his spontaneity is sometimes called in question. It should not be – even in the light of Whistler's famous put-down. Sir
Lewis Morris, author of *The Epic of Hades*, was complaining about what he considered the studied neglect of his claims to be Poet Laureate after Tennyson's
death. 'It is a complete conspiracy of silence against me,' he stressed to Wilde.
'A conspiracy of silence! What ought I to do, Oscar?' 'Join it,' said Wilde
promptly.

Wilde's reputation for spontaneous wit was established before he left Oxford.
In his *viva* he was required to translate from the Greek version of the New
Testament, which he did easily, gracefully and accurately. When the satisfied
examiners tried to stop him he continued through two interruptions, finally
pleading, 'Oh do let me go on. I want to see how it ends.'

On his arrival in America he scored two, perhaps more, considered successes.
First he was 'disappointed with the Atlantic Ocean' – and then, above all, confronted by the customs official who asked him if he had anything to declare, he
famously replied, 'No, I have nothing to declare . . .' and after a pause – 'except
my genius.' Few quips have travelled so far and so quickly.

Asked if he was going to the OP club (a theatrical society where he was likely
to have to face a hostile audience), he told the questioner, 'No, *I* go to the dinner of the OP club? I should be like a poor lion in a den of savage Daniels.'

Recalling his visit to Texas in his lecture tour, Oscar Wilde said that theatre
managers there looked diligently for real criminals to play criminal parts and
billed them accordingly. On one occasion a porter read, 'The part of Lady
Macbeth will be taken by Mrs . . . (Ten Years Hard Labour).'

She was a poisoner who had just completed her sentence.

When Wilde first met Shaw, GBS was on the threshold of his career; Wilde was established. He listened intently and politely as Shaw, delighted to have such a distinguished listener, enthused about a new magazine he was contemplating. After a long time Wilde piped up, 'Most interesting, Mr Shaw – but you haven't told us the title.' 'Oh,' said Shaw, 'as for that, what I'd want to do is to impress my own personality on the public. I'd call it *Shaw's Magazine*: Shaw – Shaw – Shaw!'

'Yes,' said Wilde, 'and how would you spell it?'

Shaw took it well.

Frank Harris was boasting one night at the Café Royal of all the great houses he frequented. Wilde grew impatient. 'Yes, dear Frank,' he suggested, 'we believe you: you have dined in every house in London, once.'

Wilde's friend Robert Ross, who long stood by him, looked back on his stormy career with Oscar when asked what he would like to have inscribed on his gravestone. He offered: 'Here lies one whose name is writ in hot water.'

To collect a few more of Wilde's judgements and dismissals. In 1889 in *The Decay of Lying* he complained, 'Newspapers have degenerated. They may now be absolutely relied upon.' He focused on gossip in *The Picture of Dorian Gray*: 'There is only one thing in the world worse than being talked about and that is not being talked about.' He was against early scandals – 'One should never make one's début with a scandal: one should reserve that to give interest to one's old age.' And, in *A Woman of No Importance*, 'It is perfectly monstrous the way people go about nowadays saying things against one, behind one's back, that are absolutely true.'

Wilde took his own theatrical ups and downs with equanimity. Meeting a friend at his club after the first performance of *Lady Windermere's Fan*, he was asked: 'Oscar, how did your play go tonight?' 'The play was a great success,' he answered, 'but the audience was a total failure.'

He was not so kind after Ellen Terry's first night in *Macbeth* with Irving. Of the famous dress immortalised by Sargent he wrote, 'Lady Macbeth seems an economical housekeeper, and evidently patronised local industries for her husband's clothes and the servant's liveries; but she takes care to do her own shopping in Byzantium.'

When Wilde and Beerbohm Tree were congratulating one another after the first-night success of *A Woman of No Importance* Wilde said to Tree, 'I shall always regard you as the best critic of my plays.'

'But I have never criticised your plays,' said Tree innocently.

'That's why,' smiled Wilde.

He had more trouble with Sir George Alexander, who produced *The Importance of Being Earnest* and sensibly insisted that Wilde cut his four acts to three. The fourth occasionally surfaces, but never to the play's advantage.

Alexander protested that Wilde could use his dialogue in another play. Wilde countered that it might not fit in another play. 'What does it matter?' smoothed Alexander. 'You are clever enough to think of a hundred things just as good.'

'Of course I am,' protested Wilde, 'a thousand if need be . . . but that is not the point. This scene that you feel is superfluous cost me terrible, exhausting labour and heart-rending, nerve-racking strain. You may not believe me, but I assure you on my honour that it must have taken fully five minutes to write.'

Wilde on journalism and literature: 'The difference between literature and journalism is that journalism is unreadable and literature unread.' On books: 'There is no such thing as a moral or an immoral book. Books are well written or badly written. On poetry: 'All bad poetry springs from genuine feeling.' As early as 1878 Walter Pater had stopped Wilde short with another observation, 'Why do you write poetry? Why do you not write prose? Prose is so much more difficult.' We should be grateful to Walter Pater. One might have thought that Wilde might admire Pope's brittle classicism but no – 'There are two ways of disliking poetry. One is to dislike it. The other is to read Pope.' Browning fared no better, neither did Meredith: 'Meredith is a prose Browning – and so is Browning.'

Wilde was similarly sharp about first novelists. 'In every first novel the hero is the author as Christ or Faust.' His jaundiced view of the general decline of literature was short: 'In the old days books were written by men of letters and read by the public. Nowadays books are written by the public and read by anybody.' Nowadays, of course, they are written by television personalities.

Gwendolyn, in *The Importance of Being Earnest,* supplied her own reading material: 'I never travel without my diary. One should always have something sensational to read on the train.' Wilde put another version of fiction into a character's mouth: 'The good end happily, the bad unhappily. That is what fiction means.' Tangentially, in *A Woman of No Importance,* Lord Illingworth speaks of 'The Book of Life'. It 'begins with a man and a woman in a garden'. But, Mrs Allonby points out, 'It ends with Revelations.' Another character in the same play observes, 'You should study the Peerage, Gerald, it is the best thing in fiction the English have ever done.'

Wilde reserved his most cutting literary criticism for Dickens. 'One must have a heart of stone to read the death of Little Nell without laughing.' For Henry James: 'Mr James writes fiction as if it were a painful duty.' And for George Meredith: 'Who can define him? His style is chaos illuminated by flashes of lightning. As a writer he has mastered everything except language; as a novelist he can do everything except tell a story. As an artist he is everything except articulate.'

On music he could take both sides. For the defence, 'Music is the condition to which all other arts are constantly aspiring.' For the prosecution he saw it in terms of its social possibilities and pitfalls. (His judgements can be found in the entry for Sir Thomas Beecham.) And it was Wilde – not Mark Twain – who observed a sign in an American saloon which read 'Please do not shoot the pianist. He's doing his best.'

When he strayed into politics, Wilde's wit was again frivolous. 'Democracy is simply the bludgeoning of the people, by the people for the people.' But class he upturned definitively: 'Really, if the lower orders do not set us a good example, what on earth is the use of them?'

Love and marriage had of course to be in his sights. In *The Picture of Dorian Gray* he wrote, 'A man can be happy with any woman as long as he does not love her.' In *Lady Windermere's Fan*, his studied perversity progressed to: 'The world has grown suspicious of anything that looks like a happily married life.' In *A Woman of No Importance*: 'Twenty years of romance make a woman look like a ruin, but twenty years of marriage make her look like a public building'; and 'The happiness of a married man depends on the people he has not married.' This often underestimated play contains more than its measure of Wildean shockers – 'Women have become so highly educated that nothing should surprise them except happy marriages'; and 'Men marry because they are tired, women because they are curious. Both are disappointed.'

Then there is Wilde the romantic. 'One should always be in love. That is the reason one should never marry'; and Wilde disenchanted. 'Niagara Falls is only the second biggest disappointment of the standard honeymoon.'

'If there is one man more deeply hated by his fellow men than any other it is the witty man,' he said with some feeling. His wit had been his triumph during his cross-examination by Carson in his first trial; but it let him down when Carson pounced on his casual dismissal of a rent boy as 'unattractive' and destroyed him 'with all the ferocity of an old friend'.

The end was awful, but the tatters of wit clung to him. When asked for a very large sum for an operation he said, 'Ah well, then. I suppose that I shall have to die beyond my means.' And there are his supposed last words in that bedroom in Paris: 'This wallpaper is killing me. One of us will have to go.'

WILDER, Billy. Anecdotes about the great Hollywood director of *Sunset Boulevard*, *Some Like It Hot*, *The Fortune Cookie*, and many other classic movies, veer between the immensely sympathetic and the barbed. Harry Kurnitz defined him at work – 'Let's face it, Billy Wilder at work is two people - Mr Hyde and Mr Hyde.'

Born in Vienna, Wilder moved to Berlin to write scenarios for early movies. After the Reichstag fire he could see little future in that town and fled to Hollywood.

He insists that during his early days in Los Angeles he lived in the ladies' room at the Chateau Marmont hotel. His idol, Lubitsch, was at Paramount. Wilder explained Lubitsch's early dabbling in German Expressionism as a practical necessity: 'They did all those angles and that lighting because they couldn't afford sets. When they got to Hollywood, they dropped all that stuff. Lubitsch,' he added, 'could do more with a closed door than most directors can with an open fly.'

It was Lubitsch who teamed him with his first great collaborator, Charles Brackett, when he moved to MGM to work on *Ninotchka*. After World War Two he served with the Psychological Warfare Division of the US Army in Germany. Among his tasks was rebuilding the German film industry. In the course of his work he had to interview ex-Nazis to decide which were the least undesirable. The director of the Oberammergau Passion play asked him for a decision on Anton Lang who had played Christ before the war and had been in the SS. The director wanted to use him again. Wilder said, 'On one condition.' He was asked what it was: 'That in the Crucifixion scene you use real nails.'

Wilder's second great collaborator was another transplanted European, I. A. L Diamond. Born Itek Dommnici in Romania, he always insisted the initials he adopted stood for Interscholastic Algebra League. Wilder said, 'The highest compliment you could get from Diamond would be "why not?" ' The Reagans once asked Wilder to the White House for dinner. He didn't want to go. Diamond agreed. 'You're right. If you go, then you'll have to invite them back to your house, then back and forth. Who knows what it could lead to?'

Working on *Some Like It Hot*, Wilder's main problem – apart from getting Tony Curtis into a dress – was Marilyn Monroe's unpunctuality and her insistence on going over the dialogue interminably. Finally, philosophically, he accepted the burden: 'My Aunt Minnie would always be punctual and never hold up production – but who would pay to see my Aunt Minnie?' He had also directed her in *The Seven Year Itch* and once said, 'The question is whether Marilyn is a person at all or one of the greatest Du Pont products ever invented. She had breasts like granite and a brain like Swiss cheese full of holes.' She explained her unpunctuality by saying that she couldn't find the studio at which she had worked for years. After some forty or fifty takes Wilder would take her aside and say soothingly 'Don't worry, Marilyn.' To which she would innocently reply, 'Don't worry about what?' 'Anyone can remember lines,' he later said, 'but it takes a real artist to come on the set and not know her lines and give the performances she did.'

Wilder's caustic side is demonstrated in his curt comments to his colleagues. He called Spyros Skouras, head of Twentieth Century-Fox studios, 'The only Greek Tragedy I know'. Of Chaplin he said, devastatingly, 'When he found a voice to say what was on his mind, he was like a child of eight writing lyrics for Beethoven's Ninth.' To an auditioning singer, 'You have van Gogh's ear for music.'

His own philosophy for directing was summoned up in his ten commandments: 'The first nine are "Thou shalt not bore." ' The tenth was 'Thou shalt have the right of final cut', or, more simply, 'The best directing is the one you don't see'. More particularly, 'The close-up is such a valuable thing - like a trump at bridge.'

Wilder has a profound distrust of the pretentious, the new wave, and the unfairly-prestigious-foreign. 'What critics call "dirty" in our movies they call "lusty" in foreign films,' he said, And when he was directing *Sunset Boulevard* he managed a jab at European movies in an aside to his lighting cameraman, John Seitz, who was querying the set-up for Gloria Swanson's attempted suicide in her vast bed. 'It's the usual slashed-wrist shot, Johnny,' he told him, 'and keep it out of focus. I want to win the foreign picture award.' He was amused by the 'usual' formula, using it again on the same movie to the same cinematographer, 'Johnny – it's the usual dead-chimpanzee set-up.' Around 1969 he was mocking the Nouvelle Vague: 'You watch, the new wave will discover the slow dissolve in ten years or so.'

However, when he first saw Eric von Stroheim at the wardrobe tests for his role as Rommel in *Five Graves to Cairo*, 'I clicked my heels and said, "Isn't it ridiculous, little me directing you? You were always ten years ahead of your time." Von Stroheim replied, "Twenty." '

One of his more blunt ripostes has stuck in the popular imagination of Hollywood. Louis B. Mayer considered *Sunset Boulevard* an insult to the film community. He was heard to say, 'Billy Wilder should be run out of town.' Wilder's response was to tell Mayer, 'Go shit in your hat.' 'That's what I'll be remembered for,' he said; 'A stupid insult to Louis B. Mayer.' To a query that surely he would be remembered for standing up to the studio head he denied it. 'No, they'll remember "shit in your hat".'

The advent in 1993 of the Andrew Lloyd Webber-Christopher Hampton-Don Black musical based on *Sunset Boulevard*, which he co-wrote with Diamond, recalled a previous attempt by Steven Sondheim and Burt Shevelove to make it into a stage show. Meeting Wilder in Los Angeles they told him what they were planning to do (the studio owned the rights). 'It can't be done,' Wilder warned them. 'Why?' they asked. 'It's not a musical,' said Wilder perceptively, 'it's an opera. It's about a queen in exile.' As Lloyd Webber was never worried about having his work compared to opera the advice would probably have not discouraged him.

Wilder considered his own style 'A curious cross between Lubitsch and Stroheim.' He attended Lubitsch's funeral in Los Angeles in 1948 – he had been in the middle of filming *That Lady in Ermine*. Lubitsch was buried in a glass-covered coffin with a cigarette in his hand. After the funeral Wilder walked to his car with William Wyler. 'Pity,' Wyler finally said. 'No more Lubitsch.' 'Worse,' said Wilder. 'No more Lubitsch pictures.'

There is no mistaking his nostalgia for pre-war cinema. 'Working at Paramount in the thirties was absolutely marvellous. You just walked across the lot and there they were: Von Sternberg, Dietrich, Gary Cooper, Leo McCarey, Lubitsch. We made pictures then. Today we spend eighty per cent of the time making deals and twenty per cent making pictures.'

He found unusual consolation in the advent of television. 'It is a twenty-one-inch prison. I'm delighted with it because it used to be that films were the lowest form of art. Now we've got something to look down on.'

Wilder once told Sam Goldwyn that he wanted to make a movie about Nijinsky. He explained that he was the greatest dancer ever, told him about his career, 'and how he ended up in a French nuthouse, thinking he was a horse.' Goldwyn said, 'What kind of picture is that? A man who thinks he's a horse?' Wilder told him, 'Don't worry, there's a happy ending. In the final scene he wins the Kentucky Derby.'

Wilder married twice. His second wife, Audrey, lived in modest circumstances with her mother. Proposing, Wilder told her, 'I'd worship the ground you walk on if you lived in a better neighbourhood.'

WILKES, John. John Wilkes, the eighteenth-century politician rake and wit, meeting Lord Townshend, remarked, 'Your Lordship is one of the handsomest men in the Kingdom and I am one of the ugliest. Yet, give me but half-an-hour's start and I will enter the lists with you with any woman you choose to name.'

Old chestnuts abound in the history of English political cut and thrust. Pre-eminent among them is the eighteenth-century classic in which Lord Sandwich, considering what his put-down for John Wilkes should be, arrived at: ''Pon my honour, Wilkes, I don't know whether you'll die on the gallows or of the pox.' To which Wilkes replied, 'That must depend, my Lord, upon whether I embrace your Lordship's principles, or your Lordship's mistress.'

On the night that the India Bill was debated, another member entreated Wilkes to be silent as the House was about to vote the way they both wished. 'My dear friend,' said Wilkes, 'I must speak, or I shall otherwise cut a most ridiculous figure tomorrow morning. For two hours ago I sent the speech which I am about to make tonight to the Press.'

WILLIAM I (the Conqueror). The bastard son of the Duke of Normandy, William had a dubious claim to the throne of England. However, his cross-Channel foray to Hastings in 1066 was one in the eye for Harold and founded the Norman dynasty. He instituted the Domesday Survey of England – 'not even one ox, nor one cow, nor one pig' escaped notice in his survey; and established the New Forest, creating 'the dreadful spectacle of thirty miles of desolation devoted to animals not subjected to the general service of mankind.'

At the battle of Hastings his soothsayer was killed, prompting the King's ironic remark, echoed down the centuries by those wishing to poke fun at astrologers who are in trouble: 'He could not have been a good one as he had not foreseen his own fate.'

This did not, however, stop William engaging a sorceress when he was bothered by the guerilla activities of Hereward the Wake. Indeed he built her tower as near Hereward's hideout in the Fens as possible so that her spells could have unlimited access. Hereward's witchcraft was more potent than the lady's and he burnt tower, guards and sorceress to a cinder.

William was tall and fat, while his queen, Matilda, was little over four feet. Their eldest son Robert inherited his father's bulk and his mother's height and was known as Robert 'Curt-hose' – perhaps best translated colloquially as 'fat-legs'. As William grew older he became so fat that his enemy the King of France taunted him with accusations of pregnancy. In response William set fire to the town of Mantes, vowing that he would set all France in a blaze. As his overburdened horse carried him through the smouldering embers of the town it shied at the timbers falling around it. The fat King was thrown onto the pommel of his saddle and suffered a rupture followed by fever and inflammation from which he was not to recover.

William took the sacrament from the Archbishop of Rouen on the night of 8 September 1087 and died next morning. Pandemonium ensued. Senior magnates rode to ensure that their estates were safe. Minor notables and servants plundered what money, plate, linen and jewels they could easily remove. Even the stately and substantial figure of the dead King was stripped of valuables to near nudity and abandoned on the floor of his bedchamber.

The indignities were not over. William's vast, embalmed frame was crammed into a stone coffin. The undertakers punctured the corpse as they forced it into the unyielding casket, and the priests scampered through the last rites to escape the appalling stench. William Rufus, his second son, commissioned an elaborate tomb, but in 1522 it was opened and the body re-interred. Forty years later the remains were destroyed; only a thigh bone survived, and despite subsequent disturbances (most recently verified by the authorities in 1987) it remains buried at Caen to this day.

WILLIAM II. On William the Conqueror's death his three stumpy sons rode in different directions after their share of the spoils as fast as their plump legs could spur their sturdy Norman horses. Robert Curt-hose, heir to the Duchy of Normandy, was hurrying back from the court of France to claim and squander his inheritance. William Rufus, heir to the Kingdom of England, was speeding to seek confirmation of his title and the blessing and support of his teacher, Archbishop Lanfranc, so that he could get down to the serious business of exploiting his new status. Henry 'Beauclerc', who alone among the brothers had been born in England, was racing to weigh the generous lump sum which had to keep him going while he waited for what more the future might bring.

William II was 31 when he came to the throne, squat and paunchy. His hair, thinning on top, hung to his shoulders around his coarse, ruddy face. His flecked eyes were of different shades and altogether he was excitable proof that plainness did not preclude vanity any more then than now. His reputation as a homosexual owes something to Church historians with whom he quarrelled.

Homosexuals did the same things to one another in 1087 as in 1887, but the law's attitude was very different. The legal records of the time do not mention these crimes, which were considered to be a problem principally for the Church, especially as churchmen were commonly supposed to be adept at such practices. It was not for another hundred years that legal texts began to spell out gruesome punishments for social and religious offenders – burning to death for sorcerers, and for any rash man who went to bed with the wife of his feudal lord (or even with his lord's children's nurse). Burial alive was suggested for those caught having intercourse with Jews, animals or people of the same sex.

There is no more vivid example of the prevailing attitude during William Rufus's reign than the failure, across the Channel, of attempts to get Pope Urban to clean up the Archbishopric of Tours, where a round of ecclesiastical couplings was danced involving the archbishop himself, his brother, the late Bishop of Orléans, the King of France, and the young incoming Bishop of Orléans, who had affairs with all three and whose popularity was so great that he was known as 'Flora', after a fashionable prostitute of the day. The archbishop's romances were a constant inspiration to popular songwriters, and 'Flora', after an investigation, was consecrated Bishop on 1 March 1098, ruling his diocese for forty years without interruption before retiring with honour.

However, the conduct of William Rufus's courtiers set the temperatures of the priests who chronicled his reign soaring. These priests' criticisms have a familiar ring – long hair and extravagant clothes were condemned – and they single out a newly fashionable boot for particular scorn. In fact this notorious forerunner of the 'kinky boots' of the 1960s was first designed to make walking

easier for Count Fulk of Anjou who had a deformed foot which, not unreason-
ably, he wished to conceal and make comfortable. William had his own troubles
with footwear. On one occasion he asked his manservant how much a new pair
of boots cost, and on hearing the price he exploded with rage, insisting that
cheap goods were an insult to a great monarch. The sensible steward continued
to buy shoes at the same rate, assured his master that they cost a great deal more,
and pocketed the difference.

William took some pleasure in squeezing money from vacant monasteries and
dioceses, and from any other promising source. Archbishop of Canterbury
Anselm's Boswell, Eadmer, tells a bizarre story of a young Jew who was convinced by a vision to convert to Christianity. His distraught father pleaded with
the King to persuade the boy to return to his former faith. Rufus could see no
profit for himself in this until the Jew promised him sixty marks. Suitably
impressed, the King called the boy before him and commanded him to
renounce his brand-new religion. 'You must be joking,' the boy effectively said,
and the script proceeds predictably as William replies, 'Me, joke with you?' He
then slips from acceptable vaudeville vocabulary into royal abuse, but the King's
oaths (he usually swore by 'the bones of Lucca') failed to persuade the boy, and
the father very reasonably asked for his sixty marks back. William argued for services rendered and in the end the two men settled for thirty marks each.

Discouraging supernatural portents were a feature of William Rufus's thirteen years of self-indulgent government. Earthquakes, 'tempests of lightning . . . and contending winds', thunderstorms, 'fast flowing rivers frozen hard',
crop failures, comets, floods and, to cap it all, in 1100 'the Devil visibly appeared
to men in woods and secret places, and spoke to them as they passed by.'
Moreover, in the county of Berkshire, at the village of Finchamstead, a fountain
flowed so plentifully with blood for fifteen days that it discoloured a neighbouring pool. William mocked the gloomy view taken of these portents throughout
his reign and he would blaspheme and pour scorn on the messenger who
brought him news of sinister visions, saying 'He is a monk and dreams for
money. Give him a hundred shillings.'

Then late in 1100 William himself had a dream which alarmed him sufficiently to halt for an instant his blaspheming course. The next day he baulked at
hunting in his favourite New Forest. However, after a heavy lunch during
which he drank more than usual, he forgot his fears and set off into the forest
with a small party. The events of the afternoon are shrouded in uncertainty but
it appears that his youngest brother Henry, now 32, was there together with
William Breteuil, the Royal Treasurer. So were two Norman lords, Gilbert and
Roger de Clare. Most significantly, there was another Norman, Walter Tirel, a
kinsman of the Clares by marriage and lord of Poix in Ponthieu. At the critical

moment, Henry is reported to have left the main party to repair his bow in a forester's hut where a witch is said to have announced to him,

> Hasty news to thee I bring.
> Henry, thou art now a king.

In another part of the forest the royal party had startled a deer and split up in pursuit. Tirel accompanied William and soon spotted the animal, pointing it out to the King. William wounded it and was scanning the shadowed pathways through the trees, his hand shading his eyes, when Tirel saw a second stag and let fly. He scored a direct hit, not on the stag; but on the monarch – leading to an unresolved conundrum. Was Tirel aiming for the stag? or for the King? Was Henry a party to a plot? Was it a jealous lover who fired the arrow? And was Tirel actually in the forest? If he was, he hurriedly left the spot where the King fell. Too badly wounded to call for help, Rufus managed to break off the shaft of the arrow, but he fell heavily on the stub, aggravating the wound and making death certain.

The King's corpse was recovered by a humble Saxon charcoal burner called Purkiss. Making his way home in the dusk, Purkiss stumbled over the dead body and threw the remains of the man from whom he would have hidden in fear a few hours earlier onto his lumbering wooden cart, bringing his gruesome burden, dripping blood, all the way to Winchester. William was buried in the Old Minster without religious rites. No bell was rung, no mass read. 'Many looked on; but few mourned. None wept for him but the mercenaries who received his pay and the baser partners of his foul vices . . .'

WILLCOCKS, Sir David. Sir David Willcocks, the distinguished director of music at Kings College, Cambridge, is rumoured to have given all the credit for the spectacularly beautiful sound his choir makes in a spectacularly beautiful building to the chapel. 'It's not the boys,' he is reported to have said, 'it's the building. That acoustic would make a fart sound like a sevenfold Amen.'

WILLIAM III and MARY II. Mary, the eldest daughter of King James II, married Dutch William and together they deposed her father. James's relationship with William was complicated. As William was a grandson of Charles I through his daughter Mary, who married the Stadtholder of the Dutch Republic, James was both uncle and father-in-law. Unlike his Queen, William was never popular with his subjects, and after her death he spent half the year abroad. William and Parliament were mutually supportive. Parliament used him as a means of restoring its authority. William used his position as King of England to shore up his defence of the Netherlands against France. To his credit

William can claim to have established a form of consitutional monarchy, the Bank of England and the National Debt.

The royal couple were married in 1677. Charles II had suggested a match in 1674 when Holland was at war. William's reply was, 'I cannot leave the battle-field nor believe it would be agreeable for a lady to be where the battlefield is.'

'Every bullet has its billet,' was a memorable aphorism of William's during the French Wars.

The Prince – although most probably gay – also had a long-standing relation-ship in Holland with one Betty Villiers; however, the marriage survived. One authority for the gay allegation is Bishop Burnet's *The History of My Own Times*. The Bishop was a supporter of William of Orange whom the King made first Bishop of Salisbury and later Governor of New York. Lord Dartmouth quotes Burnet as saying that he 'should be surprised to find he had taken notice of King William's vices; but some things,' he said, 'were too notorious for a faithful his-torian to pass over in silence.' Plainly William was firmly in the closet or as Burnet puts it, in reference to his rival favourites Portland and Albemarle, 'He had no vice, but of one sort in which he was very cautious and secret.'

'It seems to me very extraordinary that it should be impossible to have esteem and regard for a young man without it being criminal,' William said about his friendship with Keppel whom he was later to create Earl of Albemarle.

Rather like the Princess of Wales and Prince Charles, the Queen towered 4½ inches over her husband. She was outgoing and grew in popularity through her reign. He was withdrawn and had one sporting passion, hunting, which he could enjoy on his own.

William totally rejected the idea of being a consort. 'I have not come to establish a Republic or be a Duke of Venice,' he told the Lords in demanding the title of King in 1689, later adding, 'I will not be my wife's gentleman usher.' Mary took part, say-ing 'that she would take it extremely unkindly, if any, under a pretence of their care for her, would set up a divided interest between her and the prince.'

One anecdote about William and his sister-in-law (later Queen Anne) reminds me of Auberon Waugh's tale of his father greedily devouring his entire family's ration of the first bananas after the war. In this case the prize was the first fresh picked peas of the season. 'The King, without offering the Princess the least share of them, eat them every one himself . . . The Princess confessed, when she came home she had so much a mind to the Pease, that she was afraid to look at them, and yet could hardly keep her eyes off them!'

Mary died of smallpox in 1694. 'During the course of our marriage,' William wrote to Bishop Burnet, 'I have never known one single fault in her.'

William's death was caused by a fall while riding in the Park near Hampton Court. His horse, Sorrel, stumbled on a mole-hill. The King's collar bone was broken, set, broken again on a bumpy carriage ride and reset badly. The King went into a decline and, attended by Albemarle and Portland, died. The moderate mourning of the people was outmatched by the celebration of the Jacobites who created a toast: 'To the little gentleman in black velvet', by which they meant the mole on whose hill Sorrel had stumbled causing the King's death.

Of one Jacobite, Professor Dodwell, William had memorably said 'He has set his heart on being a martyr and I have set mine on disappointing him.'

WILLIAM IV. A younger brother of George IV and third son of George III, Prince William Henry, Duke of Clarence, was known as the 'Sailor King' after spending or, more accurately, misspending his early years in the Royal Navy.

As a naval lieutenant his view of Plymouth was emphatically more that of a sailor than a future king. 'Dullness rules here altogether but what is worse than all, not a woman fit to be touched with the tongs, not a house to put your head in after dark . . . If it were not for the duty of the ship I should perhaps hang myself.' A year later, aged 22, he had little hope of a hero's reception at home: 'My Christmas box or New Year's gift will be a family lecture on immorality, vice, dissipation and expense, and that I shall meet with the appellation of a prodigal son.' On his impending visit to the West Indies with his ship he wrote, 'I am sorry to say that I have been living a terrible debauched life of which I am heartily ashamed and tired. I must in the West Indies turn over a new leaf or else I shall be irreversibly ruined.'

His biographer, Philip Ziegler, casts a sceptical eye on some of the anecdotes which attached themselves to his days as a junior officer. On his first day aboard he is supposed to have said, 'My father's name is Guelph and you are welcome to call me William Guelph.' A fellow midshipman is held to have reproved him in a bumptious moment with 'Avast there, my hearty, the son of a whore here is as good as the son of a king!' After a tangle with Lieutenant Moody they shook hands and legend has it that he said patronisingly, 'You are a brave fellow – for a marine.' Since he joked, shouted, swore, drank like any other boy of his age it is hardly surprising that these incidents are given currency. He was certainly anti-intellectual. At the age of 24 he decided that, 'I know no person so perfectly disagreeable and very dangerous as an author.' A Spanish admiral was amazed and impressed to find him informing him respectfully that his barge was ready: 'Well does Great Britain merit the empire of the sea when the humblest stations in her navy are filled by princes of the blood.'

At the age of twenty he had been sent to visit Hanover where, unable to find respectable women with whom to consort, he complained that he had to satisfy himself 'with a lady of the town against a wall'. He moaned to his older brother the Prince of Wales of 'This damnable country, smoking [sic], playing at twopenny whist and wearing great thick boots. Oh, for England and the pretty girls of Westminster, at least such as would not clap or pox me every time I fucked.' One fellow officer, William Dyott, reported on his behaviour on the Halifax station in Nova Scotia when he was 23 – 'He would go into any house where he saw a pretty girl, and was perfectly acquainted with every house of a certain description in the town.' He was apt to be bested in verbal contests. When he jeered at a fellow captain for being the son of a Hackney schoolmaster, he set himself up by asking why the man, Captain Newcastle, had not followed his father's profession. 'Why, sir,' the Captain replied, 'I was such a stupid, good-for-nothing fellow, that my father could make nothing of me, so he sent me to sea.'

William's own great romance was with the actress Mrs Dorothy Jordan – who excelled as high-spirited hoydens and in 'breeches parts'. She was illegitimate and had had an illegitimate child by a theatre manager in Dublin. She was not married but assumed the name of Mrs Jordan. She had four more children early in her career at Drury Lane by a young man named Richard Ford before she left him in 1791 to become William's mistress. When George III heard of his son's liaison with an actress he was characteristically staccato. 'Hey, hey – what's this – what's this? You keep an actress, they say.' 'Yes, sir.' 'Ah well, well: how much do you give her, eh?' 'One thousand a year, sir.' 'A thousand, a thousand; too much; too much! Five hundred quite enough! Quite enough!'

Like his brother William attracted versifiers with his romance:

> As Jordan's high and mighty squire
> Her playhouse profits design to skim,
> Some folks audaciously enquire
> If *he* keeps *her* or *she* keeps *him*.

The Queen, William's mother, broke up the match in 1811. Rumour had it that he asked for repayment of the allowance he had made Mrs Jordan, which seems out of character. However, if the story is true it gave her the magnificent phrase in which she is said to have refused him: she sent him a playbill with the notice, "Positively no money refunded after the curtain has risen."

Her last appearance in London was at Drury Lane in *As You Like It*. Her farewell was in Margate. She retired to Paris where she died in poverty.

William meanwhile married Princess Adelaide of Saxe-Meiningen. He was 52 and she was 25. 'She is doomed, poor dear, an innocent young creature, to be my wife,' he said, Princess Caroline had died in childbirth, and the race was on to provide an heir. Both William and Edward, Duke of Kent decided to breed for the succession. The four daughters of William and Adelaide died – two young, two in childbirth. The Dukes of Cambridge and Cumberland then joined in . . .

Yoics! the Royal sport's begun!
I'faith but it is glorious fun,
For hot and hard each Royal pair
Are at it hunting for an heir.

The Kents were to be victorious. But William did, of course, become King himself at the age of 65. He was awakened with the news of his accession and went back to bed, he explained, 'to enjoy the novelty of sleeping with a queen'.

It was now that his ministers had to face the introduction of the Reform Bill and the Catholic Emancipation Act. The King was not enthusiastic about either measure. 'I consider Dissolution tantamount to Revolution.' he wrote to Lord Grey, who was threatening to dissolve Parliament as a means of achieving an election and reform. Debates were violent and, hurrying to Parliament, the King heard a cannon heralding his approach. He asked the Lord Chancellor, Henry Brougham, what all the noise could be. 'If it please your Majesty, it is the Lords debating.' The passage of these two measures owes something to William's unimaginative character. Sir John Plumb has called him 'the most outspoken, simple, eccentric monarch of modern times'.

His other great legacy was inspired by an accident. It is the tradition in Her Majesty's Navy to remain seated to drink the Royal toast. The Navy owes this to William, who once rose to toast his father and banged his head painfully.

He died with his last wish granted. He had fallen ill a few days before Waterloo Day 1837 and pleaded, 'Doctor, I know I am going but I should like to see another anniversary of the Battle of Waterloo. Try if you can to tinker me up to last out that day.' The doctor was successful and indeed William lasted a couple of days more.

WILLIAMS, George Emlyn. James Harding's recent biography of the play-wright and raconteur Emlyn Williams, which covers the ground about which Williams wrote with such distinction in *George* and *Emlyn* and conscientiously carries the story on until Williams' death some fifty years after the last moments charted in *Emlyn*, prompts a few Emlyn stories which 'got away' from my *Theatrical Anecdotes*.

Harding pinpoints the origin of Hugh 'Binkie' Beaumont's nickname for Williams. Richard Burton, a protégé of his fellow countryman, was under con-tract to H. M. Tennent, the theatrical production company of which Beaumont was the head. Burton was on £15 a week. As his career blossomed he reckoned he had earned a rise and asked Binkie for £20. They compromised at £17 10s. and Burton proudly reported this to Emlyn Williams who promptly told him to go back and ask for £30. After some argument he got it. Binkie's parting shot was 'I suppose that old Welsh pit pony put you up to this.'

It was a nickname Williams embraced happily. He was famous for his sharp tongue and could use it on his friends as well as others. On the Burton-Taylor *Private Lives* his verdict was 'He's miscast and she's Miss Taylor.'

Williams had introduced Richard Burton to his first wife Sybil. After he left her for Elizabeth Taylor, Burton periodically turned up for maudlin reunions. One night he suddenly said, 'Well, I'd better get back to the Dorchester or there'll be a lot of breast beating,' to which Sybil splendidly replied, 'And indeed there's quite a lot of breast to beat, isn't there?' When Williams got his CBE he wrote to Sybil Burton that it stood for 'Can't Bear Elizabeth'. When Terence Rattigan got his CBE Williams translated it as 'Chorus Boys Everywhere'.

Emlyn had his own debates with Beaumont. 'I've read your new play, Emlyn, and I like it twice as much as your last,' Binkie once said. Williams pounced. 'Does that mean you're going to pay twice my usual royalties?' he asked. It did not. When The Company of Four, a subsidiary of H. M. Tennent, revived his Shakespeare play, *Spring 1600*, at the Lyric, Hammersmith, in 1945, audiences were thin. He suggested that the Lyric housed 'The Company of Four and the Audience of Two'.

On the first night of the original production of *Spring 1600*, directed by John Gielgud, in 1934, he had been so nervous that he hid himself in the flies and watched the action from above. His anxiety was not relieved and indeed he felt a compulsive need to relieve himself. He did so in an old rusty bucket. When he told his director about it later, Gielgud said, 'You must be the first playwright who's peed over his own play.'

When he acted in *Wild Decembers*, Clemence Dane's play about the Brontës, he nearly took a solo curtain call, sure that the audience were calling 'Emlyn! Emlyn!' Just in time he realised that they were calling for Beatrix Lehmann in her character of Emily, and had the presence of mind to lead her forward for her bow. The name Emlyn often led to confusion among his fans. He listed 25 variations on the spelling of his Christian name. They included, Emelett, Emden, Emmelin, Emlyon, Emiline, Amlyn, M. Lynn, Emilio, Dmly, Mmmlyn, Melyn and Eylya.

He was adroit at word play. Once when he and Robert Helpmann were arguing about the age of Michael Redgrave he decided that they were 'splitting grey hairs'. Under General Eisenhower's regime he rechristened the White House 'The Tomb of the Well-Known Soldier'. He cherished (or invented) a wartime sign scrawled on a building: 'Abandon hope all ye who ENSA here.' And when he heard that Ivor Novello was to be imprisoned for wartime petrol offences he said to his wife, 'I suppose his great song for this war will have to be called, "Keep the Home Tyres Turning".'

He was adept at the scrambled titles which theatre people like to manipulate – though the transformation of 'Vivat! Vivat! Regina' to 'Rivet, Rivet your Vagina!' is not his. When Gielgud suggested cutting some flowery speeches in *Spring 1600* he agreed happily saying, 'We don't want James Agate to head his Sunday article, "Herrick, or little by little"!' For the musical version of *Lolita* he suggested the new title *Take Her She's Nine*, with a hit song: 'Stop the Girl I Want to Get Off.'

Referring to Merle Oberon's Eurasian background he suggested that her autobiography be called 'Lives of a Bengal Free-Lancer'.

When he found that his obituary had appeared in an American newspaper which gave the date of his death he wrote, 'I have wracked my brain and cannot recall anything untoward happening that year.'

Six years before he died in 1987, he had appeared at the Century Theatre in New York and had another great success reviving his Dickens readings. Arriving at the theatre for one performance, he found the stage door surrounded by young actors auditioning for *Jitters*, a new backstage comedy. He asked the hopefuls what was going on and one girl, noting his white hair, said kindly, 'I wouldn't bother hanging round if I were you. There aren't any parts for old men!'

WINNER, Michael. The explosive behaviour on the set of the veteran film director Michael Winner is legendary in the British movie industry – if that phrase is not an oxymoron.

However, it was best punctured on the occasion when Winner pursued a cameraman to the portable field lavatory to which he had retreated. As Winner shouted commands through the walls the reply is alleged to have come back smartish, 'Go away, Michael, I can't deal with two shits at once.'

WOODTHORPE, Peter. This anecdote of Peter Woodthorpe's somehow escaped from my theatrical collection. Woodthorpe – having had a great success as Noakes in the musical *Zuleika*, both in Cambridge and in the West End – was cast by Peter Brook in his production of Dürrenmatt's play *The Visit*, starring the Lunts. In due course it was staged in America and Woodthorpe was imported along with it. He arrived in New York – his first visit – in the early morning and left the boat for his hotel. Having checked in he set out to explore the strange city and eat breakfast. In a fast-food diner he had his first experience of American catering-speak. Seeing 'Toasted English Muffins' on the menu he ordered two and was dumbfounded to hear the waiter turn and shout through the hatch into the kitchen, 'Burn the British, twice!'

WORDSWORTH, William. The poet Wordsworth merits inclusion because of a story which illustrated his frank admission that he was without wit: 'I do not think I was ever witty but once in my life,' he confessed to a small gathering. Agog to hear the *bon mot*, his audience pressed him for it. 'I was standing some time ago at the entrance of my cottage at Rydal Mount. A man accosted me with the question, "Pray, sir, have you seen my wife pass by?" Whereupon I said, "Why, my good friend. I didn't know till this moment that you had a wife!" ' When it dawned on his audience that they had heard the punch line they burst into laughter at its pointlessness and Wordsworth in his simplicity accepted their reaction as appreciation of his wit – so both sides were happy.

It does conjure up, however, a frightening picture of Wordsworth, emboldened by his success, forever stopping one in three passersby (like Coleridge's Ancient Mariner) and bending their ears with his cumbersome anti-climax. 'If you think me dull, be it just so,' he once said to Carlyle.

He was less modest in his reactions to the news that Sir Walter Scott's next novel was to be *Rob Roy*. He took down his volume of ballads, and read *Rob Roy's Grave* to his friends. Then he put it back observing, 'I do not know what more Mr Scott can have to say on the subject.'

— X —

X-RATING. The clamour for film censorship grew during the early years of the twentieth century. The *Chicago Tribune* denounced 'The Five Cent (post nickelodeon) Theatre' as 'intolerably vicious'. An Illinois judge held that movies were responsible for 'more juvenile crime coming into my court than all other causes combined'. Chicago empowered its Police Department to preview and license all films, including such masterpieces as *Cupid's Barometer*, *An Old Man's Darling*, *My Husband Comes* and *The Bigamist*.

By 1909 American Producers had organised self-censorship through their National Board, renamed the National Board of Review of Films in 1921. Sensational titles still proliferated: *Why Be Good?*, *Sinners in Silk*, *Luring Lips*, *Red Hot Romance* and *Scrambled Wives* were accompanied by even more lurid promotional material: 'THE BLOOD IS LAVA AND THE PULSE IS ABLAZE!'

The righteous denounced Hollywood as 'Sodom by the Sea' and attacked 'Studio sewers'. The studios replied by enlisting Will H. Hays, President Harding's Postmaster-General and an elder in the Presbyterian Church, to head the Motion Picture Producers and Distributors of America (MPPDA) and maintain 'the highest possible moral and artistic standards'.

Hays was reluctant to take the job until he heard his three sons arguing which should play William S. Hart, the silent star, in a game. For the first time he realised the hold actors were beginning to exert over millions of children. It was Christmas and according to Hays he stood in the shadow of the family tree and silently made the vow of Saint Paul, 'And this I do.'

When Ben Hecht arrived in Hollywood to write screenplays in 1925 he was warned of the power of censorship by Herman Mankiewicz: 'In a novel a hero can lay ten girls and marry a virgin for a finish. In a movie this is not allowed. The hero, as well as the heroine, has to be a virgin. The villain can lay anybody he wants, have as much fun as he wants cheating and stealing, getting rich and whipping the servants. But you have to shoot him in the end. When he falls with a bullet in his forehead it is advisable that he clutch at the Gobelin Tapestry on the library wall and bring it down over his head like a symbolic shroud.' This thoroughly unhinged Hecht, whose first original screenplay, *Underworld* (1927), was mainly concerned with the villain.

In the thirties Mae West was a principal thorn in Hays's flesh. In *She Done Him Wrong*, two of her songs are 'A Guy What Takes His Time' and 'I Wonder Where My Easy Rider's Gone'. 'Easy Rider' was American thirties slang for 'pimp'.

Miss West's next film, *It Ain't No Sin*, had, to her chagrin, to be retitled *I'm No Angel* and she burst into tears – real or tactical – at the butchery of her script.

In Hollywood Joseph J. Breen, a young Catholic newsman, became the chief guardian of the Code. In a memorable 'getting nowhere' exchange with one producer, Breen vetoed the expression 'nuts to you'.

'But Joe,' said the producer, 'everybody says "nuts to you". It's accepted.'

'Not by the Code,' said Breen.

'Nuts to the Code,' said the producer.

'Nuts to you,' said Breen.

Local censors were always capable of wreaking havoc. When Cecil B. De Mille showed *Joan the Woman*, his first epic, to New York Censors in 1917 a woman board member protested that Joan's line 'My God, My God, why hast thou forsaken me?' had to go because it implied that God *could* forsake someone. It was a clergyman who pointed out that the words were Christ's on the cross, and De Mille was allowed to keep his line.

Will Hays once called a meeting of publicity directors to criticise copy that violated the spirit of the Production Code. At a crucial point two pigeons alighted on the office window. All eyes turned to watch their lovemaking. 'What's going on out there?' asked Hays.

'They're violating the Production Code, sir,' said the man from MGM.

David O. Selznick had to fight the Hays Office hard to retain Rhett Butler's line in *Gone With the Wind* – 'Frankly, I don't give a damn.' The suggested alternative was 'Frankly, I don't care.' Eventually, Hays overruled his board of advisers but fined Selznick $5,000 for violating the Production Code.

It was the Bible again which saved the denouement when Charles Laughton starred in *They Knew What They Wanted* in 1940. Laughton plays an Italian wine-maker whose mail-order bride cheats on him. A happy ending demanded that he forgive her; but Breen insisted that 'the sinner must be punished'. Laughton directed Breen to the example of the woman taken in adultery and forgiven by Christ. 'Do I understand, Mr Breen', he enquired, 'that the Code *does not recognise the New Testament?*' Breen conceded the denouement.

— Y —

YALE, Elihu. Elihu Yale, the founder of Yale university, was an Englishman who rose to become Governor of Madras. Later he retired to England, but he donated the money from some property he owned in America to found a collegiate school at Saybrook, Connecticut, in 1701. Later it moved to New Haven where it took the name of its British founder and benefactor.

YATES, Dornford (Cecil William Mercer). Dornford Yates, the popular novelist of the twenties and thirties, published two groups of novels: the 'Berry Pleydell' sequence and his 'Chandos' thrillers, both reflecting a world of wealth, prejudice and idleness which made them immensely popular between the wars.

However, Yates's early life was in stark contrast. He was born and brought up in Deal, which he came to hate after his uncle, the town clerk, embezzled £80,000 (a tidy sum in 1891) and then shot himself.

Later Yates wrote sneeringly about Deal in a novel, calling it Suet-on-Sea.

YENTOB, Alan. Alan Yentob, the Controller of BBC1, is not a Sherrin fan. A friend of mine was due to see Yentob to pitch a television series. He phoned an acquaintance whom he knew was close to Yentob to ask how to approach him. 'Oh, he's very nice and very easy,' said the acquaintance, 'and he's easily impressed. Just drop a few names.'

'But I don't know any names,' said my friend despairingly, and before he could complete the sentence with '. . . only Ned Sherrin,' he was stopped by a scream of panic down the line – 'Not *that* name!'

YOUNG, Lester. Lester 'Prez' Young, the man who named Billie Holliday 'Lady Day', features in the firing and being fired aspects of bands. When he had long been a saxophone soloist with Count Basie's band, he was hours late for a record date. When Basie finally found him in his hotel room, he declined to hurry to the studio: 'Man, I don't make no records on the thirteenth of no month.' So he was let go. Later Young hired a drummer who failed to come up to scratch on his first night. The drummer tried to ingratiate himself with Young during a break: 'Say, Prez,' he said, 'when was the last time we worked together?'

'Tonight,' said Young.

Young had a way with words and an engaging manner. Found smoking a joint near the stage at an early Newport Jazz Festival by a colleague who asked him what he was doing, he asked, 'Where are we?'

'We're at the Newport Jazz Festival!' said the concerned colleague.

Young took another puff and said, 'Then, let us be festive!'

YUSUPOV, Prince. Prince Yusupov, the Russian nobleman, was one of the aristocrats who eventually managed to assassinate the evil monk Rasputin after a combined assault with poison, pistol, bludgeon and drowning in order to rid the court of the last Tsar of all the Russias of his malign influence.

He had to wait for the payoff to his crime. It came when he sued MGM and won a substantial libel action against the company for portraying him in the film *Rasputin and the Empress*.

— Z —

ZAHAROFF, Sir Basil. The Greek billionaire, the first great international armament salesman, nicknamed the 'Merchant of Death', had the curious distinction of infuriating King George V by using the 'Sir' he had conferred on him which was only an honorary knighthood.

ZEPHANIAH, Benjamin. The rap poet and playwright, Benjamin Zephaniah, has an endearing frankness about his working methods. He told an audience of schoolchildren who asked where he wrote his poems, 'In the toilet mostly. I go in and it all comes out – the poems, I mean. It's a bit like going to the toilet, really. Sometimes I'm driving along and I feel a poem coming and I've just got to stop the car and do it. Once I was working in a shop, and I'd always be ducking out the back. I had to tell me boss, "Ooo, I've got a poem inside me and I've just got to get it out." '

Asked if he'd ever written a poem about going to the toilet he confessed, 'Not yet, but I might. Me loo at home's outside, I often go out there for a think. See, you don't need no imagination. You can write about everyday fings like that.'

ZINNEMANN, Fred. In the ups and downs of Fred Zinnemann's distinguished career as a film director I like best the story of his confrontation with one of the new, young Hollywood Turks who inhabited a new and palatial executive front office and was of that generation of executives ungrounded in movie tradition. The crass young man asked the seasoned veteran to tell him about 'a few of the things you've done'.

A tolerant Zinnemann paused for a moment and then looked up and said, 'You first.'

ZOG (Ahmed Zogu). The King of Albania's career was interesting even by

Balkan standards. He was Minister of the Interior at the age of 25; a year later, in 1921, he was Commander-in-Chief. In 1922 he was Prime Minister, only to be exiled two years later. Meanwhile the Albanians had been casting around for a king. C. B. Fry, the great English cricketer, turned them down and Prince William of Wied lasted only two years. Zog's exile was over after a year, and he returned first as President and then, in 1928, as self-proclaimed King.

Mussolini tried to marry him to an Italian princess but she plumped for Boris of Bulgaria. Zog finally married a Hungarian, Geraldine, before fleeing Il Duce's troops into exile again.

During World War Two he lived in a country house in Buckinghamshire and made a bizarre offer to buy *The Times* – which was not accepted. He told Auberon Herbert, 'I won't give a penny more than ten million for it.'

When his son, the Pretender King Leka I, lived in South Africa, his wife used to answer the phone, 'Hello, Queen Susan speaking.'

Leka qualifies – like his father – as a famous Albanian. This is a better, or at least a harder, game than naming famous Belgians. The only other two I can think of are the Belushi brothers, proudly claimed as of ethnic Albanian stock.

ZOLA, Emile. The French novelist and playwright lives on for his fiction and for his famous phrase *J'Accuse*, the title of his letter, published in 1898, which put the French government on trial and secured the eventual release of Alfred Dreyfus, the army officer unjustly imprisoned on Devil's Island.

More whimsical is his account of a food market in *The Fat and the Thin*. He describes a bouquet of cheeses which made him hear orchestral music. 'The Cantal, the Cheshire, and the goats' milk cheese seemed to be snoring out deep breaths like the prolonged tones of a bassoon, amidst which could be recognised, like detached notes, the sharp whiffs of the Neuchâtels, the Troyes and the Mont d'Or.'

We owe to the Goncourts an insight into the superstitions of Emile Zola. After the first night of a dramatised version of *Nana*, his wife asked angrily why he had not ordered supper. Zola snapped, 'You know how superstitious I am; if I had ordered it I am sure that the play would have flopped.'

ZUCKERMAN, Solly, Baron. At Solly Zuckerman's memorial service William Waldegrave recalled Mrs Thatcher's farewell lunch for the late President of the Zoological Society of London, when he stood down as President of the Parliamentary and Scientific committee. She pointed out that the reason he had survived so long in the corridors of power was that he had been trained in the world of apes.

ZUKOR, Adoph. Adolph Zukor, a pioneer of early Hollywood, president and later chairman of the board of Paramount, blended firmness with old-world politeness. Sacking his publicist Arthur Mayer he wired him: YOU'RE HERE-WITH DISCHARGED, BEST REGARDS. REMEMBER ME TO MRS MAYER.

Zukor stories often revolve around his concern for overspending. When Jesse Lasky was making *The Covered Wagon* for him in 1923 he was worried about spiralling expenses and called a halt to the production. He explained to Lasky that too many Westerns were over-flooding the market. Lasky was equal to the manoeuvre. '*Wagon* is not a Western,' he said. '*Wagon* is an epic.' Zukor was convinced: 'An epic, eh? Well, that's different. You go ahead.'

The year before, Zukor had problems with Cecil B. De Mille over *The Ten Commandments*. Initially Zukor was not impressed. 'Old men wearing table-cloths and beards,' he moaned; 'Cecil, a picture like that would ruin us.' He asked De Mille how much it would cost. De Mille estimated a million dollars. Zukor nearly had a heart attack. Trying to persuade him De Mille offered, 'We'll be the first studio in history to open and close the Red Sea.' 'You'll be the first director to close Paramount,' was Zukor's reply. De Mille got his way but half-way through shooting as the overages escalated Zukor expressed grave doubts. 'What do you want me to do?' said De Mille. 'Stop shooting and release it as *The Five Commandments*?'

Index